essays in the modern drama

essays
in the modern drama

edited by Morris Freedman, *University of New Mexico*

D. C. Heath and Company, Boston

Copyright 1964 by D. C. HEATH AND COMPANY
No part of the material covered by this copyright may
be reproduced for any purpose without written permission of the publisher.

BOSTON / ENGLEWOOD / CHICAGO / SAN FRANCISCO
ATLANTA / DALLAS / LONDON / TORONTO

PRINTED IN THE UNITED STATES OF AMERICA   (6 H 4)

introduction

FOR ALL of its richness, perhaps even because of it, modern drama has not been studied as modern fiction or modern poetry has been. At least some of the reasons are obvious. Modern drama cuts across language divisions, and critical or scholarly studies traditionally limit themselves to a national literature. The drama, too, is far more involved with theatrical matters, that is, with techniques and problems of production, than fiction or poetry is with publishing, editing, or book design. The publishing history of a novel, for example, is often a matter of indifference whereas the presentation of a play, a Stanislavsky production of Chekhov, say, or a Kazan one of Williams, is of the essence. Not infrequently, as has been remarked, a director or an actor may rise to the level of virtual collaborator with the author.

Whatever the reasons, much of the criticism of modern drama, while substantial in body, has often concentrated more on the theatrical aspects than on the literary; indeed, much of it is in the nature of reviews of particular performances, ranging, it is true, from report or routine appraisal to subtle and original analysis. We should not regret this situation, for a play is, after all, more than its mere text. One production of a play may yield quite a different work from another production, and both presentations will necessarily differ from the printed version when it is simply read.

But literature remains the starting point and the finishing point of drama; a play is first and last a work of literary art, for the words always remain after any embodiment of them. In considering drama as literature, it is necessary to make generalizations, comparisons, evaluations that have a larger intention and are apart from technique, which must always remain a momentary aspect. The emphasis in this book is on drama as literature.

Criticism can only supplement and enrich the response to a work of art itself. We cannot ever hope to understand a play, poem, novel, painting, or symphony without first encountering it ourselves. But the first act of encounter must properly be followed by thought of some sort. Sometimes, for that matter, the first act itself is not completed until it is crystallized by critical rumination. Understanding never comes to a halt, for criticism at its best sets up vibrations and reverberations that are endless.

This collection does not pretend to offer a "history" of modern drama although the major playwrights and tendencies are covered. It does present an exhibition of the immensely varied, infinitely layered nature of our response to modern drama. The selections vary from miniatures to murals. These critical portraits are sometimes as full of delight and surprise, sometimes as profound in revelation, as the drama itself which they discuss. The essays cover every modern dramatist of continuing importance and surviving value, and they deal with the most recent writers both in their achievement and in their promise.

All of modern drama may be said to stem from the work of the great pioneers: Ibsen, Strindberg, Chekhov, Shaw, Pirandello, and O'Neill. In whatever way we arrange the lines of influence, modern drama was given its largest perspectives and its major strategies by these masters.

Not least they were great innovators. Ibsen, turning his back on the well-made frivolities of Sardou and Scribe, opened a whole new territory of subject matter, so vast and compelling that his achievement still seems almost one of grand discovery, although, in fact, he worked within the technical tradition of the well-made play. Shaw worked through Ibsen but also with an awareness of (and sometimes a commitment to) the cyclical thinkers of his time—Darwin and his commentators: Henri Bergson, who proposed the notion of a "life force" in the universe; Samuel Butler, novelist and popularizing adaptor of Darwin; his fellow idealists in the Fabian Society, who hoped to remake a world by the forces of reason and sympathy. Chekhov, through the pastels of mood and thought, recorded the passing moments of a society in transition and established a dramatic form adaptable for great things and small. Pirandello assaulted the whole convention of the theater directly, pushing the stage into the audience, the audience onto the stage, reminding us of the improvisations of the older Italian *commedia del arte,* and in the process making disturbing philosophical observations about the binding tensions between art and reality. And Strindberg and O'Neill, in their different ways, at various times in their careers, explored the landscape of the passions, the landscape of the unconscious opened by Freud.

From Ibsen and Shaw on, the impact of changing contemporary society has intrigued playwrights. Wilde's examinations of the mildly changing English society of the turn of the century were polite if occasionally caustic. Later social drama, set in the more violent and less civilized contexts of civil disorder, war, widespread unemployment, the rise of totalitarianism, is bitter and angry. O'Casey is the Homer of the Irish Civil War; Brecht, of a whole world in madness, unlimited by time or place; Odets and Miller, the chroniclers of the American depression of the thirties and its lap-over into the forties;

Sartre, Camus, and Duerrenmatt, students of man's very nature as it studies itself.

Immediate as the subject matter of social drama may seem, these writers work in the shadow of the great formularizers of the past. In the background of Brecht, Odets, Miller, and the other social playwrights of the thirties and forties, and of such more recent playwrights as Osborne, is Karl Marx, the nineteenth-century German philosopher whose analyses of the political and economic structure of modern capitalistic society serve as the official source-book, the bible, for contemporary radical politics. Camus, Sartre, Duerrenmatt, and the other contemporary playwrights concerned with an existence made absurd by the excesses of totalitarianism and the fantastic promises of science, take up again the question of meaningful action examined at length by Soren Kierkegaard, the nineteenth-century Swedish philosopher of "existentialism." The social drama concerned with politics cannot be understood without reference to Marx; that concerned with philosophy, without reference to Kierkegaard and to some of the modern theologian-philosophers, like Paul Tillich.

Drama is never far from poetry. When the text of drama tightly concentrates the undertones and overtones, the ambiguities and utter mysteries, present in the most insignificant human communication, it inevitably approaches the character of poetry. Chekhov's and Strindberg's drama helped establish the modern mode for poetic drama, where actual verse is often less important than mood, intensity, and allusiveness. Beckett's *Waiting for Godot*, for example, may be read as a long, sustained "poem." A number of modern playwrights have chosen to write directly in verse, or in near-verse, of course, but some prefer a prose designed to elicit the mysteries we expect from poetry.

Poetic drama at its best calls attention to the sense of the text rather than to the sound alone. Thus, Lorca was profoundly aware of man's place in a society; his conflicts often depend on the tensions between the morality of society, which may be defined as honor, and the tensions of personal fulfillment, which is to say the morality determined by passion. Eliot was concerned with man's place in that area where the assertion and assumption of responsibility, the attempt to define meaningful action, the search for identity, mark the serious man. Williams may be said to fulfill the poetry of mood implicit in Chekhov although the psychological tensions are related to Strindberg and O'Neill. Fry is involved in an attempt to recreate the abstracted richness of poetic communication, which hopefully may, by itself, almost without regard to content, provide the sheer pleasure of sound we remember from Shakespeare. But none achieve the pure poetry of Yeats, and it is Yeats who most closely perhaps defines the character of poetic drama in our time, in his allusiveness and elusiveness, in his text being other than mere drama, in its approximating operatic libretto.

Experiment in one form or another has been prominent from the earliest days of the modern drama. But experiment reaches its fullest and most complex expression in the drama of the mid-twentieth century, when technical innovation combines with philosophical probing to yield, among other results, the drama of Genet, Ionesco, Beckett, and Pinter. The playwrights blend all previous tendencies—the discursiveness of Shaw, the naturalism and the surrealism of Strindberg, the evanescent subtleties of Chekhov, the theatricality of Pirandello, the social consciousness of Ibsen and Brecht—to open up strange, new landscapes of whose territorial treasures we are still not altogether sure. By their very work, our contemporary playwrights have been forcing a reappraisal of some of the most fundamental esthetic concepts in dramatic philosophy.

Of course, some of the playwrights noted for significant experiment are already well established, e.g., Rice and Wilder, but some of the newer ones, e.g., Beckett and Pinter, are still undergoing a continuing and relentless evaluation. Some of the most recent writers, of course, have already established themselves as belonging among those whose major concern is man's place in society, in the world at large, Brecht, Camus, Sartre, Duerrenmatt. What distinguishes them from the more obviously pioneering playwrights is perhaps only their final and clear subordinating of experiment or originality to statement; once we grasp their new idiom, which is often not all that new in any case, we concentrate on what is being said instead of on the saying. Ibsen and Shaw always lurk behind Brecht and Sartre. In the most nearly achieved art, of course, technique and substance are inseparable, but in such writers as Genet, Beckett, Ionesco, Pinter, even in the French dramatists concerned, deceivingly as straightforward adapters, with Greek themes, the emphasis is often on technique, method, device as statement in themselves. In this context, Strindberg, Pirandello, and O'Neill remain immediately relevant. Technique and message are never separate in Pirandello; Strindberg and O'Neill wrench technique to enhance statement. The masters provide a full setting in which to consider their successors and adaptors. But everything subsequent and new re-illuminates and makes richer the old. Brecht opens new perspectives in Shaw, Beckett in Chekhov, and Pinter even in Shakespeare. The thrust of understanding is never merely from the past into the present; it aims backward as well as forward; indeed, understanding in literature oscillates endlessly without regard for period or language or form.

MORRIS FREEDMAN

contents

section i
THE MASTERS

h. l. mencken

IBSEN

IBSEN, LIKE Wagner and Manet, has lived down his commentators, and is now ready to be examined and enjoyed for what he actually was, namely, a first-rate journeyman dramatist, perhaps the best that ever lived. Twenty years ago he was hymned and damned as anything and everything else: symbolist, seer, prophet, necromancer, maker of riddles, rabble-rouser, cheap shocker, pornographer, spinner of gossamer nothings. Fools belabored him and fools defended him; he was near to being suffocated and done for in the fog of balderdash. I know of no sure cure for all the sorrows of the world, social, political or æsthetic, that was not credited to him, read into him, forced into his baggage. And I know of no crime against virtue, good order and the revelation of God that he was not accused of. The product of all this pawing and bawling was the Ibsen legend, that fabulous picture of a fabulous monster, half Nietzsche and half Dr. Frank Crane, drenching the world with scandalous platitudes from a watch-tower in the chilblained North. The righteous heard of him with creepy shudders; there was bold talk of denying him the use of the mails; he was the Gog and the Magog, the Heliogabalus, nay, the downright Kaiser, of that distant and pious era.

No such Ibsen, of course, ever really existed. The genuine Ibsen was anything but the Anti-Christ thus conjured up by imprudent partisans and terrified opponents. On the contrary, he was a man whose salient quality was precisely his distrust of, and disdain for, any and all such facile heresies; a highly respectable gentleman of the middle class, well-barbered, ease-loving and careful in mind; a very skilful practitioner of a very exacting and lucrative trade; a safe and sane exponent of order, efficiency, honesty and common sense. From end to end of his life there is no record that Ibsen ever wrote a single word or formulated a single idea that might not have been exposed in a newspaper editorial. He believed in all the things that the normal, law-abiding citizen of Christendom believes in, from

Reprinted from *Eleven Plays of Henrik Ibsen*. Published by Random House, Inc.

democracy to romantic love, and from the obligations of duty to the value of virtue, and he always gave them the best of it in his plays. And whenever, mistaking his position, someone charged him with flouting these things or with advocating some notion that stood in opposition to them, he invariably called the plaintiff to book, and denied vehemently that he was guilty, and protested bitterly that it was outrageous to fasten any such wild and naughty stuff upon a reputable man.

Had he been, in truth, the extravagant iconoclast that a misinformed rabbinism tried to make him out, he would have remained, to the end of his career, a mere freak and blank cartridge in the theatre, and of no more influence than such extremists, say, as Max Stirner, Arthur Gobineau and the Marquis de Sade. So long, indeed, as he was generally held to be such an iconoclast, he actually suffered that fate. But when it began to be noticed, first by other dramatists and then by a widening public, that his ideas, after all, were really not extraordinary—that what he said, in the last analysis, was simply what every reasonably intelligent man thought—that his plays, for all their smashing air, were not actually blows at Christian culture—when this began to be understood, then he began to make his way, and all the serious dramatists of Europe began to imitate him. But they saw him, with their keener professional eyes, more clearly than the early and so absurd Ibsenites had seen him. They saw that he was not a brummagem prophet, but a play-maker of astonishing skill—one who had a new and better method to teach them. And so, when they set out to follow him, what they imitated was not the imaginary mystifications that foolish fuglemen had read into his dramas, but his direct and adept manner of clothing simple and even self-evident arguments in unusually lucid and brilliant dramatic forms—in brief, his enormously effective technique as a dramatist. He didn't teach them to think extraordinary thoughts; he taught them to put obvious thoughts into sound plays.

All this must be plain to anyone who goes through his so-called social dramas today, despite the confusing memory of all the gabble that went about in the high days of the Ibsen uproar. What ideas does one actually find in them? Such ideas, first and last, as even a Harvard professor might evolve without bursting his brain—for example, that it is unpleasant and degrading for a wife to be treated as a mere mistress and empty-head; that professional patriots and town boomers are frauds; that success in business usually involves doing things that a self-respecting man hesitates to do; that a woman who continues to cohabit with a syphilitic husband may expect to have defective children; that a joint sorrow tends to dampen passion in husband and wife, and so bring them together upon a more secure basis; that a neurotic and lascivious woman is apt to be horrified when she finds that she is pregnant; that a man of 55 or 60 is an ass to fall in love with a flapper of 17; that the world is barbarously cruel to a woman who has violated the Seventh Commandment or a man who has violated the Eighth. If you are discontented with these summaries, then turn to summaries that Ibsen made himself—that is, turn to his notes for his social dramas in his *Nachgelassene Schriften*. Here you will find precisely what he was trying to say. Here you will find, in plain words, the ideas that he started from. They are, without exception, ideas of the utmost simplicity. There is nothing mysterious in them; there is not even anything new in them. Above all, there is no idiotic symbolism in them. They mean just what they say.

As I have said, Ibsen himself was under no delusions about his dramas of ideas. He was a hard-working dramatist and a man of sense: he never allowed the grotesque guesses and fantasies of his advocates to corrupt the clarity of his own purpose. Down to the time he lost his mind—he was then at work on *John Gabriel Borkman* —he never wrote a line that had any significance save the obvious one, and he never forgot for an instant that he was writing, not tracts, but stage-plays. When the sentimental German middle classes mistook *A Doll's House* for a revolutionary document against monogamy, and began grouping him with the preachers of free love, he was as indignant as only a respectable family man can be, and even agreed to write a new ending for the play in order to shut off that nonsense. A year later he wrote *Ghosts* to raise a laugh against the alarmed moralists who had swallowed the free lovers' error. The noise of combat continuing, he decided to make an end of it by burlesquing the Ibsenists, and the result was *The Wild Duck*, in which the chief figure is a sort of *reductio ad absurdum* of the modern Drama Leaguer. In *The Master Builder* he took a holiday from social ideas, even the most elemental, and put himself into a play, shedding a salt tear over his lost youth. And in *Hedda Gabler*, as if to confute the Ibsen talmudists forever, he fashioned a thumping drama out of the oldest, shoddiest materials of Sardou, Scribe and Feuillet, nay, Meilhac and Halévy, as if to prove, once and for all time, that he was a dramatist first and last, and not a windy evangelist and reformer, and that he could meet any other dramatist, however skilful, on equal terms, and dispose of him neatly and completely.

Ibsen's chief interest, from the beginning to the end of his career as a dramatist, was not with the propagation of ethical ideas, but with the solution of æsthetic problems. He was, in brief, not a preacher, but an artist, and not the moony artist of popular legend, but the alert and competent artist of fact, intent upon the technical difficulties of his business. He gave infinitely more thought to questions of practical dramaturgy—to getting his characters on and off the stage, to building up climaxes, to calculating effects—than he ever gave to the ideational content of his dramas. Almost any idea was good enough, so long as it could be converted into a conflict, and the conflict could be worked out straightforwardly and effectively. Read his letters and you will find him tremendously concerned, from the start, with technical difficulties and expedients—and never mentioning morals, lesson, symbols and that sort of thing at all. So early as the time he wrote *The League of Youth* you will find him discussing the details of dramatic machinery with Dr. Georg Brandes, and laying stress on the fact, with no little vanity, that he has "accomplished the feat of doing without a single monologue, in fact, without a single aside." A bit later he began developing the stage direction; go through his plays and observe how he gradually increased its importance, until in the end it almost overshadowed the dialogue. And if you would get, in brief, the full measure of his contribution to the art of the drama, give hard study to *A Doll's House*. Here, for the first time, his new technique was in full working. Here he deposed Scribe and company at one blow, and founded an entirely new order of dramaturgy. Other dramatists, long before him, had concocted dramas of ideas—and good ones. The idea in Augier's *La Mariage d'Olympe* was quite as sound and interesting as that in *A Doll's House;* the idea in Augier's *Les Effrontés* perhaps exceeded it in both ways. But Ibsen got into *A Doll's House* something that Augier and Feuillet and Dumas *fils* and all that crowd of Empire dramatists had never been able to get into their plays, and that was an air of utter and absolute reality, an overwhelming conviction, a complete concealment of the dramatic machinery.

And how did he conceal it? Simply by leaving it out. Scribe had built up an inordinately complex dramaturgy. His plays were elaborate and beautiful mechanisms, but still always mechanisms. He had to sacrifice everything else—reason, probability, human nature—to make the machine run. An Augier, Feuillet and Dumas, better men all, followed docilely in his tracks. They were better observers; they were more keenly interested in the actual life about them; they managed, despite the artificiality of their technique, to get some genuine human beings into their plays. But that technique still hung around their necks; they never quite got rid of it. But Ibsen did. In *A Doll's House* he threw it overboard for all time. Instead of a complicated plot, working beautifully toward a foreordained climax, he presented a few related scenes in the life of a husband and wife. Instead of a finely wrought fabric of suspense and emotion nicely balanced, neatly hanging together, he hit upon an action that was all suspense and all emotion. And instead of carefully calculated explanations, involving the orthodox couriers and prattling chambermaids, he let the story tell itself. The result, as William Archer has said, "was a new order of experience in the theatre." The audience that came to be pleasantly diverted by the old, old tricks found its nerves racked by a glimpse through a terrifying keyhole. This thing was not a stage-play, but a scandal. It didn't caress and soothe; it arrested and shocked. It didn't stay discreetly on the stage; it leaped out over the footlights.

The audience gasped and went out gabbling, and the result was the Ibsen madness, with its twenty years of folderol. But there were dramatists in the house who, with professional eye, saw more clearly what was afoot, and these dramatists, once they could shake off the Scribe tradition, began to imitate Ibsen—Jones and Pinero and later Shaw in England; Hauptmann and Sudermann in Germany; Gorki and many another in Russia; Hervieu, Brieux and their like in France; a swarm of lesser ones in Italy, Scandinavia and Austria. Ibsen, in brief, completely overthrew the well-made play of Scribe, and set up the play that was a direct imitation of reality. He showed that the illusion was not only not helped by the elaborate machinery of Scribe, but that it was actually hindered—that the way to sure and tremendous effects was by the route of simplicity, naturalness, ingenuousness. In *A Doll's House* he abandoned all of the old tricks save two or three; in *Ghosts* he made away with the rest of them, and even managed to do without a plot; by the time he got to Little Eyolf there was nothing left of the traditional dramaturgy save the act divisions. It was not, of course, an easy reform to put through. The habits of mind of audiences had to be changed; the lunacies of the Ibsenites had to be lived down, and the moral ire of the anti-Ibsenites; above all, the actors of the time had to be untaught all that they knew about acting, and taught a lot of new things that violated their vanity and hurt their business. But Ibsen's notions had logic behind them, and they had the force of novelty, and there was in them a new and superior opportunity for the dramatist who really had something to say, and so, in the end, they triumphed in the world. Today the methods of Scribe are so archaic that they excite laughter; only the Broadhursts and Kleins of Broadway stoop to them. If an intelligent dramatist were to expose a play built upon the plans of *Verre d'Eau* or *Adrienne Lecouvreur*, even the newspaper critics would laugh at him. All that sort of thing now belongs to archeology.

But Ibsen, as I have said, was a dramatist first and last, and not a tin-pot agitator and messiah. He depicted the life of his time and he made use of the ideas of his time; he had no desire to change those ideas, nor even, in the main, to criticise them. "A dramatist's business," he used to say, "is not to answer questions, but merely to ask them." He asked a question in *A Doll's House*. He asked another, ironically, in *Ghosts*. He asked others in *The Lady from the Sea*, *The Wild Duck* and *Little Eyolf*. In *The Master Builder*, rising, so to speak, to a question of personal privilege, he abandoned his habit and ventured upon a half-answer. But is there any answer in *Hedda Gabler*? Surely not. The play is still chewed and belabored by advocates of this answer or that; the very lack of agreement shows the dramatist's neutrality. "It was not my desire," he once said, "to deal in this play with so-called problems. What I wanted to do was to depict human beings, human emotions, and human destinies, upon a groundwork of certain of the social conditions and principles of the present day." That is to say, here is your state of society, here is your woman, here is what she does—what do you think of it? So, again, in *Pillars of Society*. Here is your society, here are your pillars, here are their rascalities—what have you to say of it? Joseph Conrad, another great artist, once put the thing admirably. "My task which I am trying to achieve," he said, "is, by the power of the written word, to make you hear, to make you feel—it is, before all, to make you *see*. That—and no more, and it is everything."

george bernard shaw

THE TECHNICAL NOVELTY IN IBSEN'S PLAYS

IT IS a striking and melancholy example of the preoccupation of critics with phrases and formulas to which they have given life by taking them into the tissue of their own living minds, and which therefore seem and feel vital and important to them whilst they are to everybody else the deadest and dreariest rubbish (this is the great secret of academic dryasdust), that to this day they remain blind to a new technical factor in the art of popular stage-play making which every considerable playwright has been thrusting under their noses night after night for a whole generation. This technical factor in the play is the discussion. Formerly you had in what was called a well made play an exposition in the first act, a situation in the second, and unravelling in the third. Now you have exposition, situation, and discussion; and the discussion is the test of the playwright. The critics protest in vain. They declare that discussions are not dramatic, and that art should not be didactic. Neither the playwrights nor the public take the smallest notice of them. The discussion conquered Europe in Ibsen's Doll's House; and now the serious playwright recognizes in the discussion not only the main test of his highest powers, but also the real centre of his play's interest. Sometimes he even takes every possible step to assure the public beforehand that his play will be fitted with that newest improvement.

This was inevitable if the drama was ever again to be raised above the childish demand for fables without morals. Children have a settled arbitrary morality: therefore to them moralizing is nothing but an intolerable platitudinizing. The morality of the grown-up is also very largely a settled morality, either purely conventional and of no ethical significance, like the rule of the road or the rule that when you ask for a yard of ribbon the shopkeeper shall give you thirty-six inches and not interpret the word yard as he pleases, or else too obvious in its ethics to leave any room for discussion: for instance, that if the boots keeps you waiting too long for your shaving water

From *The Quintessence of Ibsenism*. Reprinted by permission of The Society of Authors and The Public Trustee, London.

you must not plunge your razor into his throat in your irritation, no matter how great an effort of self-control your forbearance may cost you.

Now when a play is only a story of how a villain tries to separate an honest young pair of betrothed lovers; to gain the hand of the woman by calumny; and to ruin the man by forgery, murder, false witness, and other commonplaces of the Newgate Calendar, the introduction of a discussion would clearly be ridiculous. There is nothing for sane people to discuss; and any attempt to Chadbandize on the wickedness of such crimes is at once resented as, in Milton's phrase, "moral babble."

But this sort of drama is soon exhausted by people who go often to the theatre. In twenty visits one can see every possible change rung on all the available plots and incidents out of which plays of this kind can be manufactured. The illusion of reality is soon lost: in fact it may be doubted whether any adult ever entertains it: it is only to very young children that the fairy queen is anything but an actress. But at the age when we cease to mistake the figures on the stage for *dramatis personae,* and know that they are actors and actresses, the charm of the performer begins to assert itself; and the child who would have been cruelly hurt by being told that the Fairy Queen was only Miss Smith dressed up to look like one, becomes the man who goes to the theatre expressly to see Miss Smith, and is fascinated by her skill or beauty to the point of delighting in plays which would be unendurable to him without her. Thus we get plays "written round" popular performers, and popular performers who give value to otherwise useless plays by investing them with their own attractiveness. But all these enterprises are, commercially speaking, desperately precarious. To begin with, the supply of performers whose attraction is so far independent of the play that their inclusion in the cast sometimes makes the difference between success and failure is too small to enable all our theatres, or even many of them, to depend on their actors rather than on their plays. And to finish with, no actor can make bricks entirely without straw. From Grimaldi to Sothern, Jefferson, and Henry Irving (not to mention living actors) we have had players succeeding once in a lifetime in grafting on to a play which would have perished without them some figure imagined wholly by themselves; but none of them has been able to repeat the feat, nor to save many of the plays in which he has appeared from failure. In the long run nothing can retain the interest of the play-goer after the theatre has lost its illusion for his childhood, and its glamor for his adolescence, but a constant supply of interesting plays; and this is specially true in London, where the expense and trouble of theatre-going have been raised to a point at which it is surprising that sensible people of middle age go to the theatre at all. As a matter of fact, they mostly stay at home.

Now an interesting play cannot in the nature of things mean anything but a play in which problems of conduct and character of personal importance to the audience are raised and suggestively discussed. People have a thrifty sense of taking away something from such plays: they not only have had something for their money, but they retain that something as a permanent possession. Consequently none of the commonplaces of the box office hold good of such plays. In vain does the experienced acting manager declare that people want to be amused and not preached at in the theatre; that they will not stand long speeches; that a play must not contain more than 18,000 words; that it must not begin before nine nor last beyond eleven; that there must be no politics and no religion in it; that breach of these golden rules will drive people to the variety theatres; that there must be a woman of bad character, played by a very attractive actress, in the piece; and so on and so forth. All these counsels are valid for plays in which there is nothing to discuss. They may be disregarded by the playwright who is a moralist and a debater as well as a dramatist. From him, within the inevitable limits set by the clock and by the physical endurance of the human frame, people will stand anything as soon as they are matured enough and cultivated enough to be susceptible to the appeal of his particular form of art. The difficulty at present is that mature and cultivated people do not go to the theatre, just as they do not read penny novelets; and when an attempt is made to cater for them they do not respond to it in time, partly because they have not the habit of playgoing, and partly because it takes too long for them to find out that the new theatre is not like all the other theatres. But when they do at last find their way there, the attraction is not the firing of blank cartridges at one another by actors, nor the pretence of falling down dead that ends the stage combat, nor the simulation of erotic thrills by a pair of stage lovers, nor any of the other tomfooleries called action, but the exhibition and discussion of the character and conduct of stage figures who are made to appear real by the art of the playwright and the performers.

This, then, is the extension of the old dramatic form effected by Ibsen. Up to a certain point in the last act, A Doll's House is a play that might be turned into a very ordinary French drama by the excision of a few lines, and the substitution of a sentimental happy ending for the famous last scene: indeed the very first thing the theatrical wiseacres did with it was to effect exactly this transformation, with the result that the play thus pithed had no success and attracted no notice worth mentioning. But at just that point in the last act, the heroine very unexpectedly (by the wiseacres) stops her emotional acting and says: "We must sit down and discuss all this that has been happening between us." And it was by this new technical feature: this addition of a new movement, as musicians would say, to the dramatic form, that A Doll's House conquered Europe and founded a new school of dramatic art.

Since that time the discussion has expanded far beyond the limits of the last ten minutes of an otherwise "well made" play. The disadvantage of putting the discussion at the end was not only that it came when the audience was fatigued, but that it was necessary to see the play over again, so as to follow the earlier acts in the light of the final discussion, before it became fully intelligible. The practical utility of this book is due to the fact that unless the spectator at an Ibsen play has read the pages referring to it beforehand, it is hardly possible for him to get its bearings at a first hearing if he approaches it, as most spectators still do, with conventional idealist prepossessions. Accordingly, we now have plays, including some of my own, which begin with discussion and end with action, and others in which the discussion interpenetrates the action from beginning to end. When Ibsen invaded England discussion had vanished from the stage; and women could not write plays. Within twenty years women were writing better plays than men; and these plays were passionate arguments from beginning to end. The action of such plays consists of a case to be argued. If the case is uninteresting or stale or badly conducted or obviously trumped up, the play is a bad one. If it is important and novel and convincing, or at least disturbing, the play is a good one. But anyhow the play in which there is no argument and no case no longer counts as serious drama. It may still please the child in us as Punch and Judy does; but nobody nowadays pretends to regard the well made play as anything more than a commercial product which is not in question when modern schools of serious drama are under discussion. Indeed within ten years of the production of A Doll's House in London, audiences had become so derisive of the more obvious and hackneyed features of the methods of Sardou that it became dangerous to resort to them; and playwrights who persisted in "constructing" plays in the old French manner lost ground not for lack of ideas, but because their technique was unbearably out of fashion.

In the new plays, the drama arises through a conflict of unsettled ideals rather than through vulgar attachments, rapacities, generosities, resentments, ambitions, misunderstandings, oddities and so

forth as to which no moral question is raised. The conflict is not between clear right and wrong: the villain is as conscientious as the
hero, if not more so: in fact, the question which makes the play interesting (when it *is* interesting) is which is the villain and which
the hero. Or, to put it another way, there are no villains and no heroes.
This strikes the critics mainly as a departure from dramatic art; but it
is really the inevitable return to nature which ends all the merely
technical fashions. Now the natural is mainly the everyday; and its
climaxes must be, if not everyday, at least everylife, if they are to
have any importance for the spectator. Crimes, fights, big legacies,
fires, shipwrecks, battles, and thunderbolts are mistakes in a play,
even when they can be effectively simulated. No doubt they may
acquire dramatic interest by putting a character through the test of
an emergency; but the test is likely to be too obviously theatrical,
because, as the playwright cannot in the nature of things have much
experience of such catastrophes, he is forced to substitute a set of
conventions or conjectures for the feelings they really produce.

In short, pure accidents are not dramatic: they are only an-
ecdotic. They may be sensational, impressive, provocative, ruinous,
curious, or a dozen other things; but they have no specifically dramatic
interest. There is no drama in being knocked down or run over. The
catastrophe in Hamlet would not be in the least dramatic had Polonius
fallen downstairs and broken his neck, Claudius succumbed to de-
lirium tremens, Hamlet forgotten to breathe in the intensity of his
philosophic speculation, Ophelia died of Danish measles, Laertes been
shot by the palace sentry, and Rosencrantz and Guildenstern drowned
in the North Sea. Even as it is, the Queen, who poisons herself by
accident, has an air of being polished off to get her out of the way:
her death is the one dramatic failure of the piece. Bushels of good
paper have been inked in vain by writers who imagined they could
produce a tragedy by killing everyone in the last act accidentally.
As a matter of fact no accident, however sanguinary, can produce a
moment of real drama, though a difference of opinion between husband and wife as to living in town or country might be the beginning
of an appalling tragedy or a capital comedy.

It may be said that everything is an accident: that Othello's
character is an accident, Iago's character another accident, and the
fact that they happened to come together in the Venetian service
an even more accidental accident. Also that Torvald Helmer might
just as likely have married Mrs. Nickleby as Nora. Granting this
trifling for what it is worth, the fact remains that marriage is no more
an accident than birth or death: that is, it is expected to happen to
everybody. And if every man has a good deal of Torvald Helmer in

him, and every woman a good deal of Nora, neither their characters
nor their meeting and marrying are accidents. Othello, though entertaining, pitiful, and resonant with the thrills a master of language can
produce by mere artistic sonority is certainly much more accidental
than A Doll's House; but it is correspondingly less important and
interesting to us. It has been kept alive, not by its manufactured misunderstandings and stolen handkerchiefs and the like, nor even by its
orchestral verse, but by its exhibition and discussion of human nature,
marriage, and jealousy; and it would be a prodigiously better play if
it were a serious discussion of the highly interesting problem of how
a simple Moorish soldier would get on with a "supersubtle" Venetian
lady of fashion if he married her. As it is, the play turns on a mistake;
and though a mistake can produce a murder, which is the vulgar
substitute for a tragedy, it cannot produce a real tragedy in the
modern sense. Reflective people are not more interested in the Chamber of Horrors than in their own homes, nor in murderers, victims,
and villains than in themselves; and the moment a man has acquired
sufficient reflective power to cease gaping at waxworks, he is on his
way to losing interest in Othello, Desdemona, and Iago exactly to the
extent to which they become interesting to the police. Cassio's weakness for drink comes much nearer home to most of us than Othello's
strangling and throat cutting, or Iago's theatrical confidence trick.
The proof is that Shakespear's professional colleagues, who exploited
all his sensational devices, and piled up torture on murder and incest
on adultery until they had far out-Heroded Herod, are now un-
memorable and unplayable. Shakespear survives because he coolly
treated the sensational horrors of his borrowed plots as inorganic
theatrical accessories, using them simply as pretexts for dramatizing
human character as it exists in the normal world. In enjoying and discussing his plays we unconsciously discount the combats and murders:
commentators are never so astray (and consequently so ingenious) as
when they take Hamlet seriously as a madman, Macbeth as a homi-
cidal Highlander, and impish humorists like Richard and Iago as lurid
villains of the Renascence. The plays in which these figures appear
could be changed into comedies without altering a hair of their
beards. Shakespear, had anyone been intelligent enough to tax him
with this, would perhaps have said that most crimes are accidents
that happen to people exactly like ourselves, and that Macbeth, under
propitious circumstances, would have made an exemplary rector of
Stratford, a real criminal being a defective monster, a human accident,
useful on the stage only for minor parts such as Don Johns, second
murderers, and the like. Anyhow, the fact remains that Shakespear
survives by what he has in common with Ibsen, and not by what he

has in common with Webster and the rest. Hamlet's surprise at finding that he "lacks gall" to behave in the idealistically conventional manner, and that no extremity of rhetoric about the duty of revenging "a dear father slain" and exterminating the "bloody bawdy villain" who murdered him seems to make any difference in their domestic relations in the palace in Elsinore, still keeps us talking about him and going to the theatre to listen to him, whilst the older Hamlets, who never had any Ibsenist hesitations, and shammed madness, and entangled the courtiers in the arras and burnt them, and stuck hard to the theatrical school of the fat boy in Pickwick ("I wants to make your flesh creep"), are as dead as John Shakespear's mutton.

We have progressed so rapidly on this point under the impulse given to the drama by Ibsen that it seems strange now to contrast him favorably with Shakespear on the ground that he avoided the old catastrophes which left the stage strewn with the dead at the end of an Elizabethan tragedy. For perhaps the most plausible reproach levelled at Ibsen by modern critics of his own school is just that survival of the old school in him which makes the death rate so high in his last acts. Do Oswald Alving, Hedvig Ekdal, Rosmer and Rebecca, Hedda Gabler, Solness, Eyolf, Borkman, Rubeck and Irene die dramatically natural deaths, or are they slaughtered in the classic and Shakespearean manner, partly because the audience expects blood for its money, partly because it is difficult to make people attend seriously to anything except by startling them with some violent calamity? It is so easy to make out a case for either view that I shall not argue the point. The post-Ibsen playwrights apparently think that Ibsen's homicides and suicides were forced. In Tchekov's Cherry Orchard, for example, where the sentimental ideals of our amiable, cultured, Schumann playing propertied class are reduced to dust and ashes by a hand not less deadly than Ibsen's because it is so much more caressing, nothing more violent happens than that the family cannot afford to keep up its old house. In Granville-Barker's plays, the campaign against our society is carried on with all Ibsen's implacability; but the one suicide (in Waste) is unhistorical; for neither Parnell nor Dilke, who were the actual cases in point of the waste which was the subject of the play, killed himself. I myself have been reproached because the characters in my plays "talk but do nothing," meaning that they do not commit felonies. As a matter of fact we have come to see that it is no true *dénouement* to cut the Gordian knot as Alexander did with a stroke of the sword. If people's souls are tied up by law and public opinion it is much more tragic to leave them to wither in these bonds than to end their misery and relieve the salutary compunction of the audience by outbreaks of violence.

Judge Brack was, on the whole, right when he said that people dont do such things. If they did, the idealists would be brought to their senses very quickly indeed.

But in Ibsen's plays the catastrophe, even when it seems forced, and when the ending of the play would be more tragic without it, is never an accident; and the play never exists for its sake. His nearest to an accident is the death of little Eyolf, who falls off a pier and is drowned. But this instance only reminds us that there is one good dramatic use for an accident: it can awaken people. When England wept over the deaths of little Nell and Paul Dombey, the strong soul of Ruskin was moved to scorn: to novelists who were at a loss to make their books sell he offered the formula: When at a loss, kill a child. But Ibsen did not kill little Eyolf to manufacture pathos. The surest way to achieve a thoroughly bad performance of Little Eyolf is to conceive it as a sentimental tale of a drowned darling. Its drama lies in the awakening of Allmers and his wife to the despicable quality and detestable rancors of the life they have been idealizing as blissful and poetic. They are so sunk in their dream that the awakening can be effected only by a violent shock. And that is just the one dramatically useful thing an accident can do. It can shock. Hence the accident that befalls Eyolf.

As to the deaths in Ibsen's last acts, they are a sweeping up of the remains of dramatically finished people. Solness's fall from the tower is as obviously symbolic as Phaeton's fall from the chariot of the sun. Ibsen's dead bodies are those of the exhausted or destroyed: he does not kill Hilda, for instance, as Shakespear killed Juliet. He is ruthless enough with Hedvig and Eyolf because he wants to use their deaths to expose their parents; but if he had written Hamlet nobody would have been killed in the last act except perhaps Horatio, whose correct nullity might have provoked Fortinbras to let some of the moral sawdust out of him with his sword. For Shakespearean deaths in Ibsen you must go back to Lady Inger and the plays of his nonage, with which this book is not concerned.

The drama was born of old from the union of two desires: the desire to have a dance and the desire to hear a story. The dance became a rant: the story became a situation. When Ibsen began to make plays, the art of the dramatist had shrunk into the art of contriving a situation. And it was held that the stranger the situation, the better the play. Ibsen saw that, on the contrary, the more familiar the situation, the more interesting the play. Shakespear had put ourselves on the stage but not our situations. Our uncles seldom murder our fathers, and cannot legally marry our mothers; we do not meet witches; our kings are not as a rule stabbed and succeeded by their stabbers; and when we raise money by bills we do not promise to pay pounds of our flesh. Ibsen supplies the want left by Shakespear. He gives us not only ourselves, but ourselves in our own situations. The things that happen to his stage figures are things that happen to us. One consequence is that his plays are much more important to us than Shakespear's. Another is that they are capable both of hurting us cruelly and of filling us with excited hopes of escape from idealistic tyrannies, and with visions of intenser life in the future.

Changes in technique follow inevitably from these changes in the subject matter of the play. When a dramatic poet can give you hopes and visions, such old maxims as that stage-craft is the art of preparation become boyish, and may be left to those unfortunate playwrights who, being unable to make anything really interesting happen on the stage, have to acquire the art of continually persuading the audience that it is going to happen presently. When he can stab people to the heart by shewing them the meanness or cruelty of something they did yesterday and intend to do tomorrow, all the old tricks to catch and hold their attention become the silliest of superfluities. The play called The Murder of Gonzago, which Hamlet makes the players act before his uncle, is artlessly constructed; but it produces a greater effect on Claudius than the Œdipus of Sophocles, because it is about himself. The writer who practises the art of Ibsen therefore discards all the old tricks of preparation, catastrophe, *dénouement*, and so forth without thinking about it, just as a modern rifleman never dreams of providing himself with powder horns, percussion caps, and wads: indeed he does not know the use of them. Ibsen substituted a terrible art of sharpshooting at the audience, trapping them, fencing with them, aiming always at the sorest spot in their consciences. Never mislead an audience, was an old rule. But the new school will trick the spectator into forming a meanly false judgment, and then convict him of it in the next act, often to his grievous mortification. When you despise something you ought to take off your hat to, or admire and imitate something you ought to loathe, you cannot resist the dramatist who knows how to touch these morbid spots in you and make you see that they are morbid. The dramatist knows that as long as he is teaching and saving his audience, he is as sure of their strained attention as a dentist is, or the Angel of the Annunciation. And though he may use all the magic of art to make you forget the pain he causes you or to enhance the joy of the hope and courage he awakens, he is never occupied in the old work of manufacturing interest and expectation with materials that have neither novelty, significance, nor relevance to the experience or prospects of the spectators.

Hence a cry has arisen that the post-Ibsen play is not a play, and that its technique, not being the technique described by Aristotle, is not a technique at all. I will not enlarge on this: the fun poked at my friend Mr. A. B. Walkley in the prologue of Fanny's First Play need not be repeated here. But I may remind him that the new technique is new only on the modern stage. It has been used by preachers and orators ever since speech was invented. It is the technique of playing upon the human conscience; and it has been practised by the playwright whenever the playwright has been capable of it. Rhetoric, irony, argument, paradox, epigram, parable, the rearrangement of haphazard facts into orderly and intelligent situations: these are both the oldest and the newest arts of the drama; and your plot construc- tion and art of preparation are only the tricks of theatrical talent and the shifts of moral sterility, not the weapons of dramatic genius. In the theatre of Ibsen we are not flattered spectators killing an idle hour with an ingenious and amusing entertainment: we are "guilty creatures sitting at a play"; and the technique of pastime is no more applicable than at a murder trial.

The technical novelties of the Ibsen and post-Ibsen plays are, then: first, the introduction of the discussion and its development until it so overspreads and interpenetrates the action that it finally assimilates it, making play and discussion practically identical; and, second, as a consequence of making the spectators themselves the persons of the drama, and the incidents of their own lives its incidents, the disuse of the old stage tricks by which audiences had to be induced to take an interest in unreal people and improbable circumstances, and the substitution of a forensic technique of recrimination, disillusion, and penetration through ideals to the truth, with a free use of all the rhetorical and lyrical arts of the orator, the preacher, the pleader, and the rhapsodist.

francis fergusson

GHOSTS AND THE CHERRY ORCHARD:
THE THEATER OF MODERN REALISM

Hamlet to Rosencrantz and Guildenstern—

"Then are our beggars bodies, and our out-
stretched monarchs and heroes the beggars'
shadows."

WHEN I say *modern realism* I am taking the term in the broad sense
of the strictly photographic imitation of the human scene. In this
sense modern realism is a lingua franca, a pidgin-English of the imagination which everyone in our time can understand. The camera
and the radio, continuing a process which began at least a hundred
years ago, reproduce more and more accurately the surfaces, the
sounds and sights of contemporary life: vastly distended on the screen,
or murmured in the ears of a million housewives. If we have lost our
bearings, if we automatically reject any stable picture of the human
condition, we can still gossip about the neighbors and eavesdrop on
other lives. It would seem that this medium, and the narrow scene
of human life it implies, are too meager for drama at all. Yet Ibsen
and Chekhov accepted its limitations, and made superb plays.

The theater of modern realism is greatly shrunken compared
with the theaters I studied in Part I.[1] It came out of that "diminished
scene of rationalism" which I described as the degeneration of Racine's
theater of reason: the heroes are gone, the struggle of reason itself
is lost to sight; the literal-minded Oenones and Arsaces take the stage,
with their myopic shrewdness. It is the little scene which Wagner
totally rejected, in favor of his nocturnal world of passion. If one
thinks of the theater of Shakespeare, one may place the little scene
of modern realism at the point where Hamlet meets Rosencrantz and
Guildenstern: the non-committal "center" of human awareness, the
"middle" of Fortune's favors, where the beggarly body looks sure and
solid, and all the motivations which might lead to wider awarenesses

Reprinted from *The Idea of a Theater* by Francis Fergusson by permission of Princeton
University Press. Copyright, 1949, by Princeton University Press.
[1] In Part I Fergusson discusses the classical drama of ancient Greece, seventeenth century
France, and the Romantic dramas of nineteenth century Germany. [Ed.]

look shadowy and deluded. Thus the theater of modern realism does not offer a strictly defined medium, a limited but deeply based convention for revealing human action, like the ideal Wagnerian or Racinian theater. It rejects the traditional order of myth and ritual which Shakespeare could assume. And the question is how, and to what extent, it may be used for the purposes of drama at all.

It is easy to see why Mr. Eliot should think of it as essentially anti-poetic, leading inevitably to the "desert of exact likeness to the reality which is perceived by the most commonplace mind." We have seen this desert in a thousand forms, meaningless reports of life in Paris and Pernambuco, Hoboken and Helsingfors. It is certainly true that the theater of modern realism does not offer the dramatist a defined art medium; it even imposes upon him the necessity of pretending that he has no poetic purpose at all, but truth in some pseudo-scientific sense. Yet Ibsen and Chekhov (to say nothing of other writers of less scope) were able to place in this narrow theater a certain kind of theatrical poetry. It is a hidden poetry, masquerading as reporting; it is a "poetry of the theater" (in M. Cocteau's phrase) and not a poetry of words; and it is based upon the histrionic sensibility and the art of acting: it can only be seen in performance or by imagining a performance. This property of modern realism—its close dependence upon acting—Henry James regarded as a sure sign of its vitality, and Eliot regards as a great weakness. It seems to me that James was right; it is in their direct histrionic awareness that the masters of modern realism are most closely akin to the intentions and the modes of awareness of Shakespeare and Sophocles.

Modern realism does not define an art medium, nor does it, in itself, offer the dramatist any clue to form. Ibsen and Chekhov do not enjoy the perspectives of myth or of ritual whereby action is both placed and defined in the traditional theater. . . .

Ibsen's *Ghosts* and Chekhov's *The Cherry Orchard* have little in common except the theater of modern realism itself. By considering them one may get some notion of the potentialities and the limitations of this paradoxical theater, which pretends to be not art but life itself.

THE PLOT OF *GHOSTS*: THESIS, THRILLER, AND TRAGEDY

Ghosts is not Ibsen's best play, but it serves my purpose, which is to study the foundations of modern realism, just because of its imperfections. Its power, and the poetry of some of its effects, are evident; yet a contemporary audience may be bored with its old-fashioned iconoclasm and offended by the clatter of its too-obviously well-made plot. On the surface it is a *drame à thèse,* of the kind Brieux was to develop to its logical conclusion twenty years later: it proves the hollowness of the conventional bourgeois marriage. At the same time it is a thriller with all the tricks of the Boulevard entertainment: Ibsen was a student of Scribe in his middle period. But underneath this superficial form of thesis-thriller—the play which Ibsen started to write, the angry diatribe as he first conceived it—there is another form, the shape of the underlying action, which Ibsen gradually made out in the course of his two-years' labor upon the play, in obedience to his scruple of truthfulness, his profound attention to the reality of his fictive characters' lives. The form of the play is understood according to two conceptions of plot, which Ibsen himself did not at this point clearly distinguish: the rationalized concatenation of events with a univocal moral, and the plot as the "soul" or first actualization of the directly perceived action.

Halvdahn Khot, in his excellent study *Henrik Ibsen,* has explained the circumstances under which *Ghosts* was written. It was first planned as an attack upon marriage, in answer to the critics of *A Doll's House.* The story of the play is perfectly coherent as the demonstration and illustration of this thesis. When the play opens, Captain Alving has just died, his son Oswald is back from Paris where he had been studying painting, and his wife is straightening out the estate. The Captain had been accepted locally as a pillar of society but was in secret a drunkard and debauchee. He had seduced his wife's maid, and had a child by her; and this child, Regina, is now in her turn Mrs. Alving's maid. Mrs. Alving had concealed all this for something like twenty years. She was following the advice of the conventional Pastor Manders and endeavoring to save Oswald from the horrors of the household: it was for this reason she had sent him away to school. But now, with her husband's death, she proposes to get rid of the Alving heritage in all its forms, in order to free herself and Oswald for the innocent, unconventional "joy of life." She wants to endow an orphanage with the Captain's money, both to quiet any rumors there may be of his sinful life and to get rid of the remains of his power over her. She encounters this power, however, in many forms, through the Pastor's timidity and through the attempt by Engstrand (a local carpenter who was bribed to pretend to be Regina's father) to blackmail her. Oswald wants to marry Regina and has to be told the whole story. At last he reveals that he has inherited syphilis from his father—the dead hand of the past in its most sensationally ugly form—and when his brain softens at the end, Mrs. Alving's whole plan collapses in unrelieved horror. It is "proved" that she should have left home twenty years before, like Nora in *A Doll's House*; and that conventional marriage is therefore an evil tyranny.

In accordance with the principles of the thesis play, *Ghosts* is plotted as a series of debates on conventional morality, between Mrs. Alving and the Pastor, the Pastor and Oswald, and Oswald and his mother. It may also be read as a perfect well-made thriller. The story is presented with immediate clarity, with mounting and controlled suspense; each act ends with an exciting curtain which reaffirms the issues and promises important new developments. In this play, as in so many others, one may observe that the conception of dramatic form underlying the thesis play and the machine-made Boulevard entertainment is the same: the logically concatenated series of events (intriguing thesis or logical intrigue) which the characters and their relationships merely illustrate. And it was this view of *Ghosts* which made it an immediate scandal and success.

But Ibsen himself protested that he was not a reformer but a poet. He was often led to write by anger and he compared the process of composition to his pet scorpion's emptying of poison; Ibsen kept a piece of soft fruit in his cage for the scorpion to sting when the spirit moved him. But Ibsen's own spirit was not satisfied by the mere discharge of venom; and one may see, in *Ghosts*, behind the surfaces of the savage story, a partially realized tragic form of really poetic scope, the result of Ibsen's more serious and disinterested brooding upon the human condition in general, where it underlies the myopic rebellions and empty clichés of the time.

In order to see the tragedy behind the thesis, it is necessary to return to the distinction between plot and action, and to the distinction between the plot as the rationalized series of events, and the plot as "the soul of the tragedy." The action of the play is "to control the Alving heritage for my own life." Most of the characters want some material or social advantage from it—Engstrand money, for instance, and the Pastor the security of conventional respectability. But Mrs. Alving is seeking a true and free human life itself—for her son, and through him, for herself. Mrs. Alving sometimes puts this quest in terms of the iconoclasms of the time, but her spiritual life, as Ibsen gradually discovered it, is at a deeper level; she tests everything— Oswald, the Pastor, Regina, her own moves—in the light of her extremely strict if unsophisticated moral sensibility: by direct perception and not by ideas at all. She is tragically seeking; she suffers a series of pathoses and new insights in the course of the play; and this rhythm of will, feeling, and insight underneath the machinery of the plot is the form of the life of the play, the soul of the tragedy.

The similarity between *Ghosts* and Greek tragedy, with its single fated action moving to an unmistakable catastrophe, has been felt by many critics of Ibsen. Mrs. Alving, like Oedipus, is engaged in a quest for her true human condition; and Ibsen, like Sophocles, shows on-stage only the end of this quest, when the past is being brought up again in the light of the present action and its fated outcome. From this point of view Ibsen is a plot-maker in the first sense: by means of his selection and arrangement of incidents he defines an action under-lying many particular events and realized in various modes of intelligi-ble purpose, of suffering, and of new insight. What Mrs. Alving sees changes in the course of the play, just as what Oedipus sees changes as one veil after another is removed from the past and the present. The underlying form of *Ghosts* is that of the tragic rhythm as one finds it in *Oedipus Rex*.

But this judgment needs to be qualified in several respects: be-cause of the theater for which Ibsen wrote, the tragic form which Sophocles could develop to the full, and with every theatrical resource, is hidden beneath the clichés of plot and the surfaces "evident to the most commonplace mind." At the end of the play the tragic rhythm of Mrs. Alving's quest is not so much completed as brutally truncated, in obedience to the requirements of the thesis and the thriller. Oswald's collapse, before our eyes, with his mother's screaming, makes the in-trigue end with a bang, and hammers home the thesis. But from the point of view of Mrs. Alving's tragic quest as we have seen it develop through the rest of the play, this conclusion concludes nothing: it is merely sensational.

The exciting intrigue and the brilliantly, the violently clear sur-faces of *Ghosts* are likely to obscure completely its real life and under-lying form. The tragic rhythm, which Ibsen rediscovered by his long and loving attention to the reality of his fictive lives, is evident only to the histrionic sensibility. As Henry James put it, Ibsen's characters "have the extraordinary, the brilliant property of becoming when repre-sented at once more abstract and more living": i.e., both their lives and the life of the play, the spiritual content and the form of the whole, are revealed in this medium. A Nazimova, a Duse, could show it to us on the stage. Lacking such a performance, the reader must endeavor to respond imaginatively and directly himself if he is to see the hidden poetry of *Ghosts*.

MRS. ALVING AND OSWALD:
THE TRAGIC RHYTHM IN A SMALL FIGURE

As Ibsen was fighting to present his poetic vision within the narrow theater admitted by modern realism, so his protagonist Mrs. Alving is fighting to realize her sense of human life in the blank photograph of her own stuffy parlor. She discovers there no means, no terms, and no nourishment; that is the truncated tragedy which underlies the savage thesis of the play. But she does find her son Oswald, and she makes of him the symbol of all she is seeking: freedom, innocence, joy, and truth. At the level of the life of the play, where Ibsen warms his characters into extraordinary human reality, they all have moral and emotional meanings for each other; and the pattern of their related actions, their partially blind struggle for the Alving heritage, is consistent and very complex. In this structure, Mrs. Alving's changing relation to Oswald is only one strand, though an important one. I wish to consider it as a sample of Ibsen's rediscovery, through modern realism, of the tragic rhythm.

Oswald is of course not only a symbol for his mother, but a person in his own right, with his own quest for freedom and release, and his own anomalous stake in the Alving heritage. He is also a symbol for Pastor Manders of what he wants from Captain Alving's estate: the stability and continuity of the bourgeois conventions. In the economy of the play as a whole, Oswald is the hidden reality of the whole situation, like Oedipus' actual status as son-husband: the hidden fatality which, revealed in a series of tragic and ironic steps, brings the final peripety of the action. To see how this works, the reader is asked to consider Oswald's role in Act I and the beginning of Act II.

The main part of Act I (after a prologue between Regina and Engstrand) is a debate, or rather agon, between Mrs. Alving and the Pastor. The Pastor has come to settle the details of Mrs. Alving's bequest of her husband's money to the orphanage. They at once disagree about the purpose and handling of the bequest; and this disagreement soon broadens into the whole issue of Mrs. Alving's emancipation versus the Pastor's conventionality. The question of Oswald is at the center. The Pastor wants to think of him, and to make of him, a pillar of society such as the Captain was supposed to have been, while Mrs. Alving wants him to be her masterpiece of liberation. At this point Oswald himself wanders in, the actual but still mysterious truth underlying the dispute between his mother and the Pastor. His appearance produces what the Greeks would have called a complex recognition scene, with an implied peripety for both Mrs. Alving and the Pastor, which will not be realized by them until the end of the act. But this tragic development is written to be acted; it is to be found, not so much in the actual words of the characters, as in their moral-emotional responses and changing relationships to one another.

The Pastor has not seen Oswald since he grew up; and seeing

him now he is startled as though by a real ghost; he recognizes him as the very reincarnation of his father: the same physique, the same mannerisms, even the same kind of pipe. Mrs. Alving with equal confidence recognizes him as her own son, and she notes that his mouth-mannerism is like the Pastor's. (She had been in love with the Pastor during the early years of her marriage, when she wanted to leave the Captain.) As for Oswald himself, the mention of the pipe gives him a Proustian intermittence of the heart: he suddenly recalls a childhood scene when his father had given him his own pipe to smoke. He feels again the nausea and the cold sweat, and hears the Captain's hearty laughter. Thus in effect he recognizes himself as his father's, in the sense of his father's *victim;* a premonition of the ugly scene at the end of the play. But at this point no one is prepared to accept the full import of these insights. The whole scene is, on the surface, light and conventional, an accurate report of a passage of provincial politeness. Oswald wanders off for a walk before dinner, and the Pastor and his mother are left to bring their struggle more into the open.

Oswald's brief scene marks the end of the first round of the fight, and serves as prologue for the second round, much as the intervention of the chorus in the agon between Oedipus and Tiresias punctuates their struggle, and hints at an unexpected outcome on a new level of awareness. As soon as Oswald has gone, the Pastor launches an attack in form upon Mrs. Alving's entire emancipated way of life, with the question of Oswald, his role in the community, his upbringing and his future, always at the center of the attack. Mrs. Alving replies with her whole rebellious philosophy, illustrated by a detailed account of her tormented life with the Captain, none of which the Pastor had known (or been willing to recognize) before. Mrs. Alving proves on the basis of this evidence that her new freedom is right; that her long secret rebellion was justified; and that she is now about to complete Oswald's emancipation, and thereby her own, from the swarming ghosts of the past. If the issue were merely on this rationalistic level, and between her and the Pastor, she would triumph at this point. But the real truth of her situation (as Oswald's appearance led us to suppose) does not fit either her rationalization or the Pastor's.

Oswald passes through the parlor again on his way to the dining room to get a drink before dinner, and his mother watches him in pride and pleasure. But from behind the door we hear the affected squealing of Regina. It is now Mrs. Alving's turn for an intermittence of the heart: it is as though she heard again her husband with Regina's mother. The insight which she had rejected before now reaches her in full strength, bringing the promised pathos and peripety; she sees Oswald, not as her masterpiece of liberation, but as the sinister, tyrannical, and continuing life of the past itself. The basis of her rationalization is gone; she suffers the breakdown of the moral being which she had built upon her now exploded view of Oswald.

At this point Ibsen brings down the curtain in obedience to the principles of the well-made play. The effect is to raise the suspense by stimulating our curiosity about the facts of the rest of the story. What will Mrs. Alving do now? What will the Pastor do—for Oswald and Regina are half-brother and sister; can we prevent the scandal from coming out? So the suspense is raised, but the attention of the audience is diverted from Mrs. Alving's tragic quest to the most literal, newspaper version of the facts.

The second act (which occurs immediately after dinner) is ostensibly concerned only with these gossipy facts. The Pastor and Mrs. Alving debate ways of handling the threatened scandal. But this is only the literal surface: Ibsen has his eye upon Mrs. Alving's shaken psyche, and the actual dramatic form of this scene, under the discussion which Mrs. Alving keeps up, is her pathos which the Act I curtain broke off. Mrs. Alving is suffering the blow in courage and faith; and she is rewarded with her deepest insight: "I am half inclined to think we are all ghosts, Mr. Manders. It is not only what we have inherited from our fathers and mothers that exists again in us, but all sorts of dead ideas and all kinds of old dead beliefs and things of that kind. They are not actually alive in us; but they are dormant all the same, and we can never be rid of them. Whenever I take up a newspaper and read it, I fancy I see ghosts creeping between the lines. There must be ghosts all over the world. They must be as countless as the grains of sand, it seems to me. And we are so miserably afraid of the light, all of us." [2] This passage, in the fumbling phrases of Ibsen's provincial lady, and in William Archer's translation, is not by itself the poetry of the great dramatic poets. It does not have the verbal music of Racine, nor the freedom and sophistication of Hamlet, nor the scope of the Sophoclean chorus, with its use of the full complement of poetic and musical and theatrical resources. But in the total situation in the Alving parlor which Ibsen has so carefully established, and in terms of Mrs. Alving's uninstructed but profoundly developing awareness, it has its own hidden poetry: a poetry not of words but of the theater, a poetry of the histrionic sensibility. From the point of view of the underlying form of the play—the form as "the soul" of the tragedy—this scene completes the sequence which began with the debate in Act I: it is the pathos-and-epiphany following that agon.

It is evident, I think, that insofar as Ibsen was able to obey his

[2] *Ghosts,* by Henrik Ibsen. Translated by William Archer.

realistic scruple, his need for the disinterested perception of human life beneath the clichés of custom and rationalization, he rediscovered the perennial basis of tragedy. The poetry of *Ghosts* is under the words, in the detail of action, where Ibsen accurately sensed the tragic rhythm of human life in a thousand small figures. And these little "movements of the psyche" are composed in a complex rhythm like music, a formal development sustained (beneath the sensational story and the angry thesis) until the very end. But the action is not completed: Mrs. Alving is left screaming with the raw impact of the calamity. The music is broken off, the dissonance unresolved—or, in more properly dramatic terms, the acceptance of the catastrophe, leading to the final vision or epiphany which should correspond to the insight Mrs. Alving gains in Act II, is lacking. The action of the play is neither completed nor placed in the wider context of meanings which the disinterested or contemplative purposes of poetry demand.

The unsatisfactory end of *Ghosts* may be understood in several ways. Thinking of the relation between Mrs. Alving and Oswald, one might say that she had romantically loaded more symbolic values upon her son than a human being can carry; hence his collapse proves too much—more than Mrs. Alving or the audience can digest. One may say that, at the end, Ibsen himself could not quite dissociate himself from his rebellious protagonist and see her action in the round, and so broke off in anger, losing his tragic vision in the satisfaction of reducing the bourgeois parlor to a nightmare, and proving the hollowness of a society which sees human life in such myopic and dishonest terms. As a thesis play, *Ghosts* is an ancestor of many related genres: Brieux's arguments for social reform, propaganda plays like those of the Marxists, or parables *à la* Andreev, or even Shaw's more generalized plays of the play-of-thought about social questions. But this use of the theater of modern realism for promoting or discussing political and social ideas never appealed to Ibsen. It did not solve his real problem, which was to use the publicly accepted theater of his time for poetic purposes. The most general way to understand the unsatisfactory end of *Ghosts* is to say that Ibsen could not find a way to represent the action of his protagonist, with all its moral and intellectual depth, within the terms of modern realism. In the attempt he truncated this action, and revealed as in a brilliant light the limitations of the bourgeois parlor as the scene of human life.

THE END OF *GHOSTS*: THE TASTELESS PARLOR AND THE STAGE OF EUROPE

Oswald is the chief symbol of what Mrs. Alving is seeking, and his collapse ends her quest in a horrifying catastrophe. But in the complex life of the play, all of the persons and things acquire emotional and moral significance for Mrs. Alving; and at the end, to throw as much light as possible upon the catastrophe, Ibsen brings all of the elements of his composition together in their highest symbolic valency. The orphanage has burned to the ground; the Pastor has promised Engstrand money for his "Sailor's Home" which he plans as a brothel; Regina departs, to follow her mother in the search for pleasure and money. In these eventualities the conventional morality of the Alving heritage is revealed as lewdness and dishonesty, quickly consumed in the fires of lust and greed, as Oswald himself (the central symbol) was consumed even before his birth. But what does this wreckage mean? Where are we to place it in human experience? Ibsen can only place it in the literal parlor, with lamplight giving place to daylight, and sunrise on the empty, stimulating, virginal snow-peaks out the window. The emotional force of this complicated effect is very great; it has the searching intimacy of nightmare. But it is also as disquieting as a nightmare from which we are suddenly awakened; it is incomplete, and the contradiction between the inner power of dream and the literal appearances of the daylight world is unresolved. The spirit that moved Ibsen to write the play, and which moved his protagonist through her tragic progress, is lost to sight, disembodied, imperceptible in any form unless the dreary exaltation of the inhuman mountain scene conveys it in feeling.

Henry James felt very acutely the contradiction between the deep and strict spirit of Ibsen and his superb craftsmanship on one side, and the little scene he tried to use—the parlor in its surrounding void—on the other. "If the spirit is a lamp within us, glowing through what the world and the flesh make of us as through a ground-glass shade, then such pictures as Little Eyolf and John Gabriel are each a chassez-croisez of lamps burning, as in tasteless parlors, with the flame practically exposed," he wrote in *London Notes*.[3] "There is a positive odor of spiritual paraffin. The author nevertheless arrives at the dramatist's great goal—he arrives for all his meagerness at intensity. The meagerness, which is after all but an unconscious, an admirable economy, never interferes with that: it plays straight into the hands of his rare mastery of form. The contrast between this form—so difficult to have reached, so 'evolved,' so civilized—and the bareness and bleakness of his little northern democracy is the source of half the hard frugal charm he puts forth."

James had rejected very early in his career his own little northern democracy, that of General Grant's America, with its ugly parlor, its dead conventions, its enthusiastic materialism, and its "non-conducting

[3] Jan.–Aug., 1897.

atmosphere." At the same time he shared Ibsen's ethical preoccupation, and his strict sense of form. His comments on Ibsen are at once the most sympathetic and the most objective that have been written. But James's own solution was to try to find a better parlor for the theater of human life; to present the quest of his American pilgrim of culture on the wider "stage of Europe" as this might still be felt and suggested in the manners of the leisured classes in England and France. James would have nothing to do with the prophetic and revolutionary spirit which was driving the great continental authors, Ibsen among them. In his artistry and his moral exactitude Ibsen is akin to James; but this is not his whole story, and if one is to understand the spirit he tried to realize in Mrs. Alving, one must think of Kierkegaard, who had a great influence on Ibsen in the beginning of his career.

Kierkegaard (in *For Self-Examination*) has this to say of the disembodied and insatiable spirit of the times:

". . . thou wilt scarcely find anyone who does not believe in—let us say, for example, the spirit of the age, the *Zeitgeist*. Even he who has taken leave of higher things and is rendered blissful by mediocrity, yea, even he who toils slavishly for paltry ends or in the contemptible servitude of ill-gotten gains, even he believes, firmly and fully too, in the spirit of the age. Well, that is natural enough, it is by no means anything very lofty he believes in, for the spirit of the age is after all no higher than the age, it keeps close to the ground, so that it is the sort of spirit which is most like will-o'-the-wisp; but yet he believes in spirit. Or he believes in the world-spirit (*Weltgeist*) that strong spirit (for allurements, yes), that ingenious spirit (for deceits, yes); that spirit which Christianity calls an evil spirit—so that, in consideration of this, it is by no means anything very lofty he believes in when he believes in the world-spirit; but yet he believes in spirit. Or he believes in 'the spirit of humanity,' not spirit in the individual, but in the race, that spirit which, when it is god-forsaken for having forsaken God, is again, according to Christianity's teaching, an evil spirit—so that in view of this it is by no means anything very lofty he believes in when he believes in this spirit; but yet he believes in spirit.

"On the other hand, as soon as the talk is about a holy spirit—how many, dost thou think, believe in it? Or when the talk is about an evil spirit which is to be renounced—how many, dost thou think, believe in such a thing?[4]

This description seems to me to throw some light upon Mrs. Alving's quest, upon Ibsen's modern-realistic scene, and upon the theater which his audience would accept. The other face of nineteenth century positivism is romantic aspiration. And Ibsen's realistic scene

[4] Kierkegaard, *For Self-Examination and Judge for Yourselves* (Princeton University Press, 1944), p. 94.

presents both of these aspects of the human condition: the photo-graphically accurate parlor, in the foreground, satisfies the require-ments of positivism, while the empty but stimulating scene out the window—Europe as a moral void, an uninhabited wilderness—offers as it were a blank check to the insatiate spirit. Ibsen always felt this exhilarating wilderness behind his cramped interiors. In *A Doll's House* we glimpse it as winter weather and black water. In *The Lady from the Sea* it is the cold ocean, with its whales and its gulls. In *The Wild Duck* it is the northern marshes, with wildfowl but no people. In the last scene of *Ghosts* it is, of course, the bright snow-peaks, which may mean Mrs. Alving's quest in its most disembodied and ambivalent form; very much the same sensuous moral void in which Wagner, having totally rejected the little human foreground where Ibsen fights his battles, unrolls the solitary action of passion. It is the "stage of Europe" before human exploration, as it might have appeared to the first hunters.

There is a kinship between the fearless and demanding spirit of Kierkegaard, and the spirit which Ibsen tried to realize in Mrs. Alving. But Mrs. Alving, like her contemporaries whom Kierkegaard describes, will not or cannot accept any interpretation of the spirit that drives her. It may look like the *Weltgeist* when she demands the joy of living, it may look like the Holy Ghost itself when one considers her appetite for truth. And it may look like the spirit of evil, a "gob-lin damned," when we see the desolation it produces. If one thinks of the symbols which Ibsen brings together in the last scene: the blank parlor, the wide unexplored world outside, the flames that consumed the Alving heritage and the sunrise flaming on the peaks, one may be reminded of the condition of Dante's great rebel Ulysses. He too is wrapped in the flame of his own consciousness, yet still dwells in the pride of the mind and the exhilaration of the world free of people, *il mondo senza gente*. But this analogy also may not be pressed too far. Ulysses is in hell; and when we explore the Mountain on which he was wrecked, we can place his condition with finality, and in relation to many other human modes of action and awareness. But Mrs. Alving's mountains do not place her anywhere: the realism of modern realism ends with the literal. Beyond that is not the ordered world of the tradition, but *Unendlichkeit,* and the anomalous "freedom" of unde-fined and uninformed aspiration.

Perhaps Mrs. Alving and Ibsen himself are closer to the role of Dante than to the role of Ulysses, seeing a hellish mode of being, but free to move on. Certainly Ibsen's development continued beyond *Ghosts,* and toward the end of his career he came much closer to achieving a consistent theatrical poetry within the confines of the theater of modern realism. He himself remarked that his poetry was to be found only in the series of his plays, no one of which was complete by itself.

But my purpose is, of course, not to do justice to Ibsen but to consider the potentialities of modern realism; and for this purpose Chekhov's masterpiece is essential. Chekhov did not solve the problem which Ibsen faced in *Ghosts*. He was not trying to show a desperate quest like Mrs. Alving's, with every weapon of the mind and the will. By his time the ambitious machinery of thesis and thriller had begun to pall; the prophetic-revolutionary spirit, grown skeptical and subtle, had sunk back into the flesh and the feelings, into the common beggarly body, for a period of pause, in hope and foreboding. Chekhov does not have Ibsen's force and intellect but he can accept the realistic stage much more completely, and use it with greater mastery for the contemplative purpose of art.

THE PLOT OF *THE CHERRY ORCHARD*

The Cherry Orchard is often accused of having no plot whatever, and it is true that the story gives little indication of the play's content or meaning; nothing happens, as the Broadway reviewers so often point out. Nor does it have a thesis, though many attempts have been made to attribute a thesis to it, to make it into a Marxian tract, or into a nostalgic defense of the old regime. The play does not have much of a plot in either of these accepted meanings of the word, for it is not addressed to the rationalizing mind but to the poetic and histrionic sensibility. It is an imitation of an action in the strictest sense, and it is plotted according to the first meaning of this word which I have distinguished in other contexts: the incidents are selected and arranged to define an action in a certain mode; a complete action, with a beginning, middle, and end in time. Its freedom from the mechanical order of the thesis or the intrigue is the sign of the perfection of Chekhov's realistic art. And its apparently casual incidents are actually composed with most elaborate and conscious skill to reveal the underlying life, and the natural, objective form of the play as a whole.

In *Ghosts*, as I showed, the action is distorted by the stereotyped requirements of the thesis and the intrigue. That is partly a matter of the mode of action which Ibsen was trying to show; a quest "of ethical motivation" which requires some sort of intellectual framework, and yet can have no final meaning in the purely literal terms of Ibsen's theater. *The Cherry Orchard*, on the other hand, is a drama "of pathetic motivation," a theater-poem of the suffering of change; and this mode of action and awareness is much closer to the skeptical basis of modern realism, and to the histrionic basis of all realism. Direct perception before predication is always true, says Aristotle; and the extraordinary feat of Chekhov is to predicate nothing. This he achieves by means of his plot: he selects only those incidents, those moments in his characters' lives, between their rationalized efforts, when they sense their situation and destiny most directly. So he contrives to show the action of the play as a whole—the unsuccessful attempt to cling to the Cherry Orchard—in many diverse reflectors and without propounding any thesis about it.

The slight narrative thread which ties these incidents and characters together for the inquiring mind, is quickly recounted. The family that owns the old estate named after its famous orchard—Lyubov, her brother Gaev, and her daughters Varya and Anya—is all but bankrupt, and the question is how to prevent the bailiffs from selling the estate to pay their debts. Lopahin, whose family were formerly serfs on the estate, is now rapidly growing rich as a businessman, and he offers a very sensible plan: chop down the orchard, divide the property into small lots, and sell them off to make a residential suburb for the growing industrial town nearby. Thus the cash value of the estate could be not only preserved, but increased. But this would not save what Lyubov and her brother find valuable in the old estate; they cannot consent to the destruction of the orchard. But they cannot find, or earn, or borrow the money to pay their debts either; and in due course the estate is sold at auction to Lopahin himself, who will make a very good thing of it. His workmen are hacking at the old trees before the family is out of the house.

The play may be briefly described as a realistic ensemble pathos: the characters all suffer the passing of the estate in different ways, thus adumbrating this change at a deeper and more generally significant level than that of any individual's experience. The action which they all share by analogy, and which informs the suffering of the destined change of the Cherry Orchard, is "to save the Cherry Orchard": that is, each character sees some value in it—economic, sentimental, social, cultural—which he wishes to keep. By means of his plot, Chekhov always focuses attention on the general action: his crowded stage, full of the characters I have mentioned as well as half a dozen hangers-on, is like an implicit discussion of the fatality which concerns them all; but Chekhov does not believe in their ideas, and the interplay he shows among his *dramatis personae* is not so much the play of thought as the alternation of his characters' perceptions of their situation, as the moods shift and the time for decision comes and goes.

Though the action which Chekhov chooses to show on-stage is "pathetic," i.e., suffering and perception, it is complete: the Cherry

Orchard is constituted before our eyes, and then dissolved. The first act is a prologue: it is the occasion of Lyubov's return from Paris to try to resume her old life. Through her eyes and those of her daughter Anya, as well as from the complementary perspectives of Lopahin and Trofimov, we see the estate as it were in the round, in its many possible meanings. The second act corresponds to the agon; it is in this act that we become aware of the conflicting values of all the characters, and of the efforts they make (off-stage) to save each one *his* Orchard. The third act corresponds to the pathos and peripety of the traditional tragic form. The occasion is a rather hysterical party which Lyubov gives while her estate is being sold at auction in the nearby town; it ends with Lopahin's announcement, in pride and the bitterness of guilt, that he was the purchaser. The last act is the epiphany: we see the action, now completed, in a new and ironic light. The occasion is the departure of the family: the windows are boarded up, the furniture piled in the corners, and the bags packed. All the characters feel, and the audience sees in a thousand ways, that the wish to save the Orchard has amounted in fact to destroying it; the gathering of its denizens to separation; the homecoming to departure. What this "means" we are not told. But the action is completed, and the poem of the suffering of change concludes in a new and final perception, and a rich chord of feeling.

The structure of each act is based upon a more or less ceremonious social occasion. In his use of the social ceremony—arrivals, departures, anniversaries, parties—Chekhov is akin to James. His purpose is the same: to focus attention on an action which all share by analogy, instead of upon the reasoned purpose of any individual, as Ibsen does in his drama of ethical motivation. Chekhov uses the social occasion also to reveal the individual at moments when he is least enclosed in his private rationalization and most open to disinterested insights. The Chekhovian ensembles may appear superficially to be mere pointless stalemates—too like family gatherings and arbitrary meetings which we know off-stage. So they are. But in his miraculous arrangement the very discomfort of many presences is made to reveal fundamental aspects of the human situation.

That Chekhov's art of plotting is extremely conscious and deliberate is clear the moment one considers the distinction between the stories of his characters as we learn about them, and the moments of their lives which he chose to show directly on-stage. Lopahin, for example, is a man of action like one of the new capitalists in Gorki's plays. Chekhov knew all about him, and could have shown us an exciting episode from his career if he had not chosen to see him only when he was forced to pause and pathetically sense his own motives in a wider context which qualifies their importance. Lyubov has been dragged about Europe for years by her ne'er-do-well lover, and her life might have yielded several sure-fire erotic intrigues like those of the commercial theater. But Chekhov, like all the great artists of modern times, rejected these standard motivations as both stale and false. The actress Arkadina, in *The Seagull*, remarks, as she closes a novel of Maupassant's, "Well, among the French that may be, but here with us there's nothing of the kind, we've no set program." In the context the irony of her remark is deep: she is herself a purest product of the commercial theater, and at that very time she is engaged in a love affair of the kind she objects to in Maupassant. But Chekhov, with his subtle art of plotting, has caught her in a situation, and at a brief moment of clarity and pause, when the falsity of her career is clear to all, even herself.

Thus Chekhov, by his art of plot-making, defines an action in the opposite mode to that of *Ghosts*. Ibsen defines a desperate quest for reasons and for ultimate, intelligible moral values. This action falls naturally into the form of the agon, and at the end of the play Ibsen is at a loss to develop the final pathos, or bring it to an end with an accepted perception. But the pathetic is the very mode of action and awareness which seems to Chekhov closest to the reality of the human situation, and by means of his plot he shows, even in characters who are not in themselves unusually passive, the suffering and the perception of change. The "moment" of human experience which *The Cherry Orchard* presents thus corresponds to that of the Sophoclean chorus, and of the evenings in the *Purgatorio*. *Ghosts* is a fighting play, armed for its sharp encounter with the rationalizing mind, its poetry concealed by its reasons. Chekhov's poetry, like Ibsen's, is behind the naturalistic surfaces; but the form of the play as a whole is "nothing but" poetry in the widest sense: the coherence of the concrete elements of the composition. Hence the curious vulnerability of Chekhov on the contemporary stage: he does not argue, he merely presents; and though his audiences even on Broadway are touched by the time they reach the last act, they are at a loss to say what it is all about. . . .

*   *   *

stark young

THE SEA GULL

IN THE matter of translation—I shall never be able to say this too often—a strange thing has happened with Chekhov. It is not unique among dramatists or the visual arts, but in this instance it becomes very important in the light of Chekhov's growing fame and influence in our theatre. To be brief, what we have here is a case of a dramatist coming into English with the handicap of the wrong tone bestowed upon him by the translators.

The Garnett translation is the least harmful very likely; it suffers mostly from a lack of theatre knowledge, or shall we say the sense of speakability, without which Chekhov, since he spoke through the theatre, could not be said really to be rendered into English. But that can be, and has been in various productions, somewhat got around by clipping and mending the lines for greater naturalness or plausibility as human utterance. In general, however, the idea holds that Chekhov is something smoky as to the lines, moody, complex, soulful perhaps, certainly very often vague. I once shared this notion. And lately I have been looking into some of those translations with which I began my Chekhov acquaintance, and have searched for instances that might easily excuse or justify such a conception of his style. It is no wonder we have all thought what we did. And it is no wonder that here and there my translation of *The Sea Gull* has been with the kindest and most generous intentions praised as vigorous for modern ears, or as brightening and shortening the text, or as agreeably omitting the literal translation of the original Russian and the Russian idiom. But in many respects these compliments have got the matter upside down. My translation is exactly literal, and most of the Chekhov speeches, taken in themselves, are very simple and straight. So far as I know, I made less than half a dozen departures from the word in Chekhov's text and these always for some practical theatre reason, and always with an acknowledgment in the notes to the published volume. To take one instance only, there is the title. The Russian does not mean sea gull but merely gull, which is obviously impossible for the title in English.

I even tried to keep the mere number of words in any given speech the same as in Chekhov, since the duration *per se* in a stage speech is part of its meaning.

That the translation was otherwise received by those who knew better is evinced by the comment of Dr. Nicholas Rumanceff. He says, "After reading the reviews I might have concluded that *The Sea Gull* had been rearranged for a better understanding and response on the part of American audiences. Knowing the other translations and knowing the play, I could easily have believed that this new version, to be thus successful, must be an adaptation. But such was not the case. I found almost word for word Chekhov's characteristic, it seemed to me, in Mr. Young's translation. The reason the American public loves the play and understands the play is because it is like Chekhov in English." Dr. Rumanceff was formerly Chairman of the Board of Directors of the Moscow Art Theatre.

Mr. Brooks Atkinson said in *The New York Times*: "In view of Mr. Young's discoveries in the tone-deaf and genteel translations of *The Sea Gull*, one begins to wonder how much of the other plays has been lost in opaque translations. But for this one play Mr. Young has produced a version that is clear, brisk and simple and that leaves an impression of mental alertness in the theatre. For the first time we begin to hear the voice of Chekhov as he spoke it in Russian forty years ago."

The fact must always be remembered that *The Sea Gull* is not full-blown Chekhov as to manner and mood. It was written in 1895, and was the first of his plays to get attention. The complete Chekhov quality was to come five years later in such plays as *The Three Sisters* and *The Cherry Orchard*. *The Sea Gull* is only in spots atmospheric in the sense usually applied to Chekhov; its frame is partly built and accentuated out of the older traditional European drama. Many of the critical clichés so often applied to Chekhov must, therefore, be applied to this play only with the greatest care.

Examining some of these specimens that I have picked out as examples, I am not surprised that we should have thought Chekhov's lines so complex or hard to translate. As for the Fell translation, one heard, of course, that the author had lived years in Russia and certainly, therefore, knew the language to the last degree; clearly it was conscience alone that made her willing to sacrifice naturalness of effect, ease, even English structure, much less the possibility of the lines ever being spoken by an actor on the stage. Anybody, in sum, would think that these complicated effects must certainly result from a pious effort to render with the utmost accuracy some subtle and complex original. What else would account for these contortions, solemnities, unsayabilities?

I will not try here for any startling effect, but will merely quote some of those speeches that might have misled me to those misty steppes and subtle windings of Chekhov's style as along with so many other people, I had come to imagine it. I will put down the translator's line and after it the straight and nearly always simple line that Chekhov has written.

". . . you can have no inducement to marry a man who cannot even find sufficient food for his own mouth." Chekhov merely asks how one could want to marry a man who can't feed himself.

". . . though what his provocation may be I can't imagine." Chekhov's line is "But what for?"

". . . as if the field of art were not large enough to accommodate both new and old without the necessity of jostling!" Chekhov says, "but there is room for all—why elbow?"

"I am irresistibly impelled toward her." Chekhov says, "I am drawn to her."

"I come back to the conclusion that all I am fit for is to describe landscapes, and that whatever else I attempt rings abominably false." Chekhov says, "I feel that I can write only [of the] landscape, and in everything else I am false and false to the marrow of my bones." Five of the translations refuse Chekhov that repetition of "false."

None of the others is so complicated as this Fell version of *The Sea Gull*. But at that there are wide variations in quality, and such renderings as the two following may crop up almost anywhere. Where Chekhov's manager shouts, "You don't know what a farm means," we find in one translator, "You do not know what the management of an estate involves." Where Chekhov has "Everyone must write as he wants to and as he can," we read, "Everyone must write in accordance with his desire and his capacity."

These instances, though more conspicuously off, are only bits within a larger and impinging general tone that has built up such an idea of Chekhov's lines as would make him frantic and that continue to sicken cultured Russians who encounter it. I could scarcely have been more surprised than I was when I found on coming to Chekhov in Russian that his lines are not complex or difficult at all; they are not even involved. Thinking back over it all, I see now that we should have known better all along. Chekhov's special method, the realistic-psychological, as it is called, should have taught us, I see that now only too clearly. In this method the surface of life is apparently reproduced, natural and familiar; and only by the combinations, the sequences, the underlying associations and implications, are profound meanings created. It should have followed then, if we had kept our wits about us, that his speech would have done a parallel thing. The speech would be simple, on the surface natural and easy; the inner meanings would appear but not through complex or vague lines, not through the muggy, symbolic, swing-on-to-your atmosphere sort of tone. We should have known that. I for one did not.

Apart from this complete simplicity, the other problems in translating *The Sea Gull* consisted in two things: to get the lines sayable, and thus theatre; to let Chekhov do it his own way, repeat, make images, simplify, whatever he chooses. One may at least try for that. For example when Chekhov organizes a speech where a man says he wanted to become a writer and never became one, wanted to marry and never married, etc., let us not say wanted to become a writer and didn't, wanted to marry and didn't, or remained a bachelor —not one of the six translations allows him his device of repetition here.

The most striking of these cases where Chekhov is shown a better way to do it occurs in the first act of *The Sea Gull*, where Treplev begs his mother's patience and she answers by quoting from *Hamlet*:

My son,
Thou turnst mine eyes into my very soul,
And there I see such black and grained spots
As will not leave their tinct.

Let us not assume that Chekhov did not know his business when he drew on the lines with which Shakespeare followed that speech of the queen's:

Nay, but to live
In the rank sweat of an enseamed bed,
Stew'd in corruption, honeying and making love
Over the nasty sty!

Instead of that passage, however, another and quite different one is substituted in whatever productions of this play I happen to have heard of so far, and in four out of the six translations that I have read.

Leave wringing of your hands. Peace! sit you down!
And let me wring your heart; for so I shall
If it be made of penetrable stuff.

That speech is Shakespeare, though transposed, but is not in character for Treplev; it is merely cleverish, and out of place. A fifth translation, if I remember right, gives a fragment of the Shakespeare passage but apologizes and suggests the substitution of the above. The sixth gives the Shakespeare lines verbatim.

But even that is not what Chekhov wants. The brutality of those lines is daring enough for Hamlet to speak before an Elizabethan audience, for all their strong stomachs and open audacity. If Treplev had said them to his mother, it would have brought to the moment something so appalling and obscene that he would have broken up the company gathered there to see his play. What Chekhov does is to paraphrase Shakespeare's lines into, "Nay, but why do you yield to sin, see love in the depths of wickedness?" And in addition to that milder paraphrase, he has the knocking on the floor, the horn sounding, and the play beginning, all of which serve to cut across its impact and draw us adroitly on toward his next impression.

The Sea Gull, as produced by Mr. Alfred Lunt and Miss Lynn Fontanne, and presented by the Theatre Guild, is on the whole the best Chekhov production that I have seen in English. Mr. Robert Edmond Jones' design for the first act was full of a sober, virile style rare indeed in out of door settings. Its one defect was too much light on the side farthest from Treplev's stage, where Chekhov expressly prescribes that the scene be in dusk till Treplev's curtain rises on the lake and the moon. Stanislavsky records that in their first effort to abide by this idea they got the stage so dark that the actors could scarcely be seen. Miss Fontanne in my opinion gave a brilliant performance of the actress. I have in fact the Moscow Art Theatre's Mme. Maria Ouspenskaya's word for it that she thought Miss Fontanne was better than the actress who had taken the part in Russia. Mr. Lunt seemed to me to give Trigorin the right depth, for Chekhov plainly intends him to be only a popular second-rate idol of an author. Miss Uta Hagen played Nina, the young girl, with an admirable lyric ease. Mr. Richard Whorf was at least competent as the young writer, Treplev. And Mr. Sydney Greenstreet as Sorin, the retired councilor, brother of the actress, gave a performance remarkably exact and beautiful; no performance, as Mr. John Anderson said in his *Journal-American* review, either inside or outside the Moscow Art Theatre, could be finer.

Finally there is one thing especially that should be said about Miss Fontanne's and Mr. Lunt's approach to the play: it was what Chekhov productions on our stage very seldom are, and that is an entirely honorable attitude by which there was no changing of lines, no trimming the dangerous corners of some of Chekhov's devices and motifs, no concessions to what might be easier to swallow or more popular.

david magarshack

CHEKHOV THE DRAMATIST

THE PLAYS of Chekhov, like those of any other great dramatist, follow a certain pattern of development which can be traced through all its various stages. His last four plays, moreover, conform to certain general principles which are characteristic of the type of indirect-action drama to which they belong. Chekhov himself was fully aware of that. Already on November 3rd, 1888, in a letter to Alexey Suvorin, he clearly stated that all works of art must conform to certain laws. "It is possible to collect in a heap the best that has been created by the artists in all ages," he wrote, "and, making use of the scientific method, discover the general principles which are characteristic of them all and which lie at the very basis of their value as works of art. These general principles will constitute their law. Works of art which are immortal possess a great deal in common; if one were to extract that which is common to them all from any of them, it would lose its value and its charm. This means that what is common to them all is necessary and is a *conditio sine qua non* of every work which lays claim to immortality."

Chekhov did not claim immortality for his plays. He was too modest for that. What he did claim for them, however, was something that any immortal work of art is generally supposed to possess, namely, the power so to influence people as to induce them to create a new and better life for themselves. "You tell me," Chekhov said to the writer Alexander Tikhonov in 1902, "that people cry at my plays. I've heard others say the same. But that was not why I wrote them. It is Alexeyev (Stanislavsky) who made my characters into cry-babies. All I wanted was to say honestly to people: 'Have a look at yourselves and see how bad and dreary your lives are!' The important thing is that people should realise that, for when they do, they will most certainly create another and better life for themselves. I

From *Chekhov the Dramatist* by David Magarshack. Preface Copyright 1960 by David Magarshack. Reprinted by permission of Hill and Wang, Inc. The selection here contains Chapters I and II, part of Chapter V, and Chapter VI from *Chekhov the Dramatist*.

will not live to see it, but I know that it will be quite different, quite unlike our present life. And so long as this different life does not exist, I shall go on saying to people again and again: 'Please, understand that your life is bad and dreary!'

"What is there in this to cry about?"

The misinterpretation of Chekhov's plays by the Moscow Art Theatre led to constant conflicts between their author and its two directors. These conflicts became particularly violent during the production of *The Cherry Orchard*. "The production of *The Cherry Orchard*," Olga Knipper, Chekhov's wife and one of the leading actresses of the Moscow Art Theatre, wrote, "was difficult, almost agonising, I might say. The producers and the author could not understand each other and could not come to an agreement." Chekhov himself wrote to Olga Knipper: "Nemirovich-Danchenko and Alexeyev positively see in my play something I have not written, and I am ready to bet anything you like that neither of them has ever read my play through carefully." And to a well-known Russian producer Chekhov said: "Take my *Cherry Orchard*. Is it my *Cherry Orchard*? With the exception of two or three parts nothing in it is mine. I am describing life, ordinary life, and not blank despondency. They either make me into a cry-baby or into a bore. They invent something about me out of their own heads, anything they like, something I never thought of or dreamed about. This is beginning to make me angry." And what is true of Chekhov's Russian producers is even truer of his English and American producers, though in their case the idea that the characters in Chekhov's plays represent curiously unaccountable "Russians" adequately conceals their own confusion and helplessness.

This general bewilderment would have been fatal to the popularity of Chekhov's plays were it not that, being a playwright of genius, Chekhov paints his characters with so exquisite a brush that no caricature can strip them of their essential humanity. If neither the spectators nor those responsible for the production and performance of the plays can see the wood for the trees in them, the trees themselves are so brilliantly delineated that they are quite sufficient to ensure the comparative success of any of Chekhov's famous plays. It must not be forgotten, however, that their success is only "comparative," for so far Chekhov has failed to become a really "popular" playwright either in England or America, and it is doubtful whether one in a thousand of the regular playgoers in these countries has ever seen a play of his or, indeed, knows anything about it.

Nor has Chekhov been particularly fortunate in his critics. Disregarding the host of critics in and outside Russia whose aesthetic appreciation of Chekhov derives entirely from their own sensibilities and who seem to delight in losing themselves in a welter of half-tones and feelings too exquisite for anyone but themselves to detect, two critical appreciations of Chekhov as a playwright sum up an attitude that is still prevalent among the more thoughtful admirers of Chekhov's genius. One of them comes from Tolstoy. Peter Gnyeditch, a Russian novelist and playwright who was for some years in charge of the repertoire of the Imperial Alexandrinsky Theatre in Petersburg, recounts the following observation made by Tolstoy to Chekhov in his presence: "You know I can't stand Shakespeare, but your plays are even worse. Shakespeare after all does seize his reader by the collar and lead him to a certain goal without letting him get lost on the way. But where is one to get to with your heroes? From the sofa to the . . . and back?" And to Gnyeditch himself Tolstoy remarked that Chekhov had not "the real nerve" of a dramatist. "I am very fond of Chekhov and I value his writings highly," Gnyeditch reports Tolstoy as saying, "but I could not force myself to read his *Three Sisters* to the end—where does it all lead us to? Generally speaking, our modern writers seem to have lost the idea of what drama is. Instead of giving us a man's whole life, drama must put him in such a situation, must tie him in such a knot as to enable us to see what he is like while he is trying to untie it. Now, as you know, I have been so bold as to deny the importance of Shakespeare as a playwright. But in Shakespeare every man does something, and it is always clear why he acts thus and not otherwise. On his stage he had signposts with inscriptions: moonlight, a house. And a good thing too! For the entire attention of the spectator remains concentrated on the essential point of the drama; but now everything is the other way round."

And in an interview published in the Russian journal *Slovo* on July 28th, 1904, about a fortnight after Chekhov's death, Tolstoy summarised his objections to Chekhov's plays in these words: "To evoke a mood you want a lyrical poem. Dramatic forms serve, and ought to serve, quite different aims. In a dramatic work the author ought to deal with some problem that has yet to be solved and every character in the play ought to solve it according to the idiosyncrasies of his own character. It is like a laboratory experiment. But you won't find anything of the kind in Chekhov. He never holds the attention of the spectators sufficiently long for them to put themselves entirely in his power. For instance, he keeps the spectator's attention fixed on the fate of the unhappy Uncle Vanya and his friend Dr. Astrov, but he is sorry for them only because they are unhappy, without attempting to prove whether or not they deserve pity. He makes them say that once upon a time they were the best people in the district, but he does not show us in what way they were good. I can't help feeling that they have always been worthless creatures and that their suffering cannot therefore be worthy of our attention."

The Seagull, it is interesting to note, Tolstoy roundly dismissed as "nonsense." Alexey Suvorin, the well-known Russian newspaper publisher and a life-long friend of Chekhov's, records in his diary on February 11th, 1897, that Tolstoy told him that the play was "utterly worthless" and that it was written "just as Ibsen writes his plays."

"The play is chock full of all sorts of things," Tolstoy declared, "but no one really knows what they are for. And Europe shouts, 'Wonderful!' Chekhov," Tolstoy went on, "is one of our most gifted writers, but *The Seagull* is a very bad play."

"Chekhov," Suvorin remarked, "would die if he were told what you thought about his play. Please, don't say anything to him about it."

"I shall tell him what I think of it," Tolstoy said, "but I shall put it gently. I'm surprised that you think he would take it so much to heart. After all, every writer slips up sometimes."

Tolstoy, according to Suvorin, thought that Chekhov should never have introduced a writer in *The Seagull*. "There aren't many of us," he said, "and no one is really interested in us." Trigorin's monologue in Act II he considered the best thing in the play and he thought that it was most certainly autobiographical, but in his opinion Chekhov should have published it separately or in a letter. "In a play it is out of place," he declared. "In his short story *My Life*," Tolstoy concluded with what, if he only knew, would have appeared to Chekhov the most devastating criticism of his play, "Chekhov makes his hero read Ostrovsky and say, 'All this can happen in life,' but had he read *The Seagull*, he would never have said that."

Apart from his purely moral objections to Chekhov's characters Tolstoy's main criticisms of Chekhov's plays concern their structure and their apparent lack of purpose. Accustomed to the drama of direct action, Tolstoy expected the unravelling of the knot which the playwright ties round his hero to supply the key to his character, to reveal the man as a whole. He also expected a play to solve the problems society has so far failed to solve and in this way supply the answer to the question: where does it all lead to?

Curiously enough, English criticism, too, seems to regard the same apparent lack of purpose as characteristic of Chekhov's drama, though, unlike Tolstoy, most of the critics consider that as something praiseworthy. Discussing *The Seagull*, Mr. (as he then was) Desmond MacCarthy[1] asks: "What is it all about?" and his answer is: "It is a question more than usually difficult to answer in the case of *The Sea-*

[1] *The New Statesman*, November 14th, 1925.

gull. I am obliged to turn it aside," he goes on, "and say that it is a beautiful study in human nature, penetrating, detached, and compassionate. . . . It has no theme." Still, the critic admits that he often said to himself that "a work of art to have any value must somewhere carry within it the suggestion of a desirable life," which he does not apparently find in Chekhov's plays, and he therefore suggests that it is to be found "in the mind of Chekhov himself, in the infection we catch from the spirit of the whole play; in the delicate, humorous, compassionate mind which observed, understood and forgave." The same critic, in another notice of *The Seagull* eleven years later,[2] answers the same question: "What is *The Seagull* about?" as follows: "It is a study of a group of people, penetrating, detached and compassionate." As for the purpose of the play, "the point that *The Seagull* drives home," he writes, "is that the person who possesses what another thinks would make all the difference to him or her is just as dissatisfied as the one who lacks it. By means of these contrasts Chekhov shows that what each pines for makes no difference in the end."

As for *Uncle Vanya*,[3] Mr. MacCarthy finds that Chekhov's "favourite theme is disillusionment and as far as the kind of beauty he creates, beneath it might be written 'desolation is a delicate thing.' " Generally, Chekhov's play, according to the same distinguished critic, reveals "an atmosphere of sighs and yawns and self-reproaches, vodka, endless tea, and endless discussion." And thirteen years later, the same critic, writing of *Uncle Vanya* again,[4] declared that "though Chekhov was far from ineffectual himself, the ineffectiveness of his generation was his inspiration. And his final conclusion about the play is: "Besides inventing the play without plot and theatrical effects, Chekhov was also the poet and apologist of ineffectualness." [5]

Discussing *The Cherry Orchard*,[6] Mr. MacCarthy states as a matter of fact ("we all know") that "the essence of Chekhov's drama" is "the rainbow effect, laughter shining through tears." And in a notice of *The Three Sisters*[7] he finds Chekhov's heroines to be "forlorn, ineffectual young women" and comes to the conclusion that "Chekhov's supreme gift was to bring the observation of character to a most delicate sense of justice," and that his method was "to develop character and situation by means of a dialogue which follows the broken rhythms of life, and by making every remark, every gesture of his characters reflect the influence of group relations of the moment."

[2] Ibid., May 30th, 1936.
[3] Ibid., May 16th, 1914.
[4] Ibid., February 13th, 1937.
[5] Ibid., January 27th, 1945.
[6] Ibid., October 2nd, 1926.
[7] Ibid., February 5th, 1938.

While disagreeing entirely with Tolstoy about the value of Chekhov's plays as works of art, Mr. Desmond MacCarthy, who in this respect represents English criticism as a whole, agrees with him about the absence of a well-defined aim in them as well as about the general ineffectualness of their characters. The only trouble about this now widely held view is that Chekhov himself dissented violently from it. Before, then, deciding whether Chekhov or his critics and producers are right, it is necessary to find out what Chekhov thought the final aim and form of a dramatic work ought to be, and what his attitude to contemporary drama was. For Chekhov had very definite ideas about both, and these most certainly influenced his work for the the stage.

CHEKHOV WAS not, as is generally supposed, a great short-story writer who took up drama seriously only during the last seven or eight years of his all too short life. He was a born dramatist whose first works of importance were three full-length plays, two written in his late teens and the third in his early twenties. He took up short-story writing for two reasons: first, because he had to support a large family which was entirely dependent on him, and the writing of short stories was the quickest way of doing it; secondly, because the state of the Russian stage in the eighties and the nineties of the last century was such that no serious playwright could hope to have his plays performed, let alone earn a decent living in the theatre. Even Alexander Ostrovsky, whose reputation as a playwright had long been established, was not able to do so. It was indeed this hopeless position of the serious playwright in Russia towards the end of the nineteenth century that made Chekhov look on fiction as his "legal wife" and the stage as "a noisy, impudent and tiresome mistress." But the remarkable fact about a Chekhov short story is that it possesses the three indispensable elements of drama: compactness of structure (Chekhov's term for it was "architecture"), movement, that is dramatic development of plot, and action. "The reader," Chekhov wrote to the writer Ivan Leontyev on January 28th, 1888, "must never be allowed to rest; he must be kept in a state of suspense." The dialogue in Chekhov's short stories is essentially dramatic dialogue and that is what chiefly distinguishes them from the short stories of other fiction writers. Many of these short stories, particularly the early ones, have been adapted for the Russian stage, but the "adaptation" consisted mainly in lifting Chekhov's dialogue and using the descriptive passages as stage directions. Chekhov himself "adapted" five of his short stories for the stage on the same principle, that is, he merely lifted the dialogue, adding his own stage directions, and, if his story was too short, expanding it to the necessary length of a one-act play. Commenting on a play by the Norwegian playwright Bjoernstjerne Bjoernson in a letter to Suvorin on June 20th, 1896 (that is, *after* he had written *The Seagull*), Chekhov remarked that it was of no use so far as the stage was concerned because "it has no action, no living characters and no dramatic interest." This is surely the best comment ever made on the distortion the plays of Chekhov have suffered on the stage, and especially on the English and American stage, by being denied just the quality Chekhov himself valued most both as playwright and as short-story writer, namely, action.

Chekhov, then, was a born playwright and his knowledge of the stage, too, was first-hand. As a boy in his native town of Taganrog he had often appeared on the amateur and professional stage and earned general recognition as a talented actor. Replying on March 4th, 1893, to an invitation to take part in a literary evening, Chekhov pointed out that he was a bad reader and, what was even worse, suffered from stage-fright. "This is silly and ridiculous, but I can't do anything about it," he wrote. "I have never read in public in my life and never shall. A long time ago I used to act on the stage, but there I concealed myself behind my costume and make-up and that gave me courage." And writing to Suvorin on April 18th, 1895, about an amateur performance of Tolstoy's *The Fruits of Enlightenment*, planned by a number of Moscow writers in aid of some charity, in which he had agreed to take the part of the peasant, Chekhov declared: "I used to act quite well in the past, though now I fear my voice will let me down."

His purely professional attitude towards drama (as opposed to the now so common "literary" one) can further be gauged from the fact that he did not consider a play of his completed before it had been thoroughly revised by him at rehearsals. Thus he wrote on November 27th, 1889, to the poet Pleshheyev who had asked his permission to publish *The Wood Demon*, "I never consider a play ready for publication until it has been revised during rehearsals. Wait, please. It is not too late yet. When the play has been revised at the rehearsals, I shall take advantage of your kind offer without waiting for an invitation."

Chekhov's only reason for writing a play was the likelihood of its being performed on the stage. Moreover, when writing a play he usually bore in mind the actors who were most likely to appear in its leading parts and, as in the case of *Ivanov*, he never hesitated to alter a play radically if a different actor or actress took a part he had originally intended for someone else.

"I sent you two versions of my *Ivanov*," he wrote to Suvorin on January 7th, 1889. "If Ivanov had been played by a resourceful and dynamic actor, I should have altered and added a lot. I felt in the mood for it. But, alas, Ivanov is played by Davydov. That meant that I had to write shorter and duller dialogue, keeping in mind that all the subtleties and 'nuances' will be overlooked, become ordinary and tedious. Can Davydov be gentle one moment and furious another? When he plays serious parts there seems to be a kind of handmill turning round and round in his throat, dull and monotonous, which is speaking instead of him. I am sorry for poor Savina who has to play the part of my uninspiring Sasha. I would gladly have altered it for Savina, but if Ivanov mouths his part, I can't do anything for Sasha, however much I alter her part. I am simply ashamed that Savina will have to play goodness knows what in my play. Had I known earlier that she would play Sasha and Davydov Ivanov, I should have called my play *Sasha* and made everything revolve round this part and just attached Ivanov to it. But who could have foreseen that?"

Such an attitude may appear curious to a modern playwright, but that is only because the modern playwright has become detached from the stage. To Shakespeare or (in Russia) to Alexander Ostrovsky, to playwrights, that is, whom Chekhov called "specialists of the stage," such an attitude would not have appeared at all strange, and indeed both of them wrote their plays for and around well-known members of their companies.

What was Chekhov's attitude to the theatre? What did he think of the actors of the Imperial and private stage in Moscow and Petersburg? What were his views on the problems of acting and did he think a play ought to have a well-defined aim of its own, an aim that should be intelligible to the spectator? What, finally, were his ideas on the form and structure of a play and what did he consider to be the playwright's place in the theatre?

These questions occupied Chekhov's mind continually and were of decisive importance to his whole career as a dramatist.

Chekhov left a scathing description of the state of the theatre in Moscow in an article he contributed to the Petersburg weekly *Fragments* in 1885. What Chekhov found so appalling about the Moscow Imperial stage was the reign of mediocrity on it. "At the Bolshoy Theatre," he wrote in his article, "we have opera and ballet. Nothing new. The actors are all the old ones and their manner of singing is the old one: not according to the notes, but according to official circulars. In the ballet the ballerinas have been recently joined by Noah's aunt and Methuselah's sister-in-law." The state of affairs at the Moscow Imperial dramatic theatre, the Maly Theatre, was no better. "Again nothing new," Chekhov declared. "The same mediocre acting and the same traditional ensemble, inherited from our ancestors." As for the Moscow private theatre owned by Korsh where *Ivanov* was soon to be given its first try-out, it bore, Chekhov wrote, "a striking resemblance to a mixed salad: there is everything there except the most important thing of all—meat." There were two more private theatres in Moscow at the time, one near the Pushkin memorial, known as the Pushkin Theatre, where plays were performed for only half the season, and the theatre owned by the famous impresario Lentovsky. "Whether Lentovsky's theatre," Chekhov wrote, "will be given up to operettas, pantomimes or tragedies, or whether the celebrated clown Durov will be showing his learned pig there, is so far unknown to Lentovsky himself, who is at present preoccupied with designing vignettes for some grand, stupendous, nebulous enterprise." There were, besides, "fifty thousand amateur theatres," but Chekhov had no use for them, and even the foundation three years later of the Society of Art and Literature by Stanislavsky and the actor and playwright Fedotov was looked upon by Chekhov with unconcealed derision, the pretentiousness of the name of the society being sufficient to make Chekhov sceptical about its founders.

In a letter to Suvorin on February 14th, 1889, Chekhov roundly dismissed the Russian theatre as it existed at that time as "nothing but a sport. I don't believe in the theatre as a school without which it is impossible to exist," he declared. In *A Boring Story* which he wrote between March and September, 1889, Chekhov discussed the vexed problem of the theatre as a place of entertainment at greater length and came to the conclusion that such a theatre was a mere waste of time. "A sentimental and credulous crowd," he writes, "can be persuaded that the theatre in its present state is a 'school.' But anyone who knows what a school is really like will not be deceived by such a facile statement. I don't know what the theatre will be like in fifty or a hundred years, but under present conditions it can serve only as entertainment, and as entertainment it is too expensive to be worth while. It deprives the State of thousands of gifted young men and women who, if they did not dedicate themselves to the theatre, could have become good doctors, farmers, teachers, army officers; it deprives the public of its evening hours—the best time for intellectual work and fireside chats. Not to mention the sheer waste of money and the moral injury suffered by the public from seeing a wrongly presented case of murder, adultery or libel on the stage." This criticism of the theatre as entertainment Chekhov puts into the mouth of the hero of his story, an old professor of medicine, and Chekhov was always very careful to make his heroes speak and think "in character." But there can be no doubt that, though Chekhov himself would not have expressed these ideas in so extreme a form, they were substantially his own ideas on the theatre of his day. It was certainly Chekhov the playwright who was speaking through the mouth of his hero when he condemned the music played in the intervals between the acts of a play as "quite unnecessary" and "as adding something utterly new and irrelevant to the impression created by the play." It was only with the foundation of the Moscow Art Theatre that this "unnecessary and irrelevant" custom was abolished.

*　　*　　*

The main reason for his bitter conflict with the directors of the Moscow Art Theatre was their failure to see the high moral purpose of his plays, a failure that is still characteristic of most of his producers in England and America. What differentiates Chekhov's early from his four last plays is not only a difference of technique. It is the much more important question of the final aim of the plays, the moral purpose that is absent from his early plays and forms so essential a part of his later ones. For it is these later plays that, in Chekhov's own words, "are permeated by a consciousness of an aim," and are meant to make the spectator see not only "life as it is," but also "life as it should be."

The greatest mistake English and American producers of Chekhov's plays have been making is to accept the view that Chekhov's drama is essentially a drama of frustration. This is only true of his two plays of direct action; of his last four plays the opposite is true: it is a drama of courage and hope. It was Stanislavsky who was mainly responsible for treating Chekhov's plays as plays of frustration and it was he who imposed this view on the rest of the world. But the bitter conflict between Chekhov and Stanislavsky is well known, and the most obvious mistake some producers make is in either overlooking this conflict altogether or drawing the wrong conclusion from it. They all ignore the final aim of the four great plays. Indeed, they usually go so far as to deny that such an aim exists and purposely play down or entirely ignore those parts of the plays which deal with this aim. Hence the spurious "Chekhovian" atmosphere which is laid on so thickly in every production of a Chekhov play. Ironically enough, it is they who, instead of expressing Chekhov's ideas, express the ideas of the Russian woman critic Sazonova, which appalled Chekhov when he read her strictures of his letter to Suvorin of November 25th, 1892. Suvorin himself was so astonished to read Chekhov's views on the ultimate aims of a work of art, which were so much at variance with Chekhov's former views, that he sent his letter to Sazonova for her comment and then sent those comments on to Chekhov, whose reply to Suvorin is both illuminating and decisive.

"That the last generation of writers and artists had no aim in their work," Chekhov wrote to Suvorin on December 3rd, 1892, "is quite a legitimate, consistent and interesting phenomenon, and the fact that Sazonova was aghast at my letter does not mean that I was insincere or acted against my conscience. It is you yourself who have read insincerity into it, for otherwise you would not have sent her my letter. In my letters to you I am often unjust and naïve, but I never write anything I do not believe in. But if you want insincerity, there are tons of it in Sazonova's letter. 'The greatest miracle is man himself, and we shall never grow tired of studying him.' Or 'The aim of life is life itself.' Or 'I believe in life, in its bright moments, for the sake of which one not only *can* but also *must* live; I believe in man, in the good sides of his nature,' and so on. Do you really think this is sincere, or does it indeed mean anything? This is not an outlook on life, but sheer nonsense. She underlines 'can' and 'must' because she is afraid of speaking about what is and what must be taken into account. Let her first of all tell us what is, and then I shall be glad to listen to what can and must be done. She believes in 'life,' which means that she does not believe in anything if she is intelligent or that she simply believes in the peasant's God and crosses herself in the dark as if she were a silly old woman.

"Under the influence of her letter," Chekhov goes on, "you write to me about 'life for life's sake.' Thank you very much. Why, her letter which is supposed to be so full of the joy of life is more like a graveyard than mine. I wrote that we had no aims and you rightly drew the conclusion that I considered them necessary and that I would gladly go in search of them, while Sazonova writes that it is wrong to tempt man with all sorts of benefits which he will never get— 'you must be thankful for your present mercies,' and in her opinion our misfortune consists solely in our looking for some more remote and higher aims. If this is not just female logic, then it is the philosophy of despair. He who is sincerely convinced that higher aims are as unnecessary to man as they are to a cow and that 'our whole misfortune' lies in having those aims, has nothing left but to eat, drink and sleep, and when he gets sick of all that, to take a good run and smash his head on the sharp edge of a trunk. I am not abusing Sazonova. All I mean is that she does not appear to be a very cheerful person."

MENTION HAS already been made of Chekhov's views on the paramount importance of action in a play. What are the other general conditions that Chekhov regarded as necessary to an aspiring playwright? First of all comes a thorough, first-hand knowledge of the stage. "Beginning with the next season," Chekhov wrote to a fellow-dramatist in March 1889, "I shall start visiting the theatre regularly and educating myself scenically." To his eldest brother Alexander, who had sent him a general outline of a play he was proposing to write, Chekhov wrote: "Don't forget to visit the theatre a few times and make a thorough study of the stage. You'll then be able to compare and that is important." Another rule that Chekhov was never tired of enjoining on his fellow-dramatists was the need for originality. "Try to be original in your play," he advised his brother, "and, as far as possible, intelligent, but do not be afraid to appear silly. Complete freedom of expression is necessary, but remember that only he is free to express his views who is not afraid to write stupid things. Incidentally, love declarations, infidelities by husbands and wives, and tears shed by widows, orphans and other people have been described long ago." In a further letter to his brother he gives another list of characters that a playwright should avoid: "Retired captains with red noses, drunken press reporters, starving writers, consumptive and hard working wives, honest young men without a blot on their characters, lofty-minded young ladies, and dear old nannies." Eleven years later, in a letter to Suvorin, he adds this illuminating note on the need for originality in a playwright's characters: "An educated nobleman who wants to become a priest—this is rather old-fashioned and does not arouse curiosity. You should have taken a young scientist, or a secret Jesuit who dreams of the union of the churches, or anyone else who would have cut a much more imposing figure than a nobleman who is about to take holy orders." Discussing another character in Suvorin's play, Chekhov remarks: "The father seems to have no weakness of any sort. He does not drink, he does not smoke, he does not play cards, and he is not ill. You ought to attach some kind of quality to him and give the actor something to hang on to." And he adds this rather significant note on the importance of sex in plays: "Whether the father does or does not know about his daughter's false step is not very important. Sex, no doubt, plays a great role in the world, but not everything depends on it, not by any means; and it is not everywhere that it is of decisive importance."

A play, in Chekhov's view, must above all be compact. "The more compact and the tighter a play is," he writes to a fellow dramatist, "the brighter and more expressive it is." He warns the same dramatist against becoming a professional playwright, that is to say, a playwright to whom the mere tricks of the stage are more important than the subject matter of his plays. A playwright, he insists, must above all be a poet and an artist. He must conquer the stage and not let the stage conquer him. All the same, so keen was Chekhov's perception of the requirements of the stage that in a letter to another fellow dramatist he coined the aphorism: "You must never put a loaded rifle on the stage if no one is going to fire it."

In addition to compactness and expressiveness, Chekhov laid great stress on "plasticity of phrase." He warned his brother against preciosity of language. He objected to the dialogue of one of Suvorin's plays because the language of its characters was "like a white silk dress which is all the time reflecting the sun and on which it hurts you to look. The words 'vulgarity' and 'vulgar,'" he adds, "are old-fashioned now." Writing to Gorky in January 1899, Chekhov warned him against lack of gracefulness and restraint in his first play, defining "gracefulness" in these words: "When a man spends the least possible number of movements on some definite action, then that is gracefulness."

Another principle of writing plays Chekhov stuck to all through his career as a playwright concerned the elimination of what he called "the personal element." Writing to his eldest brother in May, 1889, he declared: "Your play will be no good at all if all the characters are like you. Who cares about your life or mine or about your ideas or mine?" A further principle, which is very characteristic of Chekhov's later plays especially, is that "an author must always be humane to the tips of his fingers." But admirable as this last principle is, it has undoubtedly been responsible for a great deal of "sensitive" criticisms of Chekhov's plays which tend to obscure their more important points.

There is another piece of advice Chekhov gives to his brother which is characteristic of the external form of a Chekhov play and which might as well be noted here. Every full-length play of Chekhov's has four acts and the importance of each act in its relation to the play as a whole was defined by Chekhov as early as May 8th, 1889, in a letter to Alexander: "The first act," he wrote, "can go on as long as an hour, but the others must not last longer than thirty minutes. The climax of the play must occur in the third act, but it must not be too big a climax to kill the fourth act."

It was Chekhov's custom first to produce a rough draft of a play and then go on improving it. With *Ivanov* and *The Wood Demon* (*Uncle Vanya*) this procedure was much more drastic, the two plays in their final form undergoing vital alterations. This process of re-shaping a play Chekhov considered required much greater ability from the playwright than the initial process of writing the play. In a letter to the poet Pleshcheyev on January 15th, 1889, written soon after the completion of the final draft of *Ivanov*, he referred to this particular aspect of the playwright's craft in connexion with the "tragic laugh" that was one of the characteristics of his friend and fellow dramatist Ivan Leontyev (Shcheglov). "No," he writes, "I do not envy Jean Shcheglov. I understand now why he laughs so tragically. To write a good play for the theatre one must possess a special kind of talent (one can be an excellent novelist and at the same time write bunglingly incompetent plays); but to write a bad play and then attempt to make a good one out of it, to resort to all sorts of tricks, to delete, re-write, insert soliloquies, resurrect the dead, bury the living—to do all that one must possess a much greater talent. That is as difficult as making a silk purse out of a sow's ear. Here you will not only laugh tragically, but neigh like a horse."

One more important aspect of Chekhov's attitude to the stage still remains to be elucidated, namely his views on the playwright's place in the theatre. It was undoubtedly Chekhov's great good fortune that among the greatest admirers of his genius was Nemirovich-Danchenko, one of the founders of the Moscow Art Theatre, who prevailed on Stanislavsky almost by main force to put on *The Seagull* during the Moscow Art Theatre's first season, thus being responsible for Chekhov's close association with one of the most progressive theatres in Russia. But this association with Stanislavsky and Nemirovich-Danchenko was also one of Chekhov's greatest misfortunes inasmuch as both producers were, at the outset of their stage careers at any rate, what is commonly known as producer-autocrats who brooked no interference either from their actors or from their authors and who quite honestly held the view (all too common among producers) that they had a right to interpret a play any way they liked. Ordinarily this would have brought about an early break between Chekhov and the Moscow Art Theatre, for Chekhov would never have agreed to his elimination from the production of his plays and the complete disregard of his own interpretation of them. As early as 1887, he insisted on the playwright's right to have a deciding voice in anything that concerned the production of his plays. Writing to Nicolai Leykin, editor of the humorous weekly *Fragments* to which he had been contributing regularly during the early years of his authorship, Chekhov made it quite plain that he would never resign his position in the theatre to the producer. Leykin had written to him: "An author who habitually interferes with the production is a nuisance to the actors, his instructions being mostly silly." To which Chekhov replied: "The author is the owner of the play and not the actors. Everywhere the casting is left to the author, provided he is not absent. Besides, till now *all* my instructions were helpful and the actors did as I told them. If the author is to be completely eliminated from the production of his plays," he concluded, prophetically as it turned out, "then goodness knows what will happen. Remember how Gogol used to fly into a temper when his play was being produced! Wasn't he right?"

Holding such views, how did it happen that Chekhov let Stanislavsky and Nemirovich-Danchenko ride roughshod over his own conception of his plays? The answer to this question is simple: at the time his plays were being performed at the Moscow Art Theatre Chekhov was already a stricken man who could take no direct part in their production. He was condemned to live in the Crimea and the few rehearsals he managed to attend in Moscow were insufficient for him to correct the cardinal misunderstanding of his ideas by the two producers. (He did, however, take an active part in the rehearsals of *The Three Sisters* before the revival of the play in the autumn of 1901.) That was the reason for his frequent outbursts of anger during the rehearsals and his refusal to advise the actors how to play their parts. His stock reply to the actors, "You'll find it all in the text," was just an evasion forced on him by his complete helplessness to make his producers see the positive ideas he had taken so much pains to present in an artistic form. In face of such utter blindness on the part of his producers and their inability to raise themselves above the prevailing ideas of their time, Chekhov was powerless: he was too ill to do anything. The irony of it was that this cardinal misinterpretation of his plays seems to have agreed with the mood of that particular period in Russian history so that in spite of it the plays were (after a time) successful. There is, of course, the further fact that with so great a playwright as Chekhov the failure to grasp the ruling ideas of his plays, the inability to understand their structure, and even the plain distortion of their characters, leaves so much that is original and artistically true that the spectator has plenty left he can thoroughly enjoy. That, however, does not justify the view that Chekhov's outbursts of angry protests aganst the misinterpretation of his plays were merely the unaccountable tantrums of genius. Chekhov, as is plainly evident from his letters, does not belong to the type of writer who is devoid of critical ability. He was, in fact, a very profound literary critic as well as a man who possessed the invaluable capacity for self-criticism. It took him about seven years to work out his new formula of the play of indirect action, and there can be no doubt that he arrived at his new form of dramatic expression only after a careful and painstaking analysis of the technique of play-writing, including a thorough study of Greek drama,[8] a fact of some consequence to the understanding of the structure of his last four plays.

[8] Among the large number of well-thumbed books Chekhov sent to the public library of his native town of Taganrog were the best available translations of the complete plays of the Greek dramatists.

morris freedman

STRINDBERG'S POSITIVE NIHILISM

STRINDBERG, LIKE Ibsen, presents a surface of thesis. *The Father* appears to be a play in answer to Ibsen's "woman love." It is apparently based on woman hate and ostensibly depicts the systematic destruction by a wife of her husband. The text even contains a specific reference to *Ghosts*, in which a good word is said for Captain Alving. *Miss Julie*, although its thesis is less obvious than that of *The Father*, depicts the destruction of a "decadent" member of the aristocracy by a rising member of the lower classes. This conflict is complicated by the forces of feminine emancipation which have made Miss Julie so uncertain of her character. (Miss Julie, like Hedda Gabler, the product of the new enlightenment, cannot shape her world to suit her romantic dreams and so leaves it. Unlike Hedda, however, she has so lost possession of herself she begs to be ordered to kill herself.)

But Strindberg's thematic surface, far more obviously than Ibsen's, pulsates with disturbances that have their energy in an undertow of passion, with shocks and heavings that are generated before our eyes. Strindberg's drama is dynamically psychological. Tones, atmospheres, characters, moods change as we watch; logic and predictability, order, coherence give way before the effects of desperate needs and of violent whim; they become lost in the chaos and depths of the mental landscape.

In *The Father* we see an inflexible, principled man degenerate inexorably to a whimpering infantilism. The captain insists that it is he alone who will decide the education of his daughter; he rejects the compromise offered by his wife, which would allow the daughter to vote on her future, even though the compromise would favor his position. At his strongest, at his most assertive, we can glimpse signs of the captain's weakness; his descent to a whining dependence, to a literal swaddling by the nurse who handled him as a baby, is much less the result of his wife's attack on him than it is of his own softness of character and will, emerging at last to the determining surface. We learn very early that the captain has allowed himself to be dominated by a ménage of whimsical, willful, superstitious, fanatical women; his brother-in-law, Laura's brother, has foisted off on him at least one of them and considers it something of a joke. It was as a mother to him, both the husband and the wife agree, that the wife married him. Like a child seeking relief from some arbitrary, even terrible parental imposition, the captain implores his wife to release him from the doubt of his paternity of Bertha, but, like a child who lives under some primal taboo that is superior to his own will, the captain is actually unable to allow himself to be so released. Nor of course can he ever logically be released, for, as he points out, in a mad scene echoing Lear and Dostoyevskeyan tableaux, what father can ever be certain of his child, what father can ever be other than putative, a lament that, horrible as it may suddenly seem, is only of the nature of things (short of chastity belts): as well lament the unrelenting pull of gravity.

If the captain acts out of an absurd logic, compelled step by step in a scheme of things which seems to have an order (he is the father, he has the right to make decisions regarding his daughter; he doubts his fatherhood, which is to say his masculinity and his maturity; he ceases to decide and to act; he returns to infancy and, finally, retreats to death), Laura acts out of an illogical instinct which has its own order and inevitability. Incapable of any but the most simple strategy, a strategy shaped only by the dimmest notion of distant victory, without detail or preliminary planning, Laura is capable of the most refined, most carefully exercised tactical skill. It is the captain, after all, who first brings up the theme of the universal uncertainty of fatherhood; it is the doctor who first suggests the possibility of certifying the captain's insanity. She immediately assimilates the implicit possibilities; at once they become measures in her campaign. Yet it would be an error to consider her heartless, unaware of the nature of her behavior, indifferent to its appearance.

LAURA: But I didn't mean this to happen. I never really thought it out. I may have had some vague desire to get rid of you—you were in my way—and perhaps, if you see some plan in my actions, there was one, but I was unconscious of it. I have never given a thought to my actions—they simply ran along the rails you laid down. My conscience is clear, and before God I feel innocent, even if I'm not. You weighed me down like a stone, pressing and pressing till my heart tried to shake off its intolerable burden. That's how it's been, and if without meaning to I have brought you to this, I ask your forgiveness.

Even here, her sensitivity to the implications of things is evident. This poignant, strainingly honest, unsparing self-analysis is part of her capacious tactical instinct; she does not justify herself, that is to say, she does not find a rationale or a philosophical justification for her action, she merely describes herself. Her intentions are perhaps those of a predatory animal, of the female spider, but she lives with them, exercises them, in the cause of what she is sure is a worthy endeavor, the protection of her maternal prerogatives.

It is plain that in the background of the elemental, sexual struggle between the father and mother is the issue of the emergence of woman as an individual. Strindberg may sneer at Ibsen's idolatry of women, he may suggest that woman needs no more rights than those she already possesses in abundance (witness Laura who, as a plain matter of fact, regardless of law, states that she is the stronger, rather disarming the captain), but it is the background of Laura's ignorance, the legal dispossession of her rights, which catalyzes the explosion that is building up. The captain will not talk out his differences with his wife, answering her suggestion for a compromise by pointing out, with an adolescent preciseness, that the halfway point between the town and their residence is the railroad station. He does not trouble to inform his wife of the details or significance of his meteoritic studies, and while her confusion of a microscope with a spectroscope might have been willful, part of her campaign to have him certified as insane, it might equally well have been the result of ignorance. Nor can we blame her without extenuation for the interception of her husband's orders for books, unless we are ready to accept the captain's attitude that his meteoritic researches were none of her business, that these, essentially, preceded the whole family's welfare. All Laura can see is that the captain does not read or use all of the books he orders (common enough if one knows scholars) and that the household expenses are being squeezed. (This is especially ironic, for the captain keeps the household books, doling out expense money.)

Miss Julie, too, while it may have its roots in social questions, rises to the more airy atmosphere of psychology. Miss Julie's fate is as much the result of encountering a representative of the new proletariat and of her mother's "enlightened" upbringing as it is of her own particularity of character, her uncertainty of identity, her playfulness with passion, her alternate arrogance and submissiveness, her extravagant romanticism, her plain compulsion to perversity. Hating sex, she submits to Jean; hating men and wishing pathologically to humble them, she asks Jean to command her to suicide.

The Father gets starker and starker as it proceeds. Its movement is a steady one, an intensification at a fixed rate toward the sheer monotone of the finale. Modulation is negligible. *Miss Julie* is a chiaroscuro of tones. Before the union, there is gallantry in the air, the colors of emotion, summer perfumes, but with patterns of sudden blackness: the gentle flirtatiousness of Julie and Jean and the momentary flashes of viciousness and selfishness. After, there is dullness and greyness and the distortions and blurrings of romance (Lake Como with its incessant rains and quarrelling couples), the interplay of the changing affections of Julie and Jean toward each other, Julie's bleakness in her frustration and degradation and the red violence of her fury. Miss Julie is playing on the fringes of actuality, laughing at the depths beneath her; we are present as she totters, erratically but certainly, toward the plunge. Oppressed by will, dominated by it, she has not even the passing satisfaction of Hedda Gabler's independence, of Hedda's modest moment of control of fate (the puppetry of Lovborg), and she retains only enough will in the end to ask that Jean exercise will for her.

Miss Julie and *The Father* show characters as they move steadily toward failure and death. In *Easter* we see a man moving upward toward some degree of self-understanding and success as a person. Elis is a figure almost as obnoxious as the black Gregers in *The Wild Duck*. He is brimming with an aggressive self-pity, with pride, with a coldness of soul that excludes the rest of the universe. He is solipsistic, taking every event in his neighborhood as having a meaning only for him. (Once when the telephone rings, he hears his own voice answering.) He has been chosen, as he sees it, for endless punishment. He rises out of his pit as the result, first, of the effects on him of his fiancée, Kristina, and of his mother, who are real enough persons, but also as the result of the workings on him of his sister, Eleanora, and of the debtor, Lindkvist, who are more than real, other than real, and represent forces as well as being themselves.

Kristina works on Elis by following her bent, humoring him only just so far, letting him live with his jealousy and then with the truth. She opposes his volatility with calmness. His mother resists him openly and logically. "Your coldness," she says to him about his attitude toward Kristina, "freezes her heart." When he petulantly laments the family's fate for the hundredth time, "but why do we who are innocent suffer for his fault?" evoking the ancient dilemma of original sin, his mother dismisses him impatiently, "Oh, be quiet!" It is the mother who establishes plainly the way of redemption, the change necessary in Elis for his "punishment" to cease. "Men are human," she says, "and one must take them as they are." She says about Eleanora, "Sane or not, for me she is wise—for she knows how to bear life's burdens better than I do, better than any of us."

Eleanora, too, makes explicit the need for patience, forbearance, acceptance, self-denial. "Stop judging people," she tells Benjamin, "even those who are convicted of sin." But her effect is in her example. Even Elis sees this. "Poor Eleanora," he mutters at the end of Act I, "she's so unhappy herself, and yet she can make others happy." Her endless sweetness and gentleness, her flights of fancy (listening to the birds and to the telephone wires), her other-worldly disregard for the legal amenities of this world make it possible for her to see and state arrangements invisible and impossible to the others. She comes as close as anyone to stating the theme of the play, "Everyone has to suffer today, Good Friday, so as to remember Christ's suffering on the cross," and, indeed, at one moment or another, every one of the principal characters identifies himself with Christ.

But Elis's "sufferings"—about the family's debt to the creditor, about the failure of his student in his examination, about the rejection of him by another student, about his mother's and sister's insanity, about his father's guilt—are all external and theatrically masochistic. He flaunts his wounds and his pride in them. It is necessary for him really to suffer, to pass through agonies of character, to be redeemed. And it is here that Lindkvist plays his role. A much-imposed-on creditor, he comes to forgive, to offer mercy, not the coldness and heartlessness of justice, which Elis insists on. Almost an allegorical figure, he throws his huge shadow over the players; he knows what they have been talking about when he was away; he can, *deus-ex-machina*-like, manipulate the plot, bringing up an encounter with Elis's father that predated the swindling. He has the joviality, the comical quality (those galoshes that squish all through his scenes), but also the supernatural tone of a Santa Claus figure, which he is. He comes to bring salvation to the family at the expense of Elis's humiliation. Elis's pride must break; he must write to the student who rejected him; he must meet the governor to whom he objects so vehemently. "We're all human," Lindkvist tells him, "and in life's crises we must take one another as we are with all our faults and weaknesses—swallow each other neck and crop. Go to the Governor!"

Both Eleanora and Lindkvist represent extremes of accommodation. Eleanora works with instinct and heart; Lindkvist with logic, head, and a sense of character. They are inner and outer forces, and they meet just before the end of the play, just after Lindkvist has laid down the procedure for Elis's saving of the family.

> ELEANORA: Then you can't want to hurt us.
> LINDKVIST: No, no, dear child!
> ELEANORA: Then help us!
> LINDKVIST: Child, I can't help your father to escape his punishment. (*Looking kindly at Benjamin.*) Nor Benjamin to get through his

Latin examination. But the other help has already been given. Life won't give us everything—and nothing gratis. So you must help me too. Will you?

ELEANORA: How can I, who have nothing, help you?

LINDKVIST: What's the date today? Look and see.

ELEANORA: (*taking down the calendar.*) It's the sixteenth.

LINDKVIST: Very well, before the twentieth you must get your brother to call on the Governor and to write a letter to Peter.

ELEANORA: Is that all?

LINDKVIST: Oh, child! But if he doesn't do those things, the giant will come again with yum, yum, yum!

ELEANORA: Why does the giant come and frighten children?

LINDKVIST: To make 'em good.

ELEANORA: Yes, of course. And he's quite right.

Eleanora and Lindkvist join forces. Lindkvist may be able to lay down the rules for Elis's salvation, but it is Eleanora who will see to it that they are put into effect.

Easter modulates the harshness of *Miss Julie* and *The Father*. Elis is like the captain in his inflexible pride. He, too, cannot take people as they are, modify his stiff expectations. Unlike the captain, however, he is worked on by forces to which he must yield, the gentleness of Eleanora, the hardness of Lindkvist. He is humbled at last, and while we do not see him actually changed (for that would take another play; like Iago, he says not a word after his acknowledgment of defeat), we also do not see him go down finally. We can expect, however, since his will has not been so crumbled as Miss Julie's, since his degradation has been interior and private, that he will not take Miss Julie's ultimate solution to the enforced change of character, or collapse like the captain, all vitality spent.

Easter is a bridge between the realistic, sharp, clear-cut, monochromatic early plays (*The Father*, 1887; *Miss Julie*, 1888) and the surrealistic, complex, symphonic later plays (*A Dream Play*, 1902; *The Ghost Sonata*, 1907). The captain and Miss Julie offer portraits of persons unable, by any means, to yield to the requirements of reality. Elis does bend his nature. The large question then changes its character: just what is reality, to what are we yielding, just where and how do we live when we rise above our natures as we humble ourselves?

A Dream Play answers these questions in epic form. Whatever level we live on, whatever our occupations, "human life is pitiable." This melancholy refrain tolls throughout the play. Whatever we seek, whatever our ambitions, we are doomed to the repetition that "human life is to be pitied."

The daughter and the lawyer are depicted as married and living in an apartment adjoining his office. Their misery is unrelieved. An idiot girl, Kristin, goes around pasting up all cracks in the walls and windows to keep the heat of the apartment in. The baby's screaming frightens the clients. A cabbage smell permeates the apartment. The curtains, candlesticks, and chairs are awry. "It is not easy to be human," the wife says later after the lawyer describes how repetition turns "everything which was charming and witty and beautiful the night before" into the "ugly, stupid, repulsive. Pleasure stinks, and enjoyment falls to pieces. What people call success is always a step towards the next failure."

The secret behind the door, it is clear to us from the beginning, is that there is nothing behind the door. Theology, philosophy, medicine, law find nothing. Only the poet seems to understand this. The daughter tells him that "this world, its life and its inhabitants are . . . only a mirage, a reflection, a dream image." The poet asks the daughter, "before you go, tell me from what you suffered most down there." "From living," the daughter answers. "From feeling my vision dimmed by having eyes, my hearing dulled by having ears, and my thought, my airy, luminous thought, bound down in a labyrinth of fact. You have seen a brain. What twisting channels, what creeping ways!" And in her final summation, the daughter says:

> This then it is to be a human being—
> ever to miss the thing one never prized
> and feel remorse for what one never did,
> to yearn to go, yet long to stay.
> And so the human heart is split in two,
> emotions by wild horses torn—
> conflict, discord, uncertainty.

This would seem to be conclusively nihilistic. Out of himself, humbled into universality, the artist's only finding is that human life is to be pitied, that there is nothing behind the door of hope and expectation. But this itself is positive. To know that one is in a dream is not to expect the consequences and consolations of the real day. We cannot speak of a "logical" conclusion to *A Dream Play*. But the final resolution is one of a patient acceptance and resignation, a purging rather than a lingering discomfort; we are not angered and irritated into discomfort, as with Kafka's or Dali's very similar messages; we are eased into relaxation. If this is the way life is, and we have neither to grant nor deny the possibility, then it is the way life is.

"The labor comes first," says the girl in *The Ghost Sonata*, "the labor of keeping the dirt of life at a distance." The dirt of life is everywhere, in deceit, in fruitless repetition, even in self-knowledge.

"We are not what we seem," says the mummy, "because at bottom we are better than ourselves, since we detest our sins." We are doomed to the endless servitude of cleaning up after our vampirish servants, whether these serve us literally every day, or metaphorically, in the interest of our spirit and imagination. "Jesus Christ descended into hell," concludes the student. "That was His pilgrimage on earth."

The play is melancholy. We have unmaskings and deaths, tiredness and disillusion, frustration and disenchantment. Yet the student does not lose hope. "Where is anything that fulfills its promise? In my imagination." He feels the "vampire in the kitchen" beginning to suck him. Yet he can assert: "There are poisons that destroy the sight and poisons that open the eyes. I seem to have been born with the latter kind, for I cannot see what is ugly as beautiful, nor call evil good. I cannot." And when the girl is dying, he speaks to her in an accent of hope, of release, not resignation but expectation. "The Liberator is coming. Welcome, pale and gentle one. Sleep, you lovely, innocent, doomed creature, suffering for no fault of your own. Sleep without dreaming, and when you wake again . . . may you be greeted by a sun that does not burn, in a home without dust, by friends without stain, by a love without flaw."

But these are the ideals of earth itself, of life itself. It is the daily reward, and the agony of the play resides in the limitations of human possibility. Strindberg's plays move from the bitterness of personal anger to the hopelessness of the universal. This is a moral progression, and not simply because the universal is quantitatively more than the individual. The personal disaster, after all, matters not at all until it becomes a revelation of the total human disaster. Strindberg went from individuals and types to allegorical, all-embracing, symbolic figures: an old man, a student, a mummy, a lawyer. The microscopically sharp question "Am I the father of my daughter?" is replaced by the questions without any particulars whatsoever: "What is behind the door? How escape the dirt of living?"

It is possible, conceivably, to answer the first sort of question; Ibsen and Shaw were constantly answering questions that were specific although the implications may have been larger. It is not possible, perhaps, to answer the second sort; but there is enough achievement and art in being able just to pose it. This Strindberg finally did.

john gassner

BERNARD SHAW AND THE MAKING OF THE MODERN MIND

SHAW *knew* he was one of the creators of modern consciousness and modern conscience. He told us so himself many times, and with perfect seriousness. An apt summary of both Shaw's historical position and self-appreciation is contained in a Max Beerbohm cartoon in which the jaunty young nineteenth century Shaw offers some old clothes for sale to the great European critic Georg Brandes standing behind the counter as "a merchant of ideas."

"What'll you take for the lot?" asks Brandes.

"Immortality," says Shaw.

Brandes protests: "Come, I've handled those goods before! Coat, Mr. Schopenhauer's; waistcoat, Mr. Ibsen's; Mr. Nietzsche's trousers—"

To which Shaw blandly replies, "Ah, but look at the patches."

It is perfectly apparent that Shaw would not have been nonplussed either if Brandes had also referred to some other articles of clothing such as, shirt belonging to Samuel Butler, shoes borrowed from Karl Marx, and gloves and hat from Lamarck and Bergson. It is my suspicion that Shaw would have resented only an attribution of "cummerbund from Freud," since Shaw preferred moral passion to any other kind (his plays were once called "as unemotional as a mushroom"), and since he placed Economics above Eros as the source of good and evil, happiness and misery. And this reflection reminds me that he would have winced at some such phrase as "collar worn by Darwin" unless assured that the collar symbolized strangulation and was being rightly discarded, for Shaw was the sworn enemy of "Social Darwinism." The Darwinian struggle for existence was anathema to the intensely combative Shaw, who once proposed to revise the rules of tennis and penalize players who hit the ball too hard to be successfully returned by their opponents. The Darwinian doctrine of the "survival of the fittest," so sacred to old-line Victorian Liberals

From *College English*, XXIII, No. 7 (April, 1962). Reprinted with the permission of the National Council of Teachers of English and the author.

that they frowned on social legislation, was altogether abhorrent to this "fittest of the fit" who was in danger, indeed, of carrying survival to excess until he died of a fall in his 94th year.

Considering his virtuosity as a writer of comedies, which he appreciated even more than his audiences did at the time, Shaw declared in an early volume (*Three Plays for Puritans*), "I am a natural-born mountebank"; and Shaw was undoubtedly a born showman and devotee of pyrotechnical displays. But he was also a born preacher, and he was not in the least exaggerating when he declared as early as his 1893 Preface to *Mrs. Warren's Profession,* "I have spared no pains to make known that my plays are built to induce not voluptuous reverie but intellectual interest. . . ." Shaw, however, found it possible to reconcile his pedagogical and histrionic inclinations in the same person and the same works. In this achievement, more perhaps than in any other, lay his power as a literary and dramatic genius. And he did not truly do justice to it when he proclaimed, as he was wont to do, that he merely made Mountebank Shaw serve the sermonizing Preacher Shaw. He could advance this estimate of himself well enough, and sometimes brilliantly, for no one writing English could sustain a half-truth with more verbal skill.

Thirty years later, with the world floundering in the economic depression of the 1930's, we find him insisting, in the Preface to his aptly titled political drama *On the Rocks,* that "All great Art and Literature is propaganda." I say that Shaw did not do justice to himself in representing his art as the handmaiden of preachment, because it was often in his preachment that he found his art, as in *Major Barbara, Heartbreak House,* and *Man and Superman.* It is certainly impossible to say with respect to his plays that one side of him was the reformer and the other side the comedian; or that one side of him was the thinker and the other side the artist. Many of his most memorable lines and effective conceits, on the contrary, were inseparable from his social convictions or hopes, his will to teach and his will to create being often the same thing. What Shaw's "Serpent" says in *Back to Methuselah* applies to his best writing and explains why his work has dated so much less than the plays of his contemporaries from Pinero to John Galsworthy: ". . . imagination," says the Serpent, "is the beginning of creation. You imagine what you desire; you will what you imagine; and at last you create what you will."

It is a valid conclusion that Shaw the thinker and Shaw the artist are one and the same person. His tracts, of course, deserve a historian's consideration and can stand examination; and in their turn of phrase they too reflect his lively intelligence and talent for language. But he was not at all unique in grinding out programs of social legislation, denunciations of capitalistic laissez-faire, and unorthodox views on church, state, and economics. In retrospect, the content of the purely sociological and political writings may even seem quite outmoded if for no other reason than that the moderate social program of Shaw and his late Victorian associates was in large part adopted and made the law of the land. Besides, the program was tame from the start, even if Shaw's rhetoric was often, fortunately, unbridled. At the height of his political career as a stump speaker, London vestryman, and spokesman for the Fabian Society, founded in 1884, Shaw was committed to practical policies distinctly more evolutionary than revolutionary. With Sidney Webb, the tireless civil servant and statistician, Sidney Olivier, later the English Governor of Jamaica and Secretary of State for India, Graham Wallas, and (later) H. G. Wells, Shaw was the representative of a reformist group that picked the right label when it called itself the Fabian Society. Its program for socialization and social reform was growlingly gradualist.

At the height of its prestige the Fabian Society scarcely reached a membership of 1,500, and its policy was wisely one of permeation of established political parties. Bluster as he might, the Shaw who engaged in politics proposed the manna of reform in the middle of the road while thundering Marxism on the left. In old age he once declared, "Karl Marx made a man of me," but in the course of his life he repudiated virtually all of Marx's economics and sociology. The young Shaw, moreover, concurred at least officially with his fellow-Fabians when they called for patience with the historical process. Their slogan was "For the right moment you must wait, as Fabius did, most patiently," earning the ironic retort of a member of the Socialist Party who once said to them, "Comrades, we must not allow ourselves to be carried away by patience!"

Now this account of the Fabian Society hardly accords with our impression of Shaw, who lived on until 1950 and retained a reputation to the end of his days that was anything but suggestive of the temperament and mentality of civil servants, statisticians, and reliable sociologists. The Fabian picture is one thing; the Shaw who upset the applecart of middle-class society and recommended all sorts of public upheavals is another. What to make of Shaw became a problem as early as the 1890's when he distinguished himself as a dynamitard among music and drama critics and as a volatile and incalculable heretic among playwrights. He acquired a formidable reputation for irresponsibility while actually leading an exemplary life as the late-blooming husband of an Irish millionairess and as a hard-driving businessman in his dealings with publishers and stage producers. It was plainly his manner, more than his matter, that brought him both his notoriety and fame.

We may return then to the old clothes-and-patches theory of the Max Beerbohm cartoon, and we may end by endorsing its subject's insistence that the patches make a difference. Very much of a difference, indeed, which is tantamount to saying, as I have already done, that Shaw the thinker or maker of the modern mind is actually Shaw the *artist*. He is Shaw the essayist whose imaginative and satirical prose is the best in English after the prose of Jonathan Swift, and Shaw the playwright, for whom no peer can be found in English unless we return to the spacious stage of Queen Elizabeth and James I.

To the great variety of his interests Shaw added an impressive variety of insights and provocative presentations—the presentations of a master stylist, debater, orator, farceur, comedian, fantasist and even poet. It is safe to say that he brought more zest to debate than any of his contemporaries in England, more eloquence to oratory, more vitality to farce (with the possible exception of Oscar Wilde), more wit to comedy and more poetry to the "play of ideas" than any of his contemporaries. Moreover, in Shaw's case the manner was the man himself, so that behind all his postures and poses there was a remarkable unity of passion, energy, and levity.

This is my contention, and there is no other way to substantiate it than to examine the works themselves. A modest start can be made by reviewing in summary from Shaw's treatment of some of the tendencies, problems and challenges he encountered at the turn of the century. We can set his treatment beside that normally accorded to some particular matter by Shaw's contemporaries and so observe the singularity of his temper.

We may start with Shaw's work as a critic of the drama and theatre, since this brings us to his main form of expression. It is important to observe, in the first place, that unlike many advanced drama critics of the late nineteenth century in Europe, Shaw was not impressed by realistic dialogue, realistic play construction, and realistic theatre convention. He certainly did not write for the Stanislavskian actor and director. The only realism he had any use for was neither structural nor scenic, but intellectual and psychological. He had the astuteness to observe how easy it was to make a show of superficial reality and yet *evade* reality, to make accuracy of detail a substitute for essential truth, to feign boldness by presenting an unconventional subject but scrupulously refrain from examining it. While virtually everyone in England was crowning Arthur Wing Pinero the laureate of dramatic realism on the strength of such so-called problem plays as *The Second Mrs. Tanqueray* and *The Notorious Mrs. Ebbsmith*, Shaw was firing away at Pinero's pretensions to realism.

Shaw accused Pinero of presenting modern characters or problems and then employing shameless contrivances to reduce the action to banality and the meaning to commonplaceness. A case in point is *The Second Mrs. Tanqueray*, in which Pinero was modern enough to start with the marriage of a Victorian gentleman to a woman with a past, and conventional enough to conclude with the failure of that marriage. In order to provide a conclusion so comforting to Victorian audiences, moreover, Pinero drew upon the same contrived plot-making that discredited the so-called well-made, but actually ill-made, plays of the century. No wonder Shaw declared that Pinero's formula for popular success consisted of presenting a situation and then running away from it. This policy was the pseudo-Ibsenism that had such vogue in the English-speaking theatre. Shaw, who would have none of it and was clever enough to detect it behind all masquerades of verisimilitude, insisted that for a modern sensibility "an interesting play cannot in the nature of things mean anything but a play in which problems of conduct and character of personal importance to the audience are raised and suggestively discussed."

In attacking Pinero's realism at a time when even William Archer considered it a model of "playmaking," Shaw stood in the forefront of modern criticism. Pinero, to whom constant reference is made in Archer's classic manual on playwriting, is virtually forgotten today except for a few farces such as *The Magistrate* that possess theatrical liveliness.

It was plain that while the majority of Shaw's contemporaries were interested in "well-made" plays, Shaw was interested only in alive ones. And for him they could not really be alive unless they were provocative and constituted drama of ideas. This is important to our understanding of Shaw's own plays, too. If they belong to the genre of realism it is by virtue of their engagement to reality, chiefly by comprising a conflict of ideas, principles, ways of thinking, and ways of living. For the sake of reality, Shaw was always prepared to violate realistic structure and verisimilitude, to turn somersaults of the most farcical or fantastic kind, and to be arbitrary with his plot or to discard plot altogether.

He was ever ready to stop the overt action for a good discussion or good lecture, or even step out of the proscenium frame to harangue the audience in behalf of a relevant philosophy or sociology which is beyond, if not indeed antithetical to, the illusion achieved by plodding realists and the designers who provided scenic realism. And to serve the "reality principle" of social criticism Shaw also had no hesitation to curtail characterization, to color situations, and to invent a fantasy such as that of a Last Judgment in *The Simpleton of the Unexpected Isles* in which God removes all useless individuals, or of *Back to Methuselah,* in which the world is ruled by men who have willed themselves in some Lamarckian way into living many centuries, since little sense could be expected from the mere infants of 60, 70, or 80 who determine the fate of societies.

Shaw also availed himself of every freedom of comic invention or extravagance to overcome public indifference with provocative reversals of viewpoint, as in *Man and Superman,* in which Don Juan is turned into a paragon of virtue for whom the only passion worth having is "moral passion," and *Major Barbara,* in which Shaw maintained the cold-sober argument that all moral problems had their source in economics. In *Major Barbara,* the real benefactor of mankind, it is bizarrely argued, is none other than the munitions magnate Andrew Undershaft who builds the good society with the well paid, well housed, and well entertained employees of his factory; moreover, Undershaft is perfectly willing to sell his dynamite for peaceful purposes or for the eradication of injustice if humanity should ever have sense enough to make proper use of his product.

Shaw, to sum up, took a view of dramatic art that was essentially theatrical rather than anti-theatrical, provided true realism—that is, realism of content or idea—was well served. Mind and spirit carried him far beyond the provinciality of realism, which was already, by 1880, little more than the tired avant-gardism of the nineteenth-century European bourgeoisie. So it happened that Shaw, who greatly enriched the realistic substance of the drama by bringing economics and sociological realities into the theatre and by turning the British drawing room into a forum, actually liberated the stage from the limitations of realism. He recalled the theatre to its classic and Elizabethan heritage of freedom from picayune illusionism; in other words, he drew close to the freedom of presentational as against the stringencies of representational art. In his own work, he turned to "musical form" in discussion drama, composing plays in the manner of a theme and variations; and he exercised his flair for opera in never hesitating to stop the action in favor of a verbal aria on some subject, which is a mode of drama, too, when competently managed, as old as Euripides and Aristophanes. Granville-Barker in staging some of Shaw's early plays in London was wont to remind the actors indeed that they *were* in an opera.

Shaw was surely in the vanguard of dramatic expression whether he championed a species of dialectical realism in becoming Ibsen's most fervid advocate in the 'eighties or anticipated the imaginative styles of twentieth-century dramatic art that favor theatricalism. (It is noteworthy that he made himself an ardent champion of O'Casey's expressionist anti-war drama *The Silver Tassie*.) We move backward with him to the theatricalist art of earlier ages and forward with him to the dramatic art of Pirandello, Giraudoux, and Brecht. And lest we be misled by his championship of Ibsen, let us observe that in many pieces on Ibsen and most notably in his Fabian Society Lectures, *The Quintessence of Ibsenism*, Shaw paid little attention to the outward and rather provincial realism of the Scandinavian pioneer. Shaw analyzed each play as early as 1891, when he delivered his lectures, in terms of its challenge and reversal of accepted beliefs, its paradoxes and contradiction of commonplace attitudes. Shaw's Ibsen is a fascinating dialectician and a veritable Robin Goodfellow of the realm of comedy who plays havoc with humdrum opinion and custom. And when Shaw ultimately arrived at a view of Ibsen's real achievement he made him not the father of external realism but of discussion drama or the "play of ideas." Beginning with *A Doll's House*, Ibsen, according to Shaw, created a new form of drama by introducing a new movement into it. "Formerly," Shaw explained, "You had in what was called a well-made play an exposition in the first act, a situation in the second, and unraveling in the third. Now you have exposition, situation, and discussion; and the discussion is the best of the playwright." For Shaw modern drama and true realism started in 1879 when Ibsen's *Doll's House* heroine Nora made her husband sit down and discuss the nature of her marriage to him.

Estheticism was one of the recognized ways of revolting against nineteenth-century laissez-faire industrialism and materialism. The Pre-Raphaelite movement, the agitation of Ruskin and William Morris, and the Yellow Book estheticism of Oscar Wilde, Aubrey Beardsley and others in England, the movement of the "decadents" and "symbolists" across the English channel—these and other art-for-art's sake phenomena of the turn-of-the-century could not but be noticed and in some way or other reflected by Shaw, who was equally conscious of art and sociology. And for William Morris especially Shaw always expressed the highest regard. Against Philistine attacks on art and artists Shaw was indeed ever watchful. He was one of the few Englishmen to remain well disposed toward Wilde after his prison sentence. He wrote a vigorous defense of art against the allegations of Max Nordau that modern art was decadent and tended to be a manifestation of disease. Shaw's defense was the brilliant essay *The Sanity of Art*.

Yet Shaw's estheticism was radically different from that of most of his contemporaries or successors, and here too his originality and force are apparent. In the first place, he emphatically rejected the doctrine of art for art's sake. He rejected just as categorically the nihilistic or negativistic tendencies that have characterized estheticism from the 1890's to our own times, from the poet-drunkards and suicides of the turn of the century to the beatniks of the midcentury, from the works of Huysmans to the works of Samuel Becket. In the very depths of Shaw's disillusionment in 1932, in his play *Too True to be Good*, in which his clergyman hero mouthpiece Aubrey declared that the Western world was "damned beyond Salvation," Shaw made Aubrey conclude with a ringing disavowal of negativism. "Is No enough?" asks Shaw's desperate clergyman, and replies, "For a boy, yes; for a man never. . . . I must preach and preach no matter how late the hour and how short the day . . ."; to which Shaw the chronic activist added a postscript reading, "The author, though himself a professional talkmaker, does not believe that the world can be saved by talk alone."

For Shaw art was an act of liberation from materialistic interests, a release of the spirit, and, at the turn of the century, a weapon against Victorian Philistinism in general. He defended the right of free expression fiercely and fought British censorship. He drew that censorship down on himself indeed, most notably in the case of *Mrs. Warren's Profession*. He championed Wagner in England, especially with his pamphlet *The Perfect Wagnerite*, published in 1898. But it was Wagner the social revolutionist, as reconstituted into a semi-Marxist and Shavian artist, that Shaw championed him, interpreting *The Ring of the Nibelungs* as a drama of the overthrow of the old order and the triumph of the heroic human spirit. It was possible then for Shaw to give his allegiance almost equally to Mozart, his favorite composer, and to Wagner, his favorite musical cause. And particularly bracing was Shaw's view of the true artist as an unusually strong and independent, supremely *healthy*, individual even behind a mask of frailty and a cloud of alienation and loneliness. Nothing contrasts more sharply with the romantic idealization of the artist as an easily wilted "blue" flower in vogue during the 1890's and Shaw's portrait of Marchbanks, the boy-artist in *Candida*, written in 1893. Marchbanks may delude others and even himself, for a time, that he is a weakling, but to a perceptive "womanly woman" such as Candida he is compact of strength precisely because he is a poet at heart; he remains unimpressed by domestic felicity, refuses to submit to family authority, and is willing to learn to live without happiness.

Shaw put the matter beautifully in a letter he sent at the turn of the century to the Ibsenite actress Janet Achurch. He wrote her: "I realize the full significance of the singular fate which led me to play with all the serious things of life and to deal seriously with all its plays." To be *oneself* and at the same time labor in full knowledge of the fact that we are all members of each other was Shaw's most insistent thought on the privilege of being an artist in society. I believe that the visionary Mrs. George speaking in a trance in Shaw's discussion play *Getting Married* speaks for Shaw himself when she declares: "I've been myself, I've not been afraid of myself. And at last I have *escaped from myself*, and am become a voice for them that are afraid to speak, and a cry for the hearts that break in silence."

Inevitably with Shaw we end up—or nearly end up—with his involvement with the social conflicts and expectations and with the views on numerous specific issues such as feminism and social reform that agitated the world of his youth in the 1880's (Shaw, it may be hard to realize, was born in 1856), of his maturity before World War I, and of his old age. Characteristically, he embraced the fashion in ideas with a difference, and gave these the stamp of his individuality while employing them in some provocative synthesis of contradictions and paradoxes. For Shaw, who was one of the least ambiguous of modern authors, was also one of the most ambivalent, and we have owed much of his provocativeness and artistry to his ambivalences.

For one thing, we have owed to them his capacity for writing comedy that is serious and serious drama that is comic. And the duality of his temperament gave us both his magnificent anger and superb geniality, his zeal for reform and genuine aversion to physical aggression, well expressed in his late revision of Shakespeare's *Cymbeline*, in which Imogen says in, alas, bad verse:

> Oh, do not make me laugh.
> Laughter dissolves too many resentments,
> Pardons too many sins.

To this Iachimo replies:

> And saves the world
> A many thousand murders.

The He-Ancient in *Back to Methuselah* also recognizes the potency of laughter when he declares concerning the will to longevity that "Like all revolutionary truths, it began as a joke." One of the physicians in *The Doctor's Dilemma* also scores well for Shaw in saying, "Life does not cease to be funny when people die any more than it ceases to be serious when people laugh."

In specific cases, moreover, we find Shaw gloriously at work in the fine, and difficult, art of reconciling contradictions. We find him, for example, an ardent feminist, yet a blithe satirist of turn-of-the-century feminist fads and extravagances in so early a piece as *The Philanderer*. We find him urging war on the Victorian ideal of feminity or feminine dependency in the 1890's; and right up to the plays written after 1920, from *Saint Joan* to *The Millionairess*, he persists in glorifying the *unfeminine* woman. Yet how warmly he writes of Joan, and how constantly he creates characters who are marvelous mother-surrogates while also flourishing as clever and sophisticated women of the world. We need only glance at the marvellous portrait Shaw gave us in Candida, who is both mother-image and minx, loyal wife and flirt, housekeeper and sockmender and yet a supremely intelligent person as well. And how neatly and perceptively he reverses norms and yet rights them in the long run, so that Candida remains a loyal wife equally for unconventional and natural (or, if you will, conventional) reasons. Shaw, we may say, was progressive in his espousal of feminism in the 1880's and progressive, too, in going *beyond* feminism in the 1890's.

Shaw's variations on the themes of love and sex are too many to consider here. It is especially noteworthy, however, that he protested equally against the Victorian repressive attitude and the post-Victorian permissive one. Both seemed to him mere obsessiveness with sex when the real problem was to avoid all forms of enslavement, including enslavement to sex, and all excuses for the evasion of social reality. Unlike the run-of-the-mill opponent of Victorian prudery, Shaw endorsed progress in the relations between the sexes as a means toward achieving freedom from voluptuousness for the sake of progress in *all* relations. And with this in mind he undertook to modify evolutionary theory itself. He could not be satisfied with the established disbelief in the inheritance of acquired traits any more than he could believe that evolution had come to an end. Annexing nineteenth-century evolutionary theory to his social idealism and adopting pseudoscientific vitalism as a credo, Shaw endorsed the Lamarckian theory of the inheritance of acquired characteristics as a necessary assurance that man could progress as a species; and with that other philosophical evolutionist Nietzsche, though without the latter's advocacy of "the will to power" as a dynamic factor, Shaw reposed hope in the coming of the superman. Humanity, as he came to know it, was a race made up largely of duffers, and what was especially distressing to him was man's failure as a political animal. But Shaw consoled himself with the reflection that "We have no reason to believe that we are the Creator's last word."

Shaw, noting the unreliability of social progress, the failures of parliamentary democracy to which he devoted two plays after World War I (*The Apple Cart* and *On the Rocks*), and concluding that "every technical qualification for doing good is a technical qualification for doing evil as well"—Shaw growing impatient with the inertia of the masses and the flabbiness of their elected representatives and misleaders, tended to pin his hopes more and more on self-propelled leaders in whom he saw the superior beings who had thus far appeared among men only as sports of nature. Around this faith he was apt to spin some of his most provocative plays and vivid characterizations before and after World War I. The Caesar of *Caesar and Cleopatra* is the superman as political leader; Undershaft is the superman as industrialist; Joan of Arc is the superman (or "superwoman") as saint. The eagerness with which Shaw believed or *wanted to believe* in savior-heroes who overleap the barriers of moral sloth and general mediocrity ultimately deceived him. It betrayed him into a kinder view of Mussolini, Hitler, and Stalin than his intelligence should have permitted. In this respect he was almost pathetically a man of the divided and self-betrayed modern mind. Shaw was touchingly aware in the famous epilogue to *Saint Joan* that simple humanity was not yet ready for its saints. He could not but become aware that simple humanity was not yet ready for any other species of superman. He was less inclined to realize that the supermen who arose in the shape of the Caesars, Napoleons, and Undershafts of the world were not necessarily ready for simple humanity.

Shaw, like so many other intellectuals of his time, was also tripped up in the long run by his faith in collectivism. Apparently, it did not occur to him sufficiently that society might manifest a unified effort at a frightful sacrifice of life and liberty. He also evinced an exaggerated trust in economics as the basis of human happiness and advancement. But we can never be fair to Shaw's creative intelligence by measuring his genius by the errors of the amateur sociologist, errors he shared with many other makers of the modern mind. In speaking of Shaw we must ultimately conclude with a proper acknowledgment of Shaw the "poet"—the visionary who refused to accept limits for the human race, the believer in the possibility of a creative will ideally capable of producing perfect men in a perfected society irradiated by right reason and good will. In this faith there could be no antinomies or conflicts of reason and instinct, rationalism and religiousness, individualism and collectivism, truth and poetry.

Shaw speaks best perhaps through one of his most attractive masks, that of the unfrocked Irish priest Father Keegan of *John Bull's Other Island*. Asked by the pragmatical Englishman Broadbent "What is it like in your dreams?", Father Keegan declares that he dreams of "a country where the State is the Church and the Church the people; three in one and one in three." This ideal state is "a commonwealth in which work is play and play is life; three in one and one in three. It is a godhead in which all life is human and all humanity divine; three in one and one in three." And Shaw's heretical mystic reminds the sceptical materialist that "Every dream is a promise in the womb of time." In nothing more is Shaw so notably a man of the twentieth century as in this trust in the desirability and inevitability of progress as well as in his perilous impatience with delay after his initial faith in gradualist reform. For all his brilliant show of hard-headedness, Shaw was also at one with the post-Renaissance Western spirit in sharing its dominantly Rousseauist romanticism, its perfectibility-worship, its "Faustian" restlessness. In virtually all his work he also gave us a distinctively nineteenth- and twentieth-century translation, into by now perhaps overfamiliar, social and political terms of the words of Leonardo da Vinci, who, standing brilliantly poised between the modern and the medieval world, concluded that "Every artist has two subjects: Man and the hopes of his soul."

stark young

HEARTBREAK HOUSES

I REMEMBER how Mr. Edmund Wilson and I, some years ago in a convivial literary moment, agreed that *Heartbreak House* was probably the best of the Shaw plays. We wondered, I remember, whether in twenty years it might not be the shining light among them. Through the removal of limitations in probability, and through the opening thereby for extravagance, *Heartbreak House* is farce rather than comedy. Nor is that anything against it unless you object to the possibility that farce allows for the poetic or fantastic. The question was whether or not we had begun to be impatient with this larding of social theory and significance on to what essentially was farce, however talented, and would remain so. Mr. Wilson and I must have been thinking that *Heartbreak House* offered a more complete unity of tone than most of Mr. Shaw's plays, and that perhaps the constant effect of assertiveness which was so peculiar to Shaw, and which could get very tiresome elsewhere in his other work, was especially suited to the tone of this particular play. In *Heartbreak House* perhaps this general tone in itself effectively expressed the theme, which is the state of things that was "the cultured, leisured Europe before the War."

It must have been an impression of some different sort that had done the work, for all these reflections went flat on me when I saw *Heartbreak House* produced again these many years after. I had looked forward to seeing the play again not only from curiosity about a work of art, but also, in a way, autobiographically—which is to say curiosity about myself, as to what my state of mind and change might be. For a while, on thus revisiting this drama I took it to be the production at the Mercury Theatre that was at fault. Presently I saw that the production was fair enough—if slightly blurred—with some good performances, especially Miss Phyllis Joyce as Lady Utterwood, but that the play itself was garrulous, unfelt and tiresome.

Reprinted with the permission of Charles Scribner's Sons from *Immortal Shadows* by Stark Young. Copyright 1948 by Charles Scribner's Sons.

Evidently the impression from the Theatre Guild production of *Heartbreak House* that had remained so strongly in my mind as the years went by came from the terrace scene and the company talking there in the moonless blue night. It was a long time ago and I had forgotten nearly all they said, but not that haunting tone composed of the scene, the voices, the vibration of characters, the impending blind ruin. And presently there at the Mercury I saw that I had lost even such a response. I was sufficiently concerned to take the book down afterward and read the whole play again, the long preface included. Very likely Mr. Welles' production lacked emphasis to some extent, parts of the play needing to be speeded up, parts slowed down, the pressure lightened here, increased there, for the sake of a more distinct pattern. But at that, the design of *Heartbreak House* proved on this rereading to be no more marked than it is in the production, if as much. Gradually I concluded that there was something very amiable about the willingness of a theatre company to memorize so many lines, and to heed, or seem to heed, so much rather wilted opinion, half point and half patter. An astonishing sort of inner monotony, as it were, was apparent, and had to be coped with. Except for the different voices, you could have shut your eyes and believed not that several people were there, created and expressing themselves, but that one person was describing several people.

Since Mr. Shaw himself goes to some length in the preface to invite more or less comparison of *Heartbreak House* with Chekhov's plays, we may sketch at least the beginning of such a comparison. Chekhov, he says, had produced four dramatic studies of *Heartbreak House*, of which three, *The Cherry Orchard, Uncle Vanya* and *The Sea Gull,* so far as England went, had got as far as a couple of performances by the Stage Society. The audiences had stared and said "How Russian!" To Mr. Shaw on the contrary it seemed that these intensely Russian plays fitted all the country houses in Europe in which . . . et cetera. Such a remark as that seems to me incredibly wilful and silly. The thesis of blind chaos and selfishness and of following the part of comfortable income and securities is a definite thesis. It may readily fit into the motif of a rotting Europe. But Chekhov would have been surprised to learn that his plays were a declaration in advance of all this. The Russian world of Chekhov can be only partially compared to the England that Mr. Shaw has diagrammed in *Heartbreak House*. A great difference arises from the fact that the expressiveness of the Russian temperament, with its gift and power of outpouring the far recesses of the heart, is a far more difficult matter for the English. This is not to say that either one or the other is better, but only that they are different. Where Tolstoy, Mr. Shaw says, was no pessimist and believed in the efficacy of violent measures, Chekhov, "more of a fatalist, had no faith in these charming people extricating themselves. They would, he thought, be sold up and set adrift by the bailiff; and he therefore had no scruple in exploiting and even flattering their charm."

What a patness and charm of persuasion this Mr. Shaw has! But the mere use of the words "flatter" and "charm" give away the British rubbish, or Teutonic conception, behind the idea. The references here are plainly to *The Cherry Orchard*. But no person in it wants to be flattered as to his special idiosyncrasy, nobody in this play is talking with that self-consciousness and varying degrees of egotism or no egotism so common to modest Englishmen. The charm of these people in *The Cherry Orchard*, and often of the Russians we meet, is that nobody is thinking at all about being charming; nobody is self-conscious, nobody is affected. That sentence of Mr. Shaw's is a whole commentary on the difference between Chekhov's world and that British world which Mr. Shaw so pugnaciously caters to, rebukes so entertainingly, severely and sincerely, and makes a fortune out of.

The more you know of Chekhov's writing and of him and his life and friends, the more absurd Mr. Shaw becomes on the subject. It is all very well to use a man or a work of art to hit something or somebody over the head with; and certainly the sport is an old one. But nobody could be more astonished than Chekhov would have been to hear of his having no scruples about exploiting the people whose words and little ironic, tender or mad acts, and droll or dark life-patterns he put into plays and stories or left jotted down in his notebook. To "flatter" anything about them would not fit anything in him. What he did with his people was to turn them into theatre, just as Mr. Shaw in *Heartbreak House* turns Chekhov into a sort of literary Hyde Park soapbox dialectic for the theatre.

That such a man as Mr. Shaw could use the life that is presented in Chekhov's plays in Chekhov's way, and even some of Chekhov's ideas and attitudes, is obvious. In spite of the unsuccessful translations of the Chekhov plays into English, a great deal of him comes through; and I should think it possible enough that Mr. Shaw regards his own *Heartbreak House* as being technically related to the three Chekhov plays that he mentions, *The Cherry Orchard* especially. Whether he does so or not, the comparison is inevitable and the relationship plain. On that subject we should have to say that either he boldly exercised his usual independence in the way of doing things, or else he was blind as a bat to Chekhov's technique, stage-effects and spirit. We should be brow-beaten indeed to accept the idea that in *Heartbreak House* there is more than the merest hint or tiny reflection of Chekhov's true method, none of that pure, painstaking economy and drawing, none of that humility of vision, none of that shy certainty of intuition. And Mr. Shaw's play has none of the variety in emotional rhythm that Chekhov has, either in tone or in profound self-revelation among the characters.

Chekhov sees his people as rooted in something, which means that he begins with what they are, their quality, and from this he derives what they will express. Mr. Shaw, for all his prattle about their class, clichés, bogies, culture and complacent, urgent or ironic circumstance, sees his people in the light of their opinions. Such a course makes for certain effective dramatic patterns, for distinct *dramatis personae*, real or not real, and for straw men, to be set up or knocked over at will. But it is, I think, his greatest and his final weakness as a creative artist. And it provides the reason why no intelligent member of the traditional British ruling class has ever needed to fear Mr. Shaw very greatly. Nobody could ever take one of Mr. Shaw's magnates or autocratic ruling class characters as the real thing. They may be arresting or provocative, but—for a while at least—it is their author, not themselves, that is so articulate. The portrayal, however, could be dangerous only when it came from the centre of the character himself. It is this quality of the centrifugal that makes Chekhov different from Mr. Shaw, though centrifugal seems a word too strong for that delicate, moving security and expressive freedom that Chekhov achieves for his people, and the matrix of gentle humor, like that of a wise doctor, within which he sees what they say or do, and for which he brings no compelling benefit or reform.

Taking a work of art as a kind of biological whole, which is the only way it makes any sense, I should say that nothing Mr. Shaw presents in *Heartbreak House* to prove his case could be a better evidence of the decay, if you like, of the English scene than this play itself is, with its lack of any organic unity or exciting technique, its fuzzy lack of power, its exhibitionistic self-assertion, its futile chatter in coquettish monotone about what the first bomb could obliterate or the first ism could make stale.

domenico vittorini

PIRANDELLO'S PHILOSOPHY OF LIFE

PIRANDELLO HAS subjected to a pitiless but passionate *critique* man and life, exploring every fold and nook, and presenting to us convincingly the sad and pitiful spectacle of the tragedy of being human. In this he has the justification of sincerity and, above all, that of having lived the sadness with which he has enveloped life.

Standing before the panorama that the universe offers to every thinking man, Pirandello is struck by the fact that one is born plant, beast, or man by mere chance, and that one is fatefully and irrevocably closed in that form for the span of one's earthly existence. Man, however, is different from plants and animals in that he cannot entrust himself to instinct with the same subconscious and happy abandonment as can lower beings. For, as soon as man yields to instinct, he sets in motion the so-called intellect which is nothing more, in the majority of cases, than a mechanism of deception through which he attempts to give idealistic motives and terms to his instinctive actions. One can follow Pirandello step by step as he analyzes life and envelops it in the web of his pessimism, pointing out its harrowing contradictions. On the whole, Pirandello's philosophy is not very comforting. Standing pensively and grievingly before the spectacle of daily existence, he has concluded "that there is nothing to conclude, because it is so," which is a conclusion in itself.

This philosophy was fashioned after the experience and observation of many years, upon realizing that life constantly loses its bloom; that the faces of those he had once known as children had begun to look old; that the strength of these people had ebbed away; that their skin, once soft and velvety, was rough and full of wrinkles; that their eyes, once sparkling with youth, were dimmed by age. Deeply touched and perturbed, with the conviction of one who is stating an opinion that sums up his life, he concludes that "everything is indefinite, fleeting, and evanescent." (*Each in His Own Way*, p. 3.)

From *The Drama of Luigi Pirandello* by Domenico Vittorini (1957). Published by Dover Publications, Inc., New York 14, N. Y. and reprinted through permission of the publisher.

The author starts from the premise that our knowledge about our very self is painfully limited. Mattia Pascal, one of the best-drawn characters in Pirandello's fiction, states, in looking back at his former life: "One of the few things, indeed, perhaps the only one that I knew as a positive fact was this: that my name was Mattia Pascal." (*Mattia Pascal*, p. 1.) Man does not know much about himself beyond an intimate knowledge of his physical being and worldly possessions: his clothes, his money, his home, his estate.

This belief, instead of making Pirandello cling to the tangible sides of his life and self, leads him to a complete detachment from them. He does not understand why we give so much importance to the gross and solid aspects of tangible reality. He is unwilling to grant that the human body is our most personal possession, since it decays so steadily, though imperceptibly. Life is a short-lived dream, and shadows are the most important element in it, since we live on memories of what has been or in longings of what is yet to be. In the changes that unceasingly go on in us, we cannot cling to our tangible and actual reality, since this reality is in a constant state of flux, and therefore it offers nothing solid and permanent.

This attitude of detachment from the tangible aspects of life is brought about by the author's unsatisfied desire to find something solid on which to rest, since there is in Pirandello, as in all human beings, a great longing for life, warm and fluid, happy and joyous. If he proclaims the glory of abstraction, it is only after he has been violently and bitterly offended and disappointed by actual experience. There is therefore in him and, by way of reflection, in his characters, a constant clash between his longing for the gifts of sensuous life and the sad disappointment experienced when his lips touch a cup that is empty, or a fruit that is withered and bitter. This is one of the deepest *motifs* in Pirandello's drama, and it has been beautifully realized in *Henry IV*, although it circulates in many of his plays.

As Pirandello looks at his fellow-men and at himself, he discovers that we are all "immobilized" in the concept that each of our friends and acquaintances forms of us. Moreover, we are also crystallized in the concept that each of us forms of himself. As we grow old and youth recedes from us, we poignantly cling to that fading image. The author has no other explanation to offer upon noticing that we cover most religiously the bald spots on our heads, we dye our hair, we straighten up when we walk in the streets, and slouch into sad figures when we are unobserved. To him a portrait is a touching attempt to stem the advancing destruction of death by holding close to us the image of what we used to be.

Man not only encloses himself in a concept, but he also immobilizes in it every one of his emotions and feelings. This is a natural though tragic necessity, and it dwarfs human sentiments. The Philosopher, a character in one of Pirandello's early plays, points out that churches are nothing but the tangible form of man's religious instinct, that "not satisfied to abide in the heart of man, it has built a house for itself—and what a house: domes, naves, columns, gold, marble, precious canvases! As a house of God, the universe is unquestionably larger and richer than a church; the spirit of man in adoration before divine mystery is incomparably more noble and precious than any altar. But this is the fate of all sentiments that wish to build a house for themselves: they are, of necessity, dwarfed and become a little childish because of their vanity." According to Pirandello, this is how the infinite which abides in man fares when it takes a tangible form, without which, however, it could not reveal itself. In the clash between the beauty of what is not and the misery of what is, we are saddened by their irreconcilable contrast.

Pirandello has gone deeply into the secret chamber of man's heart and has discovered tragic wants. He has seen that there are things that we dare not confess even to ourselves, moral deeds that lie like heavy stones in the depth of our conscience. Who can go before his fellow-men with an unveiled soul? In this realization there is an echo of the great but terrifying words: "He that is without sin among you, let him first cast a stone."

The author has also been tempted to look at his existence in retrospect, and has discovered that the ideas of his youth are no longer his, and that the beliefs of yesterday have become the illusions of today. It was inevitable that at this realization a sense of emptiness should envelop him. Every basis for his thought crumbled under him, and he felt himself wandering in a universe where extinguished stars moved in a meaningless whirl as if ready to plunge into the abyss of nothingness. One of Pirandello's characters has expressed this belief in unforgettable words: "If we think over the illusions which we no longer entertain, the things which now do not *seem* as they *used to seem*, we feel suspended in a void, since we must also argue that what we feel today, that is, the reality of today, is destined to appear as the illusion of tomorrow." (*Six Characters in Search of an Author*, p. 130.) This is all the more true since history proves that in the forward advance of progress new ideas dislodge and kill old ones, just as in life children are fated to take the place of their parents, and one generation passes over the tombstones of another.

Pirandello is not abstract in his approach to the theme of his pessimism of life. He calls our attention to such aspects of the existence of his characters as may be easily compared with those of the existence of each one of us. He recalls to our mind the day when we, like the Son in *Six Characters in Search of an Author,* discovered that our parents lived as man and woman, for themselves, outside the image of father and mother which we had conceived of them and in which they lived for us. We are also compelled to mourn with another of Pirandello's characters the fact that not even the deepest affections, not even love for our mother, can resist the fatal onslaught of life. Life is a ruinous torrent and carries along in its fury men and things, irrevocably.

No happy outlook is brought to us by observing the relations between man and his fellow-creatures. Our acts appear to others as if they were enveloped in a haze and smoke which veil the flame that glows in them when we act spontaneously. With eager earnestness and passionate conviction he points out that we grow up in the belief that we are one, a definite individual, with a clear-cut contour, with definite qualities, and with a personality. Life proves that we are not, that in reality this subjectiveness of man's perceptions creates in us as many-faceted persons as are individuals who look at and know us. Closed in his subjectivism, man interprets the acts of others according to his own ideas of human behavior. The result is an incommunicability that offers one of the most recurrent and fertile *motifs* in Pirandello's theatre.

Brought face to face with the grimacing countenance of the daily tragedy, Pirandello seeks the cause of man's isolation, and he finds that words are a most inadequate means of expression. "The core of the evil is exactly here!" says the Father in *Six Characters in Search of an Author,* "In the words we use! We all have a world of things within us, each his own world. And how can we understand each other if, to the words that I say, I give the sense of things that are within me, while he who listens to them, inevitably, receives them with the sense that they have for him, from the world that he has within him?" (*Six Characters in Search of an Author,* p. 30.)

To understand the impenetrability of human beings, we must keep in mind the accusations that poor deranged Donna Antonietta hurled at her husband in her frantic state of mind. In his own flesh and soul, Pirandello lived the isolation of his characters, an isolation that leads to hostility and hatred.

All that poets have said to exalt life has appeared cold and empty to him as it echoed in his tragic soul. Man fosters the illusion of the glory of his will power, yet he has to acknowledge that his will is limited in two paramount facts: birth and death. They are both independent of his will and "between the two events many things happen that we all wish would not happen, and to which we unwillingly must submit." (*Each in His Own Way,* p. 64.) Men will say very proudly: This day which is just dawning will be ours; we shall mold it as we wish. In reality we repeat what others have done before us. Traditions and customs are there, tyrannically imposing on us what others have decreed and obeyed. We speak and must repeat the words that have always been said. "Do you believe that you live?" queries one of Pirandello's characters. "You are re-chewing the life of the dead." (*Each in His Own Way,* p. 107.)

We might argue with the author, in an imaginary conversation, that man can boast of a definite asset in human conscience. Pirandello would look at us with his wistful and whimsical eyes and say that he is aware that conscience exists in the poor of spirit who do not need it, but he is unable to find it in the over-intellectualized beings that he meets in his imaginary wanderings.

A man like Pirandello cannot think of nature in positive terms, any more than can the mariner and the aviator who know the fury of the tempest on the high sea and the slashing of the storms in mid-air. Both the mariner and the aviator see in nature an enemy to conquer, just as Pirandello sees in it the cause of the plight in which his characters are struggling in a vain attempt to free themselves. He calls our attention to the fact that life is monotonously, if not serenely, unfolding when, suddenly, an earthquake sows destruction and sorrow and leaves us uncertain whether human lives have more purpose than the Japanese beetles that the dark, callous, rough hand of a farmer snatches from the sweet-tasting ear of corn in order to throw them into a jar full of gasoline. Pirandello has allowed Leone Gala in *Each in His Own Rôle* to voice his deep-seated feeling that life is something that allures and hurts. Leone Gala proclaims his defense against the evil that life does to all, inevitably. Life is cruel: "You eat meat at the table. Who provides it for you? A pullet or a calf. You never think of it. We all hurt one another reciprocally; and each hurts himself. It is inevitable. It is life." (*Each in His Own Rôle,* p. 36.)

We are brought into the presence of evil and death while a ghastly spectacle unfolds before us. There are parents whose children are born imbeciles, unable to use their limbs, unable to speak. There are hospitals filled with pain, wars that kill millions, maim more millions, torture body and soul. At the fringe of this life lurks death, and it chills every joy and destroys every affection.

If the thought of nature is not comforting to Pirandello, that of modern civilization is not less barren of solace to him. He sees in it only the frantic efforts to escape the sadness of life. Man moves, builds cities, crosses the ocean, conquers the air, only because he tries to escape his inner torment, the torment of his intellect. He is engaged in a mad race for speed which is followed by disappointment because our thought moves faster than mechanical contrivances. The sad plight of Pirandello is that he cannot suggest contemplation in the oriental fashion. The peaceful life of a distant mythical past is beyond our reach, gone forever, the penalty that we pay for progress. Intimately and ultimately civilization is to Pirandello a synonym for tragic artificiality. Yet we must submit to it because there is no escape.

The element that contributes most in building the gloomy structure of Pirandello's pessimism is instinct. Man is compelled to yield to it even when he is perfectly aware of the dire consequences that it will entail. Pirandello considers instinct an acid which corrodes the best that life possesses. His drama begins where instinct ends. His characters are people who give themselves to passion and cannot live in it. They readily pass from passion to hatred, and they cling to it with a cruel and spasmodic tenacity. Their brain and their heart stand vigil on the flesh that yields; they rebel and the result is the lucid madness of the individuals that we see suffering in Pirandello's drama.

If we exclude the early plays conceived in the light of naturalistic principles, Pirandello's art presents a sensuality that is neither self-satisfied, beastly, nor wholesome. His drama opens at the moment when instinct has lost all its impetuousness, and the warmth of passion has been chilled by the cold dissecting power of the intellect. As a consequence, only reason predominates in the psychological life of the characters, and it leads them in their aimless wanderings over the bleak desert of their existence.

The background of most of Pirandello's plays is a wrong relation, the experience of which leaves his characters desperately disappointed. Instinct and lust appear paltry and despised, especially as the characters rebel at having their whole lives and beings identified with a moment of weakness. The rebellion of the characters is accompanied by a perplexed state of mind in the author, who seems unable to understand the power of something which is so devastating and yet seems so negligible and hateful when looked at with a certain objectivity. Pirandello is disconsolately silent before this perplexity, and often takes refuge in laughter. This thoughtful and grieving silence, mingled with a burst of laughter at human weakness, is reflected on Pirandello's countenance, and it forms the most appealing trait of his tragic personality.

There arises at this point the problem of morality as a substratum of Pirandello's art. Many people, especially if vowed to ethical orthodoxy at any cost, would call Pirandello immoral. Yet there is no other modern writer for whom morality is as intimately imbedded in the very texture of life and art as for Luigi Pirandello. This is evidenced by the fact that his drama is almost always brought about by the breaking of a moral law; by the fact that Pirandello never treats instinct as an aphrodisiac; by the unraveling of the plot that reaffirms the validity of the moral law. Pirandello does not need the glamour of immorality to make his art attractive, just as he never allows it to become laden down by the weight of didacticism. He is often provincial in the familiar tone of most of his plays, although he reaches the universal in the implications that he lends to the everyday occurrences on which he builds his drama.

Many may resent the drastic pessimism that is found at the basis of Pirandello's thought. Pirandello does not wish to give a universal value and meaning to his pessimistic sense of life. His exasperated subjectivism rejects any categorical and universal interpretation of it. If truth has as many aspects as there are thinking individuals, a life concept is the projection of each single experience. Pirandello refuses to be dogmatic.

Pessimism forms the background of Pirandello's drama, but the author has skilfully veiled his pessimism behind humor and laughter, relieving the extreme tension that oppresses his pitiful characters. In the foreground one sees ludicrous figures, victims of instinct and of Pirandello's sense of humor that expresses itself in laughter at human weakness, a laughter that hurts him although it relieves his tension.

In spite of the fact that the central part of Pirandello's picture of life is painted in dark hues, there shines in the distant horizon a feeble, iridescent light which is derived from the author's idealism. Like the idealists of all times, Pirandello contrasts the drab and sorrowful condition of man on earth with the vision of a perfect life lost in the distance of imagination whence all life originates. His idealism takes the form either of a cosmic and religious sense of universal life or of a lofty ideal existence to which man aspires when actual life offends him. This evanescent Platonism, which in its vagueness will not stand very close analysis, often echoes in Pirandello's drama, and it assumes greater importance in his latest plays. Idealism and pessimism are closer than we may at first surmise, since pessimism is often nothing but disappointed idealism.

Pirandello is fully aware of the existence and validity of man's ideal aspirations. He confesses: "We all have seen, in certain moments, appear and kindle within us a light that seems to emanate from other skies—which permits us to gaze into the most profound depths of our souls and gives us the infinite joy of feeling ourselves lost in a moment of eternity—eternal with it." (*Each in His Own Way*, p. 53.) That light shines for but a moment; it affords to Pirandello a fleeting instant of inner illumination and then disappears, leaving him in a night of terrifying darkness. This moment of inner illumination is the only eternity granted to man, but man makes the mistake of considering it a natural state and of attempting to enclose it into a system. It is natural that he should soon realize the futility of his efforts, since that moment cannot repeat itself. The result is a feeling of ennui, boredom, and nausea that stifles him, while he longs in vain for the region whence his dreams emanated.

Pirandello joins the Book of Ecclesiastes and the ascetics of long ago in proclaiming his indifference towards the gifts of the earth. Since this indifference rises through a life experience, it is beyond racial lines and outside the narrow boundaries of time limitations. It is universal, and as such it is to be found in the art of all those whose sensitiveness has been hurt by the rough hand of the daily life.

The sharp contrast that Pirandello feels between his aspiration and the result of his fearless and cold analysis of reality is determined by the objective character of his temperament that strips evil of any alluring quality, thus preventing him from abandoning himself to his belief in a good and primitive life. His drama often springs out of the conflict between the aspiration of his soul and the cold objectivity of his temperament.

It is not correct to stress unduly the term "idealism" in relation with Pirandello's thought. Idealism, outside the realm of true philosophy, has a literary patina of dubious alloy, and it points at the academic attitude of a dilettante who deals with imaginary problems and with fantastic solutions. Pirandello's idealism does not go beyond seeing grains of gold, our dreams, scattered among the ruins of the human heart—remains and echoes, but distant echoes, of the goodness that God has given to man. The ruins and the desolation of human life have attracted Pirandello's attention more than the glittering bits of the precious metal. If we chance to use the term "idealism," we should qualify it with the adjunct of "tragic."

Pirandello is inherently a primitive, with a complicated and overactive mind. His heart longs for peace and tranquillity, while his eyes long to see and his intellect to analyze what the lack of positive moral elements has produced in life. These elements have no connection whatsoever with idealism, while they testify to Pirandello's moral approach to a life concept. His ascribing to lack of simplicity and sincerity the ludicrous and painful situations in which his characters are caught points at a deep ethical attitude, and it draws a sharp line of differentiation between Pirandello and his characters, between the point of departure of the play and the final conclusion to which he is led by his deep soul. Between the beginning that portrays

Pirandello outside the precincts of the Temple of Thought, where life is mockery, and the end that shows him within the temple, in the presence of sacred life and human sorrow, there is an abyss. On one side there is Pirandello who, having reached the breaking point, bursts into broad though painful laughter; on the other there is Pirandello, the thinker and man, on whose heart experience has left deep marks and scars. Pirandello, having begun with laughter, ends by revealing to us his belief that only humility can save man from the crushing weight of his human destiny. In this fashion the element of the grotesque that permeated the plays conceived and written in the chaotic years that followed the War gives place to his attitude of passive silence with a strong religious undercurrent. Silence had been the only weapon at his disposal for many long years, and it becomes now a great force in the life of his characters.

More than an idealist, Pirandello is a modern stoic, who has found the traditional cold and stiff posture too uncomfortable and commonplace, and who has renewed stoicism, either through laughter, or through his tragic idealism. In both cases, Pirandello's art acquires a cosmic resonance which is the distinctive quality of all true and great art in which men can mirror themselves.

His art is not made out of peaceful, rhythmic life, nor is it conducive to quiet, idyllic thoughts. It bruises, it wounds, it smarts; but it presents a wide horizon of life, and it never fails to awaken in our hearts pathos and sympathy for the vicissitudes of his poor characters. His art is not made out of the plain and of the obvious, just as his characters are not pleasant people. They are not individuals that life has caught in the peaceful mold or prison of the everyday life: a nice home, a plump wife, two charming children, getting up in the morning, shaving, bathing, going to the office, lunching, going back to the office, dinner, quietly reading the newspaper while smoking a pipe, and finally going to bed. His characters have actually experienced what even our fancies dread. They have lived beyond the laws of society and humanity. They have existed in a vacuum with only their tragedy, the horror of vice in their flesh; they are, none the less, free of all fetters, primeval beings in the whirlwind of the irrational.

In spite of the statement of many critics to the contrary, the outstanding characteristic of Pirandello's thought is that of being constantly close to life. Life has always been envisaged by him in terms of man's existence on this planet. In fact, his drama centers around the consideration of what happens to a human being endowed with instinct and reason, sentiment and intellect.

In the course of literary history we find ourselves before writers who aim at transcending the actual and historical reality by losing themselves in dreams and idyls. We also meet others who do not flinch at accepting their human lot with its share of pleasure and sorrow, of ugliness and beauty. These writers followed two antithetical processes, since they either concealed what was to them the hideous countenance of daily life behind the bewitching network of their dreams, or they shunned dreams and compelled their art to portray only the massive and seamy aspects of everyday life.

In Pirandello these two processes, welded together, integrate each other, and the two planes of reality, that of the actual and that of imaginary life, are tragically fused into one. The result of this new process is, from an æsthetic point of view, that Pirandello's art can adhere more closely to life where the dispassionate observer finds a dream side by side with the most instinctive and elementary needs of man. From the point of view of sentiment, the obliteration of the boundary between the actual and the imaginary realities leads Pirandello's characters to the high plane of pure tragedy, since they are denied an escape from the talons of the grief that tortures them.

Pirandello takes into account that it is instinctive with human beings to protect themselves by allowing their fancy to picture beautiful vistas and idyllic lands, but his tragic sense of life is so impelling and overpowering that he cannot allow his characters to abide in the fantastic realm of their imagination. If the exaltation of the characters is so great that they identify themselves with their assumed reality, the illusion is only momentary, because the author shows them the fictitious quality of their attitude and how ludicrous they look. This prevents the obliteration of the original ego, and differentiates very sharply Pirandello's art from that of the traditional idealists. In the traditional process the original personality disappeared completely to give place to a new ego, primitive in the Arcadian fashion or garbed in the long robes of Platonism. In Pirandello the two personalities remain, tragically merged into one, writhing in a grief in which the truth of art defies the truth of life.

We do not speak of obliteration of reality and personality in the same sense as does Adriano Tilgher, a brilliant critic of Pirandello and of modern art.[1] Tilgher reduces Pirandello's attitude to the old transcendentalism. He also speaks of the negation of human personality in Pirandello's characters. No true dramatic art is possible without personality, and the conscious madman is in art a well-defined dramatic character. Illusion in Pirandello is forced on his characters

[1] *Voci del tempo*, 1921; *Studi sul teatro contemporaneo*, 1923.

by external circumstances, and, therefore, is no longer illusion. It is lucid madness, grief that writhes in the heart of man tied to his daily existence like a modern Prometheus.

Pirandello had ample opportunity to study this clear and conscious madness in himself as he contrasted it with that of poor Donna Antonietta. He looked at the painful circumstances of his life, at his acts and feelings, as if they were the life and acts of another being. He saw himself just as if he were a character in a strange drama, the creation of a cruel and fantastic artist. This harrowing contemplation induced the madness that he gives to his characters. His was a terrifying madness, and he felt it beating in his own veins, tormenting his brain, searing his soul, withering his body. Yet he continued to live and to work, finding in his art a solace for the tragedy that life had assigned to him.

joseph wood krutch

EUGENE O'NEILL'S CLAIM TO GREATNESS

BERNARD SHAW once called O'Neill "a banshee Shakespeare." And "banshee," as the historically minded will remember, is what Voltaire called Shakespeare. Shaw's remark was not intended to be entirely uncomplimentary and neither, for that matter, was Voltaire's. A banshee Shakespeare is still some kind of Shakespeare, and "a barbarian genius" (Voltaire's phrase) is still some kind of genius.[1]

Certain American critics, on the other hand, have hurled the insult without the qualifying compliment. Eric Bentley, after calling O'Neill "the Broadway intelligentsia's patron saint" and after explaining how hard he has tried to think well of him winds up by saying that O'Neill cannot write and cannot think. To Mary McCarthy his "lack of verbal gift was a personal affliction that became a curse to the American stage" and the most important conclusion to be drawn from *The Iceman Cometh* is that "you cannot write a Platonic dialogue in the style of *Casey at the Bat*." O'Neill, if not witty himself is, then, like Falstaff, the occasion of wit in others. And Edwin Engel, whose *The Haunted Heroes of Eugene O'Neill* is the only recent book-length study concludes: "O'Neill's style remained not only strained and turgid, but awkward, inarticulate, banal."

Of Theodore Dreiser's "style" much the same sort of things have been said. But among critics of general literature there has been, for some reason, more readiness to forgive in him what only those specifically concerned with the theatre have excused in O'Neill. And the reply to his defenders has usually been that they were, in Miss McCarthy's phrase, "Propagating the theory that a playwright was not subject to the same standards as other writers, the theory, in other words, that the theatre is an inferior art."

From *The New York Times Book Review*, September 22, 1957. Copyright by The New York Times. Reprinted by permission.
[1] Editors' note: Shaw's remark about O'Neill is frequently quoted. In the earliest form of it that we can find, St. John Ervine quotes a conversation between Shaw and Archibald Henderson in which G. B. S. called O'Neill "a Fantee Shakespeare who peoples his isle with Calibans." (St. John Ervine, "Is O'Neill's Power in Decline?" *Theatre Magazine*, vol. 43, May 1926, pp. 12, 58; also "An Appraisal of Mr. O'Neill," London *Observer*, October 29, 1933). *Fantee* apparently refers to the natives of the Gold Coast and perhaps by implication to *The Emperor Jones*.

Mr. Bentley, it is true, goes so far as to admit that an O'Neill play "comes out of a bigger head" than that of certain other contemporary playwrights and Miss McCarthy speaks grudgingly of "the element of transcendence jutting up woodenly—like a great homemade Trojan horse." But the conclusion of both can be summed up in Miss McCarthy's words: "O'Neill belongs to that group of American authors, which includes Farrell and Dreiser, whose choice of vocation was a kind of triumphant catastrophe; none of these men possessed the slightest ear for the word, the sentence, the speech, the paragraphs. . . . How is one to judge the great logical symphony of a tone-deaf musician?"

In the case of Shakespeare the final answer to Voltaire was given by that consensus which alone is capable of giving a final answer in artistic matters. Audiences are often wrong for a time. They often fail to appreciate novel excellences and they are often misled by mere fashion. But in the long run they are right, if only because, as some say, there is no other definition of what right means. And it may be that the astonishingly vigorous O'Neill revival now in progress is posterity giving its decision. Or, if this seems a premature conclusion, the revival is at least a demonstration of O'Neill's power to interest a new audience that is far more significant than his first success—for the simple reason that a second hearing in the contemporary theatre is extremely rare. Has any other American playwright ever enjoyed anything comparable to the O'Neill revival?

To suggest that posterity may even now be proving certain critics wrong is not to say that posterity will call O'Neill a great stylist or list verbal felicity among his virtues. It is to say only that it may well recognize his continued triumph over the defects his recent critics have exaggerated into intolerability.

As a matter of fact his most ardent admirers have, from the beginning, not only recognized but stressed them. Reviewing the first production of *Mourning Becomes Electra* the present writer made this comment:

> "The only thing missing is language . . . Take, for example, the scene in which Orin stands beside the bier of his father . . . What one longs for with an almost agonizing longing is something not merely good but magnificent, something like 'Tomorrow, and tomorrow and tomorrow' or 'I could a tale unfold whose lightest word . . .' But no such language does come and *Mourning Becomes Electra* remains, therefore, only the best tragedy in English which the present century has produced. This is the penalty we pay for living in an age whose most powerful dramatist cannot rise above prose."

Or consider the parody written by Lee Simonson who designed some of the sets for O'Neill's plays, was one of the directors of the Theatre Guild and, what is more important, an admirer and personal friend. In his book *The Stage Is Set* he published this version of a Hamlet soliloquy as he imagined that O'Neill might write it: "God! if I could only kill myself—get away from it all. There's nothing to live for. I'm afraid! Afraid to do anything. Afraid of death. Spooks. What they told me when I was a kid. (*Looking at the snowman*) I'm just so much mush—mush like you . . . If I could only thaw with you tomorrow—thaw, just dissolve, trickle into the earth—run off into the sewer."

This is the kind of parody that one conventionally calls "deadly," and it is no more unjust than parody has a right to be. But Mr. Simonson did not think that it was deadly, and he certainly did not want it to be. "Parody," as Oscar Wilde replied to Gilbert's *Patience*, "is the tribute which mediocrity pays to genius." It takes no great gifts to see what is wrong with O'Neill. But not all of the witty are clever enough to recognize sufficiently, as Simonson also did, what is right with him. In the classroom I used always to read this parody, and it never failed to get its laugh. But I never knew any student to dismiss O'Neill because of it.

On occasion he can write almost as badly as his detractors say. Not always, of course, and he has passages powerful simply as writing, though even in them it is not "writing" in the technical sense that one thinks of. And the case is best made for him by admitting his defects. He used dialect a great deal, and he had so little ear for it that good actors always made it better than he had written it. There are seldom any subtle overtones, never that kind of "ambiguity" now so much admired.

And it is, I think, worth remarking that with the exception of the not especially notable "That ol' debble sea" he invented no phrase which passed into current speech, even temporarily or even derisively. Though I think he is likely to be longer remembered than, say, Tennessee Williams, he had nothing comparable to the Williams' gift (shared by Erskine Caldwell) for the vocabulary, the syntax and the rhythm of Southern speech.

Why then does a new generation brought up in the theatre on the neurotic subtlety of Williams turn appreciatively again to O'Neill? What quality has he that is lacking in, to take another example, the whole contemporary French school of which Jean Anouilh is the best-known representative?

Like Williams and like O'Neill, the members of that school are, in a sense, tragic writers, and they are certainly more sophisticated. Perhaps this is, in itself, one of the answers. In Anouilh, the subtlety, the wit and the gift for words are astonishing. So, too, are the endless involutions of a mind always turning back upon itself and, as it were, dying in convulsions. The subtlety is self-destructive, leaving nothing except emptiness when the last ingenious twist has been performed. His plays seem to hope for nothing more than a display of the author's skill at playing an intellectual game.

Perhaps Americans are essentially too serious (too unsophisticated, if you insist) to accept the conclusion that the Pursuit of Truth is no more than a game. They are unwilling to look for the black hat in the dark cellar unless they believe that it may just possibly be there. O'Neill can be deeply involved in genuine passion because he is not merely playing a game to exhibit his skill. He can be black enough at times and on occasion fall a victim to the nihilism against which he perpetually struggled. But there may be "more faith in honest doubt" if "honest doubt" is not "complacent doubt." And O'Neill is never complacent, never other than deeply involved.

Man emerges from the bludgeoning he receives in O'Neill's plays with his essential dignity intact. He is still a creative being worthy of respect. That can hardly be said of either Williams or Anouilh. And it may be that the present generation has found O'Neill stimulating for precisely that reason.

Mere sincerity of intention is, of course, not enough. As one of Shaw's characters remarks: "Behind every bad poem lies a perfectly genuine emotion." Bentley has the same thing in mind when he gibes at the "recent rehabilitator," of O'Neill for "taking the will for the deed" and "applauding O'Neill for strengthening the pavement of hell." But there is a fallacy in the argument, or at least in its application. It is not merely a question of high intention versus lesser achievement. The crucial question is "To what extent and in what way is one aware of good intentions, of that genuine emotion behind a less-than-perfect poem?" Is it merely that the author says he has high intentions, that he tells you about them? Or is it that you actually perceive them in the work itself? If the second is true then more than merely the intention is present.

I have read no detraction of O'Neill whose author did not seem slightly uneasy, who did not somewhere concede more than he safely could. O'Neill's first audience did a great deal more than concede and so do the new audiences to many of whom he is a discovery. Whatever his other limitations as a writer, he had the writer's one indispensable gift. He "communicated"—the situation, the characters, and above all the depth of his concern with them. That is not everything; but it is enough.

Somerset Maugham once declared that all the great novelists—Balzac, Dickens and Dostoevsky, for example, "wrote badly." He did not say that the novels were great because they were badly written or that no writer is both a great stylist and great in other ways besides. But he did suggest that, as novelists, his favorites were superior to the Flauberts and the Jameses whom another school admires so much more. He felt that they were superior because Balzac and Dickens and Dostoevsky had virtues more important than those they lacked and because, instead of torturing themselves in the vain attempt to "get a style," they wrote what they had it in them to write. An O'Neill who wrote better would have been a better O'Neill. But he will last longer and mean more than many who can, in the ordinary sense, write rings around him.

lionel trilling

EUGENE O'NEILL

WHATEVER IS unclear about Eugene O'Neill, one thing is certainly clear—his genius. We do not like the word nowadays, feeling that it is one of the blurb words of criticism. We demand that literature be a guide to life, and when we do that we put genius into a second place, for genius assures us of nothing but itself. Yet when we stress the actionable conclusions of an artist's work, we are too likely to forget the power of genius itself, quite apart from its conclusions. The spectacle of the human mind in action is vivifying; the explorer need discover nothing so long as he has adventured. Energy, scope, courage —these may be admirable in themselves. And in the end these are often what endure best. The ideas expressed by works of the imagination may be built into the social fabric and taken for granted; or they may be rejected; or they may be outgrown. But the force of their utterance comes to us over millennia. We do not read Sophocles or Aeschylus for the right answer; we read them for the force with which they represent life and attack its moral complexity. In O'Neill, despite the many failures of his art and thought, this force is inescapable.

But a writer's contemporary audience is inevitably more interested in the truth of his content than in the force of its expression; and O'Neill himself has always been ready to declare his own ideological preoccupation. His early admirers—and their lack of seriousness is a reproach to American criticism—were inclined to insist that O'Neill's content was unimportant as compared to his purely literary interest and that he injured his art when he tried to think. But the appearance of *Days Without End* has made perfectly clear the existence of an organic and progressive unity of thought in all O'Neill's work and has brought it into the critical range of the two groups whose own thought is most sharply formulated, the Catholic and the Communist. Both discovered what O'Neill had frequently announced, the religious nature of all his effort.

Not only has O'Neill tried to encompass more of life than most

From The New Republic, September, 1936. Reprinted by permission.

American writers of his time but, almost alone among them, he has persistently tried to *solve* it. When we understand this we understand that his stage devices are not fortuitous technique; his masks and abstractions, his double personalities, his drum beats and engine rhythms are the integral and necessary expression of his temper of mind and the task it set itself. Realism is uncongenial to that mind and that task and it is not in realistic plays like *Anna Christie* and *The Straw* but rather in such plays as *The Hairy Ape, Lazarus Laughed* and *The Great God Brown,* where he is explaining the world in parable, symbol and myth, that O'Neill is most creative. Not the minutiae of life, not its feel and color and smell, not its nuance and humor, but its "great inscrutable forces" are his interest. He is always moving toward the finality which philosophy sometimes, and religion always, promises. Life and death, good and evil, spirit and flesh, male and female, the all and the one, Anthony and Dionysus— O'Neill's is a world of these antithetical absolutes such as religion rather than philosophy conceives, a world of pluses and minuses; and his literary effort is an algebraic attempt to solve the equations.

In one of O'Neill's earliest one-act plays, the now unprocurable "Fog," a Poet, a Business Man and a Woman with a Dead Child, shipwrecked and adrift in an open boat, have made fast to an iceberg. When they hear the whistle of a steamer, the Business Man's impulse is to call for help, but the Poet prevents him lest the steamer be wrecked on the fog-hidden berg. But a searching party picks up the castaways and the rescuers explain that they had been guided to the spot by a child's cries; the Child, however, has been dead a whole day. This little play is a crude sketch of the moral world that O'Neill is to exploit. He is to give an ever increasing importance to the mystical implications of the Dead Child, but his earliest concern is with the struggle between the Poet and the Business Man.

It is, of course, a struggle as old as morality, especially interesting to Europe all through its industrial nineteenth century, and it was now engaging America in the second decade of its twentieth. A conscious artistic movement had raised its head to declare irreconcilable strife between the creative and the possessive ideal. O'Neill was an integral part—indeed, he became the very symbol—of that Provincetown group which represented the growing rebellion of the American intellectual against a business civilization. In 1914 his revolt was simple and socialistic; in a poem in *The Call* he urged the workers of the world not to fight, asking them if they wished to "bleed and groan—for Guggenheim" and "give your lives—for Standard Oil." By 1917 his feeling against business had become symbolized and personal. "My soul is a submarine," he said in a poem in *The Masses:*

> *My aspirations are torpedoes.*
> *I will hide unseen*
> *Beneath the surface of life*
> *Watching for ships,*
> *Dull, heavy-laden merchant ships,*
> *Rust-eaten, grimy galleons of commerce*
> *Wallowing with obese assurance,*
> *Too sluggish to fear or wonder,*
> *Mocked by the laughter of the waves*
> *And the spit of disdainful spray.*
>
> *I will destroy them*
> *Because the sea is beautiful.*

The ships against which O'Neill directed his torpedoes were the cultural keels laid in the yards of American business and their hulls were first to be torn by artistic realism. Although we now see the often gross sentimentality of the S.S. *Glencairn* plays and remember with O'Neill's own misgiving the vaudeville success of "In the Zone," we cannot forget that, at the time, the showing of a forecastle on the American stage was indeed something of a torpedo. Not, it is true, into the sides of Guggenheim and Standard Oil, but of the little people who wallowed complacently in their wake.

But O'Neill, not content with staggering middle-class complacency by a representation of how the other half lives, undertook to scrutinize the moral life of the middle class and dramatized the actual struggle between Poet and Business Man. In his first long play, *Beyond the Horizon,* the dreamer destroys his life by sacrificing his dream to domesticity; and the practical creator, the farmer, destroys his by turning from wheat-raising to wheat-gambling. It is a conflict O'Neill is to exploit again and again. Sometimes, as in "Ile" or *Gold,* the lust for gain transcends itself and becomes almost a creative ideal, but always its sordid origin makes it destructive. To O'Neill the acquisitive man, kindly and insensitive, practical and immature, became a danger to life and one that he never left off attacking.

But it developed, strangely, that the American middle class had no strong objection to being attacked and torpedoed; it seemed willing to be sunk for the insurance that was paid in a new strange coin. The middle class found that it consisted of two halves, bourgeoisie and booboisie. The booboisie might remain on the ship but the bourgeoisie could, if it would, take refuge on the submarine. Mencken and Nathan, who sponsored the O'Neill torpedoes, never attacked the middle class but only its boobyhood. Boobish and sophisticated: these were the two categories of art; spiritual freedom could be bought at the price of finding *Jurgen* profound. And so, while the booboisie prosecuted *Desire Under the Elms,* the bourgeoisie swelled the subscription lists of the Provincetown Playhouse and helped the Washington Square Players to grow into the Theatre Guild. An increasingly respectable audience awarded O'Neill no less than three Pulitzer prizes, the medal of the American Academy of Arts and Sciences and a Yale Doctorate of Letters.

O'Neill did not win his worldly success by the slightest compromise of sincerity. Indeed, his charm consisted in his very integrity and hieratic earnestness. His position changed, not absolutely, but relatively to his audience, which was now the literate middle class caught up with the intellectual middle class. O'Neill was no longer a submarine; he had become a physician of souls. Beneath his iconoclasm his audience sensed reassurance.

The middle class is now in such literary disrepute that a writer's ability to please it is taken as the visible mark of an internal rottenness. But the middle class is people; prick them and they bleed, and whoever speaks sincerely to and for flesh and blood deserves respect. O'Neill's force derives in large part from the force of the moral and psychical upheaval of the middle class; it wanted certain of its taboos broken and O'Neill broke them. He was the Dion Anthony to its William Brown; Brown loved Dion: his love was a way of repenting for his own spiritual clumsiness.

Whoever writes sincerely about the middle class must consider the nature and the danger of the morality of "ideals," those phosphorescent remnants of a dead religion with which the middle class meets the world. This had been Ibsen's great theme, and now O'Neill undertook to investigate for America the destructive power of the ideal—not merely the sordid ideal of the Business Man but even the "idealistic" ideal of the Poet. The Freudian psychology was being discussed and O'Neill dramatized its simpler aspects in *Diff'rent* to show the effects of the repression of life. Let the ideal of chastity repress the vital forces, he was saying, and from this fine girl you will get a filthy harridan. The modern life of false ideals crushes the affirmative and creative nature of man; Pan, forbidden the light and warmth of the sun, grows "sensitive and self-conscious and proud and revengeful"—becomes the sneering Mephistophelean mask of Dion.

The important word is *self-conscious,* for "ideals" are part of the "cheating gestures which constitute the vanity of personality." "Life is all right if you let it alone," says Cybel, the Earth Mother of *The Great God Brown.* But the poet of *Welded* cannot let it alone; he and his wife, the stage directions tell us, move in circles of light that represent "auras of egotism" and the high ideals of their marriage are but ways each ego uses to get possession of the other. O'Neill had his answer to this problem of the possessive, discrete personality. Egoism and idealism, he tells us, are twin evils growing from man's suspicion of his life and the remedy is the laughter of Lazarus—"a triumphant, blood-stirring call to that ultimate attainment in which all prepossession with self is lost in an ecstatic affirmation of Life." The ecstatic affirmation of Life, pure and simple, is salvation. In the face of death and pain, man must reply with the answer of Kublai Kaan in *Marco Millions:* "Be proud of life! Know in your heart that the living of life can be noble! Be exalted by life! Be inspired by death! Be humbly proud! Be proudly grateful!"

It may be that the individual life is not noble and that it is full of pain and defeat; it would seem that Eileen Carmody in *The Straw* and Anna Christie are betrayed by life. But no. The "straw" is the knowledge that life is a "hopeless hope"—but still a hope. And nothing matters if you can conceive the whole of life. "Fog, fog, fog, all bloody time," is the chord of resolution of *Anna Christie*. "You can't see vhere you vas going, no. Only dat ole davil, sea—she knows." The individual does not know, but life—the sea—knows.

To affirm that life exists and is somehow good—this, then, became O'Neill's quasi-religious poetic function, nor is it difficult to see why the middle class welcomed it. "Brown will still need me," says Dion, "to reassure him he's alive." What to do with life O'Neill cannot say, but there it is. For Ponce de Leon it is the Fountain of Eternity, "the Eternal Becoming which is Beauty." There it is, somehow glorious, somehow meaningless. In the face of despair one remembers that "Always spring comes again bearing life! Always forever again. Spring again! Life again!" To this cycle, even to the personal annihilation in it, the individual must say "Yes." Man inhabits a naturalistic universe and his glory lies in his recognition of its nature and assenting to it; man's soul, no less than the stars and the dust, is part of the Whole and the free man loves the Whole and is willing to be absorbed by it. In short, O'Neill solves the problem of evil by making explicit what men have always found to be the essence of tragedy—the courageous affirmation of life in the face of individual defeat.

But neither a naturalistic view of the universe nor a rapt assent to life constitutes a complete philosophic answer. Naturalism is the noble and realistic attitude that prepares the way for an answer; the tragic affirmation is the emotional crown of a philosophy. Spinoza— with whom O'Neill at this stage of his thought has an obvious affinity —placed between the two an ethic that arranged human values and made the world possible to live in. But O'Neill, faced with a tragic universe, unable to go beyond the febrilely passionate declaration,

"Life is," finds the world impossible to live in. The naturalistic universe becomes too heavy a burden for him; its spirituality vanishes; it becomes a universe of cruelly blind matter. "Teach me to be resigned to be an atom," cries Darrell, the frustrated scientist of *Strange Interlude,* and for Nina life is but "a strange dark interlude in the electrical display of God the father"—who is a God deaf, dumb and blind. O'Neill, unable now merely to accept the tragic universe and unable to support it with man's whole strength—his intellect and emotion—prepares to support it with man's weakness: his blind faith.

For the non-Catholic reader O'Neill's explicitly religious solution is likely to be not only insupportable but incomprehensible. Neither St. Francis nor St. Thomas can tell us much about it; it is neither a mystical ecstasy nor the reasoned proof of assumptions. But Pascal can tell us a great deal, for O'Neill's faith, like Pascal's, is a poetic utilitarianism: he needs it and *will* have it. O'Neill rejects naturalism and materialism as Pascal had rejected Descartes and all science. He too is frightened by "the eternal silence of the infinite spaces." Like Pascal, to whom the details of life and the variety and flux of the human mind were repugnant, O'Neill feels that life is empty—having emptied it—and can fill it only by faith in a loving God. The existence of such a God, Pascal knew, cannot be proved save by the heart's need, but this seemed sufficient and he stood ready to stupefy his reason to maintain his faith. O'Neill will do no less. It is perhaps the inevitable way of modern Catholicism in a hostile world.

O'Neill's rejection of materialism involved the familiar pulpit confusion of philosophical materialism with "crass" materialism, that is, with the preference of physical to moral well-being. It is therefore natural that *Dynamo,* the play in which he makes explicit his antimaterialism, should present characters who are mean and little—that, though it contains an Earth Mother, she is not the wise and tragic Cybel but the fat and silly Mrs. Fife, the bovine wife of the atheist dynamo-tender. She, like other characters in the play, allies herself with the Dynamo-God, embodiment both of the materialistic universe and of modern man's sense of his own power. But this new god can only frustrate the forces of life, however much it at first seems life's ally against the Protestant denials, and those who worship it become contemptible and murderous.

And the contempt for humanity which pervades *Dynamo* continues in *Mourning Becomes Electra,* creating, in a sense, the utter hopelessness of that tragedy. Aeschylus had ended his Atreus trilogy on a note of social reconciliation—after the bloody deeds and the awful pursuit of the Furies, society confers its forgiveness, the Furies are tamed to deities of hearth and field: "This day there is a new

Order born"; but O'Neill's version has no touch of this resolution. There is no forgiveness in *Mourning Becomes Electra* because, while there is as yet no forgiving God in O'Neill's cosmos, there is no society either, only a vague chorus of contemptible townspeople. "There's no one left to punish me," says Lavinia. "I've got to punish myself."

It is the ultimate of individual arrogance, the final statement of a universe in which society has no part. For O'Neill, since as far back as *The Hairy Ape*, there has been only the individual and the universe. The social organism has meant nothing. His Mannons, unlike the Atreides, are not monarchs with a relation to the humanity about them, a humanity that can forgive because it can condemn. They act their crimes on the stage of the infinite. The mention of human law bringing them punishment is startlingly incongruous and it is inevitable that O'Neill, looking for a law, should turn to a divine law.

Forgiveness comes in *Ah, Wilderness!* the satyr-play that follows the tragedy, and it is significant that O'Neill should have interrupted the composition of *Days Without End* to write it. With the religious answer of the more serious play firm in his mind, with its establishment of the divine law, O'Neill can, for the first time, render the sense and feel of common life, can actually be humorous. Now the family is no longer destructively possessive as he has always represented it, but creatively sympathetic. The revolt of the young son— his devotion to rebels and hedonists, to Shaw, Ibsen and Swinburne— is but the mark of adolescence and in the warm round of forgiving life he will become wisely acquiescent to a world that is not in the least terrible.

But the idyllic life of *Ah, Wilderness!* for all its warmth, is essentially ironical, almost cynical. For it is only when all magnitude has been removed from humanity by the religious answer and placed in the Church and its God that life can be seen as simple and good. The pluses and minuses of man must be made to cancel out as nearly as possible, the equation must be solved to equal nearly zero, before peace may be found. The hero of *Days Without End* has lived for years in a torturing struggle with the rationalistic, questioning "half" of himself which has led him away from piety to atheism, thence to socialism, next to unchastity and finally to the oblique attempt to murder his beloved wife. It is not until he makes an act of submissive faith at the foot of the Cross and thus annihilates the doubting mind, the root of all evil, that he can find peace.

But the annihilation of the questioning mind also annihilates the multitudinous world. *Days Without End*, perhaps O'Neill's weakest play, is cold and bleak: life is banished from it by the vision of the Life Eternal. Its religious content is expressed not so much by the hero's priestly uncle, wise, tolerant, humorous in the familiar literary convention of modern Catholicism, as by the hero's wife, a humorless, puritanical woman who lives on the pietistic-romantic love she bears her husband and on her sordid ideal of his absolute chastity. She is the very embodiment of all the warping, bullying idealism that O'Neill had once attacked. Now, however, he gives credence to this plaster saintliness, for it represents for him the spiritual life of absolutes. Now for the first time he is explicit in his rejection of all merely human bulwarks against the pain and confusion of life—finds in the attack upon capitalism almost an attack upon God, scorns socialism and is disgusted with the weakness of those who are disgusted with social individualism. The peace of the absolute can be bought only at the cost of blindness to the actual.

The philosophic position would seem to be a final one: O'Neill has crept into the dark womb of Mother Church and pulled the universe in with him. Perhaps the very violence of the gesture with which he has taken the position of passivity should remind us of his force and of what such force may yet do even in that static and simple dark. Yet it is scarcely a likely place for O'Neill to remember Dion Anthony's warning: "It isn't enough to be [life's] creature. You've got to create her or she requests you to destroy yourself."

section ii
DRAMA AND SOCIETY

william archer

PINERO, JONES, AND WILDE

. . . I SHALL have a good deal to say of Sir Arthur Pinero which might tempt him to hint that I have not yet unlearnt my early foible of superiority. I shall have to own that his talent developed slowly, and that he has never quite shaken off certain limitations of thought and style. With all the more emphasis do I wish to say at the outset that, in so far as any one man can be called the regenerator of the English drama, that man is Arthur Pinero. We owe him a quite incalculable debt. From December, 1881, when *The Squire* was produced, until September, 1901, which saw the production of *Iris*, his principal plays may be reckoned as milestones on the path of progress. Nor do I imply that his own progress stopped with *Iris*. On the contrary, his best work was still to come. With the new century, however, other men took up the running, and he no longer stood, or rather ran, alone. But he had smoothed the way and set the pace for these other men, some of whom have shown him very scant gratitude. He was the brilliant and even daring pioneer of a great movement.

Several of his early plays have not been printed (at all events in readable form) and are remembered only by theatrical antiquaries like myself. One of them, *In Chancery*, reappeared not long ago in the form of a musical farce. Another, *Lords and Commons*, founded, I think, on a Swedish novel, made a very deep impression on me, but as I did not happen to write about it, I cannot refresh my memory of it. He made a resounding failure with a play called *Low Water*. An incident which gave rise to much hilarity was the interruption of a love-scene by the silent entrance of a man with a sack of coal, which he shot into the ottoman on which the lovers had been sitting. I fancy that the unfavourable reception of the play was on the whole justified; but it showed an earnest desire to reproduce faithfully some of the discomforts of the condition indicated in the title. In other words, it showed that the author was heart and soul in the movement

Reprinted by permission of Dodd, Mead & Co. from *The Old Drama and the New* by William Archer. Copyright 1923 by Dodd, Mead & Co., Inc. Renewal Copyright 1950 by Frank Archer. Reprinted also by permission of Curtis Brown, Ltd.

which I am trying to trace—the movement for making the stage a sincere, undistorting and unexaggerating mirror of real life. He failed in this case because his courage exceeded his tact.

It was with three brilliant farces produced at the old Court Theatre in 1885, '86 and '87 that Mr. Pinero finally established himself as a master of the stage. They are the work not only of a skilful playwright but of an original and delightful humorist. I feel sure that if *The Magistrate, The Schoolmistress* and *Dandy Dick* were republished, with stage-directions calculated to help instead of bewildering the reader, and with illustrations enabling him to visualise the characters, they would be very widely read. *Dandy Dick* is probably the best of the three, but I own to a sneaking preference for *The Schoolmistress*, the second act of which, with its fantastic supper-party and dance, is one of the most delectable episodes I ever saw on the stage.

In 1888, Mr. Pinero made a very successful plunge into sentimental comedy, with *Sweet Lavender*. Its theme was trivial and its sentiment commonplace. What assured its success was the admirable eccentric character-study of Dick Phenyl, the broken-down, somewhat whiskified barrister, who still preserves the instincts and feelings of a gentleman.

I pass over an amusing but not very significant play, *The Hobby Horse*, and come to *The Weaker Sex*, produced in March, 1889, though written some years earlier. I single it out as illustrating one of the before-mentioned limitations under which the author's talent labours. His criticism of life is coloured by that instinctive, unthinking conservatism which prevails in stageland, and among its denizens, "the profession." I am not here to talk party politics; but I think all parties must admit that there is such a thing as traditional, uninstructed conservatism, just as there is traditional, uninstructed radicalism. The stageland of Britain, and I fancy stageland everywhere, has always tended to be behind the age. You may remember a significant passage in *You Never Can Tell*, where Mrs. Clandon, newly returned after eighteen years in Madeira, is assuring her old ally, Finch McComas, that she is still in the foremost files of time, and has brought up her daughter, Gloria, upon the sincere milk of philosophic radicalism:

MRS. CLANDON: Yes: I have not gone back one inch; and I have educated Gloria to take up my work where I left it. . . . I suppose she will be howled at, as I was; but she is prepared for that.

MCCOMAS: Howled at! My dear good lady; there is nothing in any of those views nowadays to prevent her marrying an archbishop. . . . Am I howled at? No: I'm indulged as an old fogey. I'm out of everything, because I've refused to bow the knee to Socialism.

MRS. CLANDON: (*Shocked.*) Socialism!

MCCOMAS: Yes: Socialism. That's what Miss Gloria will be up to her ears in before the end of the month if you let her loose here.

MRS. CLANDON: But I can *prove* to her that Socialism is a fallacy.

MCCOMAS: It is by proving that, Mrs. Clandon, that I have lost all my disciples. . . . There is only one place in all England where your opinions would still pass as advanced.

MRS. CLANDON: (*Scornfully, unconvinced.*) The Church, perhaps?

MCCOMAS: No: the theatre.

This passage was much more pertinent in 1896 than it is today; and Pinero's play of seven years earlier may well have stood foremost among those which were in Mr. Shaw's mind as he wrote. There is some naïveté even in the title. I remember how amazed I was, even in 1889, to find that the phrase, *The Weaker Sex,* was not used ironically, but that the play deliberately set forth to prove, by the most barefaced psychological jugglery, that women were incompetent to take any serious part in the non-domestic work of the world. It seemed to me even then that such a title simply begged the whole question on which the play turned. And how did the author prove his point? By showing two middle-aged widows, prominent in the feminist movement, who accept as masculine champion a blithering idiot of an M.P., and themselves collapse into something very like idiocy the moment the prospect of a second marriage is dangled before their eyes. One of them, the heroine, makes a pathetic attempt to renew her youth and beauty, only to find that the old lover whom she hopes to recapture is now in love with her daughter. The other, who may be called the butt of the play, thinks that the idiot M.P., is proposing for herself when in fact he is proposing for her daughter, and proceeds to act with a skittish juvenility which is very painful. It is true, and fortunate, that the author argues rather by carefully-cooked example than by formal discussion; but the quality of such discussion as there is may be judged by one or two brief examples. Dudley Silchester is the *raisonneur,* the man of sound common-sense; Lady Vivash (played by Mrs. Kendal) is the heroine:

LADY VIVASH: Have any of our ladies arrived?

DUDLEY: I think so.

LADY VIVASH: Indeed?

DUDLEY: I saw some goloshes in the hall as I came in.

LADY VIVASH: I wear goloshes in the damp weather. Perhaps they are mine.

DUDLEY: Perhaps; I didn't know at first whether they *were* goloshes.

LADY VIVASH: What did you take them for?

DUDLEY: Gondolas.

LADY VIVASH: Oh! After all, the size of a woman's foot is imma-
terial. A woman doesn't carry her heart in her boots.

DUDLEY: She does—if you say "Boo" in the dark.

Now that Sir Arthur has had an opportunity of seeing how
women behave when you say "Bombs" in the dark, he is, I hope, less
impressed by Dudley's facetiousness. A little further on, when Lady
Vivash hears that her daughter, Sylvia, is returning from the Continent, she becomes utterly incapable of carrying on the ordinary business of life.

LADY: I want to see Sylvia so badly. (*Stamping her foot.*) Dudley,
you don't tell me what to do.

DUDLEY: (*Shaking his head.*) Oh, you strong-minded woman!

LADY VIVASH: I'm not! I mean I haven't seen her for so long.

DUDLEY: They're sure to be here almost directly.

LADY VIVASH: What am I to do till almost directly?

DUDLEY: There's the Committee downstairs.

LADY VIVASH: (*Impatiently.*) Oh!

DUDLEY: And your speech to prepare for tonight.

LADY VIVASH: I can't think of anything now but Sylvia.

DUDLEY: No—and it is from this material that we are to mould our
Cabinet Ministers of the future!

It is unkind, and perhaps unfair, to rake up this ephemeral chatter,
which events have rendered as obsolete as any cuneiform inscription.
I do it because we must be prepared to find, later on, that some of
Sir Arthur's best work is marred by a failure to keep abreast of
moderately enlightened political and philosophic thought.

His next play, in order of production, was one of those milestones of progress to which I have referred. *The Profligate* now seems
terribly antiquated; but we were quite right in hailing it, in April,
1889, as the strongest piece of original drama that the stage had seen
for many a long year. It dealt, sentimentally but frankly, with the
problem which Björnson had treated six years earlier in *A Gauntlet*
—the difference between the standards of moral conduct imposed
by society on men and on women. The heroine, Leslie Brudenell,
fresh from her boarding-school, has married a young man named
Dunstan Renshaw, whom she believes to be the Sir Galahad of her
dreams. She is terribly shocked when she finds that Dunstan is the
intimate friend of a certain Lord Dangars, a nobleman of the most
lurid reputation. At the Florentine villa where Leslie and Dunstan
are spending their honeymoon, there arrives, by what one of the
characters calls "an awful freak of fate," a certain Janet Preece who
has been ruined and deserted by a heartless profligate. Just as she
has told Leslie her sad story, she looks down the garden walk and,

seeing Lord Dangars and Dunstan Renshaw approaching, cries, "It's the man—the man!" Leslie assumes that she is referring to Dangars, and when Dunstan introduces his friend, declines to take his hand or to have anything to say to him. Imagine, then, the collapse of all her ideals and her happiness when it proves that Janet has never seen Dangars before, and that it is Dunstan who is her seducer. The situation, though built on an improbable coincidence, is heightened by many skilfully-devised circumstances which it would be tedious to relate, and remains one of the most powerful ever conceived. For quite a long time, as stage time is reckoned, we see the thunderbolt hanging over poor Leslie's head, and we hold our breath as we wait for it to fall. The value of the situation is of course quite independent of any judgment as to the merits or demerits of Dunstan's conduct, or as to Leslie's right to expect of him an innocence equal to her own. If we admit, as we cannot but admit, that Leslie's ideals and Leslie's ignorance are, or were, true to nature—are, or were, characteristic of an immense number of women—that is all that is required to make the situation one of tragic poignancy.

It must be owned, however, that the ethical presuppositions of the play are a little too simple, and that the absolute and universal validity of Leslie's ideals is too unquestioningly assumed. The code of retributive justice which finds Dunstan's one possible expiation in suicide belongs rather to the mid-Victorian theatre than to real life. The standard-bearer of this ideal, who permeates the play, is a sad blot upon it. He is a sentimental Scotch solicitor, Hugh Murray by name, who wears his heart on his sleeve in a way not usually held to be characteristic either of solicitors or of Scotchmen. Within five minutes of the opening of the play, we find him thus expressing himself, in his office in Lincoln's Inn, to a very remarkable confidant—none other, in fact, than the detrimental Lord Dangars, whom he detests and despises. He has told Lord Dangars that Dunstan Renshaw is that day to be married:

> DANGARS: May I beg to know who's the lady?
> MURRAY: Miss Leslie Brudenell—an orphan—my partner's ward.
> DANGARS: Money? I needn't ask.
> MURRAY: If Miss Brudenell were penniless, I should describe her as a millionaire. She is very sweet, very beautiful.
> DANGARS: You're enthusiastic.
> MURRAY: No, barely just. (*Speaking half to himself.*) I thought the same the moment I first saw her. She was walking in the grounds of the old schoolhouse at Helmstead, and I stood aside in the shade of the beeches and watched her—I couldn't help it. And I remember how I stammered when I spoke to her; because some women are like sacred pictures, you can't do more than whisper before them.

Strange talk this for Furnival's Inn, and stranger still as proceeding, not from one old friend to another, but from a solicitor to a highly disesteemed client who has just remarked, "It's a deuced odd circumstance that I have been nearly everything in divorce cases, but *never* a petitioner." Hugh Murray, however, seldom opens his mouth without emitting a flower of sentiment. He indulges in a metaphoric fantasia on the theme of wild oats, which is too long to quote. The following brief reflection may serve as a fair specimen of his style:

> Women love men whose natures are like bright colours—the homespun of life repels them. They delight to hear their fate in the cadences of a musical voice, thinking they are listening to an impromptu; it's too late when they learn that the melody has been composed by Experience and scored by other women's tears.

The fact is that Mr. Pinero, at this period, was still a rather uncritical disciple of Robertson. He had immeasurably more power than his master, but was not exempt from the characteristic Robertsonian lapses of taste.

What we may call the last work of his Robertsonian period was *Lady Bountiful*, produced in 1891. Its first three acts are very able and beautiful, containing, in Roderick Heron, a brilliantly drawn variant of the Harold Skimpole type. Its success was impaired by the fourth act, which, instead of being brief and simple, was dragged out by elaborate staging and by the tiresome chatter of conventional rustics. I believe that, if Sir Arthur could be persuaded to re-write this fourth act, the play might even now be revived with success.

Two comparatively insignificant plays, *The Times* and *The Amazons*, intervened between *Lady Bountiful* and *The Second Mrs. Tanqueray*. That play, in my opinion, opened a new period in our dramatic history—a period to be dealt with in my next lecture. In the meantime let us go back to the early 'eighties and glance at the development of Mr. Henry Arthur Jones.

From a German dissertation devoted to *Henry Arthur Jones's Dramen*, by one Hans Teichmann,[1] it appears that between 1879 and 1912 he had written fifty plays, most of them in three or more acts. Whatever else he may be, this author is a born playwright, an irrepressible practitioner of the dramatic form. And he will certainly take a prominent and honourable place in the history of what he himself has celebrated as "The Renascence of English Drama." He has dramatic instinct in plenty; he has a certain sort of originality, and a certain sort of thought, of wit, of style; he has great fervor,

[1] Otto Meyer, Giessen, 1913.

if not great clarity, of imagination; and he has often shown himself a master of the art of dramatic story-telling. His work has been throughout distinguished by an honourable ambition. We have seen how Matthew Arnold applauded his first success, *The Silver King;* and this "approbation from Sir Hubert Stanley" had a determining effect on Mr. Jones's development. He threw himself resolutely into the pursuit of culture. He read the *Nineteenth Century* and he wrote in it. He determined that his work should be a criticism of life, and especially of that British philistinism which his mentor despised, and which he himself, with his yeoman ancestry and his business antecedents, had studied at close quarters. The trouble was that his culture did not sit very lightly on him. It scarcely seemed made to his measure, and he wore it with a certain self-consciousness.

He had been cradled in melodrama and could never quite shake off its gestures and intonations. The first play in which he felt himself free to give the rein to his ambitions was *Saints and Sinners* (1884). He wrote it, as he tells us in the preface, in conscious reaction against "the cheaper and coarser art of melodrama"; yet it differs from melodrama mainly in having no mechanical sensation-scenes. Its theme is that great melodramatic stand-by, the betrayal of a village maiden by an aristocratic villain; and the subject is treated in the most ordinary melodramatic fashion, even to the death of the erring heroine in the odour of penitent sanctity. The originality of the play lies in the picture of a poor dissenting minister tyrannised over by the grasping and hypocritical tradesmen of his congregation. This is, or rather was, a new note, and did certainly differentiate the piece from ordinary melodrama. Matthew Arnold wrote of it: "You have remarkably the art—so valuable in drama—of exciting interest and sustaining it"—a very just observation, in which the critic goes nearer than he perhaps realised to the inmost secret of Mr. Jones's success. He also said: "I must add that I dislike seduction dramas— even in *Faust* the feeling tells with me"; but this remonstrance of the master did not prevent the disciple from recurring to the same motive in *Michael and his Lost Angel, The Physician, The Hypocrites,* and I fancy in other plays. Sir Arthur Pinero, as we have seen, used it once, in *The Profligate,* but I think only that once.[2]

It is impossible to attempt anything like an exhaustive review, or even a chronological enumeration of Mr. Jones's stately series of plays. They fall into two main classes: more or less melodramatic— or shall we say picturesque?—dramas of passion, and more or less frivolous comedies of intrigue. Mr. Jones is an intense believer (for dramatic purposes, at any rate) in what Racine calls

[2] *Sweet Lavender* turns upon a case of seduction in the far past.

Venus toute entière à sa proie attachée

—that sort of love which descends upon its victim like a typhoon, but, unlike a typhoon, lasts for a whole lifetime. The lifetime, indeed, is apt to be short, for the patient generally emerges from the tempest a battered wreck. Such is the love of Judah Llewellyn for Vashti Dethic in *Judah,* of Philos Ingarfield for Cynthia Greenslade in *The Crusaders,* of David Remon for Dulcie Larondie in *The Masqueraders,* of the Rev. Michael Feversham for Audrie Lesden in *Michael and his Lost Angel,* of Dr. Lewin Carey for Edana Hinde in *The Physician.* In all these plays, but especially in the first and last, there is excellent material. I should not be surprised if the playwrights of fifty years hence found in Mr. Jones's works a mine of dramatic suggestion. But in all of them there is somehow a lack of intellectual subtlety, and a search after scenic effect of the picture-poster order, which greatly detract from their ultimate value.

The theme of *Judah* is this: Judah Llewellyn, an eloquent young Methodist preacher, of partly Welsh and partly Jewish descent, falls desperately in love with Vashti Dethic, a young woman who pretends to miraculous powers of healing, and whom he regards as a creature next-door to divine. She does, indeed, work a certain number of faith-cures; and to strengthen the faith of her patients she pretends to undergo long periods of fasting, food being surreptitiously conveyed to her by her father, a charlatan and a swindler. Challenged by a certain Professor Jopp, she consents to undergo a test, being imprisoned in the keep of an old castle (great opportunity for the scene-painter!), with the Professor's daughter for her jailor. The conditions are absurdly lax, and up to the eighteenth day of the twenty-one days agreed upon, old Dethic succeeds in conveying supplies to her. At this point the watch becomes stricter; but still the father (after an amazing game at hide-and-seek) would succeed in outwitting it, were it not that there is a sentinel on whom he does not reckon—namely, Judah Llewellyn, who has ensconced himself in a convenient niche whence he can gaze upon his lady-love's windows. He sees her father handing food to her, and then solemnly perjures himself in declaring that he has seen nothing of the sort. Such is the general respect for his veracity that this testimony is held to prove her miraculous powers; but the furies of remorse pursue the perjurer until, in the last act, he confesses his sin and resigns his ministry.

This was quite a remarkable play for its date (1890) and might make a good play at any time; but the clumsy and bewildering hide-and-seek of the "picturesque" second act would have to be eliminated, along with the devastating "comic relief" afforded by the grotesque

Juxon Prall and Sophie Jopp—a pair who, under different aliases, and with slight variations of absurdity, wander through too many of Mr. Jones's plays.

The heroine of *The Masqueraders* is a young woman of the fox-hunting classes who, having come down in the world, thinks the profession of barmaid more desirable than that of nurse or governess. At a rackety hunt-ball, a subscription is raised for the family of a deceased huntsman. Someone proposes that one kiss from the beautiful barmaid, Dulcie Larondie, shall be put up to auction for this worthy purpose. The contest lies between Sir Brice Skene, a dissipated and wicked baronet, and David Remon, a virtuous astronomer. The bidding mounts up from ten guineas to twenty—thirty—forty—fifty: then to one hundred guineas—then three hundred—five hundred—one thousand—fifteen hundred. Now we have been told that David Remon's whole worldly goods amount to two thousand pounds and no more; consequently we are duly thrilled when he bids two thousand pounds—his whole fortune—for a single kiss. The wicked baronet goes one better—he bids three thousand guineas; and then, by way of keeping it all in the family, he announces his intention of marrying the lady. She, being professionally inured to alcoholic advances, offers no objection; and thus Dulcie Larondie becomes Lady Skene.

In a couple of years or so, drink and gambling bring the wicked baronet to beggary, and he not only allows, but orders, his wife to accept money from David Remon, who has meanwhile come in for a legacy of two hundred thousand pounds. Fortunately David is a man of the strictest principles—all astronomers are. But on the eve of starting on an astronomical expedition from which he has little chance of returning, he cannot bear the thought of leaving Dulcie and her child to the tender mercies of Sir Brice; so he challenges that inveterate gambler to a little flutter—he will stake his whole fortune against Sir Brice's wife and daughter. The flutter is very brief—they simply cut the cards—and David, having won the best of three, becomes (it would seem) the moral, if not legal, owner of Lady and Miss Skene. Now, for a moment, his virtue falters—he is tempted to abandon his astronomical expedition (for the result of which the whole scientific world is gasping) and devote himself to cultivating his newly acquired property. But ideal counsels prevail, and he starts for malarial West Africa, merely giving Dulcie a rendezvous in a "little star in Andromeda" which twinkles a good deal in his conversation. He has, of course, left his two hundred thousand pounds to Lady Skene, taking precautions, I hope, to keep it out of the clutches of Sir Brice, who is likely to trouble her with renewed attentions when he learns that she has come in for ten thousand pounds a year.

It is obvious that Mr. Jones is here attempting, not a realistic, but an imaginative treatment of life—a quite legitimate aim. The trouble is that the imagination is not of very distinguished quality. The talk about the star in Andromeda scarcely takes rank with the "brave translunary things" of literature. David Remon has a younger brother, Eddy, who plays the part of a sort of crack-brained Puck throughout the play. We first encounter him at the hunt-ball, where he puts his fingers in his ears, crying, "Oh! oh! oh! Those wretched musicians! They were playing horribly in tune, as if the world were full of harmony. I must get a tin kettle and put them out." The title, *The Masqueraders*, alludes to an idea on which David Remon is fond of harping, that we are not real people, but only the figures in a carnival revel—as though there were no reality beneath the masks of *Mardi Gras*. Philosophic criticism of reality is one thing, this facile fantasticating is quite another. To do Mr. Jones justice, he himself very aptly pricks his hero's bubble in this little passage between Dulcie and her sister, a hard-working nurse:

DULCIE: Nell, Mr. Remon has an odd idea that this world isn't real.
HELEN: The cure for that is to earn half-a-crown a day and live on it.

Judah and *The Masqueraders* must serve as specimens of Mr. Jones's more ambitious and imaginative work. There is a great deal of vigour and a certain individuality in it. The pity is that the world of his imagination is not sun-lit but lime-lit.

To his works of a lighter order I have applied the term comedies of intrigue. Perhaps they might better have been called satiric comedies. Sometimes they flagellate Philistinism with a scourge remotely modelled on that of Matthew Arnold; sometimes, on the other hand, they scoff at idealism. An instance of the former class is *The Triumph of the Philistines and how Mr. Jorgan preserved the morals of Market Pewbury under very trying circumstances;* an instance of the latter class is *The Crusaders*. The effectiveness of the satire is somewhat diminished by the fact that it is a little difficult to recognise either real Philistines or real idealists in the victims of Mr. Jones's persiflage. More often he leaves extremes alone and applies an indulgent, feather-weight lash, which seems to caress rather than sting, to the foibles and frailties of polite and opulent society. His masterpiece in this style is unquestionably *The Liars*, a comedy so bright and entertaining that it has a fair chance of being remembered when other pieces of the same type are forgotten—such pieces as *The Case of Rebellious Susan, The Manœuvres of Jane, Whitewashing Julia, Joseph En-*

tangled, Dolly Reforming Herself. These plays leave in the mind a composite picture of people lounging in drawing-rooms furnished by the best artists of Tottenham Court Road, and constantly fluttering round the divorce-court as birds flutter round a lighthouse, but almost always coming off with their plumage nearly as good as new. There is no sin in this society that cannot be expiated, no wound that cannot be healed, by Mr. Jones's famous panacea for all the ills of matrimonial life—a little dinner at the Savoy, to be followed next day by a visit to a Bond Street jeweller's or a fashionable fur-shop. It is not a very edifying, nor even a permanently exhilarating, picture of life; but, with all their limitations, these plays stand both intellectually and artistically in a totally different class from anything (save one or two plays of Robertson's) that passed as comedy during the century between 1777 and 1877.

Mr. Jones's great quality, however,—as I have already said and as Matthew Arnold discerned,—is his knack of "exciting interest and of sustaining it." Take, for instance, the opening of *The Physician,* produced in 1897, with Sir Charles Wyndham in the part of Dr. Lewin Carey. The scene is the doctor's consulting-room:

> *Enter, door at back, Viccars, Dr. Carey's butler, showing in Walter Amphiel. Amphiel is a pale, thin, and very delicate-looking man about thirty; striking, earnest features, with a winning, lovable expression; rather weak mouth; restless, furtive eyes with a hunted look in them.*
>
> VICCARS: Dr. Carey is attending a consultation, sir, but I expect him back shortly.
>
> AMPHIEL: I'll wait.
>
> VICCARS: What name shall I say?
>
> AMPHIEL: My name doesn't matter. I'll wait. (*Exit Viccars.*) (*Amphiel furtively watches Viccars off, and as soon as the door has closed, goes quickly to the bookshelves, runs his eye eagerly over them as if searching for something, takes out a particular book, looks at index, opens it at a certain page, sits down, reads eagerly.*)
>
> (*Enter Viccars at back, showing in Dr. Brooker, a middle-aged man, brisk, genial, robust. . . . As Brooker enters, Amphiel shows recognition and a little embarrassment, hiding his head behind his book.*
>
> BROOKER: (*Entering.*) Thank you, Viccars. Dr. Carey does expect me, doesn't he?
>
> VICCARS: Yes, sir. He left word if you came that he'd be back almost at once. Shall I get you anything after your journey, sir?
>
> BROOKER: No, thank you. Well, just a cup of tea, if you'll be so good. (*Exit Viccars at back.*)
>
> BROOKER: (*Sitting down, catches sight of Amphiel's face as he looks up furtively from his book.*) I beg pardon, my name is Brooker

—Dr. Brooker of Folkestone. I've had the pleasure of meeting you somewhere?

AMPHIEL: (*With slight embarrassment.*) I think not—I don't remember you.

BROOKER: (*Still looking at him.*) I suppose I was mistaken—your face seemed familiar to me. (*A little pause.*)

AMPHIEL: Very interesting place, a doctor's consulting-room.

BROOKER: H'm—not very—to the doctor.

AMPHIEL: This room, for instance. How many strange stories and confessions these walls must have listened to! How many men and women must have opened that door with hope in their hearts and received their death-sentence, sitting perhaps where I am sitting now.

BROOKER: Oh, don't speak of us as if we were bloodthirsty hanging judges. Say rather how many men have entered that door with despair in their hearts, and gone out cheered and comforted!

AMPHIEL: Dr. Carey is marvellously skilful in certain—certain nervous diseases, isn't he?

BROOKER: He's marvellously skilful in all kinds of diseases. He has made a great reputation with nerve diseases, simply because this is a nervous age. Everybody is suffering from neurasthenia today. Except myself, thank God!

(*Viccars re-enters with tea on salver, which he brings to Dr. Brooker. Amphiel puts book on table open.*)

BROOKER: (*Looking steadily at Amphiel.*) Surely I—didn't you consult me one Sunday evening three or four years ago?

AMPHIEL: No, no, I've never met you. (*To Viccars.*) Dr. Carey hasn't returned? (*Takes out watch.*) I'll call again by and by.

(*Exit Amphiel at back, rather hurriedly.*)

VICCARS: (*At door, looking after him, calls off.*) The door, Thomas. (*Meanwhile Brooker has taken up the book which Amphiel has put down. He looks at the page, raises his eyebrows, puts book on table again, leaving it open.*)

Not three minutes have passed since the rise of the curtain; there has not been a word of formal exposition; yet I can remember today how keenly my interest was aroused on the first night, and how I admired the skill of the thing. There is one slight and easily remediable flaw—a slip in Mr. Jones's technique. It is very unlikely that Amphiel would leave the book open on the table. In all probability, on the contrary, he would be exceedingly careful to replace it on the shelf. But it might be bound in a bright colour, so that Dr. Booker could easily pick it out, glance at the title, raise his eyebrows, and put it back again. This would be not only more probable, but a more effective piece of business. It is a measure of the delicacy of modern theatrical art that such trifles may sometimes make or mar a scene.

The solution of the mystery is that Amphiel, a rich man, noted as an enthusiastic and munificent labourer in the cause of temperance, is in fact a dipsomaniac, subject to periodical lapses into degrading debauchery. He is engaged to a seraphic young person named Edana Hinde, who has not the remotest suspicion of his infirmity. Dr. Carey conceives for her one of those intense Jonesian passions to which I have referred, but nevertheless struggles with all his might to banish the curse that weighs on Amphiel's life. His efforts are vain and Amphiel dies, which is much the best thing he can do; so that all may be said to end happily. If Mr. Jones would re-write the play and eliminate the passages of picturesque melodrama which mar the later acts, it might take a permanent place in dramatic literature.

But Mr. Jones's masterpiece in dramatic story-telling is undoubtedly *Mrs. Dane's Defence.* One scene in the third act of this play is one of the best things of its kind ever written. The heroine is trying to conceal the fact that her real name is not Mrs. Dane, but Felicia Hindemarsh, a woman of badly blemished reputation. She has thrown dust in the eyes of everyone, including Sir Daniel Carteret, a famous lawyer. He, however, requires definite information on one or two points before coming forward as her champion. He begins to question her on these points in the most gentle and considerate way. She has her story pat, and for a time all goes smoothly. Then a single slip of the tongue—nothing more than the substitution of a plural for a singular pronoun—puts Sir Daniel on his guard. His questions become more searching: she involves herself in evasions, contradictions, semi-confessions: and at last, after she has been on the rack for half-an-hour, he turns upon the poor, cowering creature with the words, "Woman, you are lying—you are Felicia Hindemarsh!" She crumples up before him, and tells her whole piteous story.

The scene is a magnificent one,[3] and it is only a consummate example of Mr. Jones's gift of wringing the last drop of drama out of a situation. And, as we listen to the dialogue, we cannot but be conscious that we have got utterly away both from the convention of wit and the convention of rhetoric—from the whole exaggerative and falsifying apparatus, in short, that had come down to our own time from the days when drama was a rite of hero-worship or a propitiation of the deities, the daimons, of corn and wine. "Flat and commonplace!" some people may say; but it is not flat and commonplace, for it is tingling with human emotion, with hope, fear, suspense, foreboding, despair; and every speech, while perfectly natural in the

---

[3] Without borrowing a single motive or incident, Mr. Jones has compressed into this play, and especially into this scene, the whole emotional effect of an intensely dramatic *cause célèbre,* the Osborne pearl case. I guessed when I saw the play that it had been suggested by this trial, and Mr. Jones told me that I was right.

situation, is placed, with the deftness of a mosaic artist, just where it is needed, now to accelerate, and again to retard, the gradual *dégringolade* of the unhappy woman from the summit of triumph to the gulf of misery. Let those who profess to think drama of this kind a despicable affair produce anything approaching it in intellectual cunning.

Some critics have exalted Mr. Jones at the expense of Sir Arthur Pinero, for no better reason than that he has a somewhat truer ear for the rhythms, or rather for the vocabulary, of everyday speech. For my part I do not think that there is any comparison between the two men. Mr. Jones is a man of robust talent; Sir Arthur Pinero, in despite of certain weaknesses, is an original dramatic genius. Remember that I have as yet spoken only of his minor works. But as I am here taking leave of Mr. Jones, I wish to point out that in his better plays we have the modern formula complete. His endeavour is to imitate with absolute fidelity the surfaces of modern life. He may often fail in that endeavour and imitate badly, and he may at best get very little below the surfaces. But we find in his work, perhaps earlier than in that of any other playwright, a form of drama in which the aims of modern realism are constantly in view and frequently achieved. The before-mentioned Herr Hans Teichmann, with true German industry, has compiled a statistical table showing how he begins by freely using the soliloquy and the aside, but how they occur less and less frequently in each succeeding play, until at last they disappear almost entirely. This is very significant.

The 'eighties and early 'nineties brought to the front several other playwrights of real note. Mr. Haddon Chambers in *Captain Swift* (1888) added a phrase to the language—"the long arm of coincidence." I well remember the laugh with which it was received when it was first spoken. Other plays, such as *The Idler* and *John-a-Dreams,* were of very moderate merit. He did not give the true measure of his talent until he produced in 1899 his admirable comedy, *The Tyranny of Tears.* In 1885 Mr. R. C. Carton produced, with the late Cecil Raleigh, a clever comic melodrama, *The Great Pink Pearl.* In the early 'nineties he devoted himself to Robertsonian sentiment in *Sunlight and Shadow, Liberty Hall* and *Robin Goodfellow.* He, too, did not show what he could really do until the very last years of the century, when he produced those brilliant light comedies, *Lord and Lady Algy, Wheels Within Wheels* and *Lady Huntworth's Experiment.*

There remains one dramatist to be mentioned before I close this survey of what may be called essentially the drama of the 'eighties: for though many of the plays I have dealt with were actually produced in the 'nineties, they were unaffected, or very slightly affected, by the new influences which came into play about 1891. The dramatist I mean is Oscar Wilde, whose theatrical career was comprised between the years 1892 and 1895. He was the most exquisite stylist that had written for the stage since Congreve, and his wit, though it often condescended to the use of a mechanical process, and often to something very like plagiarism, was copious, audacious and occasionally profound. But he treated the art of the dramatist with contemptuous insincerity. His three serious comedies, *Lady Windermere's Fan, A Woman of No Importance* and *The Ideal Husband,* are in reality mere drawing-room melodramas, and conventional ones at that. He was a born playwright in the sense that, from his very first attempt, he seemed to have the tricks of technique at his fingers' ends, and to know by instinct what would be effective on the stage. But there was no real substance in his work. One feels that in his heart he despised the stories he was telling, and took a cynical pleasure in fooling his public to the top of their bent. In *Lady Windermere's Fan* we have the old, old tale of a husband willing to risk his whole domestic happiness and incur the most injurious suspicions, in order to conceal from his wife a blot in her own scutcheon, the knowledge of which might cause her some pain, but infinitely less than that which his absurd quixotism inflicts upon her. In *A Woman of No Importance* a witty reprobate—not a baronet, but a peer—is punished for his past sins when, meeting his illegitimate son, he hears the good old *voix du sang,* and yields himself up to transports of parental affection, only to find that neither his son nor his son's mother will have anything to say to him. In *An Ideal Husband* the author ostensibly sets forth to treat the question whether a single lapse into dishonesty should necessarily end the career of an able public servant. The point is doubtless an arguable one, but only on the assumption that the peccant official has fully realised the error of his ways, and is capable of integrity. This assumption Oscar Wilde makes haste to nullify, by showing that he is as great a scoundrel as ever, and is perfectly prepared to sell his country a second time at the bidding of a blackmailer. These plays, in short, are very bad plays, clothed in shimmering robes of tinsel, not without some admixture of real cloth-of-gold. *The Importance of Being Earnest* stands on a different level. It is a delightful piece of original humour, which unfortunately degenerates in the last act into rather poor farce. The continued popularity of Wilde in Germany must, I think, be taken largely as a political demonstration—a wilful glorification of a man whom England cast out. But there is no doubt a certain section of the German public which takes drawing-room melodrama seriously. . . .

mary mc carthy

THE UNIMPORTANCE OF BEING OSCAR

ONE OF Oscar Wilde's acquaintances wrote of him that he could never be quite a gentleman because he dressed too well and his manners were too polished. The same criticism can be made of his art. There is something *outré* in all of Wilde's work that makes one sympathize to a degree with the Marquess of Queensberry; this fellow is really insufferable. Oscar's real sin (and the one for which society punished him, homosexuality being merely the blotter charge) was making himself too much at home. This is as readily seen in his comedies as in his epigrammatic indorsement of socialism or his call on a Colorado coal mine. He was overly familiar with his subjects. Shaw said of him that he did not know enough about art to justify his parade of aestheticism. Certainly, he was not intimate enough with poverty to style himself an enemy of riches. In this light, the Marquess of Queensberry's libel, that he went about "posing" as a sodomist, speaks, in the plain man's language, the true word of damnation. In his comedies, it is his audience whose acquaintance he presumes on. Where the usual work of art invites the spectator into its world, already furnished and habitable, Wilde's plays do just the opposite: the author invites himself and his fast opinions into the world of the spectator. He ensconces himself with intolerable freedom and always outstays his sufferance—the trouble with Wilde's wit is that it does not recognize when the party is over. The effect of this effrontery is provoking in both senses; the outrageous has its own monotony, and insolence can only strike once.

In *The Importance of Being Earnest* (Royale Theatre), the tedium is concentrated in the second act, where two young ladies are rude to each other over tea and cake, and two young gentlemen follow them being selfish about the muffins. The joke of gluttony and the joke of rudeness (which are really the same one, for heartlessness

Reprinted from *Theatre Chronicles 1937–1962* by Mary McCarthy, by permission of Farrar, Straus & Company, Inc. Copyright © 1947, 1956, 1963 by Mary McCarthy. Reprinted also by permission of William Heinemann, Ltd.

is the basic pleasantry) have been exhausted in the first act: nothing can be said by the muffin that has not already been said by the cucumber sandwich. The thin little joke that remains, the importance of the name Ernest for matrimony, is in its visible aspects insufficiently entertaining. That the joke about the name Ernest is doubtless a private one makes it less endurable to the audience, which is pointedly left out of the fun. To the bisexual man, it was perhaps deliciously comic that a man should have one name, the tamest in English, for his wife and female relations, and another for his male friends, for trips and "lost" week ends; but Wilde was a prude—he went to law to clear his character—and the antisocial jibe dwindles on the stage to a refined and incomprehensible titter.

Yet, in spite of the exhausting triviality of the second act, *The Importance of Being Earnest* is Wilde's most original play. It has the character of a ferocious idyl. Here, for the first time, the subject of Wilde's comedy coincides with its climate; there is no more pretense of emotion. The unwed mother, his stock "serious" heroine, here becomes a stock joke—"Shall there be a different standard for women than for men?" cries Mr. Jack Worthing, flinging himself on the governess, Miss Prism, who had checked him accidentally in a valise at a railroad station twenty-five years before. In *The Importance of Being Earnest* the title is a *blague,* and virtue disappears from the Wilde stage, as though jerked off by one of those hooks that were used in the old days of vaudeville to remove an unsuccessful performer. Depravity is the hero and the only character, the people on the stage embodying various shades of it. It is deepest dyed in the pastoral region of respectability and innocence. The London *roué* is artless simplicity itself beside the dreadnought society dowager, and she, in her turn, is out-brazened by her debutante daughter, and she by the country miss, and she by her spectacled governess, till finally the village rector with his clerical clothes, his vow of celibacy, and his sermon on the manna, adjustable to all occasions, slithers noiselessly into the rose garden, specious as the Serpent Himself.

The formula of this humor is the same as that of the detective story: the culprit is the man with the most guileless appearance. Normal expectations are methodically inverted, and the structure of the play is the simple structure of the paradox. Like the detective story, like the paradox, this play is a shocker. It is pure sport of the mind, and hence very nearly "English." The clergyman is the fox; the governess the vixen; and the young bloods are out for the kill. Humanitarian considerations are out of place here; they belong to the middle class. Insensibility is the comic "vice" of the characters; it is also their charm and badge of prestige. Selfishness and servility are the moral alternatives presented; the sinister impression made by the governess and the rector comes partly from their rectitude and partly from their menial demeanor. Algernon Moncrieff and Cecily Cardew are, taken by themselves, unendurable; the meeching Dr. Chasuble, however, justifies their way of life by affording a comparison—it is better to be cruel than craven.

Written on the brink of his fall, *The Importance of Being Earnest* is Wilde's true *De Profundis*; the other was false sentiment. This is hell, and if a great deal of it is tiresome, eternity is, as M. Sartre says, a bore. The tone of the Wilde dialogue, inappropriate to the problem drama, perfectly reflects conditions in this infernal Arcadia; peevish, fretful, valetudinarian, it is the tone of an elderly recluse who lives imprisoned by his comforts; it combines the finicky and the greedy, like a piggish old lady.

Fortunately, however, for everyone, there is a goddess in the play. The great lumbering dowager, Lady Augusta Bracknell, traveling to the country in a luggage-train, is the only character thick and rudimentary enough to be genuinely well-born. Possibly because of her birth, she has a certain Olympian freedom. When she is on the stage —during the first and the third acts—the play opens up. The epigram, which might be defined as the *desire* to say something witty, falters before her majesty. Her own rumbling speech is unpredictable; anything may come out of her. Where the other characters are hard as nails, Lady Augusta is rock. She is so insensitive that the spoken word reaches her slowly, from an immeasurable distance, as if she were deaf. Into this splendid creation, Wilde surely put all the feelings of admiration and despair aroused in him by Respectability. This citadel of the arbitrary was for him the Castle; he remarked, in his later years, that he would have been glad to marry Queen Victoria. Lady Augusta is the one character he could ever really imagine, partly, no doubt, because she could not imagine *him*. Her effrontery surpasses his by being perfectly unconscious; she cannot impose on the audience for she does not know they are there. She is named, oddly enough, after Bracknell, the country address of the Marchioness of Queensberry, where Wilde, as it turned out, was less at home than he fancied. The irony of the pastoral setting was apparently not lost on the Marquess of Queensberry, who arrived at the first night with a bunch of turnips and carrots.

herbert coston

SEAN O'CASEY: PRELUDE TO PLAYWRITING

I

DURING HIS years in Ireland Sean O'Casey's development progressed by a series of rejections. He was born into an ugly, often hostile world, and was precluded from an ordinary education and normal social contacts by weak eyes. He therefore drew into himself, finding in books both a solace and a weapon. Armed with knowledge, he later turned angrily to face the society which had forced the misery and humiliation of poverty upon him, violently rejecting and rebelling against it. At first he identified his grievances with the woes of "poor oul' Ireland"; but his experience as a laborer and unionist convinced him that the Nationalists, to whom he had given himself, wanted only to redeem Ireland for the middle class. Widened sympathies then led him to reject in turn the cause of "Irish Ireland," and to embrace the ideals of socialism. But when compromise and mediocrity threatened these ideals, he scorned the Irish labor movement, denouncing its leaders as philistines, and cast his whole hope on the day when the workers, triumphant, would realize a richer life. By the early 1920's his philosophic and political position had almost isolated him in Dublin, but he took heart in the victories of the Russian Bolsheviks, and, rejoicing, felt more confident than ever that the workers' day of glory would come. In the marching of the Red Armies he heard echoes of the workers' army that he had known, as it tramped through the streets of Dublin in 1913.

The course of his life in Dublin during his forty-six years there was filled with terrible difficulties, and disillusionment faced each new turning. He was forced to make his own way, and it was one that led him, eventually, out of Ireland. Yet by 1926, when he moved to England, he had achieved a synthesis of his experience that enabled him to go forth, not as a disconsolate exile, but as an older pioneer in search of more promising and congenial surroundings. With a stockpile of impressions and ideas, the raw material of his later work, he

From the *Tulane Drama Review*, September, 1960, pp. 102–112. Reprinted with the permission of the *Tulane Drama Review*.

set out to discover better working conditions and more personal happiness than he had found in Dublin. When he sailed that year he had many reasons for bitterness toward Ireland, but he could not blame her for depriving him of happiness, because from his beginning she had never offered him much anyway.

The last of thirteen children, eight of whom had died in infancy, John Casey (as he was christened) was born in 1880. His family lived in the North City, one of those sections of Dublin which, with the political and economic decline of the capital after mid-century, soon reflected its moribund state in slums and social decay. Those that survived infancy were still quite likely to be killed by tuberculosis— as were two of the five Casey children—but if, as luck would have it, they were missed by the major diseases, they could then look forward to a life of manual labor or clerical routine, surrounded at home in their foul tenements by unhappy wives and children they could ill afford and solaced by the Church or Irish whisky. The small miracle of O'Casey's escaping early death or a death-in-life was largely due to the determined courage and good humor of his mother, who made his home, nursed and cheered him for almost forty years. Their relationship was necessarily a close one, for an ulcerous condition of the eyes, contracted when he was very young, required frequent care and prevented his attending school. He had to rely on himself for his education, and the process was slow and erratic; despite the fact that poverty forced him to begin work at the age of about fourteen, he nevertheless managed to graduate from adventure stories to the Bible and Irish history, driven, perhaps, by a desire to emulate his late father, who had been a great reader, and by a need to assert himself in a world of authority and older brothers.

Growing awareness of his own and his country's condition then came to submerge, for some years, the interest in literature and general knowledge that he had developed. He was later to combine, in a Ruskinian fashion, his enthusiasm for culture and for social reform, but the two decades before 1915 found him intensely committed first to Irish nationalism and then to the cause of labor. In the 1890's Dr. Douglas Hyde's Gaelic League was making Irish history a topical subject, and hundreds of young men, thrilled by the challenge, were struggling fervently to arouse their torpid nation. In the Drumcondra Branch of the League, young O'Casey worked with a passion that surprised even the most devoted. He organized meetings, made speeches about the Gaelic Ideal, taught Irish, and proseletyzed for the movement, denying himself rest, fusing his destiny with that of Cathleen ni Houlihan.

Only gradually did he become aware that there were within him forces that would cause him to break with the nationalists and that his rebellion against the poverty and human misery around him, one of the factors that had led him to count himself one of the "Irish Irelanders," would bring him later to reject their ideals. What he was beginning to realize was that the Gaelic Ideal could mean little to the badly paid laborers with whom he worked, for to these men, who were scraping through their lives on a paltry wage of fifteen to twenty shillings a week, "the problem of havin' enough to eat [was] of more importance than of havin' a little Irish to speak." And it became clear to him that the members of the Gaelic League, wrapped in the glories of Ireland's past and warmed by their hatred for the English, were giving little thought to current working class misery. For O'Casey the matter came to a head during the great Dublin strike of 1913.

As a member of Jim Larkin's Irish Transport and General Workers' Union, O'Casey had been, for several years, more of a cautious sympathizer than an active unionist. But the fundamental rights which were at stake in the strike won his complete sympathy, and when his nationalist friends in the Irish Republican Brotherhood ignored his appeal for support, he abruptly severed his connections with them and made a new spiritual home for himself at Liberty Hall, where he became one of Jim Larkin's lieutenants, committing himself to the union with a passion more than equal to that with which he had served the cause of Ireland.

In 1914, trouble lay ahead and trouble was at hand. In the north loyalists armed to fight for their status as Britons; in the south nationalists, the burning vision of revolution in their minds, were preparing to fight to be Irish; and the Dublin transport workers, abused by the police as well as by their employers, were arming to safeguard the rights they had gained. The union had organized its own militia, the Irish Citizen Army, and O'Casey, one of the founders, served as its secretary for about six months in 1914. He drafted their constitution (which avowed that "the ownership of Ireland, moral and material, is vested of right in the people of Ireland"), and zealously carried out his duties, particularly that of protecting the integrity of the Army as an independent force. Mistrusting the motives of the nationalists, he vigorously fought against coalition with them, despite the attraction of the prestige and superior resources of their Volunteer militia. The Citizen Army, he maintained, must serve the workers first.

Like Ireland, O'Casey was being unconsciously propelled to independence. As forces about him swirled forward to the bloody Rising of Easter Week, 1916, they were brought into collision with the inflexible position he had taken on the role of the Citizen Army. The result was that O'Casey was deflected into a kind of political limbo, and the nationalist forces were strengthened. After fighting with the Citizen Army Council, O'Casey was rebuked by Larkin, and he resigned. Thus, though still a member of the union, he had cut himself off from its principal activity, and when his friends in the Citizen Army and the Volunteers strolled out to fight the British Army on Easter Monday, 1916, there was no question of his joining them, even had he been physically able to do so.

The price of independence was isolation, but the severance of his political ties freed him to find a new identity, for as a detached veteran, he was in a position to observe, review, and analyze the maelstrom of Irish life and to slowly distill within himself those qualities that would make him an artist. Clearly his new freedom was precious to him, for after his mother's death in 1919, he suddenly moved away from his disorderly and demanding relatives, holing himself up in a small tenement room to read, think, write, and begin a new life. Exulting in the truth of his new existence, he proclaimed that "self-realization is more important than class-consciousness," and, as he scanned from a distance the union that he had once loved, now fallen into mediocrity under new leaders, he was moved to say, "Trade Unionism may give the worker a larger dinner plate—which, heaven knows, he badly needs—but it will never give him a broader mind, which he needs more badly still."

Though a life in art was to be not quite the ideal existence that he had imagined (he would be bruised and scarred by squabbles and disappointments in the years to come), in the early 1920's he eagerly assumed the artist's role, for it meant to him not simply an opportunity for personal expression and recognition, but a way to bring order out of chaos, to reduce to essence the many experiences and questions that sprawled in his mind, and to assert the social truths that he knew. The themes of his drama lay already in his mind; his characters lived all around him; he needed only to be made aware of the dramatic possibilities of the material that he had at hand. This awareness was brought about, as we shall see, in a rather odd way after he had submitted his first plays to the Abbey Theatre.

II

O'Casey's first literary efforts, which he contributed to the "Manuscript Journal" of the Drumcondra Gaelic League about 1907, were slight pieces designed to entertain a homogeneous group of friends. Read aloud at the weekly meetings, they were, however, quite popular with the League's members, for they contained a unique blend of farce and satire. The stories concerned his alleged brother "Aloysius

Caisey [sic]," a bumbling snob inevitably tripped up by his own stupidity on every critical occasion. Aside from the rough humor of the farcical situations the Gaelic Leaguers enjoyed the demolition of social pretensions, for to them high society and social formality were associated with the despised English aristocracy. Though these early attempts can claim only passing interest, it is worth noting that the technique of blending farce and satire, which O'Casey was later to employ in many plays, was the first to appeal to him when he began to write for an audience.

An account of the blundering construction and re-construction of a "cattle bank" on the Great Northern Railway, which appeared in the union's *Irish Worker* in 1912, again exemplifies O'Casey's predilection for the weapon of farce. Here the style, as throughout his other four articles on the company's inefficiency, is loose and rambling, but the following passage, in its vividness and distinctly farcical quality, anticipates much of O'Casey's later comedy:

> It was always an exciting time on a market day when the cattle would arrive for transit from Dublin to Belfast. Then would it become a scene reminiscent of a disorderly retreat on the part of a defeated army. Everything was in confusion; running hither and thither; carts, drays, lorries, floats, horses, men, cattle, sheep, and pigs inextricably mixed together! Carters shouting for their waggons and inquiring in forcible tones from the two heartworn and harrassed checkers if they were going to be kept there all night; the checkers calling a carter to come on in an irritable manner, or cursing a dray up to the "other end of the bank"; and, louder than all, clear and unmistakable, the imprecations, full and free, of the long-suffering cattle drovers. It was chaos gone mad.

But most of the anecdotes and reminiscences in this series, clothed in heavy irony to illustrate corruption, incompetence, and labor abuses, are somewhat disjointed; they seem to comprise a rather self-conscious and diffuse attack upon the entire Great Northern Railway Company. Oddly out of place in the pages of the *Irish Worker,* they are related to its other content only by their attitude of indignation. Their lofty tone and the attempted (though unsuccessful) restraint in style are to be contrasted with the more natural, free-swinging qualities of the prose that O'Casey wrote during his dispute with "Euchan," which was going on at the same time.

An article by "Euchan" in the *Irish Worker* had, O'Casey believed, slighted the Gaelic Ideal, and he threw down his gauntlet with startling vehemence: "The Gael is here still, Euchan, stronger to suffer than hell can harm. . . . So, Euchan, you sneer. . . . It's not the

first sneer that winked at the Gael from the face of 'The Worker.' "
Pounding home his points in alliterative rhythms, O'Casey here manifests that peculiar belligerence which is characteristic of much of his
later disputatious writing; as he harangues his opponent, he seems
to long for the less restricted atmosphere of a public debate. Some
passages, indeed, are pure oratory. Consider, for instance, this paragraph which concludes one of his attacks:

> The delivery of Ireland is not in the Labour Manifesto, good and
> salutary as it may be, but in the strength, beauty, nobility and imagi-
> nation of the Gaelic Ideal. I am one of those who declare—by the
> fame of our forefathers; by the murder of Red Hugh; by the anguished
> sighs of the Geraldine; by the blood-dripping wounds of Wolfe Tone;
> by the noble blood of Emmet; by the death-wasted bodies of the
> famine, that we will enter into our inheritance or will fall one by one.

One imagines cheering.

But not all of O'Casey's literary activities in these years were
concerned with exposé and argument. About 1916 he began to write
"songs"—verses to be sung to well-known melodies—for the amusement of friends and brief verses for his own greeting cards. The
following year he was engaged by Fergus O'Connor, a Dublin publisher who was mainly interested in "songs" and in "Heart-to-Heart,
Personal, Sincere, Irish, Homely, Greetings." O'Casey confessed that
he "didn't care a lot for the job," finding it "most difficult to write to
order," but since O'Connor occasionally published serious patriotic
material this connection, which marked the beginning of O'Casey's
career as a professional writer, eventually led to more interesting
opportunities.

O'Casey's *Songs of the Wren* were published in 1918. In the
popular tradition, they are accurately described on the cover as
"Humorous and Sentimental," and are not worth so much attention
as his two "laments" for Thomas Ashe and a booklet, *The Sacrifice
of Thomas Ashe*, which were brought out the same year. Since the
latter are unquestionably sincere efforts, they afford us a measurement
of O'Casey's literary abilities at this time, just five years before the
composition of *Shadow of a Gunman*. In the "laments" the poetic
devices are hackneyed and alliteration is heavy: "The children of
Eireann are listening again / To Death [*sic*] sullen, sad, somber, beat
of the Drum. . . ." And metaphor is tortured:

> The breasts of the mountains with anger are heaving,
> Swift rivers of tears down their rugged cheeks flow;
> Their mantle of heather the wild wind is reaving
> And their proud heads are capp'd with a storm cloud of woe.

However, in *The Sacrifice of Thomas Ashe*, freed from the stale poetic devices and restrictions which surrounded his attempts in verse, O'Casey begins to develop a mode of lyric expression that he could not approach in poetry *per se*. Consider, for instance, the following paragraph from his "Forward":

> The Irish Language opened to [Thomas Ashe] the inner, secret and enchanted recesses of the Irish nature, and he understood Ireland as none but an Irish speaker can understand Her. With the passing of boyhood's years his broad heart became broader as it opened to receive the desire of freedom for his native land—desire that was nourished by the lessons taught by the sweep of the Kerry skies, the boldness of the Kerry mountains, and the untrammelled surge of the sea on the Kerry coast. And nature went on, adding strength to the body, culture to the mind and grace to the soul, so that in years to follow the whole man became a rich and ripe sacrifice for the Cause of Human Freedom and for the Cause of Ireland.

If one can ignore the rather startling and grotesque imagery, he can discern in this passage the inception of O'Casey's lyrical prose. Here the parallel phrases, the repetition of particular words, are designed to create a rolling cumulative effect which builds towards a climax in the last sentence. But the overall quality of the prose is not necessarily enhanced by this rhythmic phrasing; the repeated or alliterated word is not a significant one, the phrases in parallel are not meaningful singly and in their relationship, and these words and phrases are not maintained in a balanced contrapuntal function: as a result, only a monotonous pounding and meaningless accentuation is achieved. The noun "Kerry," for instance, which is repeated, is not a significant word in its context, and the repetition, therefore, is devoid of emotional impact. A similar earlier example is to be found in that part of the "Euchan" dispute in which O'Casey swears "by the fame of our fore-fathers; by the murder of Red Hugh; by the anguished sighs . . ." etc. Here the parallelism is at the service of unvarnished political rant.

Still other features of O'Casey's early writing are apparent in his *Story of the Irish Citizen Army* (1919), the longest work of this period, as, in several sections of his booklet, he deviates from his factual account, unable to resist the urge to break into a more colorful narrative, to heighten descriptions by figures of speech and the use of a dramatic, historical present tense. Summing up in his "After-word," he envisions "the seeds of a new life" which is blazing in Ireland, and continues:

> Parliamentarianism was a sinking fire, and, now, not all the united breath of a united party could ever again succeed in blowing it into an

inspiring flame. The new wine of new thoughts and new activities was everywhere bursting the old bottles, but though the wine has a Sinn Fein label it certainly has not an absolutely Sinn Fein flavor, for Labour has tinged it with a brighter colour and strengthened it with a stimulating cordial.

And O'Casey still adds to this plethora of unhinged metaphors as he goes on to liken the "lowly life" of Sheehy-Skeffington, whom he apotheosizes as "the first martyr to Irish socialism," to a "pearl" dissolved in the "wine." His ideas were "like the tiny mustard seed" that would grow into a tree that will afford shade and rest to many souls overheated with the stress and toil of barren politics; his "beautiful nature," we learn, was consumed in "the blazing pyre of national differences"; and he was, finally, "the ripest ear of corn that fell in Easter Week." Clearly O'Casey is not writing history here: he is composing an elegy. These layers of metaphor are not intended simply to elaborate some point of fact; their piling up is not accidental. One after the other—loosely, incongruously, one admits—they are laid in place around the central idea of destruction-procreation. The crudity of the result points to uncertainty and experiment, but here, as in *The Sacrifice of Thomas Ashe*, we note the attempt to write a lyric prose—and it is this tendency rather than the actual quality of the writing that is of primary interest.

In these excerpts from Chapter I, "The Founding of the Citizen Army," there is a description that is different in style but allied in spirit:

> Discontent had lighted a blazing camp-fire in Dublin. The ruddy light of the flame was reflected by an earnest and ominous glow in the face of every Dublin worker. Men, full of the fire of battle, thronged in dense masses the wide, expansive area facing Liberty Hall. The city was surging with a passion full, daring, and fiercely expectant; a passion strange enjoyable, which it has never felt before with such intensity and emotion. . . . .
> Suddenly the window is raised, and the tense, anxious feelings of the men crowded together burst out into an enthusiastic and full-throated cheer that shatters the surrounding air, and sends up into the skies a screaming flock of gulls that had been peacefully drifting along the sombre surface of the River Liffey.

This last is one of the most effective and original passages in the book. At the climax the tedious adjectives are forsaken and our attention is directed to a detail—the startled gulls—that instantly brings the scene to life. O'Casey briefly realizes his intention of communicating the intensity, the excitement of the experience. Too often, however, multiple adjectives and pseudo-poetic devices as, "The disappearing Artist Sun had boldly brushed the skies with bold hues of orange and crimson . . . ," or "Hope's ruddy flame was leaping in their hearts . . . ," inject a self-conscious, "literary" tone and crush his attempts; yet this writing, for all its faults, constitutes an effort to dramatize his material, to make it vivid. Here, as in O'Casey's other early writing, these deviations, almost bizarre sometimes in their context, make his work very uneven, indicating not only that his style is unsettled, but that he is uncomfortable in straight-forward narration. He must, it seems, filter his material through his personality: if it is organized by his intelligence, it must be colored by his consciousness as well. The constant tendency throughout is towards interpretation, dramatic heightening and highlighting of particular scenes, and toward the establishment of an emotional as well as an intellectual contact with his reader.

In the last few pages we have discussed those stylistic techniques which either elaborated this inclination or defeated it; and we have noticed that although none of this early work is of any notable literary merit, certain of its features foreshadow the rhythm and lyricism of O'Casey's later prose and reveal a dramatist's method and sensibility.

Just as the dialogue of his plays will reflect the language of lower-class Dublin that O'Casey spoke and heard, so the style of these early works is imbued with the rhetoric of the oratory which he had practiced and listened to for so long. His first impulse when a dispute arose was not to conduct a running literary battle, but to take up the issue with his opponent face to face in public debate, just as he had wanted to do during his controversy with "Euchan." There can be little doubt that years of training in an emphatic, flamboyant type of oratory made it natural, indeed almost unavoidable, that he duplicate its characteristic alliteration, parallelism, and reiteration in his first prose. It was a style, certainly, that was better suited to most of his needs at the time than verse forms as he knew them or a manner more restrained and precise; but it was not until he turned to writing plays that he was able to give expression to truth and deep feelings without sounding affected or pseudo-literary. Only by tapping the idiom of his daily speech was he able to express his profound concern for humanity.

III

As O'Casey's years of devotion to political and economic reforms might lead one to expect, the early plays that he wrote were, with one notable exception, portraits of social confusion and political conflict. They were, in fact, plainly didactic. It was not until a critic's chance remark shook him from his self-appointed task of prophecy and reform that he began to seek, by a distillation of his experience, to resolve some of the paradoxes that Irish life seemed to pose. Curiously enough, *Shadow of a Gunman,* which he began in 1922, was to bear more resemblance, in its half-tones and ironies, to a play that he had composed twenty years before than to the weighty dramas over which he had recently labored.

This first play, *The Frost in the Flower,* written for the Drama Club of the O'Toole Pipers about 1910–12, was never produced, since its presentation would have greatly embarrassed one of the members, upon whose recent experience it was based. The man was a teacher at St. Laurence O'Toole's Parish School who had, on a chance, applied for a better paying job that was open in a larger school. To his surprise and dismay he was accepted for the position; but being timid and unsure of himself, though he was apparently quite competent, he became frightened at the thought of the challenge which the job offered and finally refused it.

Although O'Casey's one-act play about his hesitant friend is one of those early works not extant for study, a few interesting observations can be made on the basis of accounts of it. The play began in the middle of a party which was being held to celebrate the new job and ended with the young man's agonized confession that he had decided not to take it. This ironic use of a festive occasion was to be paralleled in *Juno and the Paycock* and *The Silver Tassie;* but it is more important to note that at this early stage in his development O'Casey shows himself interested in the interplay of character and situation. The instance of this play affords some hint of the sensibility that lay for the most part dormant, neglected, during O'Casey's years of intense political activity.

About 1919–20 (just after he had moved away from his relatives), O'Casey submitted *The Frost in the Flower* to the Abbey. It was rejected, but with the comment, "not far from being a good play."

Encouraged, he went on to write a second, *The Harvest Festival,* which, in his own words,

> . . . dealt with the efforts of militant members of the unskilled unions to put more of the fibre of resistance to evil conditions of pay and life into the hearts and minds of the members of the craft unions whose gospel was that what was good enough for the fathers was good enough for the sons. The action took place in the busy preparations made by a church for holding the annual harvest festival. . . .

This play too was returned by the Abbey, the comment being "well conceived, but badly executed."

Lennox Robinson had read the first two plays and rejected them, but he considered O'Casey's third play, *The Crimson in the Tri-Colour,* good enough to send on to Lady Gregory, who recorded in her diary for November 5, 1921, "I read and wrote a long note on an interesting play, *The Crimson in the Tri-Colour,* the antagonism sure to break out between Labour and Sinn Fein, and sent it [the note] to Robinson." Five days later O'Casey came to see her about it. She praised some aspects of the play and told him, "Mr. Casey, your gift is characterisation." Regarding a production of the play, she could only say that, "we could not in any case put it on now, as it might weaken the Sinn Fein position, to show that Labour is ready to attack it. . . ." A few years later she told him, "I was inclined to put it on because some of it was so good and I thought you might learn by seeing it on the stage, though some was very poor, but Mr. Yeats was firm." Yeats had not thought much of the play and later reflected, "Casey was bad in writing of the vices of the rich, which he knows nothing about, but he thoroughly understands the vices of the poor." Lady Gregory quotes O'Casey himself as saying, in March, 1924, "You were right not to put it on. I can't read it myself now." It is interesting to compare this comment with the statement in his autobiography that "It was years after, when he had left Ireland forever, that bitterness, mingled with scorn, overtook him, for he began to realise that the plays refused by the Abbey Theatre were a lot better than many they had welcomed, and had played on to their stage with drums and colours."

In the early 1920's, however, O'Casey's faith in the judgment of the Abbey directors was complete, and he took to heart Lady Gregory's observation that his gift lay in characterization. As we shall see, his interview with her was to mark a turning point in his career. "Thereafter," he said, "I threw over my theories and worked at characters. . . ." Two of his first three plays, we may note, were heavy with political content: they were, in short, labor plays. Therefore the "theories" that O'Casey threw over in his playwriting were those that he held about the role of labor and its relation to Sinn Fein, the ruling nationalist party. Believing his ideas to be "pregnant with truth and foreknowledge," he had constructed plays to bear his message abroad, creating character and situation to demonstrate his convictions. He had confused art with propaganda.

When he set himself to concentrating upon characterization, he turned for firm footing to immediate experiences and the people he knew, just as he had in *The Frost and the Flower,* his first attempt. Clearly his redirected efforts could have resulted in non-dramatic character sketches, in the vitiation of the central action for the sake of character details; but he had absorbed a basic knowledge of dramaturgy through some theatrical experience with his brother Archie when he was young and through his subsequent play reading, and it guided his efforts securely around this hazard.

On several occasions O'Casey has indicated that one of his principal masters in dramatic technique was Dion Boucicault, whose melodramas were often staged in Great Britain and America throughout the last half of the nineteenth century. Yet in truth Lacy, Robertson, or any one of many other competent theatre writers of the period could have served him as well, for Boucicault could claim only a few minor variations on the weary themes of melodrama and none in technique. But if Boucicault was not an innovator, at least he was a sure and successful craftsman, and the violent, grandiose action of such plays as *The Coleen Bawn* and *The Octoroom* served to impress upon young O'Casey the dynamic qualities of drama and taught him the rudiments of traditional dramatic writing and stage action, so that when he later came to write plays, the form was one with which he was thoroughly familiar.

In 1922 the material of drama lay close at hand—closer than he had suspected—for the times that O'Casey lived through were violent ones. The country was convulsed by rebellion, repression, terror, civil war; and the nation's raw wounds tormented every Irishman. The true drama, however, was not in the fighting itself, nor even in the struggle of ideals that it reflected: it was, rather, in the conflict which was precipitated among friends, in families, and in the mind of the individual man.

In being referred to "characterisation," O'Casey was brought from reform to the individual, from the idea to the man. He knew his characters and their problems, for he had suffered as they had. Sifting his experience, looking about him, he found courage amidst cowardice, laughter near tragedy, and human dignity surviving in squalor. With love and indignation O'Casey turned to his art: the dramatist was ready to begin.

kenneth tynan

BERTOLT BRECHT

WRITTEN JUST after the 1929 unpleasantness, Brecht's [SAINT JOAN OF THE STOCKYARDS] is a bitter attempt to illustrate the interdependence of capitalism and religion, or—to put it more precisely—of profiteering and charity. It revolves around the friendship between Pierpont Mauler, a sentimental Chicago meat king, and a Salvation Army girl named Joan Dark. Warmed at first by Mauler's private good-heartedness, Joan slowly discovers that in an economic pinch he will go to any lengths to safeguard his profits, whereafter she realizes that by distributing soup and moral sustenance to the poor she is not alleviating hardship but accepting it as an immutable fact of life, and therefore encouraging its perpetuation. With this message on her lips, she returns to the mission hall, which Mauler and his friends have equipped with a gaudy new golden-piped organ. But her voice is drowned by the choir; exhausted by tramping the winter streets, she collapses and dies, and is thereupon hailed by the meat king's spokesman as "a fighter, and a sacrifice in the service of God." As a portrait of Chicago, the play is less than convincing, but as a satire on the relationship between those who take and those who give, its pungency is tremendous; it was by far the most successful show of the Hamburg season.

Wherever you go in Germany, Brecht is inescapable. Frankfurt, which has staged five Brecht plays since 1952, added a sixth last spring, to critical applause so tumultuous that it made half a column in the *New York Times*. The occasion was the West German *première* of Schweik in the Second World War, Brecht's version of the adventures that might have befallen Jaroslav Hašek's Good Soldier had he been conscripted by the Nazis to fight against Russia. Schweik, the beaming innocent who makes authority look most foolish when most he seems to embrace it, had an abiding appeal for Brecht, who once said that Hašek's book was one of the three literary works of this century most likely to become classics. In Brecht's play, as Schweik blunders into the Army and toward Stalingrad, the action is constantly interrupted by Hitler and his lieutenants, on a platform high above the stage; the Führer persistently, and pathetically, inquires whether Schweik, the little man, still loves him, because without the love of the little man he cannot go on. Finally, Schweik rejects his advances with unctuous obscenity. Although it is embellished with some of the loveliest lyrics Brecht ever wrote, the text is rough, acid, and brutally contemptuous of Nazi sympathizers. The night I was there, the Frankfurt audience cheered it.

The ubiquity and the influence of Brecht have been growing ever since his death, three years ago, at the age of fifty-eight. In the 1957–8 season he set a record; for the first time in the history of the German theatre a contemporary native playwright was among the four dramatists whose works were most often performed in the German-speaking countries. Shakespeare, as always, came first, with 2,674 performances, and he was followed by Schiller, with 2,000; Goethe, with 1,200; and Brecht, with 1,120. (Molière, Shaw, and Hauptmann, in that order, were the runners-up.) It is doubtful whether any dramatist in history has made a greater impact on his own country in his own era than this stubby, ribald Marxist, who spent his mature creative years—from 1933 to 1948—away from home, exiled and almost penniless, first in Scandinavia and then in the United States.

I have paid many visits to Brecht's Berliner Ensemble in the five years since it took up residence at the Theater am Schiffbauerdamm, but whenever I approach the place, I still feel a *frisson* of expectation, an anticipatory lift, that no other theatre evokes. Western taxis charge double to go East, since they are unlikely to pick up a returning fare, but the trip is worth it: the arrow-straight drive up to the grandiose, bullet-chipped pillars of the Brandenburg Gate, the perfunctory salutes of the guards on both sides of the frontier; the short sally past the skinny trees and bland neo-classical façades of Unter den Linden (surely the emptiest of the world's great streets), and the left turn that leads you across the meagre, oily stream of the Spree and into the square-*cum*-parking-lot where the theatre stands, with a circular neon sign—"BERLINER ENSEMBLE"—revolving on its roof like a sluggish weather vane. You enter an unimposing foyer, present your ticket, buy a superbly designed programme, and take your seat in an auditorium that is encrusted with gilt cupids and cushioned in plush. When the curtain, adorned with its Picasso dove, goes up, one is usually shocked, so abrupt is the contrast between the baroque prettiness of the house and the chaste, stripped beauty of what one sees on the expanses, relatively enormous, of the stage. No attempt is made at realistic illusion. Instead of being absorbed by a slice of life, we are sitting in a theatre while a group of actors tell us a story that happened some time ago. By means of songs, and captions projected on to a screen, Brecht explains what conclusions he draws from the tale, but he wants us to quarrel with him—to argue that this scene need not have ended as it did, or that this character might have behaved otherwise. He detested the reverence of most theatre audiences, much preferring the detached, critical expertise that he noted in spectators at sporting events. Theatrical trickery, such as lighting and scene changes, should not, he felt, be concealed from the customer. In his own words,

> . . . don't show him too much
> But show something. And let him observe
> That this is not magic but
> Work, my friends.

Always, as a director, he told his actors that the mere fact of passing through a stage door did not make them separate, sanctified creatures cut off from the mass of humanity—hence his practice, which is still followed to some extent by the Ensemble, of allowing outsiders to wander into rehearsals, as long as they kept quiet. He abhorred the idea that the production of plays is a secret, holy business, like the nurture of some rare hothouse plant. If actors can spend their spare time watching ditchdiggers, he said, why shouldn't ditchdiggers watch actors? Initially, the Ensemble actors were embarrassed by this open-door policy; later, however, they realized how much it had helped them to shed inhibitions. A cast that has rehearsed for weeks before strangers is unlikely to dread an opening night.

I arrived at the theatre this year during a rehearsal, and one that was loaded with nostalgia. *The Threepenny Opera*, Brecht's first decisive success, was being prepared for revival on the same stage that had seen its *première* thirty-one years earlier, with the same director in charge—Erich Engel, now looking gaunt and unwell, despite the jaunty cocksureness of his beret. As I entered, somebody was singing "Mack the Knife" with the tinny, nasal vibrato that one remembers from the old Telefunken records. Engel and two young assistants interrupted from time to time, talking with the easy, probing frankness that comes of no haste, no pressure, no need to worry about publicity, deadlines, or out-of-town reviews. I noticed that Mr. Peachum, a part usually given to a rubicund butterball, was being played by Norbert Christian, a slim soft-eyed actor in his thirties. Brecht, I reflected, would have liked that; he always detested physical type-casting. In Brecht's theatre it is what people do, not what they feel or how they look, that counts. Action takes precedence over emotion, fact over fantasy. *"Die Wahrheit ist konkret"* ("Truth is concrete") was Brecht's favourite maxim; for him there could be no such thing as abstract truth. Somebody once asked him what the purpose of a good play ought to be. He answered by describing a photograph he had seen in a magazine, a double-page spread of Tokyo after the earthquake. Amid the devastation, one building remained upright. The caption consisted of two words: "Steel Stood." That, said Brecht, was the purpose of drama—to teach us how to survive.

The rehearsal continued, the patient denuding process that would ultimately achieve the naked simplicity and directness on which the Ensemble prides itself. To encourage the players to look at themselves objectively, a large mirror had been placed in the footlights, and throughout the session photographers were taking pictures of everything that happened, providing a visual record that would afterward be used to point out to the actors just where, and how, they had gone wrong. One of the most impressive women alive had meanwhile come to sit beside me—Helene Weigel, Brecht's widow, who has directed the Ensemble since its inception ten years ago and plays several of the leading roles. At sixty, she has a lean, nut-brown face that suggests, with its high cheekbones, shrewdly hooded eyes, and total absence of make-up, a certain kind of Spanish peasant matriarch; her whole manner implies a long life of commanding and comforting, of which she clearly regrets not an instant. Her warmth is adventurous, her honesty contagious, and her sophistication extreme, and that is the best I can do to sum up a woman who would, I think, be proud to be called worldly, since a scolding, tenacious affection for the world is the main article of her faith. The Weigel—to adopt the German manner of referring to an actress—has no real counterpart in the American theatre; in appearance, and in dedication, she resembles Martha Graham, but a Martha Graham altogether earthier and more mischievous than the one Americans know. At the end of the rehearsal we exchanged gifts and greetings. I got a scarf, designed by Picasso in the company's honour; a book about the Ensemble's seminal production, *Mother Courage*; a photographic dossier comparing the performances of Charles Laughton and Ernst Busch in the title role of Brecht's *The Life of Galileo*; and—unexpectedly—a complicated game of the do-it-yourself variety, invented by Mozart to teach children how to compose country dances by throwing dice. The Weigel, alas, got only a cigarette lighter. Talking about the state of the company, she said, "When Brecht died, I was afraid this place might become a museum." Her fears have turned out to be unjustified. It is true that the Ensemble mostly performs Brecht plays, but the plays are acted and directed by people steeped in the Brecht spirit. Throughout the theatre his ghost is alive and muscular.

Or, rather, his ghosts, because there were many different Brechts, as I discovered while reading John Willett's invaluable book *The Theatre of Bertolt Brecht* and Martin Esslin's biographical study, *Brecht: A Choice of Evils*. The early Brecht was a touchy child, with a Bavarian accent, whose father ran a paper mill in Augsburg. After serving as a medical orderly in the First World War—an experience that inspired his lifelong hatred of militarism—Brecht plunged into the German *avant-garde* of the twenties, making a name for himself as an outspoken, nihilistic poet-playwright with a gift for turning gutter idiom into poetry. In Germany, where literature had always spoken a high-flying language unknown to human tongues, this was something new; as Ernest Borneman lately remarked in the *Kenyon Review*, "There was no precedent (a) for colloquial poetry; (b) for plain storytelling. There was no German equivalent to writers like Kipling, Mark Twain, or Hemingway." Brecht was impressed by, and freely borrowed from, the work of writers as disparate as Villon, Rimbaud, Büchner, Wedekind, Shakespeare, Kipling, and Luther, and he positively welcomed the charge of plagiarism, retorting that in literature, as in life, he rejected the idea of private property. Through the mouth of Herr Keuner, an imaginary character on whom he fathered many anecdotes and aphorisms, he scoffed at authors whose egotism compelled them to exclude from their work all notions and phrases that were not of their own invention: "They know no larger buildings than those a man can build by himself." (In this respect, as in several others, Brecht resembles Picasso, who once remarked, "To copy others is necessary, but to copy oneself is pathetic." In the early Montmartre days, according to Roland Penrose's recent biography, Picasso's reading matter included Verlaine, Rimbaud, Diderot, and the adventures of Sherlock Holmes, Nick Carter, and Buffalo Bill; the same list, or one very similar, would serve for the young Brecht. In addition, both men embraced Communism, yet expressed themselves in styles that were utterly antipathetic to Socialist realism; both revolutionized the arts of their choice; and both, despite shortness of stature and slovenliness of dress, were immoderately attractive to women.)

Brecht's early manner was summed up in 1922 by the German critic Herbert Ihering:

> This language can be felt on the tongue, on the palate, in one's ears, in one's spine. . . . It is brutally sensuous and melancholically tender. It contains malice and bottomless sadness, grim wit, and plaintive lyricism.

A little later there was the Brecht who, in collaboration with Kurt Weill, revolutionized the popular musical stage with *The Three-penny Opera* and *The Rise and Fall of the City of Mahagonny*, using the rhythms and slang of a depressed urban society to lacerate Western decadence, and bringing into the "serious" theatre the sardonic street-corner poetry of post-war Berlin. Already he was moving toward the vantage point that he was to make his own—"that interesting and largely neglected area," as Mr. Willett describes it, "where ethics, politics, and economics meet." In 1926 Brecht read *Das Kapital* for the first time. Marxism supplied a corrective to his anarchic tendencies, a remedy for his disgust with the world around him, and a mental discipline that delighted his love of logic and paradox. Hence, after 1928 we get Brecht the Communist didact, writing instructional plays in a new, sparse, bony style:

> When I address you
> Cold and broadly
> In the driest terms
> Without looking at you
> (I apparently fail to recognize you,
> Your particular manner and difficulties),
>
> I address you merely
> Like reality itself
> (Sober, incorruptible, thanks to your manner,
> Tired of your difficulties),
> Which you seem to me to be disregarding.

From this period come *Die Massnahme*, an austere analysis of revolutionary self-abnegation that is, intellectually, the masterpiece of Communist drama, and *Die Mütter*, Brecht's stage adaptation of the famous Gorki novel. Both plays were savagely attacked in the Marxist press—the latter for being out of touch with working-class reality, the former because it denied the thesis that a good Communist is never torn between the claims of reason and emotion. (Brecht's failure to reconcile these rival claims accounts, in Mr. Esslin's view, for the fascinating ambiguity that runs through his work. The bald statement he wants to make and the poetry with which he makes it often pull in different directions; matter and manner are exquisitely at odds.) Like many of his Leftist contemporaries, Brecht was seeking a method whereby economic processes could be effectively dramatized; he hoped to see money and food some day displace power and sex as the drama's major themes. With most bourgeois writers, he said, "the fact that moneymaking is never the subject of their work makes one suspect that . . . it may be the object instead."

The next Brecht was the director who practised, and the theorist who preached, "Epic Theatre"—a phrase he borrowed from Erwin Piscator in the twenties and went on defining until the end of his life. This, perhaps, is the Brecht who is best known in America, thanks to the energetic proselytizing of Eric Bentley. For every American who has seen a Brecht production, there are probably a thousand who are armchair experts on the "alienation effect," the abolition of suspense, the prefacing of scenes with projected captions, the use of music not to intensify emotion but to neutralize it, the rejection of "atmospheric" lighting in favour of general illumination, and the outright ban on costumes and props that do not look worn or handled.

> Of all works, my favourite
> Are those which show usage.
> The copper vessels with bumps and dented edges,
> The knives and forks whose wooden handles are
> Worn down by many hands: such forms
> To me are the noblest.

Brecht's opposition to naturalistic acting was really, as he often insisted, a return to the older forms of popular theatre, including (the list is Mr. Esslin's) "the Elizabethan, the Chinese, Japanese, and Indian theatre, the use of the chorus in Greek tragedy, the techniques of clowns and fairground entertainers, the Austrian and Bavarian folk play, and many others." His refusal to permit actors to "identify" with their roles, and thus to create strongly individualized characters, sprang from his conviction that human identity is not fixed but infinitely mutable, dependent on particular social and economic circumstances; this is the left-wing equivalent of Pirandello's theories, at once frivolous and despondent, about the many-faceted impermanence of the human ego. What Pirandello fatalistically accepted, Brecht sought to explain. His loathing of stage emotionalism is more easily accounted for. It was a violent reaction against the bombast of the conventional German theatre. Life in a Brecht production is laid out before you as comprehensively as in a Brueghel painting, and with many of the same colours—browns, greys, and off-whites. It does not seize you by the lapel and yell secrets into your ear; humanity itself, not the romantic individualist, is what it is seeking to explore. In 1936 Brecht stated his attitude:

> The spectator of the *dramatic* theatre says: "Yes, I have felt the same. I am just like this. This is only natural. It will always be like this. This human being's suffering moves me because there is no way out for him. This is great art; it bears the mark of the inevitable. I am weeping with those who weep on the stage, laughing with those who laugh."

The spectator of the *epic* theatre says: "I should never have thought so. That is not the way to do it. This is most surprising, hardly credible. This will have to stop. This human being's suffering moves me because there would have been a way out for him. This is great art; nothing here seems inevitable. I am laughing about those who weep on the stage, weeping about those who laugh."

Nobody of any critical intelligence who is familiar with what passes for "great art" in London or New York could fail to applaud this succinct, startling, and unforgettable distinction between the audience that is all heart and nerves and the audience that tempers feeling with knowledge and observation.

Two more Brechts, and the outline is complete. One was the mellow playwright who reached the peak of his creativity in exile. Between 1937 and 1945 Brecht wrote eleven plays, among them *The Life of Galileo, Mother Courage, The Good Woman of Setzuan, Puntila* and *The Caucasian Chalk Circle*. By that time the ideological element was assumed or implied more often than it was stated. The five works I have named all deal with the tension between instinct, love, and emotion, on the one hand, and, on the other, a society that perverts or exploits all three. The church defeats Galileo by playing on his weakness for the good, sensual life. Mother Courage tries to protect her family by making money out of the Thirty Years' War, but the war, in the end, destroys her children. Shen Te, of Setzuan, finds that you cannot help those you love without injuring your neighbours. The landowner Puntila, all charity and generosity when drunk, is an efficient businessman during bouts of cold-blooded sobriety, from which, unavailingly, he begs to be delivered. In the last of the great plays, *The Caucasian Chalk Circle*, good-heartedness defeats the system. Grusha, the maid, is brought to trial for having kidnapped a high-born baby, but the judge decrees that the child belongs to her, since everything should belong to those who serve it best.

The last Brecht was the sage of East Berlin, at once the pride and the embarrassment of the Communist regime, which saw him laurelled in the West (especially at the Paris International Theatre Festivals of 1954 and 1955) and accused in Russia of being a "formalist" opponent of Socialist realism. Mr. Esslin's book goes deeply into Brecht's ambivalent relationship with the Party when he returned to Germany in 1948 after an inconclusive velitation with the Un-American Activities Committee. Before moving to East Berlin, he not only contrived, with characteristic guile, to obtain an Austrian passport, which would allow him easy access to the West, but gave the copyrights of his works to a West German publisher, who still owns them. When someone asked him, toward the end of his life, why he had elected to stay in the East, he is said to have likened himself to a doctor with a limited supply of drugs who is forced to choose between two patients—a syphilitic old roué and a diseased prostitute who is, however, pregnant. It seems clear, too, that Brecht's acquaintance with Hitlerism had left him with very little faith in the possibility of turning Germany into a true democracy overnight; hence he felt able to support an authoritarian government that, whatever its faults, was at least anti-Nazi and anti-capitalist. (I suddenly remember the occasion when I took Helene Weigel to the West Berlin *première*, three years ago, of *The Diary of Anne Frank*. At the final curtain the audience sat shocked and motionless; Frau Weigel's face was rigid and masklike. Shortly afterward, in the restaurant next door to the theatre, she wept; and I should think she weeps seldom. Wiping her eyes, she shook her head and said firmly, "I know my dear Germans. They would do this again. Tomorrow.")

Early in 1949, in collaboration with his old friend Erich Engel, Brecht staged *Mother Courage* at the Deutsches-Theater in East Berlin. The style—light, relaxed, and ascetically spare—set the pattern for all his subsequent productions. As the tireless old protagonist, dragging her canteen wagon across the battlefields of the Thirty Years' War, Helene Weigel played in a manner that shrank utterly from flamboyance; her performance was graphic yet casual, like a shrug. At two carefully selected moments she was piercingly and unforgettably moving—first in the soundless cry that doubles her up when her son is executed, and again when, to avoid incriminating herself, she must pretend not to recognize his body. She walks over to the stretcher, wearing a feigned, frozen smile that does not budge from her lips until she has surveyed the corpse, shaken her head, and returned to her seat on the other side of the stage. Then she turns to the audience, and we see for an instant the drained, stone face of absolute grief. These moments apart, the production achieved a new kind of theatrical beauty, cool and meaningful, by deliberately avoiding climaxes of individual emotion; with *Mother Courage* the broad canvas and the eagle's-eye view of humanity were restored to European drama after too long an absence.

That autumn the company formally adopted the name Berliner Ensemble, and for the next five years it spent most of its time on tour. In 1952 a detailed, illustrated account of its first six presentations, complete with an analysis of the acting techniques and methods of stagecraft, was published in a huge volume of well over four hundred pages, laconically entitled *Theaterarbeit* (*Theatre Work*). In the spring of 1954 the Ensemble moved into the Theater am Schiffbauerdamm, and Brecht celebrated his homecoming with an extraordinary production of *The Caucasian Chalk Circle,* which opened in June and later astonished Paris and London. A concave white curtain covered the back of the stage, a convex white curtain swept to and fro across the front; between them, the vast revolve whirled around, bearing fragmentary settings for the journeying heroine to encounter, and long silken sheets adorned with Oriental landscapes came billowing down to indicate place and climate. Lee Strasberg, the artistic director of the Actors' Studio and a passionate upholder of Stanislavsky's quest for emotional truth in acting, as opposed to the social truth sought by Brecht, saw the play while the Ensemble was in London. He concluded that what Brecht practised was by no means incompatible with what Stanislavsky preached, and declared that the production was one of the best half-dozen he had ever witnessed.

I met Brecht, for the first and only time, in Paris during the summer of 1955, the year before his death. Ovally built, and blinking behind iron-rimmed glasses, he sported a grey tunic of vaguely Russian cut and conversed in wry, smiling obliquities, puffing on a damp little cigar. To judge by Ernest Borneman's description of him in the twenties, exile had changed his appearance hardly at all: "He was an eccentric in behaviour, speech, and dress, as well as in politics. He wore clothes that kept a neat balance between those of a soldier, a workman, and a hobo. . . . The hair was sliced off abruptly after two or three inches growth, all around the head, and hung down . . . like the coiffure you see on busts of Roman emperors." Max Frisch, the Swiss playwright and novelist, has set down perhaps the best portrait of Brecht in his later years, and I am indebted to Mr. Esslin for introducing me to it. Brecht met Frisch in Zurich in 1947 and would often, when the latter was embarking on a train journey, go to the station to see him off:

> Avoiding the crowd, he leaves the platform with rapid, short, rather light steps, his arms hardly swinging, his head held slightly sideways, his cap drawn on to the forehead as if to conceal his face, half conspiratorially, half bashfully. . . . He gives the impression of a workman, a metalworker; yet he is too slight, too graceful for a workman, too much awake for a peasant . . . reserved, yet observant, a refugee who has left innumerable stations, too shy for a man of the world, too experienced for a scholar, too knowing not to be anxious, a stateless person . . . a passer-by of our time, a man called Brecht, a scientist, a poet without incense.

After the Master's death many people in the company, as well as outside it, wondered whether it could survive without his fiery presence. An interim answer was supplied by the Ensemble's triumphant East Berlin presentation, in January 1957, of *The Life of Galileo*—a production begun by Brecht and finished by Engel. I saw it again this summer, and the play still seems to me, as it did at the first night, an incomparable theatrical statement of the social responsibilities of the intellectual. At the outset it looks as if we were in for a straight fight between religious obscurantism and scientific discovery. The only progressive art, says Galileo, is "the art of doubt," a remark that echoes Brecht's own dictum: "Scepticism moves mountains." But before long we arrive at the author's real purpose, which is to condemn Galileo for cowardice. Intimidated by the threat of torture, cajoled by the promise of a cossetted life, he abjectly recants, and emerges from the Inquisition chamber to be shunned by his pupils, one of whom shouts at him, "Unhappy is the land that lacks a hero!" Wanly, Galileo responds, "Unhappy is the land that needs a hero." Brecht goes on to show how one such concession brings a hundred in its train; within months Galileo is backing the Church in social and political, as well as scientific and theological, affairs. The final tableau epitomizes the argument: in the foreground a choir polyphonously hymns the power of science, while in the background Galileo wolfs a fat roast goose. The play contains two scenes that exemplify, as sharply as anything Brecht ever wrote, his ability to make an intellectual position visible and tangible. In the first of them a provincial ballad singer hails Galileo's challenge to Rome. As he does so, a riotous procession, reminiscent of a painting by Hieronymus Bosch, streams across the stage. Some of the marchers are clad in obscene masks, and coax a jangling music out of saucepans and brass bedsteads; others toss a straw effigy of a cardinal in a blanket; one, a child, is attired as the earth, with water squirting from its eyes at the loss of its position at the centre of the universe; another clumps in horrendously on twenty-foot stilts, surmounted by a gigantic facsimile, acclaimed on all sides, of Galileo's head. The second scene that sticks in my mind is the one in which the liberal Cardinal Barberini, newly installed as Pope, turns against Galileo. At first, skinny in his underwear, waiting to be robed, Barberini refuses to countenance the Inquisitor's demand that the scientist be brought to trial, but as the robing proceeds and he is draped, encased, and almost buried in the ceremonial vestments of his office, the Pope grows more and more receptive to the Inquisitor's plea, to which, at last, he consents. It is instructive, by the way, to contrast Brecht's attitude toward Galileo with Arthur Koestler's in *The Sleepwalkers*—bearing in mind, of course, that Mr. Koestler's Marxism was once as deeply ingrained as Brecht's. According to the Koestler version, Galileo's pride brought about a disastrous and unnecessary breach between science and religion. Brecht, on the other hand, accuses Galileo of not having had enough pride (or self-respect) to make a breach that was healthy and necessary. Koestler wants to reconcile the physical with the metaphysical; Brecht strives to keep them apart. But, whatever one thinks of the argument, it is impossible to deny the unassertive loveliness of Caspar Neher's décor for *The Life of Galileo*—three towering panelled walls of darkly glowing copper, enclosing an area into which informatively beautiful objects, such as Roman bas-reliefs and silver models of the Aristotelian universe, are occasionally lowered. The production proved that the spheres of the Ensemble would continue to revolve without the animating zeal of their great mover. Brecht thus demonstrated, posthumously, the truth of his own apothegm that no man is indispensable, or, if he is, he is up to no good.

The Ensemble today consists of sixty-two actors, plus a staff of administrators, office workers, stagehands, musicians, designers, dressmakers, scene builders, electricians, ushers, waitresses, and cooks that brings the grand total of employees up to nearly three hundred. Its yearly subsidy, paid by the Ministry of Culture, amounts to more than three million marks. Rehearsals, in this happy set-up, may go on for anything between two and six months; when I was there in June, the cast of *The Threepenny Opera* was already wearing full costume and make-up, although the opening was not scheduled until October. It sometimes worries Helene Weigel that in all its ten years of operation the Ensemble has presented no more than twenty-five plays. She need not disturb herself unduly, because the main reason for the company's low output is, quite simply, its fame. Its productions are being reverently filmed for the East Berlin archives, it is constantly being invited to foreign countries (Hungary and Rumania this summer, Scandinavia in the fall, England and China next year), and it spends a lot of time polishing and recasting its existing repertoire.

This summer I attended two productions I had not seen before. One was *Die Mutter,* Brecht's expansion of the Gorky novel about an illiterate Russian mother who begins by urging her son to abandon his revolutionary activities and ends up, after he has been shot, a convinced supporter of the cause. The play is outright *agitprop,* a mosaic of Marxist exhortations, and the last scene shows the whole cast singing in praise of Communism while a film projector fills the backcloth with newsreel shots of Lenin, Khrushchev, Mao Tse-tung, and even —fleetingly—Stalin. It all sounds crudely hysterical until one sees the stealth and subtlety of the performance. There are no exaggerated Czarist villains, no exuberantly heroic proletarians; everyone acts with a detached calm that, if anything, reinforces the message. Weigel plays the mother as a quiet but relentless nagger. ("I picked out the nagging and decided to use it all through," she told me later. "I wanted to show that nagging could be constructive as well as nasty.") Looking like Nefertiti lined by years of labour over a hot stove, she permits herself one moment of pure lyricism. Her son, who has escaped from Siberia, appears without warning at a house where his mother is employed as housekeeper. Entering from the kitchen, she sees him and instinctively registers chiding disapproval; then, uncontrollably, she flies to his arms, as weightlessly as Ulanova's Juliet flies to Romeo, letting both legs swing round the boy's waist as he catches her. Throughout the evening one feels Brecht's passion for objects that have been durably used—a sofa, a soup tureen, a hand-operated printing press. Once, in a poem, he said that his wife chose her props with the same loving precision as that with which a poet chooses his words. Weigel's props, he declared, were selected

> . . . for age, purpose, and beauty
> By the eyes of the knowing,
> The hands of the bread-baking, net-weaving,
> Soup-cooking comprehender
> Of reality.

After this, one of the company's oldest productions, I went to see the newest—*The Resistible Rise of Arturo Ui*, described in the program as *"ein Gangster-Spektakel von Bertolt Brecht."* Written in 1941, it is a jagged, raucous parody of Hitler's rise to power, told in terms of Chicago in the twenties, composed mostly in blank verse, and including several malicious revampings of scenes from Shakespeare and Goethe. Hitler-Ui is a small-time thug who, taking advantage of a falling market, blackmails the mayor of the city (Hindenburg) into allowing him to organize a really prosperous protection racket. When the mayor dies, Ui succeeds him. His plans to take over the suburb of Cicero (Austria) are disputed by some of the mob; he slaughters the dissidents with as merry a lack of compunction as Hitler showed in disposing of Ernst Roehm and his friends on the Night of the Long Knives. In the final scene Ui is the boss, high on a rostrum spiky with microphones, through which he shrieks an oration that is cacophonously reproduced, at intervals of roughly half a second, by loudspeakers all over the theatre. The whole play is performed in a style that is somewhere between Erich von Stroheim and the Keystone Cops. The Roehm murders are staged like the St. Valentine's Day massacre; a truck drives into a garage, its headlights blazing straight at the audience, and silhouetted gunmen mow down the victims. The entire cast wears the sort of distorted make-up that one associates with puppets; the revolve whizzes around; and squalling Dixieland jazz interlards the scenes. Macabre farce on this level of inventiveness was something I had never struck before in any theatre. Its quality was condensed in the performance of Ekkehard Schall as Ui—one of the most transfixing human experiments I have ever seen on a stage, and a perfect image of Brechtian acting. Schall, who is under thirty, plays Ui with a ginger moustache, a ginger forelock, a trench coat, and a hat with the brim completely turned down. He invests the part with all the deadpan gymnastic agility of the young Chaplin: clambering on to the back of a hotel armchair and toppling abruptly out of sight; biting his knuckles, and almost his whole fist, when momentarily frustrated; indulging, when left alone with women, in displays of ghastly skittishness; and learning, from a hired ham actor, that the golden rule of public speaking is to preserve one's chastity by shielding—as Hitler always did—the lower part of one's belly. Yet Schall can change gears without warning, swerving from pure knockabout to sudden glooms of fearful intensity; from Chaplin, one might say, to Brando; for the virtue of Brechtian training, as of Brechtian thinking, is that it teaches the infinite flexibility of mankind. The play itself is rowdy and Chaplinesque. What the production —and Schall, above all—has added to it is a fever, a venom, and a fury that make laughter freeze, like cold sweat, on one's lips.

> In me are contending
> Delight at the apple trees in blossom
> And horror at the house-painter's speeches.
> But only the second
> Drives me to my desk.

Thus Brecht; and this production makes one glad that he was so driven. Its directors—Peter Palitzsch and Manfred Wekwerth—are both, like Schall, young men who were shaped by his tuition. The tradition, I would hazard, is safe.

harold clurman

BERTOLT BRECHT

1948

"IN THE bloodiest times there are kind people." This line from Bertolt Brecht's play *The Caucasian Chalk Circle* might serve as a rebuttal to what I wrote . . . about some recent French plays. There are important differences, however, between Brecht and the Frenchmen. The first is that the French are dominated by a certain type of acid realism, while the German, no matter how much of a materialist he may be, generally moves toward the idealistic and the didactic. The second and more decisive difference is that the French plays are reflections of a basically middle-class psychology, while Brecht is essentially a revolutionary who identifies himself with the dispossessed. . . .

Brecht wrote *The Caucasian Chalk Circle* in 1943 and 1944 during what he once called his "exile in paradise" in Santa Monica, California. The play is one of the last in a series of distinguished dramatic works by a man who is undoubtedly the leading poet of contemporary Germany.

The plot is based on an old Chinese play which in turn was a variant of the biblical tale of Solomon's judicial stratagem in the case of the two women who claimed the same child. Brecht has transferred the locale of his play to Georgia in the Caucasus. In the Brecht play, the wise judge rules that the poor peasant girl who adopted the child shall retain it in permanent custody instead of its actual mother, the governor's wife, who lost it through selfish negligence. The point of Brecht's play is that the revolutionary mind will bring forth a new morality:

> . . . What there is shall go to those who are good for it,
> Thus: the children to the motherly, that they prosper.
> The carts to good drivers, that they are well driven.
> And the valley to the waterers, that it bring fruit.

There is a certain nobility here. It is a dangerous quality, for lofty sentiments often lead to low art. There is almost nothing more despicable than official "hope," nothing more distressing than courage displayed as propaganda. The nobility in Brecht's plays is fortunately not a self-conscious demonstration of exalted feeling but a quality immanent in his craftsmanship.

No critic of Brecht's work will fail to associate it with his theory of the Epic Theatre. It relates to Chinese as contrasted to Greek poetics. Epic theatre eschews ordinary illusion and suspense, because it does not seek to stimulate the subjective identification of the spectator with the actor on the stage. The Epic dramatist aims to encourage a certain detachment, a kind of contemplative coolness so that the spectator may take pleasure in his *understanding* of what he sees. . . . But theory does not concern me. I am convinced that Brecht writes as he does, not so much from a predetermined calculation based on what he believes to be the correct goals for the present revolutionary age, as from the dictates of his temperament.

Brecht is a kind of Gothic primitive in whom a rude simplicity is coupled with a shrewd mentality. There is a humorous canniness in his imagery and observation. ("They even have to have their weeping done for them," one of his characters says of the rich.) There is also a kind of ascetic refinement or leanness of line in his work which may be ascribed with equal justification to either the primitive or the modern aspect of his talent. The final impression is that of a great purity of utterance.

Brecht's theatre verse has inspired some of the best songs of our time—those of Kurt Weill and of Hanns Eisler. The songs and choral comments in *The Caucasian Chalk Circle* contain the essence of Brecht's meaning and the peak of his poetic diction. Whether this is proof of his limitation as a dramatist is, at the moment, difficult to ascertain. For the test of Brecht's effectiveness in the theatre must surely come from his audiences.

Except for *The Threepenny Opera* none of Brecht's plays achieved great popularity in Germany before the war. This may have been due to social as well as to artistic causes. Certainly the Brecht style is not easy to render on the stage by actors and directors schooled in an entirely different mode. In any case, Brecht has never been adequately presented in this country, despite Charles Laughton's contribution to *Galileo* and the remarkable intelligence evident in the present production. I have a feeling, however, that postwar Europe may acclaim Brecht. "Terrible is the temptation of goodness," says the narrator in *The Caucasian Chalk Circle*. It is a maxim emblematic of a force that may counterbalance the evil spirits rampant amid the ruins. The virtue of Brecht's plays is good sense carried to the point of grandeur.

BERLIN, 1956

AS I remember Berlin—which I first visited in 1922—it was a stuffily comfortable city which gave evidence of a fulsomely prosperous, unmistakably middle-class past. There were marks, too, of shock and despair—a kind of wan astonishment as of a man who, while still surrounded by substantial possessions, discovers that he is no longer solvent.

Berlin today is two towns: the one in the West strikes me like an old-fashioned ice-cream parlor built on a waste land; the other in the East resembles a shabby encampment constructed from the rubble of a formidable city. One can travel without any trouble from West to East Berlin by subway or electric train; yet the effect of the division is to make both sectors seem bloodless, ghost-like, almost unreal. There is a sense of ruin which no one, except the sightseeing guides, thinks it proper to notice or remark upon. In West Berlin people behave as if all were normal or were soon going to be; in East Berlin, as if the shattered streets were a promise of future achievement. Is this the end of a world or the beginning of a new one?

One thing has not changed: the theatre now, as in the twenties, is of the best. There were more ambitious and practiced playwrights then—in fact, the German expressionists of those days were auguries, some people believed, of a new and exalted drama—and there were innumerable actors of high rank. Today there are few new playwrights worth special mention, and most of the famous actors whose names were the pride of the European stage have disappeared through natural causes and some through causes which were not at all natural.

Yet there is no escaping the fact: in quality of production, in scenic invention, in variety of repertory, in solidity of organization, the German theatre at this moment (and Berlin is by no means the single nor even the most signal instance of it) makes the American, English, French stages look like little-theatre activities.

I had not expected this because, for one thing, such critics as Eric Bentley in New York and Kenneth Tynan in London had made it appear that the German theatre today was interesting only because of Bertolt Brecht's Berliner Ensemble Theatre. (Brecht is not the titular administrative director, but he is unquestionably its guiding spirit.) While it is true that this East Berlin company represents the most strikingly new development in the German theatre since the Second World War, it is all wrong to suggest that it is the only distinguished theatre in Germany or even in Berlin.

There is, for example, the state-supported Schiller Theatre in West Berlin, a modern and handsome construction on the site of the old building which was destroyed in the air raids. It has a seating capacity of 1,200, and its management also runs a smaller house in which intimate plays are produced. I did not inquire how large the state subsidy was, but I was informed that in the smaller city of Frankfurt the subsidy amounts to $1,500,000 a year.

The stage of the Schiller Theatre occupies one-third of the building's space. (In most American theatres the stage is confined to one-tenth of the total area.) It has several revolving tables and is equipped in most up-to-date fashion in regard to lighting, scene docks, and so on.

Almost all the actors of the Schiller Theatre are employed by the season, which is also true of the imposing technical and administrative staff. The repertory includes at present a German play of the twenties, a play by Calderón freely translated by von Hoffmansthal, Ibsen's *Peer Gynt* and *A Doll's House*, Anouilh's latest play *Ornifle*, Schiller's *Don Carlos*, Goethe's *Faust*, Shaw's *Caesar and Cleopatra*, Büchner's *Danton's Death*, Erwin Piscator's adaptation of Tolstoy's *War and Peace*, Richard Nash's *The Rainmaker*, Arthur Miller's *A View from the Bridge*, Faulkner's *Requiem for a Nun*, and a new play, being given its world premiere here, by Marcel Pagnol.

At the Berliner Ensemble Theatre in East Berlin the repertory includes, besides Brecht's plays, versions of Farquhar's *The Recruiting Officer*, Synge's *The Playboy of the Western World*, a play by the nineteenth century Russian classic Ostrovsky. Other plays being offered in other East Berlin theatres include Molière's *Georges Dandin*, plays by Schiller, Goldoni, Lorca, Hauptmann, Shaw, Shakespeare. All the East Berlin theatres are state supported, as are the opera houses in both West and East Berlin. In West Germany alone there may be as many as two hundred state-owned theatres. I paid ten marks for my orchestra ticket at the Schiller Theatre: about $2.50. The cost of a similar ticket (in dollars) is less than half that amount in East Berlin.

The audience which attends the theatre in both sectors—it is to be noted incidentally that West Berlin residents may and do attend East Berlin theatres and vice versa, just as actors living in either sector may be employed in theatres of the other—the audience, I say, appears as well "trained" as the companies themselves. They are almost invariably punctual, extraordinarily attentive and quiet during the performance, rarely applaud till the curtain is down and the house lights have been turned up. There is something almost solemn about their behavior in the theatre auditorium—they drink beer or juices and eat sandwiches during intermission in the commodious foyers intended for the purpose. They laugh discreetly, as if laughter might disturb the actors or as if the theatre were not intended for undue levity, although the biggest laugh and applause in a very bad production of *Bus Stop* I saw at one of the "private" (non-subsidized) theatres came just where it did in the New York production.

My purpose in beginning this report on the Berlin theatre with some hasty observations on the physical appearance of the city itself was not simply to introduce a bit of local color into my description. The scarred city and the atmosphere produced by the causes and consequences of its wounds stand in a vital relationship to what one sees in the theatre.

Danton's Death, at the Schiller Theatre, is the work of a German dramatist—Georg Büchner—who died in 1837 at the age of twenty-three. The play was written when he was twenty-one. A medical student, Büchner was a romantic, unhappy with the reaction which had set in in Germany after Napoleon's final defeat. But Büchner's mind had also a critical and realistic bent—he thought of drama as a form of history—and his emotions were torn between the tug of his yearning for freedom, beauty and ethical nobility and the repressive conservatism which the disillusionment with the French Revolution and the fear of Napoleon—who to most Europeans outside France somehow symbolized that Revolution—had bred.

Büchner was attracted to the purposes for which the Revolution had been undertaken—this made him a radical—but he was horrified by the physical and moral depredations of the historical process as it actually works itself out in daily needs. "Freedom has become a whore," one of the characters says in *Danton's Death;* and the play which seems buoyed up by a kind of revolutionary afflatus also has about it a quality of anguish and pessimism which a determined or doctrinaire radical would qualify as counter-revolutionary. Throughout the play, a revulsion is expressed at the nemesis of history, which seems to compel its human agents to commit criminal acts.

Because the play is wildly episodic and was utterly impracticable for stage conditions at the time of its composition, it was not produced until seventy-five years later—in 1910. I saw it done in German by the company Reinhardt brought to the old Century Theatre in New York in 1927. The production was extremely picturesque, spectacularly brilliant, but chiefly ornamental, because the play's material served Reinhardt merely as the springboard for a splendid show.

For the present director, Erwin Piscator—some twelve years in exile from Germany and only recently repatriated in West Germany, though still markedly "independent" in his views—the play is something more than an experience in sparkling modern theatrics—though it is that as well. *Danton's Death* is a romantic epic of political turmoil, a grandiose lyric statement of history's heartbreaking contradictions, a song of revolutionary ardor, and a heroic dirge on the personal misery of revolutionary action and the savage errors by which humanity progresses.

How appropriate and meaningful all this is at the state-supported theatre of West Berlin! For everything is here—on the stage, in the audience and in the streets outside: the memory and witness of "revolutionary" faiths of all kinds (we must not forget that for many Germans National Socialism represented a kind of religious revolt against capitalism and the decadent democracies) and the still harassing need to choose between different ideologies each of which is tainted with confusions, compromises and elements of shame.

Beyond all this, the energy, opulence, mechanical inventiveness of the production—which seems to move as easily and colorfully as any movie—serve in sum as an example of the sophistication, resourcefulness and imaginative exuberance of that part of the German theatre which has absorbed all the salutary influences in the world of modern art. Here are ideas, social significance, lavish showmanship, poetry—Büchner was a beautiful writer—free of the shackles of the ordinary commercial stage. The total production is a stage event of which most of us in New York, London and Paris are largely unaware —as if the theatre itself were an experience still to be discovered by us.

There are no great actors in *Danton's Death*, but the company —largely composed of people in their thirties—is virile, well endowed in voice, diction, looks, and wholly practiced in the uninhibited use of the stage. A young man, Hans Dieter Zeidler, displays a combination of temperamental dash and solidity which, while it as yet wants the modification of greater subtlety of feeling that may come with a little more living and the opportunity for repose, could well make him another of the big actors for which the German theatre is celebrated.

The setting for *Danton's Death* is a triumph of eclectic methods. Revolving platforms are used, and certain devices of constructivism: the main architectural feature of the setting is a scaffolding which resembles a modified scenic railway, itself frequently in motion, so that when people promenade on it—which is what they do in many street scenes—we get the sense of constant mobility. Images of places and people are fluently projected against screens on three sides of the stage. The result is a feeling of complete freedom in the background and environment of the play.

This setting is the work of Caspar Neher, the original designer of the Brecht-Weill *Threepenny Opera* and one of the two best designers in Germany. The other is Theo Otto, now residing in Zurich (but employed throughout Germany), who designed Brecht's *Mother Courage* at the Berliner Ensemble Theatre. Both men stand among the world's most talented stage designers of our day.

This brings me to the famous troupe whose theatrical ideology and a large part of whose repertory is the product of Bertolt Brecht's lively brain. This poet and dramatist is almost unanimously admired— certainly respected—by people of both West and East German citizenship or persuasion.

Bertolt Brecht's Berliner Ensemble Theatre in East Berlin has been called by one foreign critic the finest acting company in Europe. A number of other critics tend to discuss the productions of that remarkable organization from the standpoint of Brecht's theories. Both these approaches seem to me alien to the value or significance of any artistic phenomenon. The way to understand work in the theatre is to register and measure the effect created and the human, social and (sometimes) technical attributes which render that effect.

I begin my report on Brecht's theatre in this fashion because Brecht himself, as well as many of his admirers, lays so much stress on the unsentimental, didactic, demonstration-like nature of his art. The first thing I should like to note, therefore, is that I found *Mother Courage and Her Children*, perhaps the best of Brecht's plays, very touching.

Brecht is a poet. To overlook the extremely sensitive bareness and strength of his writing is to miss its core. It strikes me as downright silly to talk of Brecht's production methods—the tenets of his so-called Epic Theatre—without realizing that if such methods did not exist the quality of Brecht's writing would require their invention. Brecht says that his plays may be done in different ways, but it is clear that they would make no sense if one adhered to the ordinary naturalism of the contemporary stage.

Brecht's plays are morality plays as surely as anything written in the Middle Ages to demonstrate the road to Salvation or to mock the Evil One. There is in Brecht the same basic seriousness, the same need to be clear, popular, real (that is, essential). Those old plays depended a good deal on comedy—often of a primitive kind; so does Brecht, whose shrewd wit and robust humor nearly always assume a rather peasant-like bluntness. The old plays were direct: each scene had its unmistakable comic or pathetic point. They had very little of the ambiguity and indirection of the modern play. Brecht's plays do not attempt to render nuances of personal psychology: they are displays of primary action governed by primary motives. Finally, we are constantly kept aware that we are looking at an artifice, and that helps us to maintain the objectivity and critical sense which Brecht insists is the proper frame of mind for an adult in the theatre.

Mother Courage is the tale of a woman of the people who, with three illegitimate children, follows the troops during the Thirty Years' War to sell them liquor and sundry other articles soldiers crave. The play shows us how she is slowly deprived of everything she cherishes: her children, her trade, her reason for being. This woman who takes no sides, who seeks only to live and let live in the most friendly fashion, is swept along by the currents of life in a war period until nothing remains of her native honesty, good nature, moral or material possessions.

There are very funny scenes in the play, dramatic scenes and scenes which for all their brevity give us a remarkably sharp view of the epoch. But what is most important to bear in mind is that, though Brecht always endeavors to keep his writing and presentation dispassionate and rather matter-of-factly quiet—effects of climax, suspense, mood being systematically avoided—what is ultimately achieved is indelibly vivid and emotionally telling. One leaves the theatre with the unalterable conviction that war is nothing less than the greatest scourge of man's making.

In his staging, Brecht doesn't attempt picturesqueness; yet his stage has a constant visual interest. Everything is apparently being done to destroy illusion—the light, for instance, is always bright white, and the electric apparatus always in view; the revolving stage by which Mother Courage's endless wanderings are shown is plainly a stage mechanism. Songs interrupt the action arbitrarily. They sharpen the play's points like epigrams of instruction. (Splendid songs they are, too.)

The purpose of all this is to tell the audience that the play is a conscious device to present what the dramatist and his colleagues want the audience to understand—the play's moral point. But—and it cannot be repeated too often—all this does not make the play any the less moving. Everything seems congruous and right. One rarely gets any feeling of a stylistic mannerism, of a trick, labored "modernism."

Brecht is a classicist. He seeks that form of artistic truth which emphasizes the thing created above the creator, a manner which allows the spectator to appreciate the play with that repose and refinement of attention which liberate the spirit without drugging the senses. Brecht's programmatic antiromanticism is against art as magic as it is against faith as superstition. But, more deeply, Brecht's technique is a form of discipline undertaken by the artist to convey as devotedly and self-abnegatingly as possible his perception of reality. The goal is wisdom rather than excitement. It has always been the aspiration of the highest art.

Brecht's ideas and this theatre are the product of a destroyed world: Germany from 1919 to the present. The landscape of *Mother Courage* (written in exile in 1938) is that of Berlin—particularly East Berlin—today. The audience is part of a world which has been destroyed or one which may be reborn. This is not a metaphor: it is a visible, tangible fact. In such a world, one has to get down to fundamentals; everything is truly a matter of life and death. In these circumstances, an art such as Brecht's is emblematic, necessary, national.

Would Brecht's methods serve all plays? Certainly not. Still, Brecht's ideas and practice are stimulating and instructive for an understanding of the theatre everywhere. That Brecht's technique may at times be applied with happy results in certain plays other than his own is attested to by *Drums and Trumpets* (Farquhar's *The Recruiting Officer*) directed by one of the younger men of the Berliner Ensemble Theatre. It has been adapted to the uses of this theatre by making the war for which the recruiting is being done the American War of Independence (the original was written about seventy years earlier) and by making it even more than Farquhar's comedy an occasion for monkeyshines and vaudevillesque lampoon. The result is a hilarious antiwar farce of savage propaganda interlarded with all sorts of theatrical hokum—the whole giving no impression of artiness, strain or falsification.

I say "propaganda," but I must immediately add that it is of a kind which may readily be accepted by anyone at all—except a Junker or a Nazi. This explains why 30 per cent of the Berliner Ensemble Theatre audience comes from West Berlin. I have also mentioned a certain primitivism, but it should be clear that this is of a highly sophisticated sort. One striking example of this is the music. Much of it is by Hanns Eisler and Paul Dessau—Brecht's prewar musical collaborators. It reminds one very effectively of *The Threepenny Opera* and of that time in Berlin when Marlene Dietrich was driving the Emil Jannings type of boys crazy. It is an echo of the past easing the revolution of the present. . . .

❋   ❋   ❋

james h. clancy

BEYOND DESPAIR: A NEW DRAMA OF IDEAS

ONE OF the most frequently noted aspects of the contemporary theatrical scene is the triumphant arrival of unintelligibility as a major feature of many highly regarded plays. Ionesco, in his *Bald Soprano,* indicates both by the irrelevancy of his play's title and by the repetitive no-sense of his dialogue that though his play may have meaning he is dedicated to the belief that that meaning shall not be achieved by intelligible devices. His meaning exists beneath the action and the dialogue and he faithfully, and successfully, shatters the normal, intelligible form of both so that the spectator is refused the possibility of deriving meaning by a rational or intelligible process. Ionesco's success, and it is considerable, is that in many of his plays, he has matched his form and his content: both lead to the same conclusion, the revelation that life is as void of meaning and of sense as the pronouncement at the conclusion of his powerfully stated *The Chairs.* Here, before a group of non-existent people, the Orator stands to deliver at last the great message that the Old Man has bequeathed to humanity:

> *He faces the rows of empty chairs; he makes the invisible crowd understand that he is deaf and dumb; he makes the signs of a deaf-mute; desperate efforts to make himself understood; then he coughs, groans, and utters the gutteral sounds of a mute:*

> He, mme, mm, mn. Ju, gou, hou, hou. Heu, heu, gu, gou, gueue.

The Orator, and through him Ionesco, leave us with a world where intelligibility is denied by gibberish, where purpose in both life and art seems to be refuted, at least on any level subject to rational analysis, where, significantly enough, we are reminded, in idea if not in form, of Matthew Arnold's bleak prospect of nearly one hundred years earlier:

From *Educational Theatre Journal, Vol. XIII,* No. 3 (October, 1961). Reprinted by permission.

> . . . We are here as on a darkling plain,
> Swept with confused alarms of struggle and flight
> Where ignorant armies clash by night.

Ionesco and others like him have at least matched Arnold's content with a form that robs Arnold's view of cohesion and objectivity. With Arnold we see the ignorant armies clashing by night; with Ionesco we participate, in the very object of art, in the confused alarms of struggle and flight.

Ionesco's method of meaningful unintelligibility is not unaccompanied in the modern theatre. He is probably only the most successful of the practitioners of this form of dramatic art. Similar, if less striking, examples of the same approach may be seen not only in works from the continent, but also in such American performances as Jack Gelber's *The Connection.*

The heritage of such an approach to the art of the theatre goes at least as far back as the non-realistic works of Strindberg (especially *The Road to Damascus* and *The Ghost Sonata*) and gathers particular support and focus from the famous "Merdre" of *Ubu Roi* and the violent and unintelligible absurdities which expand if they do not explicate this comprehensive first line of dialogue by Alfred Jarry.

The effect of such theatrical efforts was for some time, however, extremely tangential to the main line of theatre art and it is only recently that unintelligibility has come to be reckoned as a major force in modern drama. With Franz Kafka, many contemporary playwrights feel that

> Our art is dazzled blindness before the truth; the light on the grotesquely distorted face is true, but nothing else.[1]

Though this aspect of the contemporary theatre is only an aspect, and in many respects not the most notable one, it has attracted special attention among those who write seriously about the theatre. The reason may be that such writers, who frequently demonstrate that they look with some suspicion on the respectability of their subject matter, feel that the aspect of the theatre that has aligned itself with unintelligibility has at least gained the respectability of the esoteric and raised itself to the level of the current interest in non-literate literature and the even more wide-spread acceptance of non-objective art.

To such critics, sensitive to the perverse tendency of theatrical art to remain on speaking terms with the vulgar, the vision of its increased unintelligibility has come as a belated but welcome *cachet*

[1] *The Great Wall of China,* translated by Willa and Edwin Muir (London, 1946), p. 151.

to the society of the elect. With head erect they may now walk in company with the explicator of *Finnegan's Wake* and the exegetist of the latest Jackson Pollock.

Exciting and valuable as this foray into the unintelligible is, it is not this aspect of the modern theatre that demonstrates its greatest break with the past or its most striking contribution to a possible drama of the future. Such a contribution is rather to be seen in that branch of the modern theatre that may be said to concern itself with new ideas of purpose and refurbished accent on the human will.

This theatre, as might be expected of an art that aims at unintelligibility as well as meaning, is more complicated than the theatre of no-sense. Two major phases of it may be distinguished, however, and although any such arbitrary division is more useful than accurate, it is not amiss to consider the new theatre of ideas as being represented by the otherwise opposing points of view of such authors as Bertolt Brecht and Albert Camus.

Both authors reject as a proper method for the production of an art form the tortured reflection of the emptiness and futility of man's actions and man's thoughts. Camus would not have disagreed much with the statement of Brecht, taken from the latter's essay entitled *A Little Organum for the Theatre:*

> . . . what must our images of man's life together look like? What is the productive attitude toward nature and toward society which we children of a scientific age can accept with pleasure in our theatre? The attitude is a *critical* one.

With this emphasis on the necessity of mind in the theatre, its implications of an analytical and controlled use of form and subject matter, Camus no doubt would have agreed. With the extension of Brecht's idea, he would have been utterly at variance:

> The attitude is a *critical* one. With respect to a river it consists in the regulation of its flow; with respect to a fruit tree it consists in the grafting of fruit; with respect to locomotion it consists in the construction of ships and planes; with respect to society it consists in revolution.

The revolution that Brecht foresees in this "scientific age" is not the revolution that Camus thinks is necessary. They both, however, are in favor of revolt and they both refuse to acquiesce to the resigned yea-saying of the unintelligibles. They both, in order to express their attitudes theatrically, have developed opposing aspects of a theatre concerned with a change in attitudes: a new theatre of ideas.

In a moment of complete lucidity, Caligula says, in Albert Camus' play of that name, "Men die, and they are not happy." It is this discovery of the truth of human existence that drives Caligula to a course of action that is an attempt to equal the absurdity of the world that he sees around him. To him the world is a closed universe of misery and death, and the only way to become an equal of the supposed gods who have created such a world is to become equally as cruel as they.

This is Caligula's revolt, and the term may be taken as expressive not only of an idea central to the philosophy of such writers as Sartre, Camus, Adamov, Ionesco, Brecht in a special way, and others, but also, in the frame of theatre history, as representative of one more shift in that immense and fruitful re-evaluation of the theatre that has been in process since the last part of the nineteenth century.

This re-evaluation was primarily a reaction against the nineteenth century theatre's lack of identification with the world of which it was a part, its lack of really human relationship, its lack of "idea." Pixerecourt's pride in writing for a public that could not read was, in the last quarter of the nineteenth century, no longer even an amusing paradox. The naturalistic movement was an attempt to erase the inconsequentiality of such a theatre and to re-establish a theatre that could be considered an art form, and, in a world that was teeming with new interpretations of life, a theatre that was concerned with ideas.

Of this early theatre of ideas, commemorated in the plays of Becque, Zola, Hauptmann, Tolstoy and others, Camus and Brecht are the direct inheritors. As with any inheritors of substance, however, Camus and Brecht have put their patrimony to uses other than those for which it was originally created.

This is one respect in which the word "revolt" helps explain the relationship of Camus and Brecht to the formation of a new theatre of ideas, opposed not only to the older ideas found in the theatre of the naturalists (Becque, Tolstoy, the early Strindberg, and others), but also the development of that non-ideational theatre, the theatre of unintelligibility, that is itself a revolt against a theatre of ideas, old or new.

Camus and Brecht participated (perhaps unconsciously) in a revolt against the late nineteenth century theatre of ideas not because it contained ideas (the basis of Ionesco's objection), but rather because the ideas it contained no longer seemed to be of central importance. As Brecht points out in the Introduction to his *Little Organum*, "everything had been emptied out of the contemporary theatre." It reflected "false images of the social scene on the stage (including those of naturalism so-called)."

The ideas of the naturalists, no longer valid for these new

dramatists, were mainly concerned with an attempt to place man in his environment—an environment that was on the whole seen as scientifically demonstrable, mechanistically controlled, determined by factors that could be analyzed, as Taine suggested, as accurately as vitriol and sugar.

This approach to an understanding of man and the world in which he lived might result in such overtly pessimistic works as Hauptmann's *Before Sunrise* and Becque's *The Vultures*. It might also deeply trouble such a Victorian as Tennyson, who could see in such a universe only the frightening shadow of a Nature "red in tooth and claw," of "Dragons of the prime,/That tear each other in their slime." But in the long run the point of view that was representative in this late nineteenth century theatre of ideas, and most dogmatically propagandized by such a polemicist as Zola, was of a world that, because it was subject to analysis and understanding, permitted adaptation and control. The world could be understood, however harsh its circumstances might be to those who, in ignorance, did not adapt themselves to what was ordained and inevitable. It was a material world, therefore measurable; it was, in a sense, a mechanized world, therefore predictable. It is true that Darwin had qualified his theory of natural selection by an insistence upon the elements of chance and accident, but by the end of the century this sense of the fortuitous had been minimized in the popular mind, and it is upon the popular dilution of a scientific theory that a playwright works.

Evolution and environment, these were the twin poles between which man was moved. Theoretically, the poles were measurable. Marxian dialectic confirmed this attitude by giving a meaningful picture of the past and predictable pattern for the future. Freudian psychology, as mechanistic in its philosophical aspects as the behavioristic psychology it replaced, if nebulous and personal in its method, furthered a concept of the universe that was in all things explicable. Here even the dream was subject to the yardstick; the desire was measurable; the wish not thought of as father to the deed but rather as the progeny of unconscious drives. These drives were not at the command of the person driven, but they could be made explicable by the scientifically trained.

This material and measurable world may have seemed confining to those who were nurtured upon the remnants of the humanistic spirit that had survived since the Renaissance, but these were not many nor were they finally influential. The economic growth of the latter part of the nineteenth century forced a material world upon man's consciousness. Even if he feared its power, he accepted it. The challenge was to use it. Science seemed to indicate that, massive as the world of *things* was, it was a world that could, through analysis and observation, be understood. Once understood, through energy and good-will man and the world of things could advance together in evolutionary glory.

In other words, the world of the naturalists, of Becque, Hauptmann, Zola, Chekhov, and others, was essentially an optimistic world. If it was a world not yet right, it could be made right. As an artist you could vary in your attitude from the harsh satire of Becque in *The Vultures* to the warm irony of Chekhov in *The Cherry Orchard*. In neither case did your observation of frailty imply defeat. The more angry you became at what you saw (as in Becque), the more you indicated that a change was necessary, and, in the world as then conceived, possible. *The Vultures* is constantly in danger of losing stature as a serious work because of the consideration, always lurking close at hand, that even though it might be difficult (though not impossible) to change the ways of the predatory beast in the economic jungle, a short course in a business school would have saved the Vigneron girls a good deal of trouble.

In this, as in other plays of the period, the author is always, to a greater or lesser degree, outside of his play. The evil that he saw was a thing in which he was involved critically and even sympathetically, but he was not, in the modern use of the word, "engaged" in it. He observed, he commented, he sympathized, but it was, on the whole, of others that he wrote. The naturalist playwright noted many of the crises of the period in which he lived and he presented what he saw with talent, sincerity, and warmth, but the temper of his time nudged him in the direction of aloofness, of irony, satire, or the didactic. He, and therefore the audience, saw the world around exposed. The phrase is worth noting: the world around. It implies, quite correctly, a Pisgah view. Even Moses, at such a height, thought of the world as filled with "others."

This is the aspect of the naturalistic theatre to which Brecht was objecting when he noted in his *Little Organum* that "watching and hearing are activities." The audience of the naturalistic theatre, he felt, was not allowed to participate in this activity, but, as he said, "They seem to be *people to whom something is being done.*" The audience is *being shown* a picture of life which is a result of the author's *observation*. While the play is going on, neither the author nor the audience is, in Brecht's view, participating in an activity. The crises of life in the naturalist's theatre were the crises of "others," for author and audience alike.

But the art of the naturalists, and the theatre of ideas that it presented, though it dominated the latter part of the nineteenth century, did not go unchallenged even at the time of its greatest strength. Paul Fort and his Théâtre d'Art were almost co-eval with Antoine and his Théâtre Libre. Symbolism, Expressionism, Surrealism, all were movements opposed to the naturalist doctrine in the theatre, and all were of relative importance, although Surrealism, if the word may be applied to the work of Jarry and Apollinaire, was of little importance in the art of the theatre until it finally blossomed forth in what has previously been called in this paper the theatre of unintelligibility.

Symbolism, though a more important movement in the theatre, could not argue with the ideas of the naturalists, it could only withdraw from them. It did not so much object to the naturalist's ideas as it seemed to object to ideas in the theatre. Lugne-Poe's scrim and Maeterlinck's repetitive word images are meant to obscure the ideas the better to assault directly our concept of the mysterious and the profound. The music of Debussy lay at the end of this continuum.

Thus the Symbolists do not present a new world, they make misty the old one. Touching and evocative as is the little universe of Pelleas and Melisande, of Yniold and old Arkel, it is only the old world of Zola playing at dress-up. Melisande's world, stripped of its atmosphere, is as predetermined, as materialistic, as that of Therese Raquin.

Much the same may be said of the Expressionists; they withdrew from the naturalist's world, they did not oppose another world to it. The world of *From Morn to Midnight* is again Zola's world seen from an intensely fragmentized and personal point of view. The Cashier who serves as the protagonist of Kaiser's play is as cabined, cribbed, confined by material and pre-determined circumstances as is any protagonist of a naturalistic tragedy.

Until the theatre could express a new concept of the meaning of the world, the anti-naturalist movement was lacking in those necessary philosophical limitations that turn experiment from either poverty or excess to full fruition.

A new idea of the world was necessary to complete the revolt against the naturalistic theatre of the last part of the nineteenth century, and a new theatre of ideas was necessary to express this revolt. The work of both Albert Camus and Bertolt Brecht is central to this new theatre of ideas.

The theatre of Camus, which more directly concerns itself with philosophical issues than does that of Brecht, illustrates one of the directions taken by the new theatre in a re-evaluation of man's relationship to the world. The quotation from *Caligula* noted earlier illustrates the basis from which this change was accomplished: "Men die and they are not happy." The fundamental assumption about the world is no longer, as with the naturalists, that it is material, measurable, predictable, but rather that it is unpredictable, lacks congruity, is, in a special sense, absurd.

The world of things (Sartre's *en-soi*) looms large in this new world, but man is no longer considered as a thing among things. The world of things is not man's world. The absurd is felt when man's desire that the world should be explicable is seen to be opposed by the fact that the world cannot be made explicable in human terms. Camus sees the absurd as a clash between the world's "irrationality and the desperate hunger for clarity which cries out in man's deepest soul. The absurd depends as much upon man as upon the world."

This is what Caligula understands. This is why he feels that the world is insupportable and that he needs "the moon, or happiness, or immortality; something foolish, but something that is not of this world."

But both the moon and happiness are out of his reach, as he considers them out of the reach of all men in a world where incomprehension, misery, and solitude are masters, and so, in this world where it is impossible to justify moral values, he turns to pure evil (as does Goetz in Sartre's *The Devil and God*) in order to equal the gods, who only evidence themselves by their cruelty.

Caligula has taken the first step of the creature on his way to becoming a man: he has experienced anguish and despair. He has revolted against his comprehension of the world, but his revolt is a purely negative one and as he dies he breaks the mirror that images what he has become, crying in despair that he has searched for the impossible to the limits of the world and to the very boundaries of his own nature. He has held out his hands, and all that he has seen in front of him is his own hateful image.

Martha, in *Cross-Purpose*, has, like Caligula, dedicated herself to evil because of a world that is absurd in its cruelty, its isolation, its indifference. Her defiance, like Caligula's, is hopeless and non-fruitful. She knows only that she hates the world, she has suffered injustice, but that she will not kneel:

> Deprived of my place on this earth, rejected by my mother, alone in the midst of my crimes, I will leave this world without being reconciled.

With Caligula and Martha we enter a far different world than that of Therese Raquin. Here evil is not measurable, man's nature not predictable. Evil is senseless, as is good. No moral values exist in a world that is absurd in its essence. Man exists among things, but he is not of these things, and he evidences his manhood by rebellion against a world that he can neither understand nor control.

The outlook, in *Caligula* and *Cross-Purpose*, is pessimistic as opposed to the implied optimism of the earlier theatre of ideas, but even if the vision is essentially more repugnant it is at the same time more engrossing and more personal. Camus is not presenting a world of "others," he is not dramatizing what happens to a group of people with a certain environment, a specific heredity. He is dramatizing his despair, his anguish. From the basic tenets of the play, Caligula's defeat is his, as it is ours, as it is everyman's. Camus, and his characters, and his audience, are all confronted by the same problem. If his play touches you at all, it is apt to touch you profoundly, for Camus and you have not so much observed the same phenomena as you have become engaged in the same activity. You and he are at the center of the play. What you have participated in may be a thesis play rather than a play of character, but it is intensely human because the thesis concerns you and not others.

The recognition of the absurdity of the world and man's need to rebel against it are not, however, the concluding notes of Camus' theatre. Many will maintain that his most effective work for the theatre was done when he did not advance his argument beyond these steps, but his plays are works of art and as such they followed his development as a man and reflect the increasing enrichment of his point of view.

The new conclusion that was to be expressed by Camus in the theatre in such plays as *The Just* is clearly formulated in his *Letter to a German Friend*, published in 1944. In this essay, Camus remonstrates with a Nazi for having drawn Caligula's conclusions from Caligula's premise. He blames the Nazi for adding to the injustice of the world that he sees around him. For Camus,

> . . . man must affirm justice in order to struggle against eternal injustice, create happiness in order to protest against a universe of evil.[2]

He remonstrates with the Nazi for having chosen injustice, for having, as did Caligula, thrown in his lot with the gods. As for himself, says Camus, "I have chosen justice, in order to remain faithful to the earth."

Five years after the publication of this "Letter," Camus presented the same problem dramatically in *The Just*. In this play, Kaliayev recognizes, as did Jan in *Cross-Purpose*, that one thing that must be reached for in a world of absurdity is happiness for others. "One

---

[2] Quoted in Pierre-Henri Simon, *Theatre & Destin* (Paris, 1959), p. 198.

cannot be happy," says Jan, "in exile." Kaliayev accepts becoming a criminal only in order that the world will finally "be covered with the innocent." For him there is no individual salvation, no happiness in solitude. For these reasons he is, unlike Caligula, "un meurtrier délicat," a scrupulous assassin. He has not, nor has Camus, abandoned Caligula's premise, but he has advanced beyond his conclusion. Kaliayev knows that

> Injustice separates, shame separates, suffering, the ill one does to others, living itself separates. Living is torture since being alive separates.

Therefore, Kaliayev will not "add to living justice for dead justice." He will, however, become a scrupulous assassin. He will kill the Archduke, although he refuses to accept the fact that he has killed a man and not an idea. He also insists upon paying for his crime with his own life. He says, as did the real Kaliayev before he died, "death will be my supreme protest against a world made of tears and blood."

Camus' theatre gathers its force by replacing the outworn ideas of the naturalistic theatre by newer ideas based on a re-evaluation of the situation of man and the meaning of the universe. It is a theatre founded on the dark premise of no-sense, against which man, because he is man, is forced to revolt; a world of no-values, in which man must strive, no matter what the failure, to establish value; a tragic but human-centered world in which "revolt is justified by failure and purified in death." [3]

The drama of Bertolt Brecht, much more varied and extensive than that of Camus, does not demonstrate the same tragic point of view nor depend upon the same metaphysical analysis. Starting as an expressionist in the period shortly after World War I, Brecht associated himself with the Activists of that movement and soon came to see the theatre as a political forum at the same time as it was an art form. Indeed, to Brecht, these were not opposing terms, but necessary corollaries. Even in his most didactic Lehrstück (written in the 1930's) Brecht was not in any simple sense a propaganda writer and though an avowed Marxian his plays have never been found entirely satisfactory to many of the East German reviewers.

What to some may seem his political ambivalence is a steady fact at the center of his art and one that demonstrates the propriety of linking him with Camus.

As with the latter, he assumes a world dominated by material things (in Brecht the emphasis is upon their economic aspect). Against

[3] Simon, p. 211.

this world, man must revolt. It would be simple to imply that this revolt is purely social in Brecht, philosophical in Camus. But even as Camus assumes intuitively rather than analytically that the individual must establish values, so Brecht departs from the simple Marxist concern with a revolt of the economically oppressed to an intuitive belief in the necessity of the individual to establish value within himself. The individual must change before social conditions (the world of things) can be changed.

This point of view is apparent in Brecht's comparison of the Dramatic and Epic work of art which he appended to his opera *Mahoganny*. The dramatic character, he says, is unchanging, the epic is capable of change. This change, however, is not noticeable in the characters in Brecht's plays—and here we have another similarity with the work of Camus—but is rather a desired effect in the audience. Mother Courage does not change in the play of that name. Living through the cruelties and degradations of the Thirty Years War, one after the other losing her three children, at the end of the play she pulls her wagon by herself, ready as best she can for the next phase of the war. Like the Bourbons, she has learned nothing, and forgotten nothing. But by the method of presentation, by detachment and emotional involvement dialectically opposed, Brecht has hoped to demonstrate the possibility of change in that character of the drama which is the audience. It is in this sense that the quotation given earlier is to be fully appreciated: "watching and hearing are activities."

As with Camus, the drama is an engagement of the audience as well as the actor and the playwright. The removed observation of the naturalist's theatre is completely abandoned. Brecht, more than any other modern author, has envisaged the audience as a vital part of the theatrical performance. The play is a dialogue in which the audience must participate, no matter how silently, and the devices of playwriting and production which serve to interrupt the "normal" flow of story-line, character development, empathic response, are all cues to the audience that "Watching and hearing are activities." To Brecht, the audience must not be a group of *"people to whom something is being done."* The audience must change, so that the world may be changed. Only in an active, critical approach to drama and to life can the dominance of material things be overcome in the personal as well as the social sphere.

To Brecht, the human being must change so that the order of things may be changed. In the sphere of life, man must no longer accept the happy conclusion implied by Darwin as he viewed the materially ordered world of his *Origin of Species:*

From the war of nature, from famine and death, the most exalted object which we are capable of conceiving, namely, the production of the higher animals, directly follows.[4]

Brecht could not feel such elevation at any aspect of war, or famine, or death, whether or not it were an attribute of some grand and over-riding design. Shifting to the humanistic possibilities of Marxian materialism, Brecht wrote:

Even the catastrophic bursting forth of the flood can be freely enjoyed in all its majesty by society, if society can become its master; the flood is then in society's grip.[5]

It was the material world of the social order, the catastrophic world of the economic jungle, against which Brecht felt that the revolt must be led. He was an artist, however, not a press agent for a particular system, and it is always the accent on the necessity of reform within the individual before society can be changed that allies Brecht with the humanist tradition represented in a different approach by Camus.

Brecht's *Good Woman of Setzuan* illustrates this point. Here some of the highest gods have come down to earth to find out if there are enough people living lives worthy of human beings. What they want are good people. They settle on Shen Te, a prostitute, because she is kind enough to take them in for the night. During the rest of the play we see Shen Te trying to live up to the ethical implications of this visitation and finding it impossible. Brought to her knees at last, she decides that "good deeds mean ruin," and she pleads her case before the gods by admitting:

To be good to others and to myself—
I couldn't do both at the same time.
To help others and to help myself was too hard.
Alas, your world is difficult! Too much misery, too much despair!
The hand that is extended to the beggar, the beggar at once tears off!

The gods will have none of this quibbling, however, and make no attempt to solve Shen Te's problem. They are satisfied to ascend to the comparative comfort of Heaven, singing the praises of Shen Te, the good woman of Setzuan, who calls out from below for their help, ruined by her attempts to be good, caught in the desperate paradox of the good intention that produces only unhappiness. One of the actors presents the problem to us directly in the Epilogue:

[4] (London, 1859), p. 528.
[5] *Little Organum,* para. 25.

In your opinion, then, what's to be done? Change human nature or—
the world? Well: which?

The whole drive of the play indicates that the answer is both, and
that one cannot be accomplished without the other. The grand scheme
of things, if there is a grand scheme of things, has no relationship to
the problems of man. Such a scheme is as absurd as the world of
Ionesco or the world of Camus. For Brecht, however, man does not
accept this absurdity, as in Ionesco, or defy it, as in Camus; rather
he refuses it with the assumption that another scheme of things can
be made that will have sense because "society can become its master."
This new order can be composed only with the aid of the individual's
critical understanding and his ability to incorporate within himself the
changes that he wishes to see established in the macrocosm.

This attitude is emphasized in another Brecht Parable for the
Theatre: *The Caucasian Chalk Circle.* Here the heroine is another
simple young girl, Grusha Vashnadze. She discovers in the first part
of the play that what the Storyteller says is true: "Terrible is the
temptation of goodness!"

Grusha, as had Shen Te, succumbs to this temptation and learns
that the world is not prepared to appreciate or foster her goodness.
It is only by the complete reversal of the normal processes of justice
that Grusha manages to achieve happiness. This is accomplished, however, by placing the play in a fairy-story atmosphere. The actions of
Azdak the judge that permit a happy conclusion to the sufferings of
Grusha are demonstrably abnormal and the words of the Storyteller
take them out of the world of reality:

> The people of Grusinia did not forget him but long remembered
> The period of his judging as a brief golden age
> Almost as an age of justice.

The reality of the play does not lie, therefore, in the manipulated
happy ending except as it ironically implies the rarity of the reward
of goodness. The full meaning of the play lies in its satirical and varied
exposure of the shortcomings of the average human being and his
seeming inability, in a selfish and material world, to act on other than
selfish and material principles. This is seen in many other plays of
Brecht—*Mother Courage, Three-Penny Opera, St. Joan of the Stock-
yard.* On a social level Brecht is demanding the same clarity of vision
as to man's condition and the same willed determination not to accept
the conditions as found, that characterize the dramas of Camus.
Camus' insight is personal, philosophical, and tragic; Brecht's is social,
political, and satiric. Both, however, refuse to accept the unimportance
of the individual man, even though their vision tends to tell them

that in the world as it is man's being and purpose are unintelligible. Brecht and Camus have proceeded beyond their observation to demand a kind of reason and a kind of order. Their approach and their conclusions differ widely, but they both evidence a concern with an ordered and selective art form that conveys their particular sense of the necessity of order in man and in his social and spiritual environment.

With Brecht and Camus, the domination of the naturalist's concept of the world has been revoked. Their plays are based neither upon an adjustment of man and his environment—the older drama of ideas—nor upon the more recent acceptance that such a rapprochement is absurd. They, and others like them, have written a new drama of ideas based upon fresh and challenging concepts of the universe in which man is central rather than peripheral, is the instrument rather than the product of change.

harold clurman

AWAKE AND SING AND THE GROUP THEATRE

ALTHOUGH *Awake and Sing* was a modest one-set play, Odets was unable to raise the money to produce it. Neither was I, when I addressed myself to backers interested in the "better things" in the theatre. The play, which showed people grappling with the petty details that mess up their lives, seemed in script form to make an unpleasant, harsh impression. The pettiness and mess were more apparent than the play's tenderness and pathos.

I decided to appeal to Franchot Tone in Hollywood. I called him by phone, and told him we needed $5,000 to produce Odets's play. He asked me to send a script on to him for reading. I promised to do so, but I insisted that he send the money without waiting for the script. Franchot laughed and agreed.

Though we now had the money to put the play on, no provision had been made to defray the cost of moving the heavy *Gold Eagle Guy* scenery from the stage of the Belasco, where the new production was to be housed. Part of Franchot's money had to be used to pay for this operation. Cheryl Crawford was obliged to raise another $1,500 to compensate for this unforeseen expense.

Rehearsals proceeded with remarkable efficiency and harmony. Boris Aronson, an artist whose talent had always interested me, was engaged to design the set. Stella Adler, though she first shrank from the idea of playing an unglamorous woman of fifty, took up the challenge because I suggested that perhaps after all she might not be able to do it. She wanted to prove that she could act virtually any role, no matter how removed from her in type.

Though it is true that everything at this time was done *con amore*, a few trifling circumstances cast shadows to highlight the generally creative atmosphere of our work. During the first week of rehearsal Bromberg asked if we could release him for an engagement in Hollywood, since his part in our play was only a secondary one. When I rejected the very thought of this, he said no more about it.

I was living with Odets on Horatio Street, and after rehearsal he kept me up nights to discuss the progress of the play. (We promised each other that if the play prospered at all, we would move to more respectable quarters.) I hardly slept at all. Because of over-concentration and the rapid pace of production—the play was rehearsed less than four weeks—I was in a state of almost complete exhaustion as opening night approached.

There were only nine members of the Group company in *Awake and Sing*. Most of the others were busy with rehearsals of *Waiting for Lefty* under the direction of Sanford Meisner and Clifford Odets. It was to be given at a benefit for the *New Theatre Magazine,* unofficial organ of the new insurgent movement in the theatre.

Sunday night, January 5, 1935, at the old Civic Repertory Theatre on Fourteenth Street, an event took place to be noted in the annals of the American theatre. The evening had opened with a mildly amusing one-act play by Paul Green. The audience, though attracted by the guest appearance of a good part of the Group company, had no idea of what was to follow.

The first scene of *Lefty* had not played two minutes when a shock of delighted recognition struck the audience like a tidal wave. Deep laughter, hot assent, a kind of joyous fervor seemed to sweep the audience toward the stage. The actors no longer performed; they were being carried along as if by an exultancy of communication such as I had never witnessed in the theatre before. Audience and actors had become one. Line after line brought applause, whistles, bravos, and heartfelt shouts of kinship.

The taxi strike of February 1934 had been a minor incident in the labor crisis of this period. There were very few taxi-drivers in that first audience, I am sure; very few indeed who had ever been directly connected with such an event as the union meeting that provided the play its pivotal situation. When the audience at the end of the play responded to the militant question from the stage: "Well, what's the answer?" with a spontaneous roar of "Strike! Strike!" it was something more than a tribute to the play's effectiveness, more even than a testimony of the audience's hunger for constructive social action. It was the birth cry of the thirties. Our youth had found its voice. It was a call to join the good fight for a greater measure of life in a world free of economic fear, falsehood, and craven servitude to stupidity and greed. "Strike!" was *Lefty's* lyric message, not alone for a few extra pennies of wages or for shorter hours of work, strike for greater dignity, strike for a bolder humanity, strike for the full stature of man.

The audience, I say, was delirious. It stormed the stage, which I persuaded the stunned author to mount. People went from the theatre dazed and happy: a new awareness and confidence had entered their lives.

A series of *Lefty* performances was given every Sunday thereafter at the Civic Repertory Theatre—all of them benefits. Finally on February 10 the press was invited to see *Lefty,* given together with the Group's experimental sketches.

The reviewers liked *Lefty* very much. At this time, after the Theatre Union had done three productions, and the Jewish workers' group known as Artef had won a degree of esoteric fame, one or two commentators noted that "the progress of the revolutionary drama in New York City during the last two seasons is the most recent development in the theatre."

Awake and Sing, which had been in rehearsal about ten days when *Lefty* was first presented, opened on February 19, 1935. It was accorded a very favorable but not sensational newspaper reception. In the *New York Times* Brooks Atkinson, after calling Odets the Group's "most congenial playwright," went on to say: "Although he is very much awake, he does not sing with the ease and clarity of a man who has mastered his score. Although his dialogue has uncommon strength, his drama in the first two acts is wanting in the ordinary fluidity of a play. . . . To this student of the arts *Awake and Sing* is inexplicably deficient in plain theatre emotion."

Awake and Sing was written out of the distress of the 1932 depression (not to mention Odets's whole youth). It was completed in 1933 and belatedly produced in 1935. Yet only when it was revived in 1939 did the same reviewer say: "When Clifford Odets's *Awake and Sing* burst in the face of an unsuspecting public four years ago, some of the misanthropes complained that it was praised too highly. Misanthropes are always wrong. For it is plain after a glimpse of the revival last evening that *Awake and Sing* cannot be praised too highly. . . . When it was first produced, it seemed febrile as a whole and dogmatic in conclusion. It does not seem so now; it seems thoroughly normal, reasonable, true."

Now when no one ever mentions the possibility or desirability of a repertory theatre, it might be pointed out that there can hardly be any true theatre culture without it, since most judgments in the theatre are as spotty and short-sighted as those Mr. Atkinson confessed. Indeed, the judgment of any work of art on the basis of a single hasty contact would be as frivolous as most theatre opinion. And, since I have paused to make the point, I might add that only by constant repetition through the seasons did the plays of Chekhov become box-office in Russia.

A bit of loose talk about Chekhov's influence on Odets cropped up in some reviews. Odets knew very little of Chekhov's work at this time, but quite a lot about Lawson's *Success Story*, in which he had served as Luther Adler's understudy. It was Lawson's play that brought Odets an awareness of a new kind of theatre dialogue. It was a compound of lofty moral feeling, anger, and the feverish argot of the big city. It bespoke a warm heart, an outraged spirit, and a rough tongue.

But the talk of Chekhov's influence on Odets's work was a minor note in the reception of his plays. Far more common was the bugaboo of Marxism or Communism. They constituted the specter that haunted the thirties. Rumor on these subjects was so prevalent that it reached even the daily theatrical columns. One reviewer, for example, spoke of "the simplicity of his [Odets's] communist panaceas." He preferred *Awake and Sing* to *Lefty* because in the latter "one finds Mr. Odets working now as a party member."

The Left press at the time of Odets's first success granted his importance, but was careful to make serious reservations about *Lefty*, spoke gingerly of *Awake and Sing* (in the *New Masses*), and called it "a come-down for the Group Theatre, an unimportant play whichever way you look at it," in the *Daily Worker*.

Odets became the central figure of the so-called Left movement in the theatre. But the relation of his work to Marxism or Communism was of a special sort not to be understood in terms of glib political commentary. The Marxist drift of the thirties no more "caused" *Lefty* or *Awake and Sing* in January and February of 1935 than *Lefty* and *Awake and Sing* caused the organization of the CIO in November of that year. All these phenomena, including also the NRA and the later acts of the New Deal (the National Labor Act and so on), were an outgrowth of and a response to a common dislocation that convulsed our whole society. They were all undoubtedly related, but they are by no means comprehensible if they are lumped together mechanically as if they were identical.

Odets's work from the beginning contained "a protest that is also prophecy." There was in it a fervor that derived from the hope and expectation of change and the desire for it. But there was rarely any expression of political consciousness in it, no deep commitment to a coherent philosophy of life, no pleading for a panacea. "A tendril of revolt" runs through all of Odets's work, but that is not the same thing as a consistent revolutionary conviction. Odets's work is not even proletarian in the sense that Gorky's work is. Rather is it profoundly of the lower middle class with all its vacillation, dual allegiance, fears, groping, self-distrust, dejection, spurts of energy, hosannas, vows of conversion, and prayers for release. The "enlightenment" of the thirties, its effort to come to a clearer understanding of and control over the anarchy of our society, brought Odets a new mental perspective, but it is his emotional experience, not his thought, that gives his plays their special expressiveness and significance. His thought, the product chiefly of his four years with the Group and the new channels they led to, furnished Odets with the more conscious bits of his vocabulary, with an occasional epithet or slogan that were never fully integrated in his work. The feel of middle-class (and perhaps universal) disquiet in Odets's plays is sharp and specific; the ideas are general and hortatory. The Left movement provided Odets with a platform and a loudspeaker; the music that came through was that of a vast population of restive souls, unaware of its own mind, seeking help. To this Odets added the determination of youth. The quality of his plays is young, lyrical, yearning—as of someone on the threshold of life.

It was nonsense for the New York *Sun*'s reviewer, in order to challenge the validity of *Lefty,* to check with a taxidriver on his average earnings. *Lefty* was not basically about the hackman's low wages, but about every impediment to that full life for which youth hungers. Hence the play's wide appeal.

Perhaps Odets privately harbored the belief that socialism offers the only solution for our social-economic problems. Perhaps his desire to share a comradely closeness to his fellowmen might attract him to those who hoped to bring about a socialist society, but he must also have suspected that temperamentally he might prove a trial to any well-knit party. Instead of being an adherent of a fixed program, a disciplined devotee of a set strategy or system, Odets possessed a talent that always had an ambiguous character. If because of all this the regular press was misled into chatter about his "Marxism" while the Left press was frankly perplexed and troubled by him, it may also be guessed that Odets too was pretty much in the dark on this score.

On the one hand, Odets felt himself very close to the people— the great majority of Americans—even in his bent for the "good old theatre"; on the other hand, his heart was always with the rebels. But who precisely were the rebels, and what did they demand of him? Those he knew were a small minority, and they marked out a line for him that he could not altogether accept. After the first flurry of Odets's success had passed, everyone discovered a "change" in him. The conventional reviewers were glad; the Left was disconcerted. But, in the sense they had in mind, both were wrong—Odets had not changed.

Perhaps the truth is that the vast majority, to which Odets felt he belonged as much as to any rebellious few, had not yet created for itself a cultural clarity or form, not to speak of other kinds of clarity or form—had not, for example, yet made for itself a theatre in which he could function freely. Perhaps the "few" who often criticized him more harshly than anyone else did not know how much they had in common with those they professed to scorn.

Whatever later wisdom might declare, Odets in the spring of 1935 was the man of the hour. Theatrically speaking, the climax of the Odets vogue came with the production of *Lefty* as a regular show on Broadway.

Since *Lefty* was only an hour long, we had to have a companion piece to go with it. Odets himself supplied this by dramatizing a short story purporting to be a letter from Nazi Germany he had read in the *New Masses*. The play, written to order, was finished in less than a week. Cheryl Crawford directed it, and the setting was designed by an unofficial Group apprentice, Paul Morison, who had performed similar services for us at Green Mansions.

This twin bill opened at the Longacre Theatre on March 26, 1935 at a price range from fifty cents to a dollar and a half—something of an innovation on Broadway.

In order not to disturb the casting of *Awake and Sing*, all the actors not engaged in that play took over the production of *Lefty* and *Till the Day I Die*, which, incidentally, was one of the first serious anti-Nazi plays to reach the New York stage.

Odets himself played Dr. Benjamin in *Lefty* (originally played by Luther Adler), and on opening night his appearance was greeted by an ovation. This was the last acting assignment of his career. Lee Strasberg under an assumed name played a small part in the anti-Nazi play. In the new *Lefty* cast Elia Kazan, replacing Bromberg, was thunderously effective. Everyone was sure we had picked him off a taxi to play the part—our "discovery" from Constantinople, Williams College, and Yale!

The new play was respectfully received though the *New York Times* reviewer thought: "If you want to register an emotional protest against Nazi polity, Mr. Odets requires that you join the Communist brethren"—a rather peculiar interpretation of a play that at most called for a united front against Nazism. But the plea for such a front in those days was chiefly associated with Communists.

The play actually was a rather old-fashioned piece of theatre in a style that derived from the swell of Odets's sentiment, an unavowed inclination toward romantic drama, and a feeling for social currents. It was a little artificial, yet not without some qualities of youthful sweetness and idealism.

Awake and Sing never made much money. Odets believed the failure of *Awake and Sing* to become a box-office smash was due to the Group's lack of business ability. He was wrong; the play attracted an important but small part of the theatre-going public: those who bought the cheaper tickets. *Lefty* and *Till the Day I Die* were seen by a devoted and intelligent public still too small (and poor), alas, to furnish box-office comfort.

Yet, except for their bewildered backers, the plays were an enormous success. They were the talk of the town, the thing-to-see for all who wished to remain abreast of the times. If we hadn't known this through reviews, interviews, public clamor, and an excited correspondence, I at least should have guessed it by the constant buzzing of the phone in the University Place apartment I shared with Odets.

The lion-hunters were on the trail. Actresses, publicists, bankers, novelists, editors, wanted to meet the boy wonder. There was a difference in his situation as compared to that of a young writer like Thomas Wolfe, who was similarly sought after on the publication of *Look Homeward, Angel*. The difference was that while Odets was regarded by many as the dramatic find of the day, he was in addition that new phenomenon, a radical, a revolutionary, a Red.

An interest in an important new playwright was altogether normal for people like Tallulah Bankhead, Ruth Gordon, Beatrice Lillie, Helen Hayes, Charles MacArthur, Clare Boothe (Luce). But when Bernard Baruch began to examine him, when Edna Ferber asked that he be invited to a party that she might simply "take a look" at him, when Walter Winchell sought him out to have him explain the meaning of Communism (only to decide that he preferred to get the information from the "top man," Stalin himself), we were confronted with a sign of the times as significant as it was comic.

Odets was in a whirl, pleasant at first no doubt, a little terrifying later. He bought himself more records and virtually doped himself with music. Little girls he had known in the days of our jaunts to Stewart's Cafeteria on Sheridan Square now approached him timidly (or suspiciously) and asked if they could still speak to him. This infuriated and bruised him. He began to feel rather shut off, isolated.

At the time *Awake and Sing* was written, a Hollywood scout offered him $500 a week on the gold coast. Odets asked me if it wasn't "unrealistic" to refuse it. I replied that it wasn't, if for no other reason than that he would be offered more later. When, despite all the acclaim, his earnings were relatively modest, though greater than they had ever been before, his agent called to tell him that MGM was willing to go as high as $3,000 weekly, perhaps even higher. Like a conspirator he whispered that he might be willing to consider it.

I overheard this conversation and was troubled by it. When I was at sea on my way abroad in April, I wrote him a letter confessing my reaction. It was his duty to himself, to his colleagues, and to his audience to go on writing plays. The three first plays, and the recently completed *Paradise Lost,* were a mere beginning. Odets answered that he was happy I had written him as I did. Indeed such criticism as my letter implied was always welcomed by him: it made him feel responsible. In 1937, after the success of *Golden Boy,* when I wrote him a letter in which I was very severe with him for not making better use of his time than he was wont to do at such periods, he said to me: "I received your letter. I loved it." Perhaps not all artists are so, but many flourish only when they feel a concern for their work that is eager, jealous, essential.

People from all over the country swarmed into our offices. They wanted to join us, they said, because they were in sympathy with our aims. It was often a rude shock to them when I pointed out that we were a theatre, not a cult, and that talent was still the first requirement for work with us.

The actors were now riding the crest of the wave. I do not mean this in any material sense, since most of the Group had as vague an understanding of their own economic situation as I did. They never worried over money except when they were broke, in which case a few dollars in their pockets would make them feel affluent again. They were thriving with a sense of fulfillment, the feeling that they were part of the main current, which to an extent they had helped create.

Our activity was incessant. A few of our people made experimental films with Ralph Steiner. Others helped direct plays for new groups. Kazan, for example, did this for the Theatre of Action, which produced *The Young Go First,* a play about the CCC camps. We arranged a symposium of lectures at the New School for Social Research. Lee Strasberg gave a course on stage direction at the Theatre Collective School. At Mecca Temple Morris Carnovsky did a monologue by Odets called *I Can't Sleep,* one of the pages of Odets's work most significant for its indication of the source of his inspiration—the troubled conscience of the middle class in the depression period. At the same time a playlet by Art Smith called *The Tide Rises* based on the San Francisco marine strike used the talents of the younger people in the Group and showed the Odets influence already at work.

New theatre societies were being formed all over the country to give the three Odets plays. Group Theatres shot up like mushrooms:

in Chicago, Hollywood, New Orleans, San Francisco. A Negro People's Theatre was set up in Harlem to give *Lefty* under the direction of our own Bill Challee. All in all, *Lefty* was being done in some sixty towns which had never before witnessed a theatrical performance. Thirty-two cities were seeing the twin bill of *Lefty* and *Till the Day I Die* at the same time.

Even suppressions, bans, arrests on grounds of "unlawful assembly" or "profanity," served to increase the play's prestige. These occurred in Philadelphia, Boston, New Haven, Newark, Dorchester, Chelsea, and Roxbury. On the west coast Will Geer, managing a small enterprise that had announced *Till the Day I Die*, received a menacing note: "You know what we do to the enemies of the New Germany." He produced the play, and was severely beaten up by Bundist hoodlums. In New York Odets put an extra heavy lock on the door of our apartment.

From a political or sensational standpoint, all this came to a boil when Odets went down to Cuba as head of a committee to study labor and social conditions, with emphasis on the status of students under the reactionary Mendieta regime. The visit—under the auspices of the League of American Writers—was supposed to last two weeks. It lasted a few hours; on the arrival of the S.S. *Oriente* the entire committee, composed of timid little white-collar workers and teachers, were arrested as "agitators."

The story made the headlines. Telegrams of protest were sent, meetings held, petitions signed. When I heard that some of the Group actors had called a protest meeting for the acting profession and saw one of them haranguing the small audience, beer-hall fashion, I became almost as annoyed as I had been amused.

Odets had been chosen to head the committee because in six months he had become a name. To be used in this way flattered him and appealed to his Hugoesque imagination. He wrote a few amusing reports on the matter for the *New York Post,* made highly inflammatory statements, and sounded off generally like a gay hothead in the Parisian forties of last century. He soon became bored with his own busyness, temperamentally foreign to his introverted nature.

Odets's plays aroused interest not only in theatrical and minor political circles but in the literary world generally. The book-reviewers devoted columns to him: he was being read in the same spirit as were the novels of Dos Passos, James Farrell, Erskine Caldwell, John Steinbeck, Robert Cantwell, and Thomas Wolfe. The Group as a whole drew strength from this graduation from Broadway onto the larger American scene. It also drew some false conclusions from it.

This became evident in its reaction to new plays—for example, *Winterset*. Maxwell Anderson was contemplating letting the Group, for which he had an abiding affection, produce the play if it would cast Burgess Meredith in the leading role. Despite interesting production possibilities and a fine basic theme, it left me rather cold. I could not make myself comfortable in its atmosphere of an "Elizabethan" East Side! But, considering the state of American drama, it was not a play to be dismissed lightly.

We decided, therefore, to read the play to our company. With the exception of two or three people the actors were more averse to the play than I. Though its theme was Justice and its idea sprang from a prolonged pondering on the historic Sacco-Vanzetti case, they felt no immediacy, no true life in the play, only a filtering of these matters through a sentimental literary imagination.

Lee Strasberg did not so much disagree with this reaction as he feared its consequences on the course of our development as a practical theatre. Because he felt himself under a cloud at this time, he failed to fight for his opinion. Two years later, when I admitted to the company that we had made a mistake in not doing the play, for all our reservations, since the function of a producing organization cannot be equated with that of the critic in his chair, the company maintained the integrity of its character and expressed shock at my change of view.

Yet it must not be assumed from this that the actors had become altogether complacent because of their newly won acclaim. On the contrary, there was a strong urge to make further progress. There was, for example, a movement afoot—led by Stella Adler—to take group lessons from the Russian actor Michael Chekhov. We all considered Chekhov a true acting genius, though the New York press had been unable to recognize it. The actors felt that they had achieved some measure of honesty and truth in their work, but Chekhov's gift for combining these with sharply expressive and yet very free color, rhythm, and design was something in which they knew themselves to be deficient, and which they therefore envied.

The discussion that ensued among us on this subject—a few suggested that Chekhov be persuaded to return to the Soviet Union— was a mirror of the Group's varied and lively state of mind.

Another type of discussion took place between John Howard Lawson and me. Instead of completing the play for which we had made him an advance, he had taken to writing a book. This book was intended to guide and correct himself as much as other playwrights who stood at a creative impasse. He planned to study the leading thought of the various historic epochs and to trace the manner in which this thought had been converted to dramatic use by the playwrights of each period. Then by assessing his own beliefs, by shaping them into some sort of system in tune with the most solid social wisdom of the day, he hoped to arrive at a methodology that would lead him out of the morass of his own violent mysticism and emotional anarchy.

The writing of this book, the reasons that motivated it, the changes within the author's mind during its writing, all were of utmost concern to me. They reflected not merely a personal but a typical drama in the æsthetic, moral, and social history of the period.

All that was clear to me then was that in our friendly dispute it seemed that I was advocating a greater reliance on the artist's individual instinct, and Lawson was insisting on a greater adherence to rational analysis, coherent thought, and a firmer definition of technique and objectives. Our positions had apparently reversed since the days when Lawson was fulminating rather wildly and asking: "What do you mean 'art of the theatre'?" while I had solemnly called for a more conscious approach to it. Nevertheless, I really made no issue of our debate, since I preferred to trust the testimony of works rather than the correctness of any idea.

That our success was neither universal nor equally gratifying to all who observed it, I began to suspect as soon as the first hurrahs began to die down. *Time* magazine, for instance, published besides its regular and, I believe, complimentary reviews of our three new plays a newsy report of Odets's career, which had to take the Group into account as the background from which Odets had emerged. It was all blithely factual, but there was a curious emphasis that was perhaps not accidental. The item stated that the majority of the Group were Jews (an untruth), and in another place conveyed the impression that from its inception the Group had nurtured the idea of making propaganda for a radical political philosophy. Thus our first production had been the Soviet play *Red Rust* (a misstatement of fact), and all our other productions that couldn't be interpreted in this light were either not mentioned at all or set down as subtle disguises of our fell intent.

Perhaps my announced intention of making another trip to the Soviet Union at this time served to strengthen the idea *Time*, and others, were trying to suggest. It looked even worse when Cheryl Crawford decided to join me on this trip. I expressed myself as exactly as possible when, in reply to a request for a statement from the magazine *Soviet Union Today*, I had written that, as a theatre man, I considered the theatre of the Soviet Union the most complete in our contemporary world, and added that I believed the Soviet Union was well on its way toward the creation of a truly modern culture. (What I meant by culture in this connection was the continuity of idea and sentiment between worker and artist, soldier and poet, philosopher and statesman.) With our leaving for Moscow, there was a certain amount of head-wagging and whispering.

robert warshow

CLIFFORD ODETS: POET
OF THE JEWISH MIDDLE CLASS

> Before migrating to America, all the ethnic
> groups of Yankee City possessed a family
> pattern of the patriarchal type in which the
> wife was subordinated to the husband and
> the children to the father. America has dis-
> rupted this pattern, increasing the wife's
> independence and making the children car-
> riers of the new culture—a role that has
> brought them into open conflict with their
> parents. Among Jews these developments
> manifested themselves in their most extreme
> form.
>
> "The Jews of Yankee City"
> (*Commentary*, January 1946)

THE LITERARY TREATMENT of American Jewish life has always suffered
from the psychological commitments of Jewish writers. Their motives
are almost never pure: they must dignify the Jews, or plead for them,
or take revenge upon them, and the picture they create is correspondingly distorted by romanticism or sentimentality or vulgarity.
The romantic-sentimental picture, which endows the Jews with superior wisdom and an exaggerated spirituality, is typified in an earlier
stage by the movie *The Jazz Singer*. It appears in more dignified form
in Elmer Rice's *Street Scene* and most recently in the Hollywood
biography of George Gershwin. The vulgar exploitation of the Jews
is more common; the work of Milt Gross is carried on for a later
audience in the self-conscious burlesques of Arthur Kober and the
banality of Leonard Q. Ross. A more serious and more savage type of
satire, focusing on the economic and social behavior of Jews, has
appeared recently in the work of such writers as Jerome Weidman and

Budd Schulberg, but their picture, if more honest, is still limited and superficial.

By a considerable margin, the most important achievement in the literature of the American Jews is that of Clifford Odets. No one else has been able to maintain that degree of confidence in the value of the exact truth which made his best work possible. His social understanding is limited, but he has been able to keep his eyes on reality and to set down his observations with great imagination and remarkable detachment. Jews are never commonplace to him—they are never commonplace to any Jew—but neither are they prodigies, either of absurdity or of pathos or of evil. He has perceived that they are human beings living the life which happens to be possible to them.

The elements that make up for most American Jews the image of their group are to be found in the Jewish culture of New York City; more specifically, in the culture of the Jewish lower middle class, in the apartment houses and two-family houses of the Bronx and Brooklyn, among those who all these years have had to think mainly about getting along. Not all Jews actually participate in this culture—perhaps most do not—but almost all are intimately connected with it. The New York pattern is the master pattern, repeated in its main outlines wherever there is a large Jewish population. What is especially characteristic of other areas of Jewish life is often simply the extension of this; what appears most sharply opposed to it, or furthest away from it, is often the expression of a deliberate struggle against it.

The crucial fact is that there are few who cannot immediately recognize and understand its smallest forms of behavior, its accepted attitudes, its language. If it is not "Jewish life," strictly speaking, it is for most American Jews the area of greatest emotional importance. It is what a Jew remembers, it is what he has in his mind when he experiences his more private emotions about being a Jew—affection, pity, delight, shame. Just as the life of the small town can be said in some sense to embody the common experience of the older Americans, so the life of New York can be said at this particular stage in the process of acculturation to embody the common experience of the American Jews.

Clifford Odets is the poet of this life. In the body of his work so far, with its rather specious "development" and its persistent intellectual shallowness, the spectacular achievement which makes him a dramatist of importance is his truthful description of the New York Jews of the lower middle class.

Awake and Sing, his first full-length play, remains the most impressive. He has since become a more skillful dramatist, but his progress in theatrical terms has involved a loss in the simple observation of fact which is his greatest talent: he has become more superficial and more sentimental. His significant field of knowledge is among the Jews, and what he knows about the Jews is in *Awake and Sing*.

In reading *Awake and Sing*, one is likely to be struck by its crudity: there is an illegitimate pregnancy and a hasty marriage, a life insurance policy, a suicide; the final curtain is brought down on a puerile note of "affirmation" (Odets has said, "New art works should shoot bullets"). But in the last analysis these crudities are of no great importance. The special experience of reading or seeing the play has nothing to do with the dramatics used to make it progress through its three acts.

For the Jew in the audience, at least, the experience is recognition, a continuous series of familiar signposts, each suggesting with the immediate communication of poetry the whole complex of the life of the characters: what they are, what they want, how they stand with the world.

It is a matter of language more directly than anything else. The events of the play are of little consequence; what matters is the words of the characters—the way they talk as much as the things they say. Odets employs consistently and with particular skill what amounts to a special type of dramatic poetry. His characters do not speak in poetry—indeed, they usually become ridiculous when they are made to speak "poetically"—but the speeches put into their mouths have the effect of poetry, suggesting much more than is said and depending for the enrichment of the suggestion upon the sensibility and experience of the hearer. Many of the things said on the stage are startling for their irrelevance; they neither contribute to the progress of the plot nor offer any very specific light upon the character of the participants: the hearer supplies a meaning.

The peculiarity of this poetic process is that it operates exclusively between the writer and the audience; it is not *in* the play. The characters are in a state of ignorance, always saying something different from what they think they are saying. This differs from dramatic irony in the usual sense by the cast that the ignorance of the characters is essential instead of accidental: they *do* know what is happening in the play; what they do *not* know is what they are. In a sense they are continually engaged in giving themselves away.

The effect of the method is to increase the distance between the audience and the specific facts of the play, while bringing before the audience more clearly than is usual the general facts about Jews and Jewish life which the play illustrates.

The young son, Ralph, puts into one sentence the history of his frustration: "It's crazy—all my life I want a pair of black and white shoes and can't get them. It's crazy!" The mother, Bessie, responds, betraying the bitterness of her relations with her children, the difficulty of her life, the general picture of what it must be like to live with her: "In a minute I'll get up from the table. I can't take a bite in my mouth no more." Demolishing an argument for the abolition of private property, she presents her concept of man's fate: "Noo, go fight City Hall!" She offers a scrap of worldly wisdom to justify her tricking a young man into marrying her daughter, already pregnant by another man: "Maybe you never heard charity begins at home. You never heard it, Pop?" The old man, Jacob, shows what his daughter is to him: "All you know, I heard, and more yet. . . . This is a house? Marx said it—abolish such families." Bessie's husband, Myron, demonstrates his ineffectuality: "This morning the sink was full of ants. Where they come from I just don't know. I thought it was coffee grounds . . . and then they began moving." A sentence exhibits his tenuous grasp on American culture: "My scalp is impoverished," he says, out of nowhere. Sam Feinschreiber, the unfortunate object of Bessie's choice for her daughter ("In three years he put enough in the bank . . ."), reacts to the news that the baby is not his own: "I'm so nervous— look, two times I weighed myself on the subway station." Uncle Morty, the successful dress manufacturer, replies to the suggestion that he might send a little more money to take care of his father: "Tell me jokes. Business is so rotten I could just as soon lay all day in the Turkish bath." Uncle Morty prepares to leave the house: "Where's my fur gloves?"

To the experienced ear, every speech tells again the whole story, every character presents over and over the image of his particular kind, the role of his kind in the culture which contains it. The characters are diminished as human beings in favor of their function as instruments of poetic evocation. Rich or poor, happy or not, they serve their purpose. The responses called forth by the play are responses to the life of the Jews, to the psychological roots of one's own life, never to the individual lives of the people on the stage.

In the end you really get something like a direct apprehension of sociological truth, the whole picture built up out of the words spoken on the stage, the tones of speech and thought, all is added to the knowledge already possessed by the audience.

It is not the whole picture of the Jews; there is no whole picture of the Jews. And even as a partial picture it calls for some reservations. Assuming all necessary reservations, the picture might be called: what happened to the Jews in New York.

The adult immigrant had some advantages. Whatever it was that drove him to come, he was able to carry with him a sense of his own dignity and importance. He had a kind of security, though it is a strange thing to say of a Jew. In Europe, with the club over his head, he had nevertheless lived in a community which was in important ways self-sufficient, and which permitted him to think of himself as a man of value: he was a scholar, or a revolutionist, at the very least he knew himself to be a more serious man than his Gentile persecutors. To be a Jew was a continual burden, even a misfortune, but it could not have seemed to him a joke or a disgrace.

He came off a boat, he had to find a job the very next day, and for the rest of his life he was likely to be taken up by the numberless techniques of getting by: how to make a dollar, how to pursue the infinitesimal advantages which made it possible for him to survive from day to day. The humiliation of his poverty and impotence was tremendous, but he was already equipped with a mechanism for separating from it some of the needs of his personality. In his own mind, and in the semi-European atmosphere he created in the synagogues or the cafés and radical groups, he could contrive for his sad life the appearance of a meaning that went beyond the everlasting pettiness of which it actually consisted. He had a past.

For his children, helping after school with the family's piece-work or going themselves to work in the shops, and often suffering in addition under a savage moral discipline with no apparent relevance to the real world, the pretensions of the father could be nothing but nonsense. He could create in the minds of his children only an entirely generalized ideal of moral and intellectual superiority absolutely without content. (Bessie Berger: "I raise a family they should have respect.")

If the parents had a great deal of love and wisdom, or if the family made money soon enough, the children could sometimes arrive at a tolerable balance between dignity and economic pressure. But the familiar pattern was not often to be avoided: the children holding before them the image of a suffering and complaining mother and of a father whose life went outside of the home, who was somehow responsible—with his "ideas"—for the family's hardships. It was remembered with undying resentment that he had given money to the synagogue or the Party—to "make a show"—while his family went hungry, and the things he believed in came to represent a wilful refusal to understand the principle that charity begins at home. ("Go in your room, Papa. Every job he ever had he lost because he's got a big mouth. He opens his mouth and the whole Bronx could fall in. . . . A good barber not to hold a job a week.") If he made money at last, then his demonstrations of allegiance to the things he thought valuable might be received with more tolerance, even with pride, but they still remained for his children outside the area of practical life.

For his part, he was always disappointed in his children, and his sense of disappointment was often the only thing he could clearly communicate to them. He succeeded at least in becoming a reproach to them, and the bitterness of the personal conflict which ensued was aggravated by the fact that they could never quite see from what he derived his superiority or what it was he held against them.

The children took hold of what seemed to them the essential point —that they were living in a jungle. It would not be accurate to say that they failed to understand the rest; so far as they were concerned, the rest was not there to see, it had retired into the mind.

They tried to act reasonably. Every day they could see more clearly the basic truth: without a dollar you don't look the world in the eye. This truth was not for a moment welcome to them, they accepted it with all suitable reluctance, they doffed their hats continually in the direction of the "other things," but they really saw no alternative to following out the implications of what they knew. After all, their analysis of the situation was virtually a matter of life and death. ("Ralphie, I worked too hard all my years to be treated like dirt. . . . Summer shoes you didn't have, skates you never had, but I bought a new dress every week. A lover I kept—Mr. Gigolo! . . . If I didn't worry about the family who would? . . . Maybe you wanted me to give up twenty years ago. Where would you be now? You'll excuse my expression—a bum in the park!")

Between the facts as they saw them and the burden of undefined moral responsibility laid upon them by the father, no decision was possible. Money was at least effective, it could really solve their worst problems. It was what they *had* to have. What they wanted was not money, but it was nothing very definite. The best basis they could find for their life was a worldly compromise: money is filth, but money is all you'll ever get.

In general terms, the kind of life they established for themselves is not different from the characteristic life of the rest of their society: its primary concerns are economic security and social prestige; its day-dreams are of unlimited economic security and unassailable social prestige. ("Ralph should only be a success like you, Morty. I should only live to see the day when he drives up to the door in a big car with a chauffeur and a radio. I could die happy, believe me.") Indeed, they were especially quick to perceive the underlying pattern of the society and to conform to it. Looking from the outside, and suffering from the hostility of those around them, they naturally understood the significant facts thoroughly; for Jews, that had always been one of the necessities of life.

But it was not merely a matter of a generation moving from one culture into another. As it happened, the newer culture had already come to a point where it was unable to provide much security or dignity even for those who indisputably belonged to it. Understanding was in this case a bar to adjustment, and the life of the Jews has been colored by their awareness of the terms of the compromise they have had to accept. Their frustration is part of a universal frustration, but their unhappiness is more acute because all along they have known what they were doing.

Sometimes their special situation gave them a kind of edge, as if they were a day older in history than everybody else. They were capable of phenomenal success. Errand boys made themselves into millionaires simply by shrewd and unremitting attention to the possibilities of capitalist enterprise. Entertainers, exploiting the contrast between what they were and what they wanted, found a huge audience suddenly ready to see the point. Hollywood became a gold mine, demonstrating that the Jews were not different from everybody else, only a little further along: they could feel the exact level to which culture had come.

Success made no essential difference. A million dollars was a great and wonderful thing—how can you refuse money if you don't know what would be better?—but they could never believe that it was really enough to make a man important. Uncle Morty says "Where's my fur gloves?" not to impress the others but to remind himself of how far he has come.

They wanted also to be good and wise men. Having no frame of reference by which to attach a meaning to "good" and "wise," even a false meaning, they were forced to seek what assurance they could find in the tangible evidences they knew to be valueless: money, prestige, the intellectual superiority of one man to another. Thus from the complex of their fears and desires they evolved the three imperatives that govern them: be secure, be respected, be intelligent. In their world a dentist is better than a machinist, a doctor is better than a businessman, a college professor is best of all. But an unsuccessful intellectual is worse than an unsuccessful businessman: he should have known better than to try.

Their economic strength comes from their ability to act as the situation demands even though the situation is abhorrent to them. But the gap between moral man and the requirements of reality has seemed to them so wide that they have been able to function successfully only by imposing cynicism on themselves as a kind of discipline. They have gone further than most in the acceptance of reality, and this is perhaps the strongest kind of subversion—to take capitalism without sugar.

What it costs them is their characteristic mental insecurity, a mixture of self-pity and self-contempt. Self-pity because their way of life was forced upon them, self-contempt because they can accept no excuse.

Awake and Sing is a depression play, and its picture of Jewish life is sharper and more brutal than it would have been a few years earlier. The hidden framework of need and compulsion had come out. If it had ever been possible for the Jews to lull themselves completely in the material benefits of capitalism, that possibility was gone. With the depression, their painfully built structure of defenses shook and fell, respectability itself was threatened, and they looked again into the abyss of poverty, all the more frightening because it was so familiar, because they had given so much to get out of it.

The characters contemplate the meaninglessness of their lives. The image of their failure is constantly before them; they cannot contain themselves, they must burst out every minute in a fury of bitterness and impotence, justifying themselves, calling for pity, enveloping themselves and the world in indiscriminate scorn. They have ceased to communicate; each confronts his own unhappiness, using language primarily as an instrument of self-expression and a weapon of defense.

It is as if no one really listens to anyone else; each takes his own line, and the significant connections between one speech and another are not in logic but in the heavy emotional climate of the family.

> RALPH: I don't know. . . . Every other day to sit around with the blues and mud in your mouth.
> MYRON: That's how it is—life is like that—a cake-walk.
> RALPH: What's it get you?
> HENNIE: A four-car funeral.
> RALPH: What's it for?
> JACOB: What's it for? If this life leads to a revolution it's a good life. Otherwise it's for nothing.
> BESSIE: Never mind, Pop! Pass me the salt.
> RALPH: It's crazy—all my life I want a pair of black and white shoes and can't get them. It's crazy!
> BESSIE: In a minute I'll get up from the table. I can't take a bite in my mouth no more.
> MYRON: Now, Momma, just don't excite yourself—
> BESSIE: I'm so nervous I can't hold a knife in my hand.

MYRON: Is that a way to talk, Ralphie? Don't Momma work hard enough all day?

BESSIE: On my feet twenty-four hours?

MYRON: On her feet—

RALPH: What do I do—go to night clubs with Greta Garbo? Then when I come home can't even have my own room? Sleep on a day-bed in the front room!

BESSIE: He's starting up that stuff again. When Hennie here marries you'll have her room—I should only live to see the day.

HENNIE: Me too.

They live on top of one another, in that loveless intimacy which is the obverse of the Jewish virtue of family solidarity, and their discontentment is expressed in continual and undisguised personal hostility. The son, Ralph, is in love:

BESSIE: A girl like that he wants to marry. A skinny consumptive . . . six months already she's not working—taking charity from an aunt. You should see her. In a year she's dead on his hands. . . . Miss Nobody should step in the picture and I'll stand by with my mouth shut.

RALPH: Miss Nobody! Who am I? Al Jolson?

BESSIE: Fix your tie!

RALPH: I'll take care of my own life.

BESSIE: You'll take care? Excuse my expression, you can't even wipe your nose yet! He'll take care!

Someone is slow about coming to the dining-room: "Maybe we'll serve for you a special blue-plate supper in the garden?" Morty responds to one of Jacob's dissertations on the class struggle: "Like Boob McNutt you know! Don't go in the park, Pop—the squirrels'll get you."

In a brilliant climax, Bessie Berger reveals the whole pattern of psychological and moral conflict that dominates her and her family: when Ralph discovers that his sister's husband was trapped into marriage, Bessie, confronted inescapably with her own immorality, and trembling before her son's contempt, turns upon her *father*, who has said nothing, and smashes the phonograph records that are his most loved possessions and the symbol of his superiority. This act of fury is irrelevant only on the surface: one understands immediately that Bessie has gone to the root of the matter.

Purposeless, insecure, defeated, divided within themselves, the Bergers made a life like a desert. The process which produced them was not ironbound; one way or another, there were many who escaped. But the Bergers are important. The luckiest is not out of sight of them; no consideration of the Jews in America can leave them out; in the consciousness of most of us they do in some sense stand for "Jew."

robert warshow

THE LIBERAL CONSCIENCE IN *THE CRUCIBLE*

ONE OF THE THINGS that have been said of *The Crucible,* Arthur
Miller's new play about the Salem witchcraft trials, is that we must
not be misled by its obvious contemporary relevance: it is a drama
of universal significance. This statement, which has usually a somewhat
apologetic tone, seems to be made most often by those who do not
fail to place great stress on the play's "timeliness." I believe it means
something very different from what it appears to say, almost the contrary, in fact, and yet not quite the contrary either. It means: do not
be misled by the play's historical theme into forgetting the main point,
which is that "witch trials" are always with us, and especially today;
but on the other hand do not hold Mr. Miller responsible either for
the inadequacies of his presentation of the Salem trials or for the
many undeniable and important differences between those trials and
the "witch trials" that are going on now. It is quite true, nevertheless,
that the play is, at least in one sense, of "universal significance." Only
we must ask what this phrase has come to mean, and whether the
quality it denotes is a virtue.

The Puritan tradition, the greatest and most persistent formulator
of American simplifications, has itself always contained elements dis-
turbingly resistant to ideological—or even simply rational—understanding. The great debate in American Calvinism over "good works"
versus the total arbitrariness of the divine will was won, fortunately
and no doubt inevitably, by those who held that an actively virtuous
life must be at least the outward sign of "election." But this interpretation was entirely pragmatic; it was made only because it had to be
made, because in the most literal sense one could not survive in a
universe of absolute predestination. The central contradiction of Calvinism remained unresolved, and the awful confusions of the Puritan
mind still embarrass our efforts to see the early history of New England as a clear stage in the progress of American enlightenment. Only

Hawthorne among American writers has seriously tried to deal with these confusions as part of the "given" material of literature, taking the Puritans in their own terms as among the real possibilities of life, and the admiration we accord to his tense and brittle artistry is almost as distant as our admiration of the early New Englanders themselves; it is curious how rarely Hawthorne has been mentioned beside Melville and James even in recent explorations of the "anti-liberal" side of our literature.

The Salem witch trials represent how far the Puritans were ready to go in taking their doctrines seriously. Leaving aside the slavery question and what has flowed from it, those trials are perhaps the most disconcerting single episode in our history: the occurrence of the unthinkable on American soil, and in what our schools have rather successfully taught us to think of as the very "cradle of Americanism." Of Europe's witch trials, we have our opinion. But these witch trials are "ours"; where do they belong in the "tradition"?

For Americans, a problem of this sort demands to be resolved, and there have been two main ways of resolving it. The first is to regard the trials as a historical curiosity; a curiosity by definition requires no explanation. In this way the trials are placed among the "vagaries" of the Puritan mind and can even offer a kind of amusement, like the amusement we have surprisingly agreed to find in the so-called "rough justice" of the Western frontier in the last century. But the more usual and more deceptive way of dealing with the Salem trials has been to assimilate them to the history of progress in civil rights. This brings them into the world of politics, where, even if our minds are not always made up, at least we think we know what the issues are. Arthur Miller, I need hardly say, has adopted this latter view.

Inevitably, I suppose, we will find in history what we need to find. But in this particular "interpretation" of the facts there seems to be a special injustice. The Salem trials were not political and had nothing whatever to do with civil rights, unless it is a violation of civil rights to hang a murderer. Nor were the "witches" being "persecuted"—as the Puritans did persecute Quakers, for instance. The actual conduct of the trials, to be sure, was outrageous, but no more outrageous than the conduct of ordinary criminal trials in England at the time. In any case, it is a little absurd to make the whole matter rest on the question of fair trial: how can there be a "fair trial" for a crime which not only has not been committed, but is impossible? The Salem "witches" suffered something that may be worse than persecution: they were hanged because of a metaphysical error. And they chose to die—for all could have saved themselves by "confession"

—not for a cause, not for "civil rights," not even to defeat the error that hanged them, but for their own credit on earth and in heaven: they would not say they were witches when they were not. They lived in a universe where each man was saved or damned by himself, and what happened to them was personal. Certainly their fate is not lacking in universal significance; it was a human fate. But its universality—if we must have the word—is of that true kind which begins and ends in a time and a place. One need not believe in witches, or even in God, to understand the events in Salem, but it is mere provinciality to ignore the fact that both those ideas had a reality for the people of Salem that they do not have for us.

The "universality" of Mr. Miller's play belongs neither to literature nor to history, but to that journalism of limp erudition which assumes that events are to be understood by referring them to categories, and which is therefore never at a loss for a comment. Just as in *Death of a Salesman* Mr. Miller sought to present "the American" by eliminating so far as possible the "non-essential" facts which might have made his protagonist a particular American, so in *The Crucible* he reveals at every turn his almost contemptuous lack of interest in the particularities—which is to say, the reality—of the Salem trials. The character and motives of all the actors in this drama are for him both simple and clear. The girls who raised the accusation of witchcraft were merely trying to cover up their own misbehavior. The Reverend Samuel Parris found in the investigation of witchcraft a convenient means of consolidating his shaky position in a parish that was murmuring against his "undemocratic" conduct of the church. The Reverend John Hale, a conscientious and troubled minister who, given the premises, must have represented something like the best that Puritan New England had to offer, and whose agonies of doubt might have been expected to call forth the highest talents of a serious playwright, appears in *The Crucible* as a kind of idiotic "liberal" scoutmaster, at first cheerfully confident of his ability to cope with the Devil's wiles and in the last act babbling hysterically in an almost comic contrast to the assured dignity of the main characters. Deputy Governor Danforth, presented as the virtual embodiment of early New England, never becomes more than a pompous, unimaginative politician of the better sort.

As for the victims themselves, the most significant fact is Miller's choice of John Proctor for his leading character: Proctor can be seen as one of the more "modern" figures in the trials, hardheaded, skeptical, a voice of common sense (he thought the accusing girls could be cured of their "spells" by a sound whipping); also, according to

Mr. Miller, no great churchgoer. It is all too easy to make Proctor into the "common man"—and then, of course, we know where we are: Proctor wavers a good deal, fails to understand what is happening, wants only to be left alone with his wife and his farm, considers making a false confession, but in the end goes to his death for reasons that he finds a little hard to define but that are clearly good reasons —mainly, it seems, he does not want to implicate others. You will never learn from this John Proctor that Salem was a religious community, quite as ready to hang a Quaker as a witch. The saintly Rebecca Nurse is also there, to be sure, sketched in rapidly in the background, a quiet figure whose mere presence—there is little more of her than that—reminds us how far the dramatist has fallen short.

Nor has Mr. Miller hesitated to alter the facts to fit his constricted field of vision. Abigail Williams, one of the chief accusers in the trials, was about eleven years old in 1692; Miller makes her a young woman of eighteen or nineteen and invents an adulterous relation between her and John Proctor in order to motivate her denunciation of John and his wife Elizabeth. The point is not that this falsifies the facts of Proctor's life (though one remembers uneasily that he himself was willing to be hanged rather than confess to what was not true), but that it destroys the play, offering an easy theatrical motive that even in theatrical terms explains nothing, and deliberately casting away the element of religious and psychological complexity which gives the Salem trials their dramatic interest in the first place. In a similar way, Miller risks the whole point of *Death of a Salesman* by making his plot turn on the irrelevant discovery of Willy Loman's adultery. And in both plays the fact of adultery itself is slighted: it is brought in not as a human problem, but as a mere theatrical device, like the dropping of a letter; one cannot take an interest in Willy Loman's philandering, or believe in Abigail Williams' passion despite the barnyard analogies with which the playwright tries to make it "elemental."

Mr. Miller's steadfast, one might almost say selfless, refusal of complexity, the assured simplicity of his view of human behavior, may be the chief source of his ability to captivate the educated audience. He is an oddly depersonalized writer; one tries in vain to define his special quality, only to discover that it is perhaps not a quality at all, but something like a method, and even as a method strangely bare: his plays are as neatly put together and essentially as empty as that skeleton of a house which made *Death of a Salesman* so impressively confusing. He is the playwright of an audience that believes the frightening complexities of history and experience are to be met with a few ideas, and yet does not even possess these ideas any longer but can only point significantly at the place where they were last seen and where it is hoped they might still be found to exist. What this audience demands of its artists above all is an intelligent narrowness of mind and vision and a generalized tone of affirmation, offering not only particular insights or any particular truths, but simply the assurance that insight and truth as qualities, the things in themselves, reside somehow in the various signals by which the artist and the audience have learned to recognize each other. For indeed very little remains except this recognition; the marriage of the liberal theater and the liberal audience has been for some time a marriage in name only, held together by habit and mutual interest, partly by sentimental memory, most of all by the fear of loneliness and the outside world; and yet the movements of love are still kept up—for the sake of the children, perhaps.

The hero of this audience is Clifford Odets. Among those who shouted "Bravo!" at the end of *The Crucible*—an exclamation, awkward on American lips, that is reserved for cultural achievements of the greatest importance—there must surely have been some who had stood up to shout "Strike!" at the end of *Waiting for Lefty*. But it is hard to believe that a second Odets, if that were possible, or the old Odets restored to youth, would be greeted with such enthusiasm as Arthur Miller calls forth. Odets's talent was too rich—in my opinion the richest ever to appear in the American theater—and his poetry and invention were constantly more important than what he conceived himself to be saying. In those days it didn't matter: the "message" at the end of the third act was so much taken for granted that there was room for Odets's exuberance, and he himself was never forced to learn how much his talent was superior to his "affirmations" (if he had learned, perhaps the talent might have survived the "affirmations"). Arthur Miller is the dramatist of a later time, when the "message" isn't there at all, but it has been agreed to pretend that it is. This pretense can be maintained only by the most rigid control, for there is no telling what small element of dramatic *élan* or simple reality may destroy the delicate rapport of a theater and an audience that have not yet acknowledged they have no more to say to each other. Arthur Miller is Odets without the poetry. Worst of all, one feels sometimes that he has suppressed the poetry deliberately, making himself by choice the anonymous dramatist of a fossilized audience. In *Death of a Salesman*, certainly, there were moments when reality seemed to force its way momentarily to the surface. And even at *The Crucible*—though here it was not Miller's suppressed talent that broke through, but the suppressed facts of the outside world—the thread that tied the audience to its dramatist must have been now and then under some strain: surely there were some in the audience to notice uneasily that these witch trials, with their quality of ritual and their insistent need for "confessions," were much more like the trial that had just ended in Prague than like any trial that has lately taken place in the United States. So much the better, perhaps, for the play's "universal significance"; I don't suppose Mr. Miller would defend the Prague trial. And yet I cannot believe it was for this particular implication that anyone shouted "Bravo!"

For let us indeed not be misled. Mr. Miller has nothing to say about the Salem trials and makes only the flimsiest pretense that he has. *The Crucible* was written to say something about Alger Hiss and Owen Lattimore, Julius and Ethel Rosenberg, Senator McCarthy, the actors who have lost their jobs on radio and television, in short the whole complex that is spoken of, with a certain lowering of the voice, as the "present atmosphere." And yet not to say anything about that either, but only to suggest that a great deal might be said, oh an infinitely great deal, if it were not that—what? Well, perhaps if it were not that the "present atmosphere" itself makes such plain speaking impossible. As it is, there is nothing for it but to write plays of "universal significance"—and, after all, that's what a serious dramatist is supposed to do anyway.

What, then, *is* Mr. Miller trying to say to us? It's hard to tell. In *The Crucible* innocent people are accused and convicted of witchcraft on the most absurd testimony—in fact, the testimony of those who themselves have meddled in witchcraft and are therefore doubly to be distrusted. Decent citizens who sign petitions attesting to the good character of their accused friends and neighbors are thrown into prison as suspects. Anyone who tries to introduce into court the voice of reason is likely to be held in contempt. One of the accused refuses to plead and is pressed to death. No one is acquitted; the only way out for the accused is to make false confessions and themselves join the accusers. Seeing all this on the stage, we are free to reflect that something very like these trials has been going on in recent years in the United States. How much like? Mr. Miller does not say. But *very* like, allowing of course for some superficial differences: no one has been pressed to death in recent years, for instance. Still, people have lost their jobs for refusing to say under oath whether or not they are Communists. The essential pattern is the same, isn't it? And when we speak of "universal significance," we mean sticking to the essential pattern, don't we? Mr. Miller is under no obligation to tell us whether he thinks the trial of Alger Hiss, let us say, was a "witch trial"; he is writing about the Salem trials.

Or, again, the play reaches its climax with John and Elizabeth Proctor facing the problem of whether John should save himself from execution by making a false confession; he elects finally to accept death, for his tormentors will not be satisfied with his mere admission of guilt: he would be required to implicate others, thus betraying his innocent friends, and his confession would of course be used to justify the hanging of the other convicted witches in the face of growing community unrest. Now it is very hard to watch this scene without thinking of Julius and Ethel Rosenberg, who might also save their lives by confessing. Does Mr. Miller believe that the only confession possible for them would be a false one, implicating innocent people? Naturally, there is no way for him to let us know; perhaps he was not even thinking of the Rosenbergs at all. How can he be held responsible for what comes into my head while I watch his play? And if I think of the Rosenbergs and somebody else thinks of Alger Hiss, and still another thinks of the Prague trial, doesn't that simply prove all over again that the play has universal significance?

One remembers also, as John Proctor wrestles with his conscience, that a former close associate of Mr. Miller's decided some time ago, no doubt after serious and painful consideration, to tell the truth about his past membership in the Communist party, that he mentioned some others who had been in the party with him, and that he then became known in certain theatrical circles as an "informer" and a "rat." Is it possible that this is what Mr. Miller was thinking about when he came to write his last scene? And is he trying to tell us that no one who has been a member of the Communist party should admit it? Or that if he does admit it he should not implicate anyone else? Or that all such "confessions" may be assumed to be false? If he were trying to tell us any of these things, perhaps we might have some arguments to raise. But of course he isn't; he's only writing about the Salem trials, and who wants to maintain that John Proctor was guilty of witchcraft?

But if Mr. Miller isn't saying anything about the Salem trials, and can't be caught saying anything about anything else, what did the audience think he was saying? That too is hard to tell. A couple of the newspaper critics wrote about how timely the play was, and then took it back in the Sunday editions, putting a little more weight on the "universal significance"; but perhaps they didn't quite take it back as much as they seemed to want to: the final verdict appeared to be merely that *The Crucible* is not so great a play as *Death of a Salesman*. As for the rest of the audience, it was clear that they felt themselves to be participating in an event of great meaning: that is what is meant by "Bravo!" Does "Bravo!" mean anything else? I think it means: we agree with Arthur Miller; he has set forth brilliantly and courageously what has been weighing on all our minds; at last someone has had the courage to answer Senator McCarthy.

I don't believe this audience was likely to ask itself what it was agreeing to. Enough that someone had said something, anything, to dispel for a couple of hours that undefined but very real sense of frustration which oppresses these "liberals"—who believe in their innermost being that salvation comes from saying something, and who yet find themselves somehow without anything very relevant to say. They tell themselves, of course, that Senator McCarthy has made it "impossible" to speak; but one can hardly believe they are satisfied with this explanation. Where are the heroic voices that will refuse to be stilled?

Well, last season there was *The Male Animal*, a play written twelve or thirteen years ago about a college professor who gets in trouble for reading one of Vanzetti's letters to his English composition class. In the audience at that play one felt also the sense of communal excitement; it was a little like a secret meeting of early Christians—or even, one might say, witches—where everything had an extra dimension of meaning experienced only by the communicants. And this year there has been a revival of *The Children's Hour*, a play of even more universal significance than *The Crucible* since it doesn't have anything to do with any trials but just shows how people can be hurt by having lies told about them. But these were old plays, the voices of an older generation. It remained for Arthur Miller to write a new play that really speaks out.

What does he say when he speaks out?

Never mind. He speaks out.

One question remains to be asked. If Mr. Miller was unable to write directly about what he apparently (one can only guess) feels to be going on in American life today, why did he choose the particular evasion of the Salem trials? After all, violations of civil rights have been not infrequent in our history, and the Salem trials have the disadvantage that they must be distorted in order to be fitted into the framework of civil rights in the first place. Why is it just the image of a "witch trial" or a "witch hunt" that best expresses the sense of oppression which weighs on Mr. Miller and those who feel—I do not say think—as he does?

The answer, I would suppose, is precisely that those accused of witchcraft did *not* die for a cause or an idea, that they represented nothing; they were totally innocent, accused of a crime that does not even exist, the arbitrary victims of a fantastic error. Sacco and Vanzetti, for instance, were able to interpret what was happening to them in a way that the Salem victims could not; they knew that they actually stood for certain ideas that were abhorrent to those who were sending them to death. But the men and women hanged in Salem were not upholding witchcraft against the true church; they were upholding their own personal integrity against an insanely mistaken community.

This offers us a revealing glimpse of the way the Communists and their fellow-travelers have come to regard themselves. The picture has a certain pathos. As it becomes increasingly difficult for any sane man of conscience to reconcile an adherence to the Communist party with any conceivable political principles, the Communist—who is still, let us remember, very much a man of conscience—must gradually divest his political allegiance of all actual content, until he stands bare to the now incomprehensible anger of his neighbors. What can they possibly have against him?—he knows quite well that he believes in nothing, certainly that he is no revolutionist; he is only a dissenter-in-general, a type of personality, a man frozen into an attitude.

From this comes the astonishing phenomenon of Communist innocence. It cannot be assumed that the guiltiest of Communist conspirators protesting his entire innocence may not have a certain belief in his own protest. If you say to a Communist that he is a Communist, he is likely to feel himself in the position of a man who has been accused on no evidence of a crime that he has actually committed. He knows that he happens to be a Communist. But he knows also that his opinions and behavior are only the opinions and behavior of a "liberal," a "dissenter." You are therefore accusing him of being a Communist because he is a liberal, because he is for peace and civil rights and everything good. By some fantastic accident, your accusation happens to be true, but it is *essentially* false.

Consider, for example, how the controversy over the Hiss case reduced itself almost immediately to a question of personality, the "good" Hiss against the "bad" Chambers, with the disturbing evidence of handwriting and typewriters and automobiles somehow beside the point. Alger Hiss, for those who believe him innocent, wears his innocence on his face and his body, in his "essence," whereas Chambers by his own tortured behavior reveals himself as one of the damned. Hiss's innocence, in fact, exists on a plane entirely out of contact with whatever he may have done. Perhaps most of those who take Hiss's "side" believe that he actually did transmit secret documents to Chambers. But they believe also that this act was somehow transmuted into innocence by the inherent virtue of Alger Hiss's being.

In a similar way, there has grown up around figures like Whittaker Chambers, Elizabeth Bentley, and Louis Budenz the falsest of all false issues: the "question" of the ex-Communist. We are asked to consider, not whether these people are telling the truth, or whether their understanding of Communism is correct, but whether in their "essence" as ex-Communists they are not irredeemably given over to falsehood and confusion. (It must be said that some ex-Communists have themselves helped to raise this absurd "question" by depicting Communism as something beyond both error and immorality—a form of utter perdition.)

Or, finally, consider that most mystical element in the Communist propaganda about the Rosenberg case: the claim that Julius and Ethel Rosenberg are being "persecuted" because they have "fought for peace." Since the Rosenbergs had abstained entirely from all political activity of any sort for a number of years before their arrest, it follows that the only thing they could have been doing which a Communist might interpret as "fighting for peace" must have been spying for the Soviet Union; but their being "persecuted" rests precisely on the claim that they are innocent of spying. The main element here, of course, is deliberate falsification. But it must be understood that for most partisans of the Rosenbergs such a falsification raises no problem; all lies and inconsistencies disappear in the enveloping cloud of the unspoken "essential" truth: the Rosenbergs are innocent *because* they are accused; they are innocent, one might say, by definition.

In however inchoate a fashion, those who sat thrilled in the dark theater watching *The Crucible* were celebrating a tradition and a community. No longer could they find any meaning in the cry of "Strike!" or "Revolt!" as they had done in their younger and more "primitive" age; let it be only "Bravo!"—a cry of celebration with no particular content. The important thing was that for a short time they could experience together the sense of their own being, their close community of right-mindedness in the orthodoxy of "dissent." Outside, there waited all kinds of agonizing and concrete problems: were the Rosenbergs actually guilty? was Stalin actually going to persecute the Jews? But in the theater they could know, immediately and confidently, their own innate and inalienable rightness.

The Salem trials are in fact more relevant than Arthur Miller can have suspected. For this community of "dissent," inexorably stripped of all principle and all specific belief, has retreated at last into a kind of extreme Calvinism of its own where political truth ceases to have any real connection with politics but becomes a property of the soul. Apart from all belief and all action, these people are "right" in themselves, and no longer need to prove themselves in the world of experience; the Revolution—or "liberalism," or "dissent"—has entered into them as the grace of God was once conceived to have entered into the "elect," and, like the grace of God, it is given irrevocably. Just as Alger Hiss bears witness to virtue even in his refusal to admit the very act wherein his "virtue" must reside if it resides anywhere, so these bear witness to "dissent" and "progress" in their mere existence.

For the Puritans themselves, the doctrine of absolute election was finally intolerable, and it cannot be believed that this new community of the elect finds its position comfortable. But it has yet to discover that its discomfort, like its "election," comes from within.

wallace fowlie

SARTRE

BY THE nature of the philosophy he expounds and by the forcefulness of his writing, Jean-Paul Sartre has divided the French intellectual public during the past fifteen years. Violent quarrels have punctuated the development of every phase of existentialism, the appearance of every book, and the early performances of every play. Political theory and political affiliation have had their part in these quarrels. Sartre has been denounced by Thorez and the extreme left as well as by the extreme right, whose exponents seem to be asking to have the writer burned alive. This atmosphere of argumentation and battle is not unusual in France. Every literary movement has tried—and usually in a belligerent way—to adopt and assimilate and illustrate a philosophy. Sartre's case represents this phenomenon in reverse order. He is a philosopher who uses literary forms for the expression of his philosophy. Almost at its inception as a highly technical philosophy, existentialism annexed literary genres: novels, plays, essays, in order to explain itself to an ever-widening audience. Its principal literary products are literary without any doubt, and can be approached as literature. They are also demonstrations. Critical writings on Sartre and existentialism have, on the whole, been a medley of philosophical explanation and literary judgment. And they will probably remain such a medley for some time to come.

M. Sartre, however, has said that it is not necessary to understand his philosophical system as such in order to read his novels and to attend performances of his plays. His doctrine, elaborate and meticulously constructed, is still unfinished. Any final judgment, either praise or condemnation, will have to be suspended, at least for a time. Meanwhile, Sartre belongs to literature in his multiple roles as novelist, dramatist, essayist, and polemical writer. His mind is as active and engaging as his pen is prolific. He has all the resources, all the capabilities of becoming a major writer. In fact, he is that already for

From *Dionysus In Paris: A Guide to Contemporary French Theater,* by Wallace Fowlie; Meridian Books, The World Publishing Company, Cleveland, Ohio. Copyright © 1960 by Wallace Fowlie. Used by permission of The World Publishing Company.

many critics who have not hesitated to couple his name with that of Voltaire, and to compare his influence with that of Voltaire in the eighteenth century.

The style of his writing is always close to his thinking. In reading him, one has the impression of following his thought in all of its complexity and immediacy. Writing that remains so faithful to philosophical thinking is bound to appear verbose and overabundant. Is this prolixity or richness? Such a question often comes to mind in the presence of a Sartre text. God is deliberately and doctrinally omitted from his considerations, and there is an absence of spirituality in the usual sense of the word. But there is sincerity and conviction. His characters seem separated from him and often appear more as arguments than as living human beings. But he places them in a world, in an atmosphere that is very much his own creation. There is a Sartrean "world," recognized as such in many countries of the real world today, and this is the result of a vigorous productive temperament, of an intellect and a sensibility that have redefined and agitated some of the eternal problems of humanity.

Three terms or themes concerning man's fate in the world occur so often in the writing of Sartre that they can justifiably be taken as the pivotal points of his considerations. First is man's solitude, his aloneness and even, in its extreme form, his alienation. Each of us is a body, separated from all other bodies, irreparably alone, a world unto itself which can never be fully communicated to another world. There are passages in Proust's novel on the separateness of every human life to which I believe Sartre would fully subscribe. The second term is man's freedom, a power residing in each isolated body which may or may not be used. Freedom, in the Sartrean sense, is closely associated with the third term, responsibility, because it is usually defined as that freedom which man may use in assuming some kind of responsibility which is outside of him, an autonomous responsibility.

These three terms, with the emphasis given them by existentialist philosophy, place the work of Sartre close to that of other systematic thinkers in the twentieth century. They announce considerations that are central in the work, for example, of the humanist André Malraux and the Catholic Georges Bernanos. Sartre does not believe that there is any system or any philosophy that assures man of enduring comfort and security and peace. Bernanos has expressed very similar convictions about Catholicism, which he defines as a daily struggle and adventure, and not at all as peace found within an established order.

The feeling of aloneness, of man's solitude, is constantly being contradicted by his desire to assume responsibility as a human being, to join with some cause. In fact, it is more than a contradiction or a paradox; it is a tension that often grows into such proportions that it can be called anguish or destiny or absurdity. These are the familiar existentialist terms and they designate the principal problem upon which Jean-Paul Sartre has thus far based most of his writing. His approach to this problem seems more systematic, more rigorously organized than the more dramatic approach of Malraux (in *La Condition humaine*) or the more lyric approach of Bernanos (in *Sous le soleil de Satan*). And yet it would be erroneous to look upon the novels and the plays of Sartre as propaganda literature, as *pièces à thèse*. They have their own unity and independence, their own settings and themes. They emphasize, more than the works of other twentieth-century writers, the restricted and yet all-embracing world of the human conscience.

Traditionally in France, the theater is looked upon as a domain that the leader of a new movement is anxious to capture and utilize. This was true for Voltaire in the eighteenth century and for Hugo in the nineteenth. Without being a professional dramatist, in the sense that Jean Anouilh is a dramatist, Sartre has used the theatrical form with considerable ease and naturalness and spontaneity. His thought about the great problems that his philosophy raises, such as man's solitude, and freedom and responsibility, has a greater clarity in the plays than in the other forms of his writing. As a dramatist, in the highest sense of the term, however, he lacks some of those mysterious bonds that join the heroes of the stage with their creators, and he lacks the full power of poetic expression by means of which spectators are able to follow the deepest dramas in the souls of dramatic heroes and even to see the most subtle expressions visible on their faces. The overwhelming facility of Sartre and his disarming intelligence are almost impediments in his more purely literary works and especially in his plays. One feels that the writing of his dialogue has been accomplished without effort because it is dominated by the very clarity of the subject matter as he sees it. But this dialogue, in its freshness, spontaneity, liveliness, is dramatic in itself, and because of these very qualities. One follows so many ideas, as they multiply rapidly in scene after scene, that they hold our full attention and we end by not missing, in any serious sense, the psychological hesitations and subtleties, and the dramatic insights of poetic metaphor that are pervasively present in such playwrights as Shakespeare, Pirandello, and Claudel. So substantial is the intellectual nourishment of a Sartre play, that we forget what it lacks.

When *Les Mouches* (*The Flies*) was first put on in 1943, under the direction of Charles Dullin, at the Théâtre Sarah-Bernhardt, Sartre was known to a fairly limited public for his volume of stories *Le Mur* and his novel *La Nausée*. He was writing at that time his treatise *L'Etre et le Néant*. His new treatment of the fable of Orestes seemed to the public of 1943 to bear a strong relationship to the moral dilemma of the Occupation. The Parisians went to the theater not only to see a new play but also to feel united one with the other in this interpretation of the daily drama they were living through. The theme of the Resistance was far less obvious to the public that attended the revival in 1951.

Some of the essential elements of the *Oresteia* are preserved in *Les Mouches:* Clytemnestra has married Aegisthus, who has usurped the throne and is tyrannizing the people. Electra, daughter of Clytemnestra and legitimate heiress, is impoverished. Full of hate, she sits at the door of the palace. Her brother Orestes returns from exile, brought back by fate and the persistent prayers of his sister. To these familiar elements Sartre has added the figure of an ironic Jupiter and a swarm of gigantic flies, evil-smelling and avenging spirits who hold the city of Argos in a mysterious plague. Orestes returns to the plague-ridden city of his birth, in obedience, as he explains it, to a need to return home, to feel himself one with his own people. (*Je me soucie bien du bonheur! Je veux mes souvenirs, mon rôle, ma place au milieu des hommes d'Argos. . . .*) Such speeches as this, in which a facile kind of comfortable happiness was derided, seemed to the public of 1943 to extoll the life of risk and peril that they were living through in Paris.

The newest theme of the play is that of Orestes as redeemer. After sixteen years of exile in Corinth, he returns to Argos and witnesses the poverty and wretchedness and fear of his city. Aegisthus maintains in the people of Argos, by means of a yearly evoking of the dead, an obsession with their past sins. In slaying his mother, Orestes will commit a crime far worse than all the other crimes of the city. He commits this deed of his own free will, as an act of justice, because he makes the discovery, in his dialogue with Jupiter, that the gods are not just. His crime will draw down upon him the swarm of avenging flies. As he leaves the city, the citizens of Argos are recovering their former lightness of heart and a conscience relieved of the obsession of guilt and fear. This concept of redemption, brought about by means of crime, is of course the opposite of the Christian concept of redemption, of sanctity and martyrdom.

The relationship between Orestes and the people of Argos is a moving dramatic situation in *Les Mouches,* and it is also the source of much of the existentialist philosophy in the play. Orestes makes a choice, and thereby exercises his freedom, when at the end of the play he takes on the fear and the guilt of his people and thereby experiences alienation. The reign of Aegisthus (which is also the reign of Jupiter) has made the people slaves to a dead myth. At the beginning of the play, Orestes wants to acquire the memories of the people and thereby fill the void of homelessness in himself. But at the end of the play, by killing Aegisthus and Clytemnestra, he takes on the remorse of the people and frees them from their guilt. The people of Argos represent, for the existentialist philosopher, the old collective power that is enslaved and propagandized. By making his choice, Orestes exists and creates his self. Electra, who at the beginning of the play appears as a revolutionary, is terrified at the end by her brother's violence. When threatened by Jupiter, she quickly falls back into conformity and into the state of terror from which Orestes wanted to liberate her. She criticizes Orestes' freedom and thereby announces in *Les Mouches* the unexpected theme of misogyny.

At the beginning of the play, Orestes returns to his origins and to his city. He finds in the city of his origins a people ruled by the authority of Jupiter and Aegisthus. Moreover, he finds that his mother has become the consort of the tyrant-usurper. Although he expresses contempt for the people of Argos, he kills for the sake of the people. This is a social gesture that is quite in keeping with the program of existentialism. The antithesis that the play establishes between the people and Orestes would seem to illustrate the antithesis that Sartre the philosopher establishes between "being" and "existence." The people of Argos, representative of being, are part of a system into which they were born, which they had not chosen and which they accept passively and guiltily. Orestes, on the contrary, demonstrates the existentialist creed of "commitment." By choosing to act, he emerges into the transcendent state of existence. By this function of his active will, he passes from the nondescript state of being to that of a dedicated existence. We do not see in the play how this emergence takes place, and yet we realize that the hero has renounced the collective (which the philosopher calls essences and systems) and has accepted as the condition of his existence a state of estrangement and anguish.

This freedom, practiced by Orestes in *Les Mouches*, is defined by the philosopher as the need in each man to choose at each moment of his life the way in which he should see the world. Man's freedom is therefore his conscience, which functions only when it is thinking something. In himself man is nothing. In order to exist he has to create his own existence. As his conscience, in its free functioning, separates him from all things in the world, he feels exile. But exile in his freedom. Jupiter says to Orestes that he is not at home in the world, that he is an intruder, a splinter in the flesh, a poacher in the lord's forest. (*Tu n'es pas chez toi, intrus; tu es dans le monde comme l'écharde dans la chair, comme le braconnier dans la forêt seigneuriale. . . .*)

Man is therefore called upon, during the unfolding of his existence, to create the very meaning of that existence. This admonition of existentialist philosophy dominates all the plays of Sartre. Man's conscience has to be perpetually lucid, perpetually choosing. What may possibly be called the psychology of Sartre is his study of the various means by which man tries to evade the necessity of choosing and creating his existence. Man's dream is to become placidly immobile like a stone, insensitive. This is his fundamental cowardice, his desire to play the social comedy of conformity, to appear before all other men as one of them. One of the characters in *Huis Clos* describes the six mirrors in the bedroom. In them she used to enjoy seeing herself as other people saw her and that kept her awake. (*Il y a six grandes glaces dans ma chambre à coucher. Je parlais, je me voyais parler. Je me voyais comme les gens me voyaient, ça me tenait éveillée. . . .*)

Huis Clos (*No Exit*) was first performed at the Vieux-Colombier in May 1944, just before the liberation of Paris. Three characters, a man and two women, find themselves in hell, which for them is a living-room with Second Empire furniture. Each of the characters needs the other two in order to create some illusion about himself. Since existence, for Sartre, is the will to project oneself into the future— to create one's future—the opposite of existence, where man has no power to create his future, is hell. This is the meaning of the Sartrean hell in the morality play *Huis Clos*. Garcin's sin had been cowardice, and in hell he tries to use the two women, who are locked up forever with him in the same room, under the same strong light, as mirrors in which he will see a complacent and reassuring picture of himself.

This play, an example of expert craftsmanship so organized that the audience learns very slowly the facts concerning the three characters, is Sartre's indictment of the social comedy and the false role that each man plays in it. The most famous utterance in the play, made by Garcin, when he says that hell is everyone else, *l'enfer, c'est les autres,* is, in the briefest form possible, Sartre's definition of man's fundamental sin. When the picture a man has of himself is provided by those who see him, in the distorted image of himself that they give back to him, he has rejected what the philosopher has called reality. He has, moreover, rejected the possibility of projecting himself into his future and existing in the fullest sense. In social situations we play a part that is not ourself. If we passively become that part, we are thereby avoiding the important decisions and choices by which personality should be formed.

After confessing her sins to Garcin, Inès acknowledges her evil and concludes with a statement as significant as Garcin's definition of hell. She needs the suffering of others in order to exist. (*Moi, je suis méchante: ça veut dire que j'ai besoin de la souffrance des autres pour exister.* . . .) The game a man plays in society, in being such and such a character, is pernicious in that he becomes caught in it. *L'homme s'englue* is a favorite expression of Sartre. The viscosity (*viscosité*) of such a social character is the strong metaphor by which Sartre depicts this capital sin and which will end by making it impossible for man to choose himself, to invent himself freely. The drawing-room scene in hell, where there is no executioner because each character tortures the other two, has the eeriness of a Gothic tale, the frustration of sexuality, and the pedagogy of existentialist morality. The least guilty of the three seems to be Garcin, and he suffers the most under the relentless intellectualizing and even philosophizing of Inès. At the end of the play, Garcin complains of dying too early. He did not have the time to make his own acts. (*Je suis mort trop tôt. On ne m'a pas laissé le temps de faire mes actes.*) Inès counters this (she has an answer to everything, Garcin is going to say) with the full Sartrean proclamation: "You are nothing else but your life." (*Tu n'es rien d'autre que ta vie.* . . .)

No further argument seems possible after this sentence, and the play ends three pages later when the full knowledge of their fate enters the consciousness of the three characters and Garcin speaks the curtain line: *Eh bien, continuous.* . . . This ultimate line which, paradoxically, announces a continuation of the same play, was to be echoed ten years later in the concluding line of Samuel Beckett's *En attendant Godot*. The two plays bear many resemblances both structurally and philosophically.

In 1946, shortly after the *maquis* activities of the Resistance under the German occupation, Sartre's play *Morts sans sépultures* (*The Victors*) projected in a highly tragic form the drama of *maquisards* captured and tortured by other Frenchmen who were collaborating with the Occupation forces. Of all of Sartre's plays, this is the most classical in structure, the most concentrated in intensity, the most rewarding in psychological study. The action of *Morts sans sépultures* takes only a few hours. It begins very close to its denouement. At the time of the first performances, the tragedy was so close to the actual events that had inspired it, that the experience of the spectacle was almost too painful to witness. Now, after a decade, the play can be more easily considered outside of its immediate context. The horror of its action can still be felt, but as a more universal horror than in 1946. It reaches extremes in the feelings of pain and horror it arouses in the public, and in fact the play may be criticized for passing beyond the horrors that an audience can stand.

Five members of the *maquis,* one a woman, have been captured by the French militia. Their prison is an attic where they are hand-cuffed and trying to prepare themselves for questioning and the inevitable torture. After a scene with those about to be tortured, we see the torturers, whose markedly sadistic tendencies are made clear, and finally we see the two groups mingled: victims and executioners. Three events, or what classical dramaturgy would call three peripeteia, give to this situation a dramatic action.

The prisoners know that their jailers mean to extract from them the real name and whereabouts of their leader Jean. Their principal consolation is that they do not know these answers and that therefore no matter what torture is imposed, they will not be able to reveal the truth. This is the situation at the beginning of the play. The first change (or peripeteia) is Jean's being pushed into their group. He has been taken by soldiers who had no suspicion of his identity. This new capture changes the atmosphere. The prisoners know now that under torture they may reveal a valuable piece of information.

During the first round of questioning, when one prisoner kills himself by jumping from the window, the others do not talk. But one of them, fifteen-year-old François, is not questioned. He is shaken with fear and almost collapsing in the attic and the others realize that he will not be able to withstand the torture. The cause is at stake, and they do not hesitate long before they strangle the boy. This is the second change, one of horror and tragedy. The third is a stratagem arranged by Jean, who is about to be released. He plans to place papers in the pocket of a dead comrade whom the militia, when they come upon the body, will take for himself. The prisoners are therefore to reveal the hiding place of "Jean." But this is of no avail, for after the confession, the most sadistic of the jailers shoots one after the other.

The anguished moral debate that goes on in the mind of each prisoner makes of this play primarily a psychological drama. We follow the thoughts of these characters far more closely than their actions. The situation in which they find themselves is extreme. Their reaction to it constitutes the drama. The physical aspect of this struggle is at no point omitted or softened by Sartre. Physical suffering is at every moment joined with moral agony. The individuals of the group, each one of whom suffers in a different way, are related to the vast numbers of people they represent. We are constantly reminded of the reality of the cause for which the prisoners are being sacrificed. A play that might easily have emphasized the anecdotal and the horrifyingly realistic, is raised to a high degree of spirituality. The sacrifice of François, for example, in the third tableau, is carried out as a ritualistic act. The individual is sacrificed to the group, as the group is sacrificed to the people. The meaning of sacrifice enables the prisoner Henri to strangle the boy François, as it enables the others to turn their heads away as the deed is done.

The melodramatic effects and the lofty moral theme of *Morts sans sépultures* are present in Sartre's next important play, *Les Mains sales* (*Dirty Hands*) of 1948. The atmosphere again is one of suspicion, espionage, and the insignificance of a single individual life in terms of the cause or the party. In 1948 Sartre was an intellectual leader for a vast number of young Frenchmen. Since his play underscored a tyrannical comportment among the leaders of the party, and an almost stupid submission among the subordinates, the very orthodox Communists in France claimed that the play gave a false picture.

The action of the play takes place in a buffer state between Germany and Russia, and which resembles Hungary. Deliberately Sartre raises in *Les Mains sales* doctrinal problems of the day. He is one of the few contemporary French dramatists who have attempted to treat directly the political tragedy of the twentieth century. The plot has improbabilities and exaggerations. It describes a kind of underground Communism that it is hard to believe existed in one of Germany's satellite countries. Hoederer is the veteran Communist leader. Hugo is the young convert to Communism from his bourgeois background. To choose him as the assassin of the party leader, who is suspected of weakness and infidelity, is the outstanding improbability. The character and strength and passion of Hugo are well drawn. Raised by an adoring family, he has turned against them and against their indulgences. The picture of his background is stilted and his revolt against it seems far out of proportion to its significance. Those to whom he has turned, suspect him. He works hard to be accepted. He has learned the doctrines of Communism as a child learns his catechism. He believes every article of the doctrine and recites it uncritically.

He comes to Hoederer to serve as a kind of secretary and brings with him his wife Jessica. She is lively and talkative, but shrewd also. The contrast between Hoederer and Hugo is striking. Hoederer knows the rules of the game as well as the novice. He has served the party for a long time and has moved beyond the age of theory. Moreover, he is strongly patriotic and has no desire to see the Red Army take over his government for long. It will be enough if it withstands the invasion of the German army. This is the origin of the quarrel between Hoederer and the other party leaders whose hands are "clean." In speaking with Hugo and Jessica, he unbends somewhat and undertakes to explain to them the reason for his work, the reason why at times his hands are "dirty."

But Hugo has the intolerance of the young and the ardor of the convert. Twice he shoots at Hoederer. Once when a grenade is thrown into the room, which indicates the party's scorn for his delay in killing the leader. And the second time, a more theatrical device, when he enters the room and finds Hoederer embracing his wife. This time he does kill Hoederer. Not for a political crime, however, but because of a surge of jealousy. Later, in prison, Hugo learns that the party has given up its position and officially taken Hoederer's stand. But Hoederer had been murdered because of this stand, and Hugo realizes that he murdered a hero. This moment of the play (which curiously enough has been criticized), when Hugo feels that his political faith has been betrayed, seems movingly tragic. It is the struggle of a purity in thought against the ways of the world, and surpasses even the intense argumentative scene when Hoederer tries to win Hugo over to his own political position.

The work of Jean-Paul Sartre was placed on the Index at approximately the time of the first performances of *Le Diable et le Bon Dieu* (*Lucifer and the Lord*) in 1951. When it was learned that the play was set in sixteenth-century Germany and that the hero was named Goetz von Berlichingen, Sartre was of course asked whether he had been influenced by Goethe's play of that name. He replied in the negative in an interview in *L'Observateur* and acknowledged some influence from a play of Cervantes (*El Rufián Dichoso*). *Le Diable et le Bon Dieu* has been called the opposite or the reverse of Claudel's *Le Soulier de satin*. During the first half of the play, Goetz is constantly deriding God. During the second half, he expresses religious aspiration, but this is impeded by men who do not reward holiness and by God, who does not exist. Sartre's philosophy redefines in this play man's fate as something absurd.

The steady flow of language, filling four hours in performance, has all tones and modes: impiety, mockery, atheistic existentialism: nothingness of man, the emptiness of heaven, the power of evil and its persistent logic, the impotence of the good and its ridiculousness. The play is almost a parade, an assembly of characters and arguments. It has an impressive majesty about it in the richness of the ideas and their provocative violence. There are a few truly dramatic scenes and others where the rhetoric of dialectic dominates. To sustain such a long and vigorous role, such an actor as Pierre Brasseur was needed in the part of Goetz. There are few actors today with his physical power and impeccable diction. Jean Vilar matched him as the priest of good will who was forced to treachery and casuistry.

The play is a chronicle and presented in the manner of classical Spanish plays, in three acts and eleven tableaux. Goetz, a captain, is fighting his brother Conrad, and besieging the city of Worms. This pleases the archbishop-prince who is dissatisfied with the bourgeois of Worms. Goetz wants to destroy the city, for the joy of massacre and pillage. He is on the side of evil and looks upon himself as contender against God. The wretched priest Heinrich fails to understand his duty and gives over the keys of the city to Goetz for a few religious imprisoned by the bourgeois. Then the unexpected takes place. Goetz cheats in order to lose. He chooses the good and distributes his lands to the peasants. But it is hard for him to do good, and Sartre demonstrates that he will win nothing and understand nothing about his experiment.

The generosity of Goetz is welcomed with suspicion and even open hostility. He tries to assume the suffering of the prostitute Catherine, who has been his victim. At one point, he deliberately wounds himself and pretends he has received the stigmata. He founds a new city (Cité du Soleil) dedicated to peace and nonresistance. The city easily succumbs to a general massacre. The defrocked priest Heinrich convinces Goetz that his reasons for doing good are the same reasons for his once doing evil. This leads Goetz to his conclusion that God does not exist. Here *Le Diable et le Bon Dieu* joins with an important theme of Sartre's first play *Les Mouches*. Crime appears as the condition for a true communism among men.

In a sense, the play is a vast elaborately staged demonstration of Sartre's atheism. (Catholics may easily wonder why Sartre worries so intensely about God who he decides does not exist!) At the end of *Les Mouches* some degree of hope for man's future is offered. Orestes had killed his mother and was leaving his native land, but at least he had been convinced that the gods are powerless when man learns that he is free. *Le Diable et le Bon Dieu* is on the theme of *Les Mouches,* namely the relationship between man and God, to which Sartre has given a more drastic answer. In the *Observateur* interview Sartre said that if God exists, good and evil have the same result. Goetz is responsible for general massacres when he is evil and when he is good. At the end of the play, Goetz accepts a limited human morality. The conclusion for man would seem to be social, but the play is confusing in its philosophical implications as well as in its structural organization. The strongest part of the text is in the opening tableaux, where Goetz appears as the incarnation of evil, as powerful as Lucifer and as convincing as Mephistopheles.

With these plays and with others not so successful (*La Putain respectueuse* [*The Respectful Prostitute*], *Nekrassov,* and *Kean*), Sartre emphasizes predicaments in which the characters find themselves. The situation is unusual and highly dramatic: a plague of flies in Argos (*Les Mouches*), a living-room in hell (*Huis Clos*), a torture chamber (*Morts sans sépultures*). The analysis of the characters in these plays is limited to the necessity they feel to adapt to the situation, to identify themselves with the situation, to choose the situation. There is a strong Corneillean tradition in this existentialist theater where will power is depicted at the heart of stricture and suffering. Whatever situation Sartre constructs for his characters, he is intent upon studying the conflict that takes place between the sincerity of the character in his effort to choose his own life and the power of his conventional world as it seeks to trap and distort him. The predecessors of Sartre, each in his own way, have analyzed this familiar struggle between convention and honesty. As studies of the conflict between sincerity and insincerity, Sartre's plays mark one moment in a literary theme that is both ancient and contemporary.

Such a lesson is almost ludicrously clear in *La Putain respectueuse,* where social morality is purely hypocritical and where the rights of men are in the hands of those in power. In the play the United States is satirized as representing a purely social morality. Behind such a play is an age-old quarrel over the source of evil: is it in an unjust unfair society, as Rousseau would claim, or is it in man himself, in the psychic life of man, as Pascal would say. Sartre, on the whole, takes the latter view. Whenever man is ruled solely by conventions that are hypocritical for him, he has failed in his own existence, failed in assuming his own rights.

One of the goals of literature for Sartre, defined in his elaborate theory of literature as commitment, is to reveal the petrification of man when as a coward he becomes fixed in a social pose. This immobilization is a glue, a stickiness, in Sartre's favorite image. Orestes in *Les Mouches* demonstrates the possibility of avoiding it. There is a danger at the beginning of the play that he will not change, that he will remain in a comfortable routine existence. When he learns of the crime that holds the city in its power, he has an intuition concerning his mission. If he perpetrates an act contrary to social conformity (in this case, the attitude of the people of Argos), he will liberate the city and create his own existence. In this choice of Orestes', Sartre very clearly defines the greatness of man as his willingness to accept responsibility.

If the realization of freedom is the first stage in Sartrean morality, the use of this freedom—its commitment—is the second stage, which will coincide with the discovery of reality. Orestes makes this discovery, and Hoederer, in *Les Mains sales*, represents in his life of action an acceptance of responsibility. Man, who before the realization and the employment of his freedom is nothing and is comparable to the immobile things around him in the world, becomes a "project." He becomes his own value. After killing Clytemnestra, Orestes explains to his sister Electra that he has committed *his* act, that he will bear its responsibility, and that henceforth he will follow his own road. (*J'ai fait mon acte, Electre. Je le porterai sur mes épaules comme un passeur d'eau porte les voyageurs. . . . Dieu sait où il me mène, mais c'est mon chemin. . . .*)

The plays of Sartre have the dynamics of existentialist exercises. In them he tracks down the alibis we make in our daily lives and flails the system of routines by which so much is carried out in history. The fear of standing alone forces us to these routines, exemplified in the plays by fear in the people of Argos (*Les Mouches*), by the static quality of hell (*Huis Clos*), by the goal of security in the bourgeois world (*Les Mains sales*).

gerald weales

WHATEVER HAPPENED TO JEAN-PAUL SARTRE?

IN ONE of the *Shoestring Reviews* there was a number in which the
chorus did an elaborate tango to a song, the words of which might
have been pieced together from the remembering conversation of
movie lovers whose first passion was more than two decades old, who
wondered what had become of Rochelle Hudson, of Bobby Breen.
I was reminded of that song when I fished from my mailbox the new
collection of plays by Jean-Paul Sartre[1] and carried it, uncovered,
down the hallway to my office. A dozen years ago such a burden
would have caused excitement—well, genuine interest, at least. Today, mild curiosity, obvious indifference. I was tempted to sweep one
of my colleagues into my arms—an absurd if not an existential act—
and tango to my destination, chanting, *Whatever happened to Rochelle
Hudson, whatever happened to Jean-Paul Sartre?*

By now it is a commonplace of mass-circulation sociology that
American culture, whatever continuity and solidity it may have at its
base, is on the surface a changing pattern of fads and enthusiasms. It
has become almost impossible for the American intellectual (the man
who insists on the label the way the Shriner insists on his hat) to
cling to the old pose that he is above the impulse that has recently
put Fabian on the front of fan magazines and stereo equipment into
living rooms. He knows that he has to have seen the movies of Ingmar
Bergman and the *nouvelle vague,* to have attended the plays of Beckett
and Ionesco, to have read the beats and the angries, if only to condemn. Literary booms are as artificial as those in show business and
the clothing industry, and their pattern is as easy to follow. A single
work attracts attention for some reason—its quality, its rightness for
a particular moment, its eccentricity—and stirs up comment—analyses
in the quarterlies, reviews in the weeklies, attacks often in the large-
circulation magazines and the newspapers. The comment in its turn

Reprinted by permission from *The Hudson Review,* Vol. XIII, No. 3, Autumn 1960.
Copyright 1960 by The Hudson Review, Inc.
[1] *The Devil and the Good Lord and Two Other Plays,* by Jean-Paul Sartre. Knopf. $5.00.

forces the publishers, the play producers, the film distributors to present more works by the same author (or the same group), which proliferation increases the comment and changes its nature—attacks in the quarterlies, articles in the weeklies discussing the phenomenon of the new success, favorable notices in the large-circulation magazines and the newspapers. The increased comment in its turn . . . and so it goes until the saturation point is reached, until the new fad dies of what the television boys, every time they bury a new comedian, call over-exposure. The object of all the excitement, the recipient of all the applause, his bubble burst, is forced then into a decline as artificial as his rise. In time, when he has ceased to be a fashionable success and an ex-fashionable success, he reaches the point where someone may finally look at his work for its own sake.

The Sartre boom was a kind of classic. Talk about him and his existentialism got to this country before his works did, smuggled in, one supposes, in the barracks bags of returning literate GIs. After the Broadway production of *No Exit* in 1946, a commercial failure and a critical success (it won the Drama Circle award for the best foreign play of the year), the sluice gates were opened and the deluge began. Between 1947 and 1949 more than a dozen books by Sartre were published—novels, plays, stories, film scripts, philosophical works, literary criticism. All of his plays were performed in New York. Erwin Piscator's group at the New School did *The Flies* in 1947; during 1948, New Stages, one of the first of the ambitious post-war off-Broadway groups, presented *The Victors,* Thornton Wilder's adaptation of *Morts sans sépultures,* and *The Respectful Prostitute,* which moved uptown and became a Broadway hit; a version of *Les Mains sales,* called *Red Gloves,* played on Broadway for three months, over the protests of Sartre, who disowned it. For three years, everyone wore Sartre in his buttonhole. It was impossible to open a journal of any kind without running into Sartre as author or Sartre as subject. College students, the reading variety, clutched Sartre volumes as they hurried across campuses to coffee klatches where everyone declared himself an existentialist. Anyone who was anyone read the first volumes of *Roads to Freedom,* which Knopf still calls "his famous tetralogy" although the fourth novel has yet to be written. Then, the bandwagon began to run down. Between 1950 and 1956 only five books by Sartre were published, partly because his early work had been pretty much worked over (the Philosophical Library should be able to mine a few more volumes out of his *Situations*), but mainly because the Sartre market was bearish. None of his plays of the fifties managed a New York production and only now, with this new collection, are they being published in this country.

Sartre's roller-coaster career as a borrowed American art-and-idea hero is so neat an example of the boom-and-bust course of our imported intellectual enthusiasms that he might be labeled Example A and forgotten. It is possible, however, to make a few guesses about why he should have had the success of the late forties and the relative decline of the fifties. His work was the first European work to come to us after the end of World War II. Since it came from France, it carried an automatic seal of approval, the one that became current in the twenties when the expatriates invented (or accepted) the myth that Paris was the cultural capital of the world, a myth, incidentally, which still has vitality despite the fact that the provincialism of French intellectuals has been smothering it for years. But Sartre's work not only evoked old loyalties to the France of Gide and Cocteau, but new loyalties to the French Resistance movement, the New France in the making.

Beyond the happy national label, Sartre brought a supposedly new philosophy, one which could be used as excuse or banner, depending on the user's particular psychological and philosophical set. The freedom of the existential hero became, for some people, particularly for those who knew Sartre's ideas only by reputation, a kind of license, a lifting of moral restraint, a downpayment a decade early on the big beatnik sell that was to be the noisiest domestic product of the fifties. On the other hand, the freedom of the existential hero, which included the necessity for each man to create himself and to bear the responsibility for his creation, could be seen and was seen as a positive philosophy, a road by which a man might make his tough way through a world which God had deserted and in which the economic and psychological determinisms could no longer be used as excuses. I still feel a sense of excitement at the end of *The Flies* when Orestes steps down from Apollo's protective pedestal and strides off, carrying the guilt of the city on his back, having made a real Orestes of himself by acting and demanding the responsibility for his own act. In the years right after the war, the brief period of hope that carried the United Nations in its womb, there was a suspicion that political action could make a new world. As the ideals of the French Resistance carried over into the first awakening of post-war France, so the sense of working together—brotherhood *is* the word—managed to stay alive briefly in a world at peace. So, in the late forties, the political Sartre was as acceptable as the philosophic Sartre or the French Sartre. Then, too, there was the artistic Sartre. Whatever final verdict one wants to bring in on the merit of the man's work, there is little doubt that that work, particularly the plays, was provocative when it first appeared. In sum, success.

After the boom, the lowering of it. The intellectual climate of the early fifties was something else again. There is no need really to bring up the late Senator McCarthy—although Sartre probably would—for McCarthy, who once seemed to be an important force, has become, in retrospect, a by-product. Anti-Communism, which was a meal-ticket to the McCarthies, was a fact to most American intellectuals, even to those who disowned the Senator and refused to proclaim themselves New Conservatives. The time was no longer ripe for the political Sartre and the spectacle of his own twistings and turnings in relation to the French Communists made him even less palatable. New American attitudes helped create new European attitudes, and the kind of imbecile anti-Americanism represented by Simone de Beauvoir's *America Day by Day* rubbed off on Sartre. Finally, his celebrated quarrel with Albert Camus, which, as Herbert Luethy said in *France Against Herself*, was not really understandable outside Paris literary circles, was settled on this side of the Atlantic in Camus' favor, and Sartre's old Resistance colleague was taken up—less flamboyantly, it is true—in his place.

The changing political climate was, however, not the most important contribution to the decline of Sartre. There were philosophic and artistic forces at work. The success of Sartre's existentialism was its executioner. Serious students went back to Sartre's sources, embraced Kierkegaard and flirted with Heidegger; the Christian existentialists, from Marcel to Tillich, stole some of Sartre's thunder in the face of what was once and briefly called a religious revival. Those humanists who had been finding in Sartre their own image of responsible man suddenly saw existentialists on every bush. When I read a speech of Judge Learned Hand in which he talked about making his own motley, I knew that he and Sartre's Orestes were brothers and that I had come home to a tradition as old as Western culture. If the freshness had worn off the philosophy, how much more it had worn off the literature. Giraudoux and Anouilh finally found their places on the American stage; Beckett, Ionesco, Genêt were introduced. Although none of these playwrights is like Sartre, they detracted from his uniqueness. Sartre had almost been French literature and philosophy in the late forties; by the fifties one could pick and choose.

What of the three plays in the new volume? those which have only now been picked and chosen—for publication in this country? As is usual with Sartre's plays, all three of them are concerned, directly or indirectly, with his philosophy; each one, in its way, deals with the problem of identity, the protagonist's assumption of a role which may become him as he plays it, appearance becomes actuality. Despite the ideational similarity, each of the three plays retains its structural, its generic individuality. *The Devil and the Good Lord,* set in Germany at the beginning of the Reformation, is philosophic discussion masking as historical chronicle; *Kean* is an adaptation from Alexandre Dumas which retains a hint of its romantic origins; *Nekrassov* is political satire that calls itself farce.

The most ambitious of the plays, *The Devil and the Good Lord,* seems to me the least interesting and the least successful. Like *The Flies,* it is an existential parable, but unlike the early play, it fails to provide a hero whose metaphysical struggle is also a human one. Goetz's long quarrel with God and the weapons he uses, the attempts to achieve absolute evil and absolute good, place him in a world of abstraction, like that of Camus' *Caligula,* which sex and slaughter, war and wild flowers cannot make real. In the last act Goetz finally realizes that "Silence is God. Absence is God. God is the loneliness of man." Having worked his way to the despair of existential freedom, Goetz is ready to become imperfect man in a universe that does not judge him; only then can he lead the Peasants' Revolt, become a butcher again, but this time for men not against God. The point is made; the lecture is over. Although there are a few strikingly theatrical scenes—part of Sartre's early success with *No Exit* and *The Respectful Prostitute* came surely from his inclination for arresting situations—the end result is the feeling that one has read a serious play, but not necessarily a good one. The general pedagogical tone of the piece is heightened by the fact that it deals not only with Goetz's troubles with God, but with the political problems of *Dirty Hands*—how much can one lie to a man for his own good—and in terms that suggest the tactics of contemporary revolutionary parties.

In *Kean,* Sartre has retained Dumas' romantic story in which, with the help of the Prince of Wales, the actor saves the good name of the Danish ambassador's wife, and he has even out-Dumased Dumas by transferring Kean's passionate collapse on stage from a scene from *Romeo and Juliet* to one from *Othello.* Sartre has used the story for its own purposes, however; he has made very explicit the problem of identity implicit in the Dumas play when Kean, unhappy in love, cries out, "Je ne suis pas Romeo . . . Je suis Falstaff. . . ." Sartre's play is primarily an intellectual comedy which retains the grand gestures of the original, a pleasure in their own right, and heightens that pleasure by making Kean continually aware that he is gesturing. A happy marriage of Dumas and Anouilh.

The most startling play in the volume is *Nekrassov.* It is often very funny, and the idea of Sartre being funny—except by accident —is something of a surprise. The play is a blending of slapstick and satire that suggests Nigel Dennis in *Cards of Identity*. The plot concerns a swindler who pretends to be a high Soviet official seeking refuge in France, where his revelations give Sartre a chance to attack the rightist press and the professional anti-Communists. If that were all there were to it, the play would be no more interesting than any quickly dated political quarrel, but beyond the immediate satirical situation—the pamphleteer's concern—the play kids the whole idea of deception and self-deception. Behind the kidding of course—but lightly, lightly—lies the hero's existential problem, whether he should create himself George de Valéra, master criminal, or Nekrassov, professional turncoat; at one point, he even makes a Sartrean declaration, "Good and evil, I take it all upon myself. I am responsible for everything." These philosophical echoes do no harm to *Nekrassov*, but there is one obvious weakness in the play. No farce can withstand sentimentality and as soon as the farceur begins to go soft, so does the play. Sartre fails with Véronique, the Communist heroine, and with the problem of the two off-stage leftist editors who are willing to go to jail for their cause; whenever Véronique appears or her friends are mentioned the play goes sticky. For most of the way *Nekrassov* rises above the political occasion that brought it forth, plays with human weakness rather than political error, but Sartre fails finally to differentiate between the two and in the end his own allegiance (as always, a temporary one) reduces *Nekrassov* to a partisan pamphlet. But a funny one.

None of the three plays is likely to convince anyone that Sartre is a great playwright, but all of them testify that he is a versatile one.

martin esslin

FRIEDRICH DURRENMATT AND THE
NEUROSIS OF NEUTRALITY

AN INTERVIEWER once asked Friedrich Durrenmatt to define what he understood by "theater." The Swiss dramatist hesitated a moment; then he said: "Take, for example, two people who are drinking coffee. That is nothing in particular. But if you knew that their cups contain poison, it might become drama."

And this definition certainly applies to Durrenmatt's own theater. This son of a Swiss Protestant clergyman, who celebrated his forty-second birthday on January 5, and is recognized as one of the two most powerful dramatists now writing in German, is obsessed with murder, executions and violence: a hangman climbing through the window to carry out clandestine executions; a public prosecutor taking it upon himself to execute an adulterous wife; a horrifying ruin of a fabulously rich old woman (who was inexcusably prettified to suit Lynn Fontanne in the English-American productions of the *The Visit*, thereby making nonsense of the play) arriving in a small town offering the citizens vast sums if they murder the seducer of her youth; a "private bank" conducted on the principle that any depositor threatening to withdraw his funds is murdered—these are just a few of Durrenmatt's subjects.

He regards the crime story as the most appropriate art form for our age: "How is the artist to survive in a "world of 'educated' people, of literates?" he has asked, and replied: "It is a question that depresses me, to which I know no answer. Perhaps best by writing crime stories, by creating art where nobody suspects art. Literature will again have to become so light that it will weigh nothing on the scales of today's literary criticism. Only thus can it regain some weightiness."

Why should a Swiss, a citizen of one of the few spots in Europe to escape the violence of two cataclysmic world wars, a country so affluent, so faultlessly organized that life runs smoothly and placidly

Reprinted in *The Washington Post*, February 17, 1963 from *The Manchester Guardian*. Reprinted here by permission of *The Manchester Guardian*.

from the cradle to the grave, be so preoccupied with violence? Precisely because he is a citizen of a country so hygienic, so antiseptically germ-free, that he is bound to suffer agonies of guilt about not being afflicted with the hideous diseases of his time.

Durrenmatt, and his countryman Max Frisch, the other leading dramatist of the contemporary German-speaking world, are both deeply preoccupied with this problem, are both giving expression to a deep malaise which one might call the "neurosis of the neutrals." For young men of spirit to sit idly on the sidelines while the world was being purged by fire and violence cannot have been other than agonizing and frustrating beyond endurance.

In Frisch's case it produced a violent, romantic yearning for the great wide world, a contemptuous dismissal of his own secure and complacent countrymen as fat, insensitive Biedermanns (in *The Firebugs*) or as the puny-minded Andorrans, citizens of a dwarf mountain republic who escape the guilt of their anti-Semitic neighbors merely by dint of living in a country so small that it is always a victim, never an active agent of history. Durrenmatt has said, "there are no more guilty or responsible human beings. Everybody claims that *he* is not to blame, that *he* did not want it to happen. And, indeed, things would have happened without anyone in particular doing anything towards making them happen. We are far too collectively guilty, far too collectively embedded in the sins of our fathers and of their fathers. We are merely the children of their children. That is our bad luck, not our guilt. Guilt presupposes personal action, a religious act. Only comedy can deal with *us*. Our world has led us into the realm of the grotesque, as it has led us to the atom bomb: just as the apocalyptic paintings of Hieronymus Bosch are also merely grotesque."

If guilt and personal accountability for our actions are no longer possible, our misfortunes become like the pitfalls of people who stumble over banana skins. That is why the drama of our time has to be a drama of pitfalls—tragic farce.

"Fate," Durrenmatt says, "has departed from our scene . . . In the foreground of our stage everything is reduced to mere accident, disease, or crisis. Even war will become dependent on whether electronic brains will predict its profitability . . . Woe to us if someone tampered with our machines, interfered with our artificial brains. And even such possibilities would be less calamitous than the possibility that a screw might be loose somewhere, a coil entangled, a button out of order—the world might end because of a short-circuit, a technical mishap. So we are no longer threatened by God, Justice, Destiny, as we find it in Beethoven's Fifth Symphony, but by traffic accidents, dam bursts owing to faulty construction, explosions in atomic plants caused by an absent-minded apprentice."

Hence tragedy becomes impossible as a subject for drama. It is also impossible because there is no longer an audience for it: "Tragedy presupposes a community . . . that is, a common shared view of the world and its purpose. Such a community cannot nowadays be pretended to exist without embarrassment. There is nothing more comic than to sit through the mystery plays of the anthroposophists without sharing their views."

And yet, Durrenmatt maintains, tragedy can enter through the back door. His grotesque farces may reveal it, in a flash, suddenly, as a yawning abyss that opens up for a moment in the midst of grotesquely hilarious proceedings.

Nor, he says, are such tragic farces an expression of despair: "True, he who realizes the meaninglessness, the hopelessness of this world, may be led to despair; but this despair is not a consequence of the world being thus constituted, but an answer he gives to this world. And there could be another answer: his refusal to surrender to despair, his resolution to face this world, in which we often live like Gulliver among the giants . . . It is still possible to show man as a being of courage . . . The world (and therefore the stage which stands for the world) appears to me as something monstrous, an enigma made up of calamities that have to be accepted, but before which there must be no capitulation . . ."

And so Durrenmatt confronts his audiences with a world that may be horrifying and grotesque but which, he hopes, they will face with courage and a sense of humor. It is much to ask of a theater public still largely conditioned to light after-dinner entertainment. But perhaps this time they will live up to this provocative dramatist's high expectations.

a. alvarez

THE ANTI-ESTABLISHMENT DRAMA

MORE THAN any other art the drama is dominated by fashion, for the good reason that it is the art most dominated by personalities. Theater people know, for the most part, only theater people. If they are important enough, actors have plays written for them and playwrights have reviewers rooting for them. Whatever its gossip, its factions, its hatreds, the theater looks after its own. To reverse Lionel Trilling's famous dictum, it will preserve at any cost the illusions its own snobbery generates. With enough personal force and style, a man of the theater—playwright, actor, or critic—can create a fashion which nothing, except the laws of inertia that govern all performances, will destroy.

There is a simple explanation of all this: the theater is the only art which, in England at least, has no truck with the intellectuals. Sooner or later every other art form, with the possible exception of the cinema, is subjected to dispassionate analysis by men who are as committed to the implications of the work as to the practical details. Granted, the intellectuals usually create theories of art which, like the artist's own, are more interesting than useful. But they also create standards; they argue out their judgments; they reason from their personal impressions. In a word, they think. And this makes for a certain free and disinterested space around the subject in which fresh air can circulate. Now thinking is a tradition that has hardly affected the British theater since the death of Ben Jonson. A few maverick foreigners have managed it: Goethe, Buechner, Brecht or, on a more superficial level, Sartre. But the English stage has had to make do with, at best, conversation pieces. From time to time, of course, ideas go around; Shaw's plays are full of them. But as one knows from elsewhere than the theater—from coffee bars, cocktail parties or faculty meetings—ideas can flourish independently of thinking. Shaw's characters exchange ideas with the canny enthusiasm of small boys exchanging marbles, but they have no truck with the endless difficulty

From *Partisan Review,* Fall, 1959. Reprinted by permission.

of registering experience freshly, of organizing and judging it according to standards one has lived out. A good dramatist may master ideas well enough to create from them lively conversation, but the pressure of lived experience which gives them life and validity is not usually his concern. To judge from these prose statements, for example, John Osborne and Arnold Wesker might be rather muddled schoolboys, not the enormously talented playwrights they in fact are. Of course, the theater is a peculiarly specialized art, technical beyond any other literary form. As such it has attracted a special kind of intelligence and has its own specialized satisfactions. But there is no reason in the world why anyone or any art should be specialized to the point of inanity, or conventionalized to the point where it is cut off from the ordinary processes of the intelligence.

I have made so much of this rather obvious point because the conventions of the London theater have altered a great deal in the last few years. There is a healthy sign of decreasing specialization; there are stirrings of significance and life. Early in the 'fifties nothing seemed deader than the British stage. The standard of acting, of course, was very high and notable justice was done to the routine classics. But every new play went according to a fixed plan. "The scene," the program would say, "is the drawing-room of Mr. and Mrs. Murgatroyd-Winterbotham's house overlooking Regent's Park. The time is the present. One morning in May." The curtain would duly rise on the usual sham but tasteful Regency. The phone would ring. The usual maid would enter.

> MAID: The Murgatroyd-Winterbotham residence. No, I'm afraid Madam is not at home. Oh yes, of course, Mrs. Manningham-Gillingham. No, I don't know when she'll be back. (*Confidentially and rather excited*) She went out last night after dinner and hasn't returned. The master seems very worried. He scarcely touched his kidneys at breakfast. (A noise off) Yes Mrs. Manningham-Gillingham, I'll tell her (replaces receiver). Oh *Madam!* (Enter Mrs. M.W. a smart little blonde in her mid-thirties. She looks tired and upset. Her mink coat is awry.)

Not even T. S. Eliot, when he turned popular playwright, had the energy or imagination to break the mode. Hence those disastrous Happy Families of his, with their gin-and-water omniscience and martyrdom.

Yet somehow, in the last three or four years, the miracle has happened, the conventions have changed. To be sure, conventions of a kind still abound but at least they are new. The theater is still very much a middle-class entertainment; the booking, the trek to the West End remove all spontaneity from play-going; it becomes a major family event. Hence the success of Frederick Lonsdale, Noel Coward, Terence Rattigan and the rest depends on the manner in which they all, in their slightly different ways, cater to the spacious suburban dream; while Christopher Fry is to poetry what Stockbrokers' Tudor is to architecture. Now in the late 'fifties, the audience is much the same but the middle-class image of itself, its known facts and willed fantasies, have changed. After all, during the last few years the gen-teel have taken a terrible beating. The wealthy remain what they were, but the middle income group has been taxed to the point of collapse. Their facade of cheerful respectability grows more and more precarious and their prospects are grim. So the world of drawing-room comedy, with its servants, Bentleys, night-clubs and more or less dis-creet extra-marital relationships, no longer corresponds even to the haziest yearnings, much less to the cold facts of life in Wimbledon, Kensington and Maida Vale. Niceness is all no longer. So the drawing-room drama plays to smaller and smaller audiences for shorter and shorter runs. Not even the most conventional registers of lower middle-brow taste, the critics in the evening papers, feel they have to take it particularly seriously. When one of Lonsdale's plays was revived recently with great elaboration and a particularly glowing cast, the producer made a telling alteration: he shifted the time of the thing from the mid-Depression 'thirties to 1913, that fabulous age before the flood, when England and the bourgeoisie were still something. The implication was that drawing-room comedy, to be enjoyed, now had to be taken as a period piece, like its Restoration ancestor or Romantic tragedy.

The change in taste and convention is largely the work of two theater groups: George Devine's English Stage Company, whose thea-ter is the Royal Court in Sloane Square, and Joan Littlewood's Theater Workshop, who perform at the Theater Royal in the Stratford of East London, not Upon Avon. Between them they have altered the whole theatrical scene. First, they have given the stage a new freedom by introducing a great deal of modern work from abroad: Beckett, Arthur Miller, Lorca, O'Neill, Ionesco and many others. In this way the whole domain of drama has changed, the drawing-room furniture has been scrapped, and the inertia of sensibility that ruled over it has gone too. A new range of experience as well as a profusion of new theatrical techniques has been made possible. And suddenly it has become clear that England in its turn has a whole generation of experimental writers and producers who had been waiting for the chance to say their say. Granted, their say has been patchy, much of it bad, the avant-gardism is mostly tiresome *chi-chi*, and the Court has been conned by some terrible frauds. But the new work has been performed; after the long winter the river has begun to flow again.

The second change in the theater might be called a Left-Wing conversion. It has been a muddled process but it began, as it may well end, with the discovery of Bertolt Brecht. Five years ago hardly anyone in England had even heard of him. Then the Berliner Ensemble performed in London in German; Theater Workshop gave a translated *Mother Courage* its British premiere; and the Royal Court staged *The Good Woman of Setzuan*. One of the most influential of the drama critics met Brecht in Berlin and underwent a positively Pauline conversion to socialism. Since then, social realism has been the word.

The direct influence of Brecht is still small, though most of Miss Littlewood's distinctive mannerisms as a producer can be traced back to his theories. His indirect influence, however, is very large. I mean something rather more than his politics. For Brecht was a major writer before he was a Communist, and in spite of it. This means that in his best work his politics make themselves felt not by any tiresome didacticism but by serious human concern with justice and goodness which— at his best, I repeat—have nothing to do with any party line. But politics he had, and this, in a century in which nearly all major writers have either kept wholly apart from politics or been on the Right—the last significant Left-Wing poet was Shelley—makes Brecht an extraordinarily powerful exception, who had a whole new language of drama to offer. Moreover it was a theatrical language which had been translated most eloquently in the production of Joan Littlewood; hence it seemed the language most likely to produce significant and fresh effects.

I do not, for a moment, wish to give the impression that this change of theatrical style is any sign at all of a great change of heart in the British electorate. Nor fundamentally in the British dramatists. None of the four most promising playwrights who had gotten a hearing as a result of the new fashion—John Osborne, Arnold Wesker, Brendan Behan and Shelagh Delaney—seem to have much more than a bright socialist gloss on their work. They are not so much pro-Labour as anti-Establishment. And this is perfectly understandable. Behan apart (he is Irish; therefore his politics are something quite special and, for the non-Irishman, not quite comprehensible), they were all born too late to have lived through any real domestic political conflict. Osborne is the oldest and he, I believe, is my age. That means he was about fifteen when the Labour government was elected after the war; politically, I imagine, he could remember nothing at all of the 'thirties.

Wesker is two or three years younger than Osborne, and Miss Delaney about six years younger than Wesker. This means that their most lively political experience has very little to do with mass unemployment, strikes and union-busting, and a great deal to do with the forlorn sight of the Welfare State sinking under the paralyzing weight of the bureaucrats until it achieved what J. W. Aldridge has called Welfare Stasis. Their political ideas are probably less defined by enthusiasms and causes than by irritation.

On the stage this irritation takes a specific technical form. They are all determined at least not to hoax their own creations. If nothing else, they will stick to the facts and rhythms of modern life. In the new plays toast is burned, clothes are ironed, bobs have to be found for the gas-meter, the empties have to be returned to the pub. The heroes lose their jobs rather than their fortunes, their wives more often than their mistresses. And most important, they talk like living people. The extraordinary thing about the old drawing-room drama was the way even the light social chatter had been formalized until it seemed almost a separate language. T. S. Eliot may, after all, have had a reason for chopping into verse lines the cocktail party repartee of his later plays. He did not succeed in making poetry out of it, in any intensive sense of that term, but he did cannily indicate the degree to which the conventions of this kind of social back-chat had become formal and apart.

The new writers have changed all this. Miss Delaney is said to have been prompted into writing her play by seeing a Terence Rattigan piece while she was still a nineteen-year-old millhand. As everyone does on these occasions, she came out saying "I could do better than that." But unlike most other people, she went away and did so. In all fairness, Miss Delaney does not have anything like as sharp an eye for a dramatic situation as Rattigan. A measure of her and her colleagues' superiority is their ear for speech. Their language is slangy, gay, messy, irreverent; it is, in short, the real thing, just as their feelings come from a shared experience rather than from some trumped-up device. It is this straight-forwardness of pity and gusto that makes Behan's *The Hostage* superior, I think, to Dylan Thomas's *Under Milk Wood*. In both works there is a certain spurious, cossetted vitality. As with so much modern Celtic art, the line between Life—with a capital L—and Blarney is so delicate as not to be always discernible. But Behan's vitality at least manifests itself in terms of people rather than in a willed excess and trickery of language.

The strength of Osborne, Wesker, Delaney and Behan is precisely in their commitment to realism. This guarantees them such an immediate impact that it often masks the fact that social realism has itself become a convention. It is a convention of talk. Provided the drama-tists can create a truth of talk they are absolved from that other truth of dramatic inevitability. Without exception their plays all fade out in the last act. The audience is left simply with "a slice of life," while the cycle of life—the process in which character and circumstance act upon each other until they are resolved in an irresistible action—is ignored. I suggest that despite appearances, the dominant influence in the new British drama is not Brecht, who was a master of dramatic tension; it is instead the documentary film. For the documentary merely presents, while the artist presents in order to resolve; which brings us back to that question of thinking.

Arnold Wesker's *Roots,* for example, is unquestionably the best play now on in London. Wesker has extraordinary insight into unlikely people, an uncannily accurate ear for dialogue, and a nice sense of irony at his own expense. Moreover, he has also flung an idea or two into the ring. But he has, as yet, no sense at all of what it feels like to live ideas so that they are implicit in every action. He may talk about intellectuals, but his own intelligence works through the shrewdness of his ear. The result is that his work, like Osborne's, leaves you most strongly with a great impression of artistic muddle. At the end of *Roots* all the implications of family loyalty and hatred, all the criticism of the seemingly blameless young intellectual cad, are left in the air. The heroine's revelation is simply a gift of the gab, which apparently makes all the trickery and corruption worthwhile. No doubt Wesker is per-fectly sincere about what he says; but sincerity only counts in a work of art when it is transformed into *artistic* conscience, forcing the material to whatever its latent but inevitable conclusion may be. Fundamentally, all satisfying drama is Aristotelian.

Perhaps all four of these dramatists have yet to produce objective works of art; so far they have been concerned with portraits of the artists as young men. If their work is inconclusive, that may be because not enough has happened to them. The danger is that their talent to do the partial thing is such that it has created of itself a convention and a fashion. Before the age of thirty they are becoming models for other writers. In, for instance, a recent Royal Court production called *Sugar in the Morning,* the author Donald Howarth was so obviously delighted with his ability to put real people on the stage and make them talk as he has heard them, that he apparently never bothered to think up a plot until, at the last moment, he found himself stuck for an ending.

There is plenty of writing talent in England, just as there are talented producers like Joan Littlewood and William Gaskill to do it justice, and at least one brilliant new stage designer—Sean Kenny, a pupil of Frank Lloyd Wright, who got his start at the Royal Court and has now been given a much bigger chance at the new Mermaid Theater. But the question is whether the talent will develop according to its own toughest artistic instincts, or whether the anti-intellectual esotericism of the theater will turn it into just another transient and self-stultifying fashion.

henry popkin

WILLIAMS, OSBORNE OR BECKETT?

Each is a leader in the drama of his nation.
Which will most affect the world stage?

THIS YEAR the New York theatre is undergoing an invasion of British plays, written by authors relatively unknown here—Brendan Behan, Shelagh Delaney, Arnold Wesker and Harold Pinter—all of them full-grown playwrights with full-grown reputations in their own country. Also, this season will see the French invasion of last year continue. The new French names are a little less fresh, but they are still in the process of being established here; to the current plays by Jean Genet and Samuel Beckett, France will soon add Eugene Ionesco's latest work, *The Rhinoceros*.

On the other hand, our own big names remain the same old ones. The dominant tendency in American drama is represented by the plays of Tennessee Williams and William Inge and, despite a few quick flashes of light off-Broadway, no new stars have joined our firmament.

The drama of each of these three nations—Britain, France and the United States—preserves its individual flavor. American drama is psychological; it serves up untidy neuroses usually garnished with pat solutions. Britain has a new social drama which nightly slays the dragons of poverty, prejudice and war. The French dramatists contrive experiments in form that continue man's endless conversations on the timeless issues. A closer examination will show how these differences arise out of differences among the nations themselves.

In the days before psychologizing swallowed Broadway, we had our own social drama, of which Arthur Miller and Lorraine Hansberry are the last, isolated exponents. Formerly, we had dramatists like Elmer Rice, Robert Sherwood and Sidney Kingsley, who were liberal social reformers; Sherwood was especially identified with the New Deal of Franklin Roosevelt, whose speeches he helped to write. Clifford Odets, Lillian Hellman and many others expressed a more radical criticism of society.

From *The New York Times Book Review*, November 13, 1960. Copyright by The New York Times. Reprinted by permission.

In the past fifteen years, Tennessee Williams has established the priority of the psychological play. His most typical works examine emotional maladjustments which may have their roots in abrupt social change, but he directs our attention to the flower, not the root.

His first Broadway plays, *The Glass Menagerie* and *A Streetcar Named Desire*, showed women who could not adapt themselves to the death of the old, aristocratic South that they had known. Still, the main fact about Amanda Wingfield and Blanche Du Bois is not that they illustrate any social law. First of all, they are human beings, sometimes ludicrous, sometimes pitiful; they have the misfortune to be special cases of incurable emotional ailments.

Williams is equally pessimistic in such later plays as *Sweet Bird of Youth* when he shows Bohemian rebels in hopeless revolt against society, but he has now promised to be more cheerful, and has made a start with his newly opened comedy, *Period of Adjustment*.

A cheerful Williams would surely resemble William Inge, who supplies happy endings to similar dilemmas. Thus, in *The Dark at the Top of the Stairs*, the husband feels he was born out of his time and the daughter seems invincibly shy, but, in Inge's happier world, such problems can be solved.

The emphasis of Paddy Chayefsky and William Gibson is, like Inge's, psychological and optimistic. The oddly matched lovers of Chayefsky's *Middle of the Night* and *The Tenth Man* need only remember that love's the best doctor—for old age and other ailments. A generation ago, Gibson's *Two for the Seesaw* might have got by as a play about a love affair, but, in our time, the affair must provide therapy for the young lovers.

Even our social dramatists are responding to this tendency. Clifford Odets pointed the way years ago with *The Country Girl*, a play about an alcoholic who is also a pathological liar. Lillian Hellman's latest play, *Toys in the Attic*, shows a man trapped by his family, not by society. And even in Arthur Miller's latest play, *A View from the Bridge*, the chief character is an emotional "case," in the Williams manner; his troubles begin with his incestuous passion for his niece.

Our old and new dramatists are alike in one further respect: their techniques are generally objective and realistic, and, in fact, the realism of the stage has been reinforced by the realism of television, a medium for which Chayefsky and Gibson have written.

The Americans are psychologists and psychiatrists; the British are, on the other hand, social rebels. They are critics of the existing order. After decades of tepid drawing-room comedy, their drama has entered the real world and has even admitted the lower orders to serious consideration. A leading director, Joan Littlewood, has written of "those dear departed days when . . . the voice of the Cockney was one long whine of blissful servitude."

Those days are gone forever. Only a few years ago, John Gassner could write that "the British social play generally displays a moderation as unfortunate in the theatre as it is theoretically admirable in politics." But now the working classes dominate a blatantly immoderate social drama.

A four-year renaissance has turned up a number of lively dramatists—John Osborne, Brendan Behan, Shelagh Delaney, Arnold Wesker, John Arden, Willis Hall, and, writing in a somewhat different vein, Harold Pinter and N. F. Simpson. Each one argues sharply and bitterly for social change to solve the problems arising out of poverty, war, colonialism and prejudice.

Everything began with John Osborne and *Look Back in Anger* which opened in May, 1956. Osborne speaks for the young rebel with no firm place in society, for Jimmy Porter who shocks his conventional wife out of her upper-class complacency, for George Dillon who is gobbled up by middle-class society and by the vulgarization of art. His entertainer, in the play of that name, debases the art of the stage while the Suez campaign debases politics.

Brendan Behan's *The Hostage* is a freewheeling attack on practically everything, including Irish nationalism, demonstrative religion, the royal family and armed conflict. In *Roots* and other plays, Arnold Wesker examines the various aspects of socialism and touches especially upon the communion that socialism creates. Shelagh Delaney's *A Taste of Honey* is less direct, but it implicitly attacks poverty and prejudice against Negroes and homosexuals. John Arden's anti-war, anti-colonial play, *Serjeant Mumgrave's Dance,* was preceded and followed by plays assailing conformist social planning.

The verse dramatist, Ronald Duncan has charged that these playwrights "are writing within the convention of Mrs. Tanqueray," that is, of nineteenth-century realistic drama. But the conventional realism furnishes only the background to most of these plays and the new dramatists will employ any variations to drive home their meaning. In Joan Littlewood's productions especially—they have included *The Hostage* and *A Taste of Honey*—we may expect song, dance and speeches addressed to the audience.

When Osborne's entertainer does his act, he addresses the audience in the theatre which is his audience in the music hall. Arden's characters often break into rhyme or song and in the last act of *Ser-*

jeant Musgrave's Dance, the theatre audience impersonates the spectators gathered to hear the serjeant.

Wesker's realism is stricter, but the heroine of *Roots* makes orations in imitation of her absent lover and ends an act with song and dance. The reason is simple—these writers start with something vital, and quite specific, to say; they need many voices to say it to every indifferent ear in the theatre.

In France, the new masters of the stage—Beckett, Ionesco and Jean Genet—write experimental drama. Instead of showing the recognizable surfaces of our existence, they distort average life and dramatize their exasperation with it.

Ionesco, who has said the most about his intentions, notes that his colleagues (including Beckett and Genet) differ from the social critics "because they question the whole state of man, and offer us clear proofs that man is more than merely a social animal."

And what is more than social man? These writers offer the timeless man of any age or society, by turns bully, slave, wit and imbecile, capable of occasional flights of lyricism or contemplation. His problems are more deeply rooted than even neurosis and social injustice.

These dramatists take up the most general issues. Genet's favorite subjects seem to be the universality of illusion, of the theatrical impulse and of the will to subjugate others. In his latest play, *The Blacks*, Negroes enact a ritual murder of their white masters (impersonated by Negroes) and then enact their own revolt and the execution of their masters. Obviously, Genet is commenting upon the antagonism of black and white and upon colonialism, but he does not write with any reformist purpose.

Quite as little reform is possible for the mysterious, unidentified figures of Beckett's *Waiting for Godot*, who illustrate both the inevitability and the folly of waiting. Beckett's later plays, *Endgame* and *Krapp's Last Tape*, take as their subjects loneliness and old age—equally universal complaints for which no remedies can be found.

In Ionesco's plays, human relations are made nonsense when humanity is stifled by the interference of things, or words. When the characters of *The Bald Soprano* mechanically exchange trite phrases taken from a manual of English conversation, the effect, says Ionesco, is "criticism . . . of all societies, of language, of clichés—a parody of human behavior."

If his longer plays have more traditional plots, they still insist upon the same vague atmosphere and the same general issues. *The Killer* is about death and *The Rhinoceros* about conformism, but the deliberate vagueness permits a variety of readings. The Germans played *The Rhinoceros* as a somber political drama, the French as a gay comedy; Kenneth Tynan found it a criticism of "all change," while others read it as an attack upon de Gaulle.

The objective slice of life is to be seen almost nowhere in France except in the most commonplace boulevard plays. Anouilh takes liberties with the old conventions in his latest works. If Françoise Sagan's *Chateau in Sweden* is technically realistic, its characters are so wildly unconventional that they break the old form.

Here, experiment becomes the rule, and society subsidizes it. A year ago, the French Government dedicated two theatres to experimental drama. The whole atmosphere of French art provides a sympathetic home for experiment, for Genet's plays within plays, for Beckett's tireless talkers, for Ionesco's paper-thin exemplars of society.

Why do these different developments take place?

I can offer several explanations for the American trend. First, the positive one—psychiatry and the circumstances that make it necessary now flourish in urban America. For whatever reasons, we have turned psychoanalysis into a major industry. Perhaps the trouble is that, collectively, we are more prosperous than ever before and so we become nervously busy and furtively guilty. Leisure encourages self-examination which continues even in the theatre, where our current problem plays furnish a sweetened, simplified psychiatry, a painless analysis by proxy at the hands of amateur analysts.

Solid negative reasons explain why the French and British tendencies are not transforming American playwriting. First, box-office survival is more difficult than ever, even in our prosperity, and theatrical experiment is a doubtful commodity. Only one of the new experimental French plays was attempted on Broadway—*Waiting for Godot*. Genet's *The Balcony* was the only French importation to succeed last year, but it succeeded off Broadway.

Also, the new French drama clashes with the popular American belief that all problems have solutions; we are made uncomfortable by permanent problems—like death and taxes, which fit, respectively, into the French and British scheme of things.

We are not now writing native plays in the British fashion because politics is a divisive issue—at a time when the box office needs every dollar. On the other hand, love, as the Gershwins once reminded us, is sweeping the country. (Curiously, the divisive nature of politics does not bother the British. More than half the nation is Tory; if there is a Tory dramatist, I have not heard of him.) Our social drama has had its day, and it still suffers from the bad scare that McCarthyism gave it.

The new British drama reflects Britain's social mobility. Sons of the working class and the lower middle class are writing plays, expressing themselves and their social classes on the stage for the first time. Shelagh Delaney worked in a factory, Arnold Wesker was a pastry cook, Brendan Behan was a house painter. All of them embody the new energy of the lower orders of society, released by the effect of the war in jumbling social rank and also by current prosperity.

But prosperity has not, as in America, deadened social issues. Nothing like McCarthyism ever checked the naturally leftist bent of British intellectuals, and new events have recommended certain public issues to them—such events as race riots in London, insurrection in Kenya, the Suez invasion, protests against the big bombs. And now, for the first time, this social criticism takes to the stage. A prominent director, Tony Richardson, has observed: "Everyone is writing plays —all the young creative talent is directed at the theatre."

But why the theatre? For one thing, everyone knows that a playwright earns more than any other sort of writer, and that fact ought not to be underestimated. Furthermore, the dramatic renaissance has a snowball effect. By this time, everyone has also learned that an actor named John Osborne and a factory-hand named Shelagh Delaney came out of nowhere and made good overnight; armies of new dramatists hope to do the same. And fortunately, London has a few adventurous little theatres, far from the West End, where some of their plays can be tried out with a minimum of economic danger.

Without these theatres, the new drama would be inconceivable. They are unlike our own off-Broadway theatres because almost all the new dramatists write for them and because their plays, if successful, move to the West End.

The theatres which have contributed most to the new drama are the Royal Court (a "dramatist's theatre," the home of Osborne's, Wesker's, Arden's and Simpson's plays) and Joan Littlewood's Stratford Theatre Royal (a "people's theatre," more deliberately proletarian, the home of Behan's and Miss Delaney's plays).

Another circumstance helps to make a vital drama possible— the recent mildness of the Lord Chamberlain's censorship, which has been imposed upon the stage since 1737. For years, plays banned for obscenity or for touching upon delicate social issues might be shown only in private clubs. In 1934, when our own social drama was burgeoning, a producer protested that, because of this censorship, the British drama was "twenty years behind the times."

He was a prophet, for, in the Nineteen Fifties, the British started writing plays that recall our own Nineteen Thirties. The Lord Chamberlain has moved with the times, but at his own slow pace.

Paris has had its little theatres for a long time and also its old tradition of artistic experiment. In addition, the French enjoy an intimate knowledge of the modern realistic play. They had their own early realistic dramatists, like Becque and Brieux and, in institutions like the Théâtre Libre, they did more than any other nation to convert the world's stage to realism.

The realistic play is old stuff to them; they have written it, staged it, digested it, and so they move on. Accordingly, André Barsacq, who directed Françoise Sagan's play, finds American drama passé: "I am a little insensitive to this style of drama. It seems to take us back to the time of the Free Theatre in France."

But why must the themes of Genet, Beckett and Ionesco flourish in France? Let us consider the alternatives. Political themes are difficult because political life is frozen. For most literary people, the only possible political activity is protest against particular injustices. In the main political arena, the splinter groups so precariously balance one another that the only alternatives seem to be chaos and de Gaulle.

To follow French political discourse is to become, like Ionesco, persuaded of the impossibility of all discourse. The main political alternative in the French theatre is Marxist epic drama in the style of the Brechtians, with whom Ionesco is continually quarreling.

American psychological themes are superfluous because the French are frank, and they have less to hide. The oddities of conduct which Williams defends are casually taken for granted and tolerated in France. For example, a character in one of last year's plays describes his wedding. The justice of the peace asks: "Do you take this woman?" "Certainly," says the bridegroom, "wouldn't you?" The justice replies: "Personally, I'm a pederast."

An American might base a solemn play on this exchange but in Paris the line is good for a laugh, and that is all. In short, the only stable, serious issue is the kind that Genet, Beckett and Ionesco treat. They have the further advantage of belonging to well-established traditions of French literature, to an old inheritance of ironic and meditative pessimism. And Ionesco has a special ancestor in Flaubert. In his highly stylized manner, he does what Flaubert did more calmly in the novel: he exposes the vulgarity of the middle class.

The future will surely see some interbreeding of dramatic types. American plays are everywhere, and the new British dramas are beginning to travel. France's *The Rhinoceros* was performed last season in Paris, London and Duesseldorf: it will soon be done in New York, Amsterdam, Oslo, Ljubijana and, no doubt, other cities.

Influences are slower to become established and, as yet, I find no new ones in American drama. The experimental form of Jack Gelber's *The Connection,* an off-Broadway success which shows drug addicts in their native environment, may owe something to the French theatre. Normally, we leave experiment to off-Broadway and social criticism to "sick" comedians, but perhaps we can hope for stimulation from the British invasion of the new season.

In France, of course, everyone is receptive to everything; Paris is, and always was, the most cosmopolitan of cities. Every kind of drama seems to be attempted first in Paris, but not everything takes root. One supposes, however, that especially if French politics pursues its present turgid course, the French will continue to favor dramatic experiment.

In Britain, where the pace of dramatic activity is quickest, so is the pattern of international influences. The new dramatists are eager to catch any new dramatic idea or influence, from whatever source. Bertolt Brecht's plays, with their social lessons set to music, have obviously stimulated the social critics in the London theatre.

England also has a French school in N. F. Simpson, whose *One Way Pendulum* suggests Ionesco, and Harold Pinter, whose *The Caretaker* recalls Beckett. Fortunately for Simpson, Ionesco's spade-work was done in England a century ago by the nonsense of Lewis Carroll. Fittingly, Pinter's most loyal defender is Harold Hobson, the British critic who has most identified himself with the cause of French drama. "American" energy abounds, but specific American influence is less visible than formerly.

Currently, the theatre's most provocative group of playwrights is, I think, the British. Individual disappointments are always possible, but the continuing activity of Osborne, Behan, Miss Delaney, Wesker and the rest should keep Britain's dramatic renaissance alive. A brilliant generation of this sort invariably becomes an international influence and helps to remind us that, as the world grows smaller, its stage grows larger.

section iii
POETIC DRAMA

edwin honig

LORCA'S FOLK TRAGEDIES

THE FEW YEARS immediately following his early experimental works
offer the first signs of Lorca's maturity as a dramatist. The folk tragedies, his best achievement, are the work of a poet become director-
playwright who used his familiarity with folklore and music to elaborate the drama's structural design. This multiform talent was the stuff
out of which a reawakened dramatic art emerged. For his single theme,
Lorca went to the folk; and for his protagonist, he went to woman.

The strength of Lorca's folk drama lies precisely in his use of
woman as bearer of all passion and earthly reality: the wild superb
nature of which Synge had spoken. With Lorca it is not simply an
accidental choice. The Spain which let its blood for Christ secretly
admired the Virgin more. The Virgin prevailing over all early Spanish
church art was the symbol of earthly fecundity as well as the mother
of divine mercy. The Spaniard often seems to mistrust his male saints
for not suffering enough or convincingly. Spanish women saints, however, were always known to suffer magnificent and terrible martyrdom.
The character of the *dueña*, the woman chaperon, very early became
a convention in the Spanish theatre. And she, as the repository of good
earthy frankness, knew the world's tricks and provided the audience
with the protective motherly domination which it sought in woman.
The Don Juan legend has been a popular and recurrent theme in
Spanish literature because it re-affirms the generously fertile nature of
woman as distinct from the abstract and essentially barren male lover
who finds no permanence except in the arms of death. The Spaniard
has been somewhat contemptuous of his philandering Don Juan, who
instead of conquering women should have been conquering the New
World, or even his own small plot of ground.

Lorca's heroines are modern versions of the warm matriarchal
type found in all Spanish literature. They are magnetic fields inevitably
drawing tragedy to themselves from a too ardent faith in the right of
their natural instincts. Again, they are islands which the world cannot

From *Garcia Lorca* by Edwin Honig. Copyright 1944 by New Directions. Reprinted by
permission of New Directions.

touch with its soiled and makeshift logic. Because their humanity is such an extremely procreative answer to life, they threaten to disrupt the mere man-made machinery of social law, which is, finally, a substitution for life. They are the affirmation to the question of the ultimate which man, with the beam of social exigency in his eye, is always begging. When they lose the sense of integration in life which is necessary to them, the world trembles and comes apart. Thus it is as martyrs of frustrated love, from the heroine of *Mariana Pineda,* who dies on the gallows, to the suicide of the youngest daughter in *La Casa de Bernarda Alba,* that Lorca's women uphold the insistent theme of his tragedies.

With increasing subtlety, the musical conception is woven into the dramatic. If *Mariana Pineda* can be compared to a sonata, then *Bodas de Sangre, Yerma,* and *Doña Rosita la Soltera,* constructed with infinitely more complicated motifs, must be compared to concertos. The supplementary use of a musical pattern introduced with *Mariana Pineda* becomes a function integrated in the dramatic form of the latter three. The scene is more variegated, spectacular; the characters multiply, while the principals are more definitely individualized. Only the simplicity of plot with its relentless argument remains the same.

Bodas de Sangre (*Blood Wedding*) was written and produced in Madrid during 1933. Within a few years, it traveled to Latin America, reaching Argentina and Mexico; it was translated into French, English and Russian, and produced in Paris, New York and Moscow. In the original, or where the barriers of translation did not hinder it, its appeal lay in the strong characterization of the peasant struggling with the immutable laws of nature. It tells the story of an unconsummated marriage among the hill folk of Castile. The atmosphere of imagery and speech is transformed with the dry landscape into the repressed emotion of violence which fills the play. A Mother's only remaining son is planning to marry a girl living beyond the hills with her father. Following the recent feud murder of her husband and several sons, the Mother is obsessed with knives and death. The prospective bride, a strong, silent girl "accustomed to solitude," was previously engaged to Leonardo,[1] who is now married to her cousin. But the members of Leonardo's family were guilty of the feud murder. The Mother suspects her son's Betrothed because of the latter's past relationship with Leonardo. And Leonardo, a wild, maladjusted creature, still secretly yearns for the girl he did not marry. The first scene announces the Mother's obsession and the involvement of persons sharing a common destiny.

---

[1] The only character in the play with a proper name is thus identified with the strength and rapacity of a *lion.*

The second scene is practically a lyrical interlude. It takes place in Leonardo's house where his Mother-in-Law and Wife are putting the children to sleep with a lullaby:

> *Duérmete, rosal,*
> *que el caballo se pone a llorar.*
> *Las patas heridas,*
> *las crines heladas,*
> *dentro de los ojos*
> *un puñal de plata.*
> *Bajaban al río.*
> *¡Ay, cómo bajaban!*
> *La sangre corría*
> *más fuerte que el agua.*
>
> (Go to sleep, my rosebay,
> for the horse has begun to cry.
> His hoofs wounded,
> his mane frozen,
> a silver dagger
> between his eyes.
> They took him to the river.
> Ay, how they went down!
> His blood was flowing
> more swiftly than water.)

Leonardo comes in from the fields, irritated by the news of his Wife's cousin's approaching marriage. In his coarse black mood, he leaves his Wife weeping. She spreads her anxiety, enacting it within the verses of the lullaby.

In the third scene, the prospective Groom and his Mother visit the wasteland home of the Betrothed and her father. In conversation, their language becomes clipped like the sandy landscape. When the financial details are discussed and the marriage date is set, they leave. The Betrothed, silent and dutiful till now, suddenly shows her bitterness by biting her own hand. She is physically as strong as a man. Her Maid tells her of the rider who came the night before. The Betrothed is frightened and incredulous. But at that moment, there is the sound of a horse at the window. She looks out. It is Leonardo.

Thus the first act shifts within a dark and light motif: hard imagistic language, natural and colloquial, when people converse together; and symbolic, aerated language when feeling passes into the anonymity of the scene and is translated into poetry. But throughout, the atmosphere is stark, devoid of desire, and the human will is left out. This is the proper emotional setting to a play which turns more and more on a passionate release of the instincts.

The first scene of the second act is in the house of the Betrothed, the morning of her wedding day. She is trying hard to contain herself when, alone and before the other guests, Leonardo enters—a tight root of bitterness. She bids him leave, while the others come singing wedding songs. When the Groom arrives, she asks him to rush her off to church, for she is impatient with the pre-nuptial ceremony while the thought of Leonardo still roams in her mind:

> I want to be your wife, to be with you alone, and not to hear any voice but yours. And to see none but your eyes. To have you embrace me so tightly that even if my mother, who is dead, should call me, I could not be separated from you.

This, however, is not said with a lover's passion, but with the desperation of one who is almost equal to committing a crime.

The second scene sharpens the conflict between the social fact of the marriage and the impending irruption of anarchic instinct. The wedding not yet consummated, the Groom's Mother joins the talk of the neighbors and begins to accentuate her characteristic obsession. She speaks of Leonardo's family as those "handlers of knives and people of the false smile." Her heightened eloquence enlarges the images of blood and murder: how she found one of her sons dead in the square, and how, after touching the body, "I moistened my hands in his blood and licked them with my tongue. Because it was my blood." The Betrothed appears downcast, while Leonardo passes back and forth across the scene. At the same time that the main action approaches a climax, the song and talk of the people grow animated and more naturally lusty than ever. The Betrothed, who has become increasingly recalcitrant with her Groom, finally leaves, complaining of dizziness. Leonardo's Wife, who has the strongest instinct in the matter, finds her husband gone and agonizedly blurts out her suspicion that the two have run off together. The Groom's Mother violently spurs her son on in pursuit and urges everyone to follow him. There is the smell of blood in the air. She says, "The hour of blood has arrived again. Two camps." It is the hour of tragedy which she has been expecting like the thrust of a blade ever since her first foreboding speech.

The third act turns on the symbolism of song and the strategy of the spectacle. The first scene is a dim forest where two violins are heard playing in the background. It is filled with the supernatural air of a Calderón allegory. Three Woodsmen are singing in verse, like an improvised chorus of fates. They argue the efficacy of the lovers' escape: "One should follow his instinct. They have done well to flee," or "One should follow the road of blood," or "But blood which sees the light is drunk by the earth," or "What then? It is better to die with one's blood flowing than to live with it stagnating." Suddenly the Moon itself enters, dressed as a young woodsman, its white face diffusing a blue light, sorrowing, lost, restless, and singing—the very height of Lorquian moons! "The moon leaves a knife/ abandoned in the air . . ./ How I should like to enter some breast/ that I might warm myself there," it moans. It is a moon made by a child's fairy-tale imagination, of white chalk and eggshell. Then an old Beggar Woman appears—the personification of Death. She describes the pursuit into the forest and commands the Moon to aid her: "Light up the vest and open the buttons,/ and then the knife will know its way." The Groom enters, white with destiny, and she agrees to lead him to Leonardo. The Woodsmen pass again, and echo the impending tragedy. For a moment the scene focuses upon the escaped lovers—a scene which Lorca says should be "full of great sensuality." Accepting the inevitability of their situation and the tragedy to follow, they blame not themselves but the blind lusts which the earth has created in them. They go deeper into the wood to hide. But suddenly, there are two loud cries, and the double murder has been accomplished. The Moon advancing from the background stops short; the music of the violins ceases as the Beggar Woman reappears. She opens her cloak in the center of the stage like a bird with huge wings. Then the blue light of the Moon is shut off.

As it concerns the three main actors, the violence of this scene is human. With the others—the Woodsmen, who are the fates, the Moon, who is the messenger of Death, and the Beggar Woman, who is Death itself—the scene rises to the supernatural plane, suggesting the Greek *deus ex machina*. There is also the growing sense of similarity with the Tristan-Isolde legend, and with the mythologies of all nations that ever boasted a folk to conserve them. The communication runs on two levels: the classical artistic convention, and the folk-legend character of violence and tragedy.

The short final scene, much of it in verse, is the summation of the tragic statement slowly become impersonal. It takes place in a bare massive enclosure suggestive of a church. Two seated girls are winding out a red skein, singing:

> *Jazmín de vestido*
> *cristal de papel.*
> *Nacer a las cuatro,*
> *morir a las diez.*
> *Ser hilo de lana,*
> *cadena a tus pies*
> *y nudo que apriete*
> *amargo laurel.*

> (Jasmin dress,
> crystal paper.
> Born at four o'clock,
> and dead at ten.
> To be the woolen yarn,
> the chain to your feet,
> and the knot that ties
> your bitter laurel wreath.)

Through their song, these girls spread an atmosphere of transparent lyricism. One feels that they uphold the tragedy through the simplicity of understatement in the words. In another way, these verses are a counterpart of the chorus of Woodsmen in the previous scene. Their extreme delicacy echoes the ageless old melody breathed on the wind at the coming of birth and death. Destiny here is woman. There is no male character in the final scene.

The first recognizable player to enter is Leonardo's Mother-in-Law, who has become nameless and somewhat like all relatives who come when death requires their mourning. Her appearance is a prelude to the more important actors: the Beggar Woman, and the Mother and the Betrothed who follow. The Beggar Woman dissolves the personal tragedy in her description of the double murder in the wood:

> *Yo los vi; pronto llegan; dos torrentes*
> *quietos al fin entre las piedras grandes,*
> *dos hombres en las patas del caballo.*
> *Muertos en la hermosura de la noche.*
>
> .   .   .   .   .   .
>
> *Los dos cayeron, y la novia vuelve*
> *teñida en sangre falda y cabellera.*
>
> .   .   .   .   .   .
>
> *Así fué; nada más. Era lo justo.*
> *Sobre la flor del oro, sucia arena.*
>
> (I saw them suddenly appear like two torrents
> quiet at last among the huge rocks:
> two men buried in the horse's hoofs.
> Dead in the beautiful calm of night.
>
> .   .   .   .   .   .
>
> Both fallen, and the betrothed returning,
> her skirt and hair stained with blood.
>
> .   .   .   .   .   .
>
> And so it was; nothing more. It was just.
> Over the flower of gold, dirty sand.)

When the Mother hears a neighbor weeping, she is annoyed; her own tears are dry. Now all her sons are dead.—

Your tears are only tears of the eyes—nothing more; and mine will come when I am alone, from the soles of my feet, from my roots, and will be more fiery than blood.

Out of my dream I shall make a cold dove of ivory, bearing camellias of frost over the cemetery. But no; not "cemetery," not "cemetery": bed of earth, bed which protects them and wafts them to heaven.

For her, the death of her last son ends the earth's terrible hunger for blood. The ritual now accomplished, her knowledge can no longer bring her pain. What should she care, therefore, for the protestations of the Betrothed, who comes to her now, wanting to die—to die so that the world may be convinced of her innocence and "honor."

What does your honor mean to me? What does your death mean to me? What does anything matter to me any more? Blessed be the leaves of grain because my sons are beneath them; blessed be the rain because it washes the faces of the dead; God be blessed, who lays us down together to rest.

Death is constantly washing the accumulation of personal grief away from the cloth of life; it cannot bring more tragedy than that. Yet, the acceptance of death on these terms is seen less through Catholic morality than through the knowledge of biological ritual. Lorca wished to take abstract death and the passage to heaven out of thought, and to substitute the knowledge of death in everything directly perceptible on earth. He does not enlarge his symbols of decay. For death, like life itself, is neither foul nor ugly: it is only the withering of strong mountainous things and weak colorful things. Weighing Catholic morality as it is conventionally preached, Lorca finds that it does not safeguard the innocent of spirit. On the contrary. Innocence invites a terrible fate which not even martyrdom can sanctify. In the deed itself, life is minimized, endangered, and finally atrophied. What exists in man and all of nature is that perfection of sensual reality which needs no compensation in an afterlife. Perhaps of death, then, it is only possible to say with the Beggar Woman, "It was just. Over the flower of gold, dirty sand."

For the first time, with *Bodas de Sangre*, one can speak of Lorca as poetic dramatist rather than as dramatic poet. Action is no longer static, nor congealed in the frames of "three prints." To be sure, there are evidences of a lyricism seeking to arrest the action in the lullaby scene of the first act; later in the forest scene with the Woodsmen, Moon and Beggar Woman; and finally in the first part of the last scene where the seated girls sing to their weaving. But these are not interludes which have been created as ends in themselves; rather, they operate as a respectable dramatic device: as projectors of the action on an inner screen, catching all the emotion previously rehearsed by the actors. Moreover, the central motifs are emphasized by economy of symbols and imagery in these scenes: the horse, the knife, the stream, the flow of blood. Likewise, spectacular and supernatural effects like the personification of Moon, Death, and Fates, add to the conciseness of dramatic statement. From the standpoint of the play's imaginative development, they are not artifices by which extra-human forces intrude into the dramatic situation, as in the old Greek tragedy. Rather, they serve to indicate most powerfully the fate which the human actors have been nursing in themselves from the very beginning. Death is the personal creation of each character and not a masked figure in sanctified descent from a hidden scaffold above.

Those who criticized *Bodas de Sangre* as typical of the lyric poet's deviations on the stage, were actually blind to the significance of the dramatist's intention. Far from being an amateur playwright, Lorca was exploring the primitive dramatic structure, the Catholic mass, the tribal ritual, and attempting thereby to create a tragic form which might fit the modern condition without relinquishing the spontaneity of the ancient. No mere poetic trickster would prescribe such an arduous discipline for himself in the theatre; nor could any poet simulate it who was not aware of some impelling drive to universalize his art. Though touched by every man, tragedy can be re-created only by those whose imagination, born of a sense of mass and weight in human suffering, is continually being purified in the struggle against it.

Written and produced in 1934, the year following *Bodas de Sangre, Yerma*[2] is Lorca's first tragedy constructed on a broad base of dramatic realism. Whereas the characters of *Bodas de Sangre* are dominated by a common sense of sharing a tragic fate (where the blind action of lust which results in tragedy arises from the earth, involving everyone in its consequences), the whole tragic burden in *Yerma* is borne by a single woman, and is measured by the deepening of her struggle with the problem of frustrated motherhood. While *Bodas de Sangre* follows in the tradition of Lope de Vega, who insisted on the spectacular and collective conception of tragic action, *Yerma* follows in the tradition of Calderón de la Barca, who insisted on the individual conception of tragedy, formulated by a religious code setting certain moral bounds to action. This makes not only for a natural difference in dramatic construction, but for the resolution of tragedy on a higher spiritual plane in *Yerma* than in *Bodas de Sangre*.

Although there is less verse in *Yerma* than in any other Lorca play,[3] the author still insists, in his subtitle, on its essential poetic

[2] Literally translated, *yerma* is *desert, sterility*.
[3] This was written before *Bernarda Alba* was published.

character: "A Tragic Poem in Three Acts and Six Scenes." When the
curtain rises on the first scene, Yerma is found asleep with her needle-
work at her feet. Bathed in a strange white light, the scene portrays
the last moment of her dream: a shepherd crosses on tiptoe, leading a
child by the hand. The two regard the sleeping figure for a moment
till a clock strikes. When they leave, the light changes "into the happy
light of a spring morning." Whereupon Yerma wakes. This bit of stage
décor effectively introduces the character of Yerma and the whole
motif of the tragedy. With the first few speeches in the home of Juan
and Yerma, the source of tragedy is opened wide. The theme of
fecundity and death, love and marriage, as symbolized in Yerma and
Juan, is vividly announced. Yerma is a malleable, richly poetic girl, but
frank and definite in her need. She opposes the earth which Juan is
working as an energetic farmer. She is herself the earth. Juan does
not like to be reminded of her desire for a child. Because he is impotent, he cannot actually "see" her. She, on the other hand, sees
everything. And this is the tragedy of her life: that what she sees,
though simple, is unmitigated; and that her need for a child, though
natural, is unsatisfied and begins to obsess her like a disease. Further,
Yerma's friend María, a simple peasant girl, is introduced. She is going
to have a child, and Yerma is delighted and more excited than María
herself. There is a lovely pathos in the advice she gives María: "Don't
walk about too much and when you breathe, breathe as softly as if you
had a rose between your teeth." Towards the end of the scene, Victor
appears. He is a shepherd, robust, physically attractive. (And Victor's
appearance seems like a re-entrance, for he suddenly becomes identified with the dream-shepherd of the beginning.) He hints at her
preoccupation: her desire for a child and her fear of Juan's frigidity.
Already we come to see Juan as the symbol of the materialist, the
blind provider. There is some sense too that Yerma is drawn to Victor
in a way she cannot account for. Her eyes linger over the spot where
he has been standing. And while spinning alone, she sings to the child
of her imagination:

> ¿De dónde vienes, amor, mi niño?
> "De la cresta del duro frío."
> ¿Qué necesitas, amor, mi niño?
> "La tibia tela de tu vestido."
> ¡Que se agiten las ramas al sol
> y salten las fuentes alrededor!
>
> .   .   .   .   .   .
>
> ¿Qué pides, niño, desde tan lejos?
> "Los blancos montes que hay en tu pecho."
>
> .   .   .   .   .   .

¿Cuándo, mi niño, vas a venir?
"Cuando tu carne huela a jazmín."
¡Que se agiten las ramas al sol
y salten las fuentes alrededor!

(Where do you come from, love, my child?
"From the heights of bitter cold."
What do you need, love, my child?
"The warm cloth of your dress' folds."
Let the branches shake in the sun
and the fountains leap about us!

.　　.　　.　　.　　.　　.

What do you ask for, my child, so far?
"The white mountains of your breasts."

.　　.　　.　　.　　.　　.

When are you coming, my child?
"When your flesh smells of jasmin."
Let the branches shake in the sun
and the fountains leap about us!)

In the second scene the dramatic complications are well under way. Yerma has a long passionate talk with an old peasant woman—Lorca's name for her is simply the old Pagan Woman—twice married and bearer of fourteen sons. A powerful creature, her nature is full of deep earth roots. Yerma has been married three years now and is still childless. The Pagan Woman, who senses the tragedy, is silent. Yerma keeps questioning her, however, and is answered cautiously, in hints. The Pagan Woman asks whether Yerma loves her husband. Yerma does not know, but exclaims, "God will aid me." At this, the old woman turns on her abruptly:

When are you going to realize that he does not exist? Only man can help you. But there should be a God, even a very tiny one, to send lightning down on those men whose seed is rotten and who puddle up the happiness of the fields.

It is a strong denunciation of Juan, and the Pagan Woman leaves on this. But Yerma understands that there is no solution for her in the experience of others.

Then two young women enter. Like Yerma, they have come to carry food to their husbands working in the fields. The First Woman has left her child asleep at home. Immediately Yerma's anxiety is aroused. "Children must not be left alone. Are there pigs about your house?" And the surprised mother rushes off at Yerma's alarming suggestion. The Second Woman, who is recently married and without children, pokes fun at her. She admits no interest whatever in having children. Yerma tells her she is only a frilly little girl. Frilly, yes, the Woman answers; but she didn't want to marry in the first place; she was forced into it. Marriage is an imposition of the old upon the young. She would much rather play in clear streams, ring bells, and occasionally take a drink of anisette. She rushes off laughing when Victor enters, singing a shepherd's song:

> *¿Por qué duermes solo, pastor?*
> *¿Por qué duermes solo, pastor?*
> *En mi colcha de lana*
> *dormirás mejor.*

> (Why, shepherd, do you sleep alone?
> Why, shepherd, do you sleep alone?
> You'd sleep much better
> in my warm wool cover.)

And Yerma picks up the refrain directly:

> *Los robles ponen agujas, pastor,*
> *debajo de tu almohada, pastor,*
> *y si oyes voz de mujer*
> *es la rota voz del agua, pastor, pastor.*

> (Beneath your pillow, shepherd,
> the oaks stick needles, shepherd;
> if you hear a woman's voice there,
> it's the broken call of waters, shepherd.)

> *Por el llano ya vino*
> *mi marido a cenar.*
> *Las brasas que me entrega*
> *cubro con arrayán.*

> *Por el aire ya viene*
> *mi marido a dormir.*
> *Yo alhelíes rojos*
> *y él rojo alhelí.*

> *Hay que juntar flor con flor*
> *cuando el verano seca la sangre del segador.*

> (Down the mountain my husband
> is coming to eat.
> He brings me a rose
> and I bring him three.

> Through the fields
> my husband came in to dine.
> The hot coals he brings me
> I cover with myrtle.

> Through the night air my husband
> is coming to sleep.
> He like a gillyflower red
> and I like red gillyflowers.
>
> When summer saps the blood of the sower,
> then let us join our flowers together.)

The women continue their songs in the rhythm of fertility, accentuating Yerma's isolation. They can hardly imagine a barren woman.

In the second scene it is twilight in Yerma's house. Juan is seated, attended by his two sisters. Here the emotional restraint contrasts sharply with the songs of the Washerwomen in the previous scene. Juan is seen more clearly, in a light becoming hard and austere. The Sisters-in-Law begin to move about in the background like ghosts. When Yerma comes in the conversation between her and Juan is clipped and full of violent repressed feeling. Estrangement has opened like a chasm between them. Yerma cannot live in stoical forbearance, which she regards as deathly. Still, the word from everybody is "humility," "acceptance"—but she cannot accept what is without passion or fruit. This knowledge is a little maddening for her.

> ¡Ay, qué prado de pena!
> ¡Ay, qué puerta cerrada a la hermosura!,
> que pido un hijo que sufrir, y el aire
> me ofrece dalias de dormida luna.
> Estos dos manantiales que yo tengo
> de leche tibia son en la espesura
> de mi carne dos pulsos de caballo
> que hacen latir la rama de mi angustia.
> ¡Ay, pechos ciegos bajo mi vestido!
> ¡Ay, palomas sin ojos ni blancura!
> ¡Ay, qué dolor de sangre prisionera
> me está clavando avispas en la nuca!
> Pero tú has de venir, amor, mi niño,
> porque el agua da sal, la tierra fruta,
> y nuestro vientre guarda tiernos hijos,
> como la nube lleva dulce lluvia.
>
> (Oh, what a field of pain!
> Oh, what a door shut on loveliness!
> When I ask a child for my suffering, the wind
> gives me dahlias from a sleeping moon.
> These two streams of warm milk
> I possess become in the closeness
> of my flesh two quiverings of a horse
> which make my branch of anguish beat.

Oh, blind breasts beneath my dress!
Oh, eyeless doves of no whiteness!
Oh, such sorrow of imprisoned blood
sticking wasps to my neck!
But you must come, love, my child,
because water yields salt, and earth fruit,
and our belly holds dear children
as clouds bear sweet rain.)

Later María comes with her child, saying she has been afraid to visit heretofore because of Yerma's envy. Yerma explains that it is not envy but her feeling of poverty. And the fixation of five years is now turning to the conviction that "I shall end by believing that I myself am my own child." She feels humbled by the fertility about her:

> Yes, I am offended, offended and forever humbled, seeing how the wheat grows tall, how the fountains never cease flowing and how the sheep give birth to hundreds of lambs, and the dogs, and it seems that the whole field is suddenly standing on its toes to show me its lovely dozing creatures, while I feel two hammer blows here instead of the mouth of my child.

María is a natural woman who grows uneasy listening to Yerma. Victor is a natural man with a fine instinct, but he cannot answer Yerma. She seeks an answer; and Juan knows it, but infers that she wishes to dishonor him morally thereby. He therefore forbids her to leave the house. But at the end of the act, seeking a supernatural source, she goes to the Conjurer.

We see this act clearly in two terms: the Christian symbol of work and order, which is the world of Juan, María and Victor, and the pagan world of passion, which is disorder—all of nature—and the sensual landscape of Yerma's imagination. She is being forced into a martyred position which is obnoxious to her. She seeks efficacy from life, not fermentation or glory, since she cannot conceive that the functions of man are other than the functions of nature. Her obligation is to herself, a conscience which will not allow her an artificial solution to the problem.

In the third act, Yerma learns from the Conjurer about women who have borne children with supernatural aid. She is told of a woman who stood in the river, "with her shoes and petticoats drenched in blood . . . but her face shining," and conceived. Yerma's idea of child-bearing is a mixture of milk and light: a pure form. Her reality is the whole of inviolable nature existing within her; but when ghostly frigidity is placed there instead, she would tear it out rather than have it sit on her heart. Her relation to Juan is that of a mountain of fire to a mountain of frost. But she has her honor: "I don't love him, I don't love him, and still he is my only salvation. For honor and chastity, my only salvation." Dawn comes and Juan enters with his two sisters. He accuses her of dishonoring him out of doors. Yerma defends herself simply and unanswerably, as a woman:

> Draw close to me and smell my clothing; come, come close! See if you can find an odor that is not yours, that has not partaken of your body. Take me nude, stand me in the middle of the street and spit on me. Do with me what you wish, for I am your wife, but be careful not to insinuate another man's name between my breasts.

But what bothers Juan is that "the people will begin to talk" about her wanderings. And when he asks what she is looking for, she embraces him passionately:

> I am looking for you. I am looking for you; I seek you day and night without finding a shade to breathe in. It is your blood and your help I want.

This goes against the grain; he throws her away from him. Now she sees herself, frustrated, really seeking herself. She cries, "Cursed be my father who left me his father's blood of a hundred children. Cursed be my blood which seeks them knocking against the walls." Then her final outburst reveals the crux of the whole play:

> It is one thing to want something with the head and another thing is when the body—cursed be the body!—does not answer us. It is all written down somewhere and I am not going to begin fighting the seas with my bare hands. So it is! Let my mouth be struck dumb!

From this point on, one expects only the extremest consequences of frustration—suicide or murder. Yerma commits both.

The last scene is enacted at a mountain shrine where women have come to pray for children. As night falls, Yerma is there watching the celebration of a popular masque. It is played by two women: one disguised as "a robust male," and the other as "a fertile female." Some children who are present immediately recognize the characters as The Devil and His Wife. Singing duets in the rhythm of the popular ballad, the "man" grasps a bull's horn in each hand, and the woman, a collar of bells. Lorca cautions against an exaggerated interpretation of this scene: "These characters should not be made to seem in the least grotesque, but of great beauty, as products of the pure earth." Guitars ring out. There is the smell of a primitive fertility rite, the lost art of peoples which flourished before the spread of tribes into towns—a heavy, steady, fiery music of flesh and earth.

The old Pagan Woman reappears to tell Yerma what she could

not before, when Yerma was a young wife. Juan is to blame, she says, and Juan's whole family, for

> . . . neither his father, nor his grandfather, nor his great-grandfather behaved like pure-blooded men. For them to have sons, it has been necessary that heaven and earth meet—they were made with spit . . . On the other hand, your family, no! You have brothers and cousins a hundred miles around. See what a curse has been thrown over your loveliness.

The Pagan Woman adds that her son is waiting nearby.

> My house needs a woman. Go with him and all three of us shall live together. . . . If you enter my house you will still find the odor of cradles there. The ashes of your quilt will turn to bread and salt for your children. Come. Don't worry about what people will say.

Yerma, however, who knows the responsibility of form, of honor, cannot abide by this. She upbraids the old woman sharply and concludes, "Mine is a sorrow which has already departed from the flesh." Thus her frustration seems to have turned almost into mysticism. She is a woman who has gone the complete round of her being, until she is "inverted." She is ready for anything, yet not in her old way, if she do it now, as she must, but in a way that is suddenly revealed to her. The old Pagan Woman leaves in search of some other woman for her son.

When Yerma moves, she discovers that Juan has been spying behind a rock. The ensuing scene is short, with words and images that are sharp direct arrows aimed at the tragic center. There is no pretense between them. Juan comes to give her his grief, to bring her back to his ashen life once and for all: "The moment has finally come to throw off this continual lamentation after obscure things, things outside of life, things empty as air." Outside of life, things of no substance? Yerma replies with anger and amazement. It is her very core he is denying, full of life and substance. Yet, they do not concern him: "What is important to me is what I have in my hands, what I see with my eyes." But this is just what Yerma has been waiting to hear from him. "It's true," she cries, suddenly capturing the significance of the tragedy, "one does not know the truth when it is wrapped up inside, but how huge it is and how it cries when it walks out and raises its arms!" But he is dumb to her catastrophic meaning. "Life is sweeter without children . . . I am happy not having them." What then do you want of me? Yerma asks. You, yourself, he answers. But finally she sees him clearly, and defines his words: "That's it! You want a house, peace, and a wife. But nothing more. Isn't that so?" And Juan agrees. Never has he really been troubled about her desire

for a child—his own impotence admitted or not; it has meant nothing
to him. Now she is equal to the deed. At last she knows her silence
broken, her answer given to her. Juan moves close to kiss her. I am
searching for you, he says, echoing her words. No, Yerma replies, you
search for me only when you are hungry, "when you feel like eating
a bird." And knowing now the final betrayal and no answer, she
chokes him for his impurity which is worse than the desert he has
imposed upon her. She kills him with her own hands, cleanly, with
the strength of her passion.

A chorus of women approaches. Yerma, relieved of her burden,
says:

> I'm going to rest without ever waking anxiously to see whether my
> blood has announced the coming of new blood. My body barren for-
> ever. What would you know? Don't come near me, because I have
> killed my child. I myself have killed my child!

Having killed him, she has also committed suicide within herself; for
according to her self-created code, she is at last certain, now that her
husband is dead, never to bear children.

In both the moral and dramatic sense, *Yerma* is the highest
achievement of Lorca's theatre. The character of Yerma rises out of
the anonymity of a universal problem into real tragic stature. Lorca
has departed in this play from the use of merely the elementary fact
of historical statement as found in *Mariana Pineda;* he has shown
resolution in terms of consistently self-impelled motivation. Thus,
Yerma is not simply an expanded ballad, but a consciously created
drama with a beginning, a middle, and an end. The supernatural has
become an organic part of the whole. When he employs chorus and
dance here, it is a technique integrated with every movement of the
plot, so that even Yerma's final resolution, the murder of Juan, gathers
impetus if not immediate inspiration from the dionysiac ritual at the
shrine in the last scene. There is no quality of emotional expression
in this drama which is false to, and which does not find basis in, the
immediate character of the land.

In any other context, the murder would be highly grotesque, if
not incomprehensible. If it were not an act of passion, then, or if it
were not a compulsion rising from a free identification with the land,
the whole meaning of the drama would be lost. But Yerma's character
and situation, if they are nothing else, are consistent and meaningful.
They create a logic of circumstance which becomes absolute on its
own terms. If she could have accepted any other terms, of course,
Yerma's violence would not have been inevitable. For she might have
become reconciled to her plight by yielding to the standardized

stoicism of the society about her. She might even have turned further into the bare emotion of Catholic humility or the conviction of martyrdom, as Mariana Pineda did—except that in her own situation, Yerma could not possibly reap the social recognition which was Mariana's reward. On the other hand, she might have chosen to accept the suggestion of the old Pagan Woman, or even of a more conscious Victor, and having left Juan for another, forsaken the moral conventions of society, as the Betrothed did in *Bodas de Sangre*. Only her unique conception of honor made none of these contingencies possible. She sought out all the forms of efficacy, both natural and supernatural, which her own sense of decency might sanction. But when these did not avail, only her unmet passion remained to dictate the extremity of her action. Her law was not the mere self-constituted amorality of the anarchist which concludes that since God does not exist, everything is possible; but the tragic form of truth which is as instinctive and imaginative as a poem's.

In her flight from frustrated struggle, Yerma gains nobility and is raised above vain tears. In being poetic, Yerma's solution is an act of creative liberation and an ultimate criticism of Spanish stoical morality. She proves that stoicism is a philosophy suited to a people or to an individual enslaved, for whom the world has grown too large. Instead of fortifying the soul, stoicism extracts the soul and makes it a dead letter in the name of perverted vanity. For the human being who must find some excuse for breathing in and breathing out, life becomes a biological pulp finally dissolved in the earth. Yerma, for whom the world is rich and intimate, is an island of green in a vast sea of stoicism—an island which we feel the angry sea always takes by storm . . .

The publication in 1946 of Lorca's suppressed drama *La Casa de Bernarda Alba*, makes possible a summary statement regarding the poet-dramatist's use of theme in the theatre. Thus far the traditional character of his subject has been stressed. It has also been shown that esthetically his drama developed from the more subjective treatment of character and conflict noted in hs experimental plays to the more objective presentation of the plight of woman in her pathetic condition of frustrated love. It is now possible to go further and show that what was implicit throughout, with *La Casa de Bernarda Alba* becomes completely manifest: that Lorca's drama as a whole is an act of social criticism as well as a document of unresolved personal dilemma.

The kind of society in which woman may be made to enact a dominant role is essentially "pre-romantic." In such a society her action is functional and not sentimental. As a life-binding force her obligation as mother and matriarch is to reproduce and keep together the family group, which is still the most significant social unit. Out of such a role, and the more her function is realized in the life of the community, arise the rituals and religious taboos which ensure the continuance of the society. Whether she attends the god of the vine in his seasonal orgies or is made the repository of religious mysteries in the temple or later becomes the symbolic figure representing social virtue or man's fate, her role is always positive, preservative and undebatably integrative of society's ideals. In Spain, where the maternal and matriarchal ideals have always predominated, they have given birth to a literature of Mariolatry, feminine martyrdom, the ethical norms of the *dueña* and a castigated Donjuanism. What Lorca is saying in all his folk dramas is that the ritual which for centuries apotheosized those ideals has now succeeded in devitalizing them. What is left is a value which propels its representative to certain tragedy since it is no longer capable of being fulfilled in either personal or social terms without detriment to the individual or to society. Thus the dual failure of Mariana Pineda as a woman and the cause of freedom urged by her irresponsible love, in Lorca's first play. Thus the suicide of Adela as a fertile question and the hypocritical survival of the frigid and class-stratified answer of the mother, Bernarda Alba, in Lorca's last play. Virtue which was once a creative personal principle safeguarding in the individual the life of order against the threat of social anarchy becomes a negative abstraction and a destructive shibboleth in a society which has made it an instrument for chaos.

The personal dilemma of the poet reflected in his plays, which to some extent are the enactment of that dilemma, is precisely that of his heroines in the folk dramas: frustrated love. In personal terms lack of fulfillment suggests a conflict of sexuality through its insistence on unresolved impasse in the plays, and through it increasingly an uncontainable eroticism which *wills* the impasse.

It may be seen now why in choosing to stay close to the traditional habits of culture perception, Lorca was able to identify his dilemma with that of a society already consuming itself in its own contradictions, and why in rescuing the creative ethic which it had subdued he was able to give his theme poetic significance without strictly imaginative or dramatic resolution.

Lorca's dramatic experiments like *Mariana Pineda, Don Perlimplín, Así Que Pasen Cinco Años,* etc., all treat the problem of romantic love ironically. In *Mariana Pineda,* where the poet identifies himself with the heroine, he takes refuge with her in a martyrdom of sentimental mysticism. In *Don Perlimplín,* where he sees himself as both the erotic Belisa and her imaginative but impotent old husband, his refuge is a sadistic revenge: the creation of an imaginary young lover who betrays himself and Belisa in an act of pathetic irony. In *Así Que Pasen Cinco Años,* the cruelly materialistic heroine who rejects the Young Man for the Football Player and a car, is juxtaposed to a second-best but equally unavailing love, the Stenographer, who flees from him, while he is consoled by the voice of his imagination in the figure of an animated mannikin. His end is a half-willed suicide dictated by the card players, his own irresponsible fate.

In the folk dramas which culminate with *La Casa de Bernarda Alba,* romance no longer exists even as an ironic statement. The poet, identified with all his heroines, perpetuates desire endlessly in an eroticism which, like Yerma's, ends in a metaphysical suicide, or like Doña Rosita's, spreads itself through the fields and wells and walls of Granada's circumambience. The refuges into which all his protagonists escape are in a sense fatally predetermined by the enormity of their excessive and unfulfillable need which they realize cannot be ratified by the society and situation in which they find themselves. And they correspond, in this way, to the poet in the jail of his richly surging world of sexuality whch can neither be contained without a sympathy as gigantic as his own or broken through without catastrophe. But just as the first is never encountered, so the second gradually seems, as the dénouement of play after play, more a result of the same paralyzed circumstance than a revealing resolution of a many leveled tragic insight. It is the personal dilemma which prevents Lorca's folk dramas as well as his other plays from rising so often out of pathos to real tragedy. At the same time, however, it makes for Lorca's unique sincerity as an artist and shows why a tragedy of personal validity must fail in the modern world, where it remains unresolved finally in terms of social criticism, in terms of a society which inevitably degrades as it makes meaningless personal integrity.

f.o. matthiessen

THE PLAYS OF T. S. ELIOT

> A verse play is not a play done into verse,
> but a different kind of play: in a way more
> realistic than 'naturalistic drama,' because,
> instead of clothing nature in poetry, it
> should remove the surface of things, expose
> the underneath, or the inside, of the natural
> surface appearance. It may allow the char-
> acters to behave inconsistently, but only
> with respect to a deeper consistency. It may
> use any device to show their real feelings
> and volitions, instead of just what, in actual
> life, they would normally profess or be con-
> scious of; it must reveal, underneath the
> vacillating or infirm character, the indomita-
> ble unconscious will; and underneath the
> resolute purpose of the planning animal, the
> victim of circumstance and the doomed or
> sanctified being. So the poet with ambitions
> of the theatre, must discover the laws, both
> of another kind of verse and of another kind
> of drama.—Eliot, Introduction to S. L.
> Bethell's *Shakespeare and The Popular Dra-
> matic Tradition*, 1944.

THE INTERPLAY between Eliot's created work and his criticism, so illuminating to the comprehension of his poems, is inevitably something different in the case of his dramas. His theory of poetry has been borne out by his practice, and both have been greatly influential now throughout the generation. But his conception of drama, his belief in the need for poetic drama, still remain more in the realm of theory even in his own experiments, as well as in their limited effect on the general course of the drama in our time. As he observed in his "Dia-logue on Dramatic Poetry," which he wrote as a preface to Dryden's

From *The Achievement of T. S. Eliot* by F. O. Matthiessen, pp. 155–176. Third Edition © 1958 by Oxford University Press, Inc. Reprinted by permission.

great discussion of the subject, "It is one thing to discuss the rules of an art when that art is alive, and quite another when it is dead."

At the start of Eliot's career Yeats and the Abbey Theatre were making a limited revival of plays in verse, but the prevailing relation between English poetry and drama was summed up in one of Eliot's early statements: "Browning wrote dull plays, but invented the dramatic monologue or character." For several years it appeared as though Eliot would confine his strong dramatic impulses to the realm of Browning's successes, but by 1926, a year or two before he wrote his "Dialogue," he had already experimented with *Sweeney Agonistes*. He had always been absorbed with the great age of the English theatre, as his many essays on Elizabethan playwrights bear witness. But his earliest comprehensive formulation of what he demanded from drama and did not find on the contemporary stage remains buried in an uncollected review, "The Beating of a Drum," where in the course of discussing Olive Busby's *Studies in the Development of the Fool in Elizabethan Drama,* he remarked:

> The essentials of the drama were, as we might expect, given by Aristotle: 'poetry, music, and dancing constitute in Aristotle a group by themselves, their common element being imitation by means of rhythm—rhythm which admits of being applied to words, events, and the movements of the body.' It is the rhythm, so utterly absent from modern drama, either verse or prose, and which interpreters of Shakespeare do their best to suppress, which makes Massine and Charlie Chaplin the great actors they are, and which makes the juggling of Rastelli more cathartic than a performance of *A Doll's House.*[1]

You do not have to agree with his final example—which was a sally in the war he shared with Yeats against the limitation of realism —in order to perceive that he has grasped the conception of poetic drama as an organic whole. He realizes, as the nineteenth-century imitators of Shakespeare did not, that verse is not something merely added to a play as an extra ornament or trimming, but that the poetic pattern and the dramatic pattern must subsist together as integral products of one act of imagination. This, incidentally, is what Granville-Barker, who knew both the stage and poetry, has demonstrated again so persuasively in relation to Shakespeare's plays.

To the extent that the nineteenth century, following in the wake of Coleridge, divorced the poetic philosopher from the workaday playwright, it misunderstood and falsified Shakespeare. To the extent that it confined poetry to the closet, it also, in Eliot's view, impoverished the drama. In a radio broadcast in 1936, the year after

[1] *The Nation and Athenaeum,* 6 October 1923. The quotation within the passage is from Butcher's commentary on *The Poetics.*

the considerable success of *Murder in the Cathedral* on the stage, he made his position as explicit as possible: "I believe . . . that poetry is the natural and complete medium for drama; that the prose play is a kind of abstraction capable of giving you only a part of what the theatre can give; and that the verse play is capable of something much more intense and exciting." [2]

By then the drive for realism had become far less dominant in the theatre, which could so easily be beaten on this ground by the film. Consequently Eliot could hold it

> reasonable that the stage should not attempt to compete with the film in illusion of scenery . . . and event. It should turn to the voice, to movement which is meant to be seen from several angles, and to things which can be done by the actor himself and which cannot be done by his pictures. And all this points to the verse play.
>
>   To work out a play in verse . . . is to see the thing as a whole musical pattern. . . . The verse dramatist must operate on you on two levels at once. . . . It is fatal for a poet trying to write a play, to hope to make up for defects in the movement of the play by bursts of poetry which do not help the action. But underneath the action, which should be perfectly intelligible, there should be a musical pattern which intensifies our excitement by reinforcing it with feeling from a deeper and less articulate level.

This describes what Eliot has striven for in his own plays. As usual his work is of greatest interest in its technical experiments, and in the reasons he gives for them. One of his strongest convictions about the nature of a living tradition is the unlikeliness that any verse form can be renewed for the same purpose for which it was widely current in the past. He would doubt that either the Popean couplet or the *Don Juan* stanza could serve any longer for satire, except as an occasional *tour de force*. He would be even more certain that the expectedness of blank verse for drama would keep it from being anything more than a poor imitation of Shakespeare, would prevent it from "contributing anything to the life of our own time."

'The problem for us, therefore,' he continued in his radio talk,

> is to get away from Shakespeare. . . . That is not so easy. I have found, in trying to write dramatic verse, that however different a metre from blank verse I was working with, whenever my attention has relaxed, or I have gone sleepy or stupid, I will wake up to find that I have been writing bad Shakespearean blank verse: and I have had to scrap the lot and start all over again. Hence we have to make use of suggestions from remote drama, too remote for there to be any danger of imitation, such as *Everyman,* and the late medieval morality and mystery plays, and the great Greek dramatists.

[2] This was printed in *The Listener,* 25 November 1936.

When he was writing *Sweeney Agonistes,* Eliot was already convinced that "the recognized forms of speech-verse are not as efficient as they should be; probably a new form will be devised out of colloquial speech." He expressed that conviction in his self-revelatory introduction to *Savonarola* (1926), his mother's closet drama, in rhymed couplets, where he also declared that after the discursive conversational pieces of Shaw, the drama needed an intensification, a tightening, that "the next form of drama will have to be a verse drama but in new verse forms."

Eliot subtitled his first brief scenes "fragments of an Aristophanic melodrama," but the source of the verse spoken by Sweeney and his friends was much nearer at hand. The poet was trying to utilize vaudeville rhythms for reasons that he had recently articulated in his appreciation of Marie Lloyd as "the greatest music-hall artist of her time." He felt that she "represented and expressed that part of the English nation which has perhaps the greatest vitality and interest"; and that any hope for a popular drama would spring from the robust entertainment of the lower class, and not from the "morally corrupt" middle class, already given over to the lifeless mechanism of the standardized cinema. The songs in Eliot's play, "Under the bamboo tree" and "My little island girl," found their stimulus in American jazz, as did the syncopation of the dialogue. As a result Eliot's verse here seemed less novel than usual to American ears, but it became one of the starting points for Auden's charades.

In the method of projecting his content Eliot was indebted again to Henry James. The hero is so different a character from the "apeneck Sweeney" of the poems that Eliot might better have given him a different name. And while the epigraphs from St. John of the Cross and Aeschylus' *Choephori* may seem at first glance another of Eliot's pieces of elaborate irony, the words quoted from Orestes' speech about the Furies—"You don't see them, you don't—but *I* see them: they are hunting me down"—are directly relevant to Eliot's intention. For, like James, Eliot was presenting characters of differing degrees of consciousness. Doris and Dusty and the visitors to their flat were meant to be "material, literal-minded, and visionless." Sweeney, in his meditations on "birth, copulation, and death," can not communicate his feelings to them, but only to the sentient members of the audience. This complete isolation of Sweeney from the rest of the cast was well conveyed both in Hallie Flanagan's production at Vassar (1933), and in Rupert Doone's for the Group Theatre in London (1935). But such an extreme development of James' device would hardly seem workable for a play of much length, and it is not surprising that Eliot left Sweeney's "agon" a fragment.

His "Dialogue on Dramatic Poetry" suggests—half a dozen years before he undertook *The Rock*—where he would turn next. He cites again the satisfying formality of the ballet, the elimination of all inessentials in its concentrated "liturgy" of "traditional, symbolical, and highly trained movements." As one of the speakers in the "Dialogue" remarks, "Here seemed to be everything that we wanted in drama, except the poetry." But the mention of liturgy leads on to the remark that "the consummation of the drama . . . is to be found in the ceremony of the Mass." Another speaker takes exception. Granted that the origin of drama is in religious liturgy, granted that "the Mass is a small drama, having all the unities," and that "if you consider the ritual of the Church during the cycle of the year . . . you have represented the full drama of Creation," nevertheless, "even if you are a believer, you will have dramatic desires which crave fulfillment otherwise. . . Religion is no more a substitute for drama than drama is a substitute for religion."

The consensus to which Eliot's speakers come is the same that he had voiced in his introduction to *Savonarola:* "In genuine drama the form is determined by the point on the line at which a tension between liturgy and realism takes place." In reaction against the photographic tendencies of realism, Eliot wanted to move again towards heightened convention. William Archer's *The Old Drama and the New* was a central point for attack, and in the position he took up against this apostle of Ibsenism, Eliot revealed a break with current standards of drama even more complete than his poetry had made with Tennyson and Swinburne. In answer to Archer's charge that the weakness of Elizabethan drama lay in its unrealistic conventions, Eliot said that on the contrary it had never been conventional enough.

> "The great vice of English drama from Kyd to Galsworthy has been that its aim of realism was unlimited. In one play, *Everyman,* and perhaps in that one play only, we have a drama within the limitations of art."

We may gasp, as often in Eliot, at the astringency of his example, which seems to close more doors rather than to open the possibility of any. But he made clearer the grounds of his admiration, in a lecture on "Religious Drama: Medieval and Modern" (1937): "In *Everyman* the religious and dramatic are not merely combined, but wholly fused." [3] Even if that fusion is the mark of classic wholeness, Eliot can still perceive that something lay beyond the medieval drama's scope. It may be a relief to turn back to "the austere close language" and to "the simplicity of the mysteries," but "if new influences had

[3] *The University of Edinburgh Journal,* Autumn 1937.

not entered, old orders decayed," we should not have had the less orderly magnificence of *King Lear*.

But in our time of broken standards and beliefs he wanted to see what reinvigoration for drama might lie in a return to its source in liturgy. The structure of *Ash Wednesday*, as we have observed, draws upon the drama of the Mass. In *The Rock*, performed at Sadler's Wells in 1934, Eliot set himself to write a play on behalf of the fund to preserve the old churches of London. Strictly speaking, *The Rock* is a pageant, not a drama. That is to say, its situation does not give rise to any intense struggle or conflict; its structure consists of a series of scenes of a related tone, scenes which decorate the theme of the building of the Church, the hardships it has encountered in various crises of the past as well as the present, and the firmness of its triumph. The scenario was not original with Eliot, but provided for him by Martin Browne; Eliot's task was to produce the dialogue, the bulk of which is in prose. Many of the scenes are hardly of interest beyond their original purpose of furnishing the text for a formal spectacle, which was accompanied by music and ballet. And some of them, in their very conception, do not escape from unctuousness. But the passages of verse, which run to several hundred lines, though spoken mostly by the Chorus, include also the whole of the most energetic scene, that in which the Church is confronted by Redshirts, Blackshirts, and Plutocrats. This scene shows Eliot trying his hand at the kind of material that Auden, whose first experiments owed so much to Eliot, had already made ambitious efforts to handle in *The Dance of Death*.[4]

Although its choruses give voice to some of the same profound kind of meditative poetry that he was to develop in his *Quartets*, *The Rock* hardly meets Eliot's test for a religious play, "that it should be able to hold the interest, to arouse the excitement, of people who are not religious." Nor, through the very nature of its inception, could it possibly rise to his far more exacting demand of creating an indisseverable double pattern of poetry and drama. Such a set piece could not possess the wholeness of vision and movement of a *Polyeucte* or an *Athalie*. But the case was very different with the play which Eliot wrote for the Canterbury Festival the following year.

Murder in the Cathedral, like many of the morality plays, is a drama of temptation, but Becket as the great archbishop proves su-

---

[4] This interchange suggests an interesting sequence. Without Eliot's revolt against the art for art's sake of the 'nineties, his steady insistence that no part of life should be barred from poetry, and his growing example of how a poet can turn for his material both to religion and to politics, Auden's generation would not have found the ground so clear for their own handling of contemporary affairs. But Auden's political plays, as well as Spender's *The Trial of a Judge*, are much more implicated in immediate events, and owe a great deal to the theatre of Berthold Brecht.

perior to his tempters. One of the most conspicuous technical triumphs
in all Eliot's poetry is in the choruses that were designed to be spoken
by the working women of Canterbury. Here he carried further his
experiments in finding verse forms suitable for ritualistic drama. He
had no living stage tradition upon which to draw, but he believed that
a chorus could still perform something of the same fundamental function that it had for the Greeks. It could "mediate between the action
and the audience"; it could "intensify the action by projecting its emotional consequences, so that we as audience see it doubly, by seeing its
effect on other people."

Eliot's women are there to watch and suffer, and their feelings
are nearly all in the most sombre key. Their gamut is from nameless
dread of foreboding to horror at the fact of Becket's murder. Their
lines are generally iambic, of greatly varying lengths, though, as in
The Rock, Eliot usually avoided the pentameter. He explored some
of the possibilities of Hopkins' sprung-rhythm, and carried it on occasion into a patterned prose, quickened by alliteration and internal
rhyme. He was very dexterous throughout in organizing his speeches
according to natural breath lengths.

His actors are also characterized by the verse they speak, so that
there is a marked difference between the lilting cadences of the First
Tempter, who tries to lure Becket by the memory of old pleasures,
and the bluntness and force in the lines of those who tempt by power,
either of the Chancellorship or of a new alliance with the barons
against the King. The Fourth and last Tempter is at the top of a rising
scale. For while the resumption of the role of Chancellor lay almost
as remote from Becket's present desires as did worldly pleasure, and
while a coalition with the barons could stir him only momentarily,
the Fourth Tempter alone is unexpected by Becket, and tempts him by
his own deepest thoughts:

> You know and do not know, what it is to act or suffer.
> You know and do not know, that acting is suffering
> And suffering is action. Neither does the actor suffer
> Nor the patient act. But both are fixed
> In an eternal action, an eternal patience
> To which all must consent that it may be willed
> And which all must suffer that they may will it,
> That the pattern may subsist, for the pattern is the action
> And the suffering, that the wheel may turn and still
> Be forever still.

This had been Becket's first speech in the play, reflecting on the
lot of the Chorus, and the Fourth Tempter flings it back at him almost
word for word. The firmness of its doctrine reveals how far Eliot has

advanced in his possession of Dante's conception of grace, "la sua voluntade è nostra pace." [5] Eliot no longer dwells as he did earlier on "the eternal burden" alone, but, in this subtle interweaving of suffering, striving, and acceptance, on the possibility of "the perpetual glory." But by making the Fourth Tempter penetrate to the same deep level of understanding, Eliot dramatizes Becket's chief peril, the temptation to the proud mind to become so confident in its wisdom that it seeks—and takes for granted—a martyr's crown as its reward.

> The last temptation is the greatest treason:
> To do the right deed for the wrong reason.

In the meditation that closes the first act Becket wins through to the recognition that no man can will his way to martyrdom. "I shall no longer act or suffer to the sword's end," he concludes, and submits his will to God's.

In the sermon that serves for an interlude between the two acts, Becket reveals himself secure in this deeper reliance, and then, holding fast to his belief in the supremacy of God's law above man's law, he encounters the wrath of the Knights, who are the same as the four Tempters of the first act, and goes to his death unflinchingly. The blasphemy of the Knights' deed is underscored by the fact that they advance to their bloodshed with phrases borrowed from spirituals and revival hymns just after the Chorus has voiced a despairing passage, "Numb the hand and dry the eyelid," in the cadences of "Dies Irae." The Knights then turn to the audience and in a passage of dramatic shock (which seemed too sudden in some performances, though highly effective in others) they drop into the prose of modern debate, and try to justify their act by all the rationalizations of expediency. But the ending belongs to the Priests and the Chorus mounting to a prayer of intercession to "blessed Thomas."

Murder in the Cathedral was immensely successful for its immediate purpose in the chapter house at Canterbury. It demonstrated what Eliot meant by saying, in the final lines of his "Dialogue": "A continuous hour and a half of *intense* interest is what we need." Despite the problem created by a chorus on the modern stage, the play demonstrated this again in a long run at the Mercury Theatre in London under Ashley Dukes and Martin Browne. It was one of the great successes of the WPA theatre in New York, where the Chorus was handled by dividing its lines among several individual speakers,

[5] Eliot's passage is also closely akin to Jonathan Edwards: 'In efficacious grace we are not merely passive, nor does God do some, and we do the rest. But God does all and we do all. God produces all, and we act all. God is the only proper author and fountain; we are the proper actors. We are, in different respects, wholly active and wholly passive.' In moving towards Catholicism Eliot has also preserved the rigor of his Puritan forebears, and his dramas of pride are still in the tradition from Hawthorne.

and where Harry Ervine's interpretation brought more vitality to the title role than the somewhat too ritualistic performance of Robert Speaight. In the spring after the liberation of France it scored a renewed triumph at the Vieux Colombier in a translation by Henri Fluchère.

Stimulated by his first reception on the regular stage, Eliot attempted in *The Family Reunion* something far more difficult, a play that would use the setting and characters of drawing-room comedy and that would still include the Eumenides in its cast. He seems to have been thinking of the method evolved by James for his "ghost" stories, where the design was to have "the strange and sinister embroidered on the very type of the normal and easy." [6] "Nothing is more dramatic than a ghost," observed one of the speakers in Eliot's "Dialogue," but it is one thing to suggest an eerie presence in fiction, quite another to present the Eumenides in evening dress in the embrasure of a window on the modern stage, and here Eliot's inexperience in the theatre betrayed him into a device that failed badly in its effect.

He may have been thinking also of Chekhov's haunted world of social decay, and it is significant that two other Americans of Eliot's generation, O'Neill in *Mourning Becomes Electra* and Jeffers in *The Tower Beyond Tragedy,* have dramatized the theme of a curse on a house by a rehandling of the Orestes story. Eliot's device for his chorus here is also comparable to some of O'Neill's previous experiments in having his characters withdraw momentarily from the action to voice their inner thoughts. Eliot's choric group consists of the hero's uncles and aunts, who are on hand for his return, after a long absence, for his mother's birthday. They are unlike the usual Greek chorus in that their role is not to illuminate the action, but to express their baffled inability to understand what is happening:

> *We do not know what we are doing. . . .*
> *We have lost our way in the dark.*

[6] That Eliot had in mind James' story, "The Jolly Corner," while composing his play is made apparent by one of the opening speeches describing how Eliot's hero, like James' exile returning to his old home, will be confronted everywhere by the specter of his past:

> *The man who returns will have to meet*
> *The boy who left. Round by the stables,*
> *In the coach-house, in the orchard,*
> *In the plantation, down the corridor*
> *That led to the nursery, round the corner*
> *Of the new wing, he will have to face him—*
> *And it will not be a very jolly corner.*

The reference was even more pointed in the manuscript draft, which continued:

> *I am sorry, Gerald, for making an allusion*
> *To an author whom you never heard of.*

Eliot is absorbed again, in much the same fashion as he was in *Sweeney*, in projecting different levels of consciousness, but one danger here is that his country-house social group is so inert and lifeless that we can hardly become interested in them even as a contrast with the hero, the titular head of the house, Harry, Lord Monchensey. Most of the verse that they speak has a deliberate flatness, and seems, indeed, to have been designed to sound on the stage hardly distinguishable from prose. In this kind of effort to approximate colloquial speech, Eliot seems to have forgotten his earlier and wiser principle that verse should always be used for a heightening, that whatever can now be said just as well in prose is better said in prose.

The hero is in a state of mind which he finds it almost impossible to explain to anyone else. Seven years before, after a brief and disastrous marriage, while travelling on an ocean liner, he either pushed his wife overboard or at least watched her slip and drown. He is not quite clear which, but he had wanted to kill her, and has felt himself pursued ever since, as though by the Furies. The difference from the Furies in Aeschylus is profound, and suggests that in handling his ambiguous material Eliot failed to keep to his realization that the action in a play must be "perfectly intelligible," that, in fact, he failed on this occasion to find an adequate "objective correlative."

Only in the last play of Aeschylus' trilogy are the Erinys transformed into the Eumenides. The moment is of the widest social significance. The baleful Furies who have tracked down the murderer Orestes are forced by Athena to yield and to become benevolent guardians of the state. What is dramatized thereby is the immense step that was taken by mankind in giving up primitive blood-vengeance, a life for a life, and submitting to the ordered process of courts of law. Orestes is then released as having done sufficient expiation for his terrible vengeance of his father's death upon his mother, and the curse on the house is at an end.

Eliot wanted to suggest a comparable transformation. Harry has long felt himself followed and watched, but it is only upon his return to Wishwood that he finally sees his pursuers and comes to recognize their true meaning. The two scenes in which they appear on the stage are between Harry and his cousin Mary, whom his strong-willed mother had once designed for his wife, and between Harry and his Aunt Agatha, the one deeply perceptive and sympathetic member of his family. But these scenes, though here Eliot quickened and intensified his verse, are very obscure, owing to Harry's own obsessed state, and do not begin to convey to the audience the intention that Eliot outlined in a letter to Martin Browne:

The scene with Mary is meant to bring out, as I am aware it fails to, the conflict inside him between . . . repulsion for Mary as a woman, and the attraction which the *normal* part of him that is left, feels toward her personally *for the first time*. This is the first time since his marriage ("there was no ecstasy") that he has been attracted towards any woman. The attraction glimmers for a moment in his mind, half-consciously as a possible "way of escape," and the Furies (for the Furies are *divine* instruments, not simple hell-hounds) come in the nick of time to warn him away from this evasion—though at that moment he misunderstands their function. Now, this attraction towards Mary has stirred him up, but, owing to his mental state, is incapable of developing; therefore he finds a refuge in an ambiguous relation— the attraction, half of a son and half of a lover, to Agatha, who reciprocates in somewhat the same way. And this gives the cue for the second appearance of the Furies, more patently in their role of divine messengers, to let him know clearly that the only way out is purgation and holiness. They become exactly "hounds of heaven." And Agatha understands this clearly, though Harry only understands it yet in flashes. So Harry's career needs to be completed by an *Orestes* or an *Oedipus at Colonnos.*

In the scene with Agatha, Harry comes at least to know his situation. She tells him, to relieve his mind, that his father, long since dead, had fallen in love with her and had wanted to kill Harry's mother, but that she, Agatha, had kept him from doing so. Nevertheless, the thought was there, and Harry must now expiate a repetition of the same crime. Or rather,

> *What we have written is not a story of detection,*
> *Of crime and punishment, but of sin and expiation. . . .*
> > *It is possible*
> *You are the consciousness of your unhappy family,*
> *Its bird sent flying through the purgatorial flame.*
> *Indeed it is possible. You may learn hereafter,*
> *Moving alone through flames of ice, chosen*
> *To resolve the enchantment under which we suffer.*

By finding an equivalent for the transformation of the Furies through the difference between Hell and Purgatory, in the acceptance of the purifying fire, Eliot has tied the Eumenides into his pattern of thought, but he has hardly been explicit enough to take an audience with him. Also, the inferiority for dramatic purposes of Harry's story to that of Orestes is manifest, since the hatred of a wife, though repeated in two generations, does not, as Eliot handles it, assume much more than private significance.

There are also some echoes of *Hamlet* in Harry's situation. As he says,

> *It is not my conscience,*
> *Not my mind, that is diseased, but, the world I have to live in.*

And when his family, still maintaining that he suffers from delusions, sets the old family doctor to spy out the cause of his neurosis, they suggest the behavior of the King and Polonius. Strangely enough, there is also a reminder of what Eliot found unsatisfactory in *Hamlet* as a play: that Shakespeare gives the sense there of struggling with some "intractable" material that he could not bring to light, that the

> supposed identity of Hamlet with his author is genuine to this point: that Hamlet's bafflement at the absence of objective equivalent to his feelings is a prolongation of the bafflement of his creator in the face of his artistic problem. Hamlet is up against the difficulty that his disgust is occasioned by his mother, but his mother is not an adequate equivalent for it; his disgust envelops and exceeds her.

Eliot has found the peculiar genius of Cyril Tourneur to consist in his expression of "the loathing and horror of life itself." Something of that quality is infused into Harry, Lord Monchensey, but his objective situation simply will not support it. After Agatha's revelation, Harry accepts the fact that his destiny is to suffer more, not to evade, no longer to flee from but to "follow the Furies"—a phrase which at one time was Eliot's tentative title for the play. Yet Harry can speak of his future in only the most general terms:

> *Where does one go from a world of insanity?*
> *Somewhere on the other side of despair.*
> *To the worship in the desert, the thirst and deprivation,*
> *A stony sanctuary and a primitive altar,*
> *The heat of the sun and the icy vigil,*
> *A care over the lives of humble people,*
> *The lesson of ignorance, of incurable diseases.*
> *Such things are possible. . .*
> *I must follow the bright angels.*

But when, in lieu of the traditional chariot of the *deus ex machina,* we have the highpowered car in which his faithful valet, after returning to pick up his Lordship's cigarette case, is to drive him away, the break between the surface of the play and the depth it is meant to symbolize becomes ludicrous and irreparable. By no suspension of disbelief can we conceive how Harry, whose life seems to have been passed mainly in resorts and luxury hotels, can undergo the discipline of suffering in any broadly meaningful sense. And when, after his departure, Agatha closes the play by reciting a rune to end the curse while she and Mary make a stylized dance around the birthday cake and blow out the candles, so that the "last words shall be spoken in the dark," as in the service of *tenebrae,* the effect seems an unintentional parody of liturgy rather than a reinvigoration from it.[7]

Eliot's belief in the value of poetic drama is based on its richer resources for transcending "the ephemeral and superficial," and for concentrating upon "the permanent struggles and conflicts of human beings." Only through such struggles is character revealed. One of Eliot's greatest gifts in his earlier dramatic lyrics was the power to suggest the essence of a character in a few lines. But a play requires more than the flash of suggestion; it requires development through a significant action.[8] The most devastating aspects of *The Family Reunion* are the unexamined implications of Harry's conduct. Whether or not he pushed his wife overboard, she went to her death by drowning; but the loss of her life, other than as a phase of the hero's education, is made a ground of no remorse. It seems only a re-enactment of Sweeney's macabre statement:

> *Any man has to, needs to, wants to*
> *Once in a lifetime, do a girl in.*

Harry's heightened awareness, through his talk with Agatha, of the meaning of what has happened to him produces no access of pity for his wife, but only a renewed ruthlessness towards his mother. Unlike Orestes, he does not murder her, but he becomes none the less the instrument of her death. Warned by the doctor that his mother is at an age where she cannot stand a shock, he produces one by breaking with her and leaving Wishwood; and we learn that she is dead before the curtain falls. Hers is the character of blind pride and selfish will that brings on *nemesis,* but Harry's utter lack of compunction seems none the less unnatural. We are reminded very forcibly of the sentence from St. John of the Cross that Eliot prefixed to *Sweeney:* "Hence the soul cannot be possessed of the divine union, until it has divested itself of the love of created beings." Though Agatha may tell Harry that "Love compels cruelty/To those who do not understand love," Eliot has not succeeded in persuading us that Harry has anything of the overmastering love of God that alone could give sanction to the mystic's terrible renunciation.

---

[7] This seems to have been the case both in the play's limited run in London (1939), under the direction of Martin Browne, and in the amateur performance by the Harvard Dramatic Club (1940).

[8] Matthew Arnold's realization of his failure to find such "human actions" for his plays gave rise to the formulation quoted as an epigraph to my chapter on "The Objective Correlative" (p. 56 above).

Maud Bodkin, in *The Quest for Salvation* (1941), pointed out some of Eliot's limitations when contrasted with the archetypal patterns of Aeschylus. C. L. Barber's essay, "T. S. Eliot after Strange Gods" (*The Southern Review,* Autumn 1940), utilizing a Freudian technique, is the most extensive examination of the inadequacy of the play's symbols.

The contrast with Eliot's Becket is revelatory. His presentation of the archbishop was limited but coherent. He was not writing a drama of disastrous pride like *Lear*, but a drama of pride overcome. His Becket, after resisting the tempters, is a "sanctified being," such as Eliot described in the epigraph to this chapter. Such an image, to be sure, greatly simplifies the actual figure concerning whom historians are still divided as to whether he fought at the last "for an idea" or "for the humiliation" of his opponent Henry II. In Eliot's Anglo-Catholic belief Becket is a martyr, but the poet makes him a saint even in this life. He gives none of the flare-up of the natural man who was reported to have met Reginald FitzUrse, the leader of the murderers, with the angry denunciation, "you pander." But if Eliot lost something of the human being in the ritualistic priest, even if his Becket, in the consciousness of his mission, barely escapes from "the pride that apes humility," Eliot managed to dramatize permanent issues.

He could do it since—as was not the case in *The Family Reunion*—he had grasped and interpreted a social context. He was aware that his conception of history ran contrary to that of a secular age, and one of his most striking passages is that in which Becket addresses the audience with a prophetic vision:

> *I know*
> *What yet remains to show you of my history*
> *Will seem to most of you at best futility,*
> *Senseless self-slaughter of a lunatic,*
> *Arrogant passion of a fanatic.*

The Fourth Tempter also looks ahead to the Reformation, when Becket's shrine will be pillaged, but adds:

> *later is worse, when men will not hate you*
> *Enough to defame or to execrate you,*
> *But pondering the qualities that you lacked*
> *Will only try to find the historical fact.*
> *When men shall declare that there was no mystery*
> *About this man who played a certain part in history.*

One reason why Eliot could give an urgency to these reflections is that he was not writing about the past alone. As Becket went on to denounce indifference, oppression, and exploitation, as he gave his life "to the Law of God above the Law of Man," Eliot was writing also against the then rising menace of Fascism, when violent men comparable to Reginald FitzUrse took power into their own hands. Eliot bore out again thereby what he asserted about Pound's translations, that in possessing the past a poet could suggest the present. When he wrote *The Waste Land,* he had also proved the converse, but he could not do so in *The Family Reunion.* Perhaps his increasing sense of the degradation and decay of the modern world had gradually numbed him against any strong feeling for such immediate issues as Becket had faced. Although he wrote an essay about "the idea of a Christian society," when confronted with one of the sharpest-drawn crises of our own time, he replied to a questionnaire on loyalist Spain: "While I am naturally sympathetic, I still feel convinced that it is best that at least a few men of letters should remain isolated, and take no part in these collective activities." One wonders whether such detachment could be possible for any dramatist who would meet the exacting standards held up by Granville-Barker: that the dramatic art in its fully developed form "is the working-out . . . not of the self-realization of the individual, but of society itself."

Whatever the reason, Eliot could not contrive to endow his Eumenides with any of the collective significance that they possessed for the Greeks. It may also be argued that a mind as saturated with St. John's "dark night of the soul" as Eliot has revealed himself to be in his *Quartets* may produce profound contemplative poetry, but is unlikely to have sufficient closeness to human beings to present their conflicts concretely. In a recent essay on "The Social Function of Poetry," [9] Eliot wrote:

> "We may say that the duty of the poet, as poet, is only indirectly to his people: his direct duty is to his *language,* first to preserve, and second to extend and improve."

Eliot was careful to emphasize, once again, that this is not a duty merely to form, in isolation from content, since the poet "discovers new variations of sensibility which can be appropriated by others. And in expressing them he is developing and enriching the language which he speaks."

In spite of the failure of *The Family Reunion,* therefore, one should not underestimate the new possibilities that Eliot has already opened for poetic drama. We have only to turn to Tennyson's *Becket* to perceive how far *Murder in the Cathedral* has gone towards revitalizing the genre. Tennyson used the loose five-act structure of a chronicle play in which the nineteenth century imitated the Elizabethans, and though he presented Becket as a spiritual man, in answer to the sceptics, he did not succeed in creating much tension. He ranged over Becket's whole career from the days of his earliest friendship with the King, he introduced an immense cast of characters,

[9] In *The Norseman,* November 1943, and, in a more extended form, in *The Adelphi,* July 1945.

and provided a love interest through Henry's affair with Rosamund. Only in his final scene did he come to Becket's return, after his long exile in France, to the situation out of which Eliot made his whole play. But even more remarkable than Eliot's dramatic concentration is the resonance of his verse, the variety that he gains through its stylized patterns. For one symptomatic instance of why he felt traditional blank verse to be played out, take the difference in dramatic energy between Becket's two speeches to his priest at the moment when the Knights attempted to break into the Cathedral:

Tennyson

Undo the doors: the church is not a castle:
Knock, and it shall be open'd. Are you deaf?
What, have I lost authority among you?
Stand by, make way.

Eliot

Unbar the doors! Throw open the doors!
I will not have the house of prayer, the church of Christ,
The sanctuary, turned into a fortress.
The Church shall protect her own, in her own way, not
As oak and stone; stone and oak decay,
Give no stay, but the Church shall endure.
The church shall be open, even to our enemies. Open the door!

Murder in the Cathedral, including the sombre magnificence of its choruses, is the most sustained poetic drama in English since *Samson Agonistes,* and playable as that work was not designed to be. In spite of its stiffly restricted content, Eliot's drama is particularly impressive when set off against the dead background of the commercial theatre during the past decade. With the radio, as Auden and MacLeish have also argued, we have returned to a period when an audience can again depend entirely upon the spoken word. That may have something to do with the fact that even large moving-picture audiences now respond to Shakespeare's verse as delivered by Laurence Olivier, and that stage revivals of Webster and Middleton and of Yeats's translation of *Oedipus* are again being attempted. At least we are faced with a situation that might challenge the fullest resources of a dramatic poet. Despite the long interruption of the war and the isolating rigors of Eliot's thought, it may be hoped that his play-writing is not yet a finished chapter.

marion magid

THE INNOCENCE OF TENNESSEE WILLIAMS

A EUROPEAN whose knowledge of America was gained entirely from the collected works of Tennessee Williams might garner a composite image of the U.S.: it is a tropical country whose vegetation is largely man-eating; it has an excessive annual rainfall and frequent storms which coincide with its mating periods; it has not yet been converted to Christianity, but continues to observe the myth of the annual death and resurrection of the sun-god, for which purpose it keeps on hand a constant supply of young men to sacrifice. Its young men are for the most part beautiful and fawnlike; an occasional rough customer turns up, but in the end he, too, is revealed as beautiful and fawnlike. Its women are alternately in a state of heat or jitters; otherwise they are Mediterranean. The country does not observe the traditional Western sexual orientation which involves the pursuit of the female by the male; instead, its young men reluctantly allow themselves to be had on those occasions when there is no way of avoiding it and when the act is signaled and underscored by portents of Elizabethan proportions. They are right in general to be of two minds regarding the sexual embrace, for it is as often as not followed by the direst consequences: cannibalism, castration, burning alive, madness, surgery in various forms ranging from lobotomy to hysterectomy, depending on the nature of the offending organ.

Perhaps the European would not be very far wrong. A culture does not consistently pay the price of admission to witness a fable which does not ensnare some part of the truth about it. Perhaps that feverish tropical set by Jo Mielziner is the land of heart's desire for Americans, as Italy has been the land of heart's desire for Englishmen, huddled all winter long around their shilling meters and damp fireplaces. In any case, watching the ladies in flowered hats queuing up for a matinee of *Sweet Bird of Youth* inevitably raises questions: How much do they understand? How much do they suspect? What do all these goings-on mean to them? Do they flock to a new play by Ten-

From *Commentary*, January, 1963. Reprinted by permission.

nessee Williams because it is sensational, because it is "poetic," because it is both at the same time and the one quality redeems the other? Finally, do they find anything of their own experience—of love, marriage, desire, loneliness—reflected in that peculiar mirror which Williams holds up to nature?

Probably they do. Tennessee Williams is not our best, but our only American playwright since O'Neill. His imagination, magnetized though it is by the outlandish and the outré, is a kind of fever chart of our national ailments. There is, for instance, an image which runs obsessively through Williams' plays—the beautiful young man at bay, the quarry ringed by his pursuers. The mind, the sensibilities, the stomach, all recoil from this image when it is served up with obvious relish in a darkened theater, snakily choreographed by Kazan or distended on wide screen in all the glory of MGM technicolor. Yet that image is frighteningly akin to the one emblazoned not so long ago on all the front pages of the land: Meredith ringed by the Mississippi National Guard on the campus at Ole Miss; and in the background, blurred figures with clenched fists. Who knows what goes on behind those flat faces with steel-rimmed eyeglasses and slits for mouths? One has a sense that Williams dwells closer to that knowledge than other dramatists writing about us, for us, today. Though Williams has not, so far as I know, delivered himself of a single pronouncement on the question of integration, though his signature is never to be found on a petition or a full-page ad in the New York *Times,* he seems to have located the trouble spots more precisely than Arthur Miller, for instance, who deals so conscientiously with "social" questions. Williams is American in his passion for absolutes, in his longing for purity, in his absence of ideas, in the extreme discomfort with which he inhabits his own body and soul, in his apocalyptic vision of sex, which like all apocalyptic visions sacrifices mere accuracy for the sake of intensity. Intensity is the crucial quality of Williams' art, and he is perhaps most an American artist in his reliance upon and mastery of surface techniques for achieving this effect.

One result is that Williams' plays cannot be talked about except in their performance. Ever since 1947, when *A Streetcar Named Desire* was produced under the direction of Elia Kazan and starring Marlon Brando, Jessica Tandy, and Kim Hunter, with a stage setting by Jo Mielziner, the pattern for rendition of a Williams play has remained as fixed as a Kabuki dance. Other hands than Kazan's have since dimmed the lights, set the underbrush to quivering, and on occasion gilded the lily, yet the results have always been, when successful—that is, when "like a play by Tennessee Williams"—approximations of that *ur*-Williams production.

THERE IS first of all the matter of lighting. As Eric Bentley observed, Kazan sees the world, especially Williams' world, as phantasmagoria. "Don't turn the lights on," Blanche gasps in *Streetcar* and Kazan passed the word on to the electricians. Nor have they been turned on since. Doing so would dispel the shadows, the evanescence, the sense of undefined shapes and meanings lurking in the foliage. In Hollywood, the word "air" is used to designate atmosphere, the intangible stuff of which dreams are made. Directors in the throes of creation have been known to cry out for "more air"—which means the opposite of what it seems to mean: not clarity nor breathing space nor the light of day, but the baying of bloodhounds, the waving of palm fronds, the lonely clarinet solo, the voices of offstage potion peddlers raised in song. The milieu of Williams' plays lends itself especially well to this hot (Southern) "air" treatment. One suspects that, after *Streetcar,* Williams worked with an image in his mind's eye closer to the South of Broadway than to the actual South.

The second element is timing. Kazan is the virtuoso of a certain kind of tension on stage. His method might be called the technique of unexpected syncopation. The regular to-and-fro buildup of a climactic scene, particularly of an encounter between two actors, is slightly distorted. Pauses are a trifle longer than expected, or a trifle shorter. Long speeches are broken up in eccentric ways, so that unexpected words ring out in the electric silence. No Williams play is complete without the participation of at least one, preferably more, actors who have been trained at the Actors' Studio or temples of the same persuasion, where they have perfected their versions of this curious syncopation.

This mode of diction has by now become a convention of contemporary American theater in the past two decades. Its components are mainly twofold: since it was originally developed by the Group Theater in its attempt to render "realistically" the rhythms of urban, and especially New York, life, it has more than a trace in it of Yiddish inflection as well as Yiddish phrasing; at the same time it has been updated by hipster gesture and talk. The diction can now be heard nightly on those serious hour-long television dramas which frequently give the impression of being dubbed, so many preparatory lip movements does the actor go through before he works around to the crisis of utterance. This nervous medley acts as an assurance to the spectator that harrowing as the content is of what is spoken, what is unspoken is even worse. What is said is the less important half; the better half is the silence.

Williams writes the ideal "line" for this mode of delivery. It is a long line, which achieves its most striking effects through a Steinian repetitiveness, through the use of unexpected archaisms, and the insertion of unexpected "literary" words and ironically elegant turns of phrase. It is a stylized rendering of Southern diction, which is more self-conscious, more evasive, but also more imaginative than Northern speech. The odd thing is that nearly all of Williams' characters speak this language, regardless of class or place of origin, and it is to be heard even in the grunts of Stanley and Mitch in their more pensive moments.

When a Williams libretto is placed in the hands of an actor whose rendition is tailored to it, the result is an orgy of syncopation just this side of hysteria. It has been remarked that Williams writes great parts for actresses, but only for a certain kind of actress. She must bring to the part a fund of that particular kind of nervous intensity that we associate with Geraldine Page, Maureen Stapleton, or Lois Smith. The champion performance of all time in The Syncopated Mode was the one given by Geraldine Page in *Summer and Smoke* in 1951. It was this performance which brought her stardom and spawned legions of imitations that are still among us—actresses who express emotion by plucking at their forearms and the ever present brooch at their throats, who issue declarations with an upward inflection and ask questions with a downward one.

The actress who lacks this particular intensity is as fatally out of place as a prima donna singing in English with an Italian opera company. A case in point was that of Shelley Winters, who played the female predator in *The Night of the Iguana*. Miss Winters is not on the brink of hysteria, she does not even seem neurotic, much less bizarre. Dressed in blue jeans and a hastily buttoned man's shirt, she romped through the part of the bitch hotelkeeper looking like nothing so much as a plump athletics counselor at a girl's camp. Common sense as well as the sense of humor rebelled against the idea that she represented that ogre-female, the hideous embodiment of the life force, which is central to Williams' vision of life. Lacking its center, the play slowly fell apart.

ALL OF which are some of the reasons why a successful Williams play in full regalia does not seem written and produced so much as masterminded; it is more like the perfect crime than an artistic undertaking. Williams' vision is not only fulfilled, it is over-fulfilled by Kazan's technique, which is to keep the play in a state of constant explosive motion. Perhaps this is one reason why it does not linger in the mind. Its effect is all in the seeing and quivering at the moment of seeing, a series of shocks to the eye and to the nervous system which renders the viewer captive. Occasionally one has an impulse to shout "Stop!"

when some particularly questionable assertion has been made onstage, but it has already flitted away, been swallowed up in the chiaroscuro. It is this shimmering motion that most of the critics praise when they invoke Williams' good qualities—his "elusiveness," his "poeticism." It is as though on Broadway that larger ambiguity which is a characteristic of great art can be achieved merely by a blurring of outline. Dim the lights, provide a clarinet solo or the tinkling of a jukebox, buttress the action with a gathering storm and if possible add a symbol or two which seems to flicker on and off like a neon light, saying: "I may look like an iguana, but what I really am is a symbol." Then all efforts to discern what the playwright is actually saying will be dismissed as pedantry, offensive to the "magical" nature of the theatrical occasion.

Lately, however, Williams has been getting a bad press, though for the wrong reasons. Certain of his motifs have become so insistent and so unmistakable that they no longer quite scurry away unnoticed into the underbrush. Yet Williams' vision has not really changed so much between *Streetcar*, which was hailed as our only American tragedy, and *Sweet Bird of Youth*, which outraged even Kenneth Tynan. It seems unjust of the critics to have taken Williams to their bosoms when he hinted coyly at the unspeakable and to chide him when he speaks a bit more clearly about it.

THE TOTAL effect of Williams' work has been to plunge ordinary conceptions of the male-female relation into such disorder that the services of a Harry Stack Sullivan seem needed to straighten them out again. The first of these grand subversions was the figure of Stanley Kowalski, which appeared before the American public and before the world in the person of Marlon Brando. Though numerous actors have since played the part, Brando remains forever etched in memory as the embodiment of American malehood, and Kowalski is probably the most famous male figure in modern drama. Doubtless at this moment Brando's Korean counterpart is playing the role in whatever passes at the Seoul Repertory Company for a torn t-shirt.

Kazan, who likes to get down to brass tacks, described Kowalski in his celebrated notes to the production of *Streetcar* as "a walking penis." Whatever that would look like (the imagination is certainly compelled), Brando's rendition of it came out as something more ambivalent. His mincing interpretation of the role may even have struck sophisticated members of the audience as a brilliant example of post-Freudian insight: the walking phallus must necessarily take on some suspicious mannerisms: we all know about overcompensation, and what is brutality but the fear of cowardice and impotence?

Leaving Brando's performance out of it and taking Kowalski at face value, as written by Williams—what are we to make of him? Even forgetting temporarily certain cultural data—that members of the lower middle class are rather more inclined toward the sham genteel in their sexual mores than toward the nobly savage, and that it is primarily college graduates who are as conscientious about their sex life as though it were some humanist obligation—one still wonders how Stella and Stanley ever got together. How did Stella ever get over those initial hurdles—Stanley's table manners, Stanley's preferences in dress, Stanley's recreational interests, Stanley's friends, Stanley's stupidity? If we accept Stanley as ape, the character of Stella ceases to be interesting except clinically. Williams claims allegiance with Lawrence in his philosophy of sex, yet in the creation of Kowalski he forgets utterly Lawrence's basic lesson—that profound sexual experience civilizes, humanizes, lends grace and delicacy. Lady Chatterley is attracted specifically by the natural aristocracy of the gamekeeper which his skill and power as a lover only confirm. Despite his presence on the stage in satin pajamas and his continued invocation of the "colored lights" we do not really believe in the instinctive animal beauty (purity?) of Stanley in bed because out of it he behaves with such benighted crudity. Did Stanley rape Stella, too, just by way of a how-do-you-do? Do all women burn to be raped? Is this the locker-room fantasy that is Williams' version of animal purity?

"They come together with low, animal moans," the stage directions say. Earlier Stella launches into the first of those hushed sexual confidences which run through all of Williams' plays and ring such an astonishingly false note. "I can hardly stand it when he's away for a night," says Stella. "When he's away for a week I nearly go wild. . . . And when he comes back I cry on his lap like a baby. . . ." It is hard to know what is more unpleasant in this image: the overt sentimentality it expresses, or the latent brutality it masks: a fascination with the image of the helpless creature under the physical domination of another, accepting his favors with tears of gratitude. That the emotion of gratitude is not the predominant one that women feel for their lovers seems to have escaped Williams, fixated as he seems to be upon the delights his heroes must be capable of affording. Later Stella's breathless sexual confidences will be echoed by Serafina della Rose, describing her husband's prodigious feats in bed, and by Margaret describing the absolute "indifference" of Brick, which makes him the perfect lover. When there is no woman on the scene to give testimony, the heroes themselves oblige with weary chronicles of the services they have rendered scores of women: Val in *Orpheus Descend-*

ing, refusing to serve any longer as "stud" to women like the impatient Carol; Chance Wayne in *Sweet Bird Of Youth* describing the legions of lonely women whom he has taught about love; Shannon in *Night of the Iguana* confiding his rape at the hands of an adolescent girl. At the center of most of Williams' plays there is the same slightly repellent pas de deux: the man austere, eager to keep his purity; the woman turning to him like Potiphar's wife unto Joseph.

The foregoing belongs, in Williams' world, to the category of "corruption." When he describes "pure" love, one expects hoots from the gallery—but perhaps again the gallery is hungering for any version of that fabled sentiment that Williams can manage to offer. "Pure" love in Williams—which antedates the hero's initiation into "corruption" (spoken darkly, with a faint slurring)—generally takes place in aquatic environs when both the hero and the heroine were very young. The heroine—Val's chance encounter on a houseboat off the Florida coast, Chance Wayne's true love by the Gulf Stream—is generally an exceedingly pale girl with long blond hair—ethereal to the point of incorporeality. In *Sweet Bird,* dramatizing one of those fervid paradoxes that Williams so loves, Heavenly, the "corrupted" pure love, rides at the head of a political caravan, dressed "all in whaat . . . laak a virgin . . ." though she's had that—operation— (spoken darkly and crooningly) "done" on her. . . . How strange to find Williams, the disciple of Lawrence, talking about physical (corrupt) and spiritual (pure) love.

IN ANY EVENT it is difficult to credit those dossiers of sexual achievement that Williams' heroes carry around with them like traveling salesmen with a new fall "line." They seem, when actually confronted with it, to go to great lengths to avoid going to bed with women. They would, in general, prefer to go bowling, to throw each other high forward passes, to wander off in quest of correspondences in the world of nature to their own sense of themselves. When authentic warmth is generated in the plays of Tennessee Williams, it is most often on the occasion of an encounter between two men, and at the expense of their temporarily absent womenfolk—as, for instance, in the moving and very beautiful scene between Brick and Big Daddy in *Cat on a Hot Tin Roof.* It takes Brick three long acts to be persuaded into bed, and it is only the threat of having his liquor supply cut off that finally does it; in the play *Night of the Iguana,* two acts elapse and the hero goes off reluctantly, as to a martyrdom, only when his resistance has been worn down through sheer fatigue; in *Sweet Bird of Youth* the bribe of a checkbook and the use of the Cadillac are necessary before Chance Wayne succumbs to the Princess. The filmed version, recording the moment in closeup and with a directness mercifully lacking in the theater, had Paul Newman's classic features wearing an expression of which the verbal equivalent could only have been "aw shucks!" as Geraldine Page undulated rapidly toward the windows to pull down the blinds. Surely even a gigolo enjoys his job somewhat, and Alexandra del Lago is supposed to be a famous and alluring movie queen; but the feeling communicated is of a child being forced to stay indoors and practice his scales for an hour before he will be released to go out and play with the other kids.

INDEED, WILLIAMS' heroes seem more compelled by the mysteries of the nursery and bathroom than by the mysteries of the boudoir, or any more epic battleground. Throughout his plays there is a continuous fascination with the intricacies of bodily processes, the unlovely data of mortality, which suggests a small boy eavesdropping on the talk of a couple of old maid aunts. In almost every Williams play there recurs the clinical-medical set piece, in one version or another; sometimes for comic purposes, as in the detailed evocation of Big Daddy's "spastic colon," which provides a sort of running gag to the play; or for darker purposes, as in the dark references to the imminent demise of Lady's husband in *Orpheus Descending*, or the hushed recitation of what the knife did to the young life of Heavenly Findley. Williams is one of the few dramatists writing who can get a nervous laugh from the audience simply by showing a group of pregnant women on-stage. That shrouded Southern setting becomes a metaphor for an equally threatening landscape—the landscape of the body, interior and exterior, made actual in *Summer and Smoke* when Dr. John, standing before an anatomy chart gives the hypnotized Alma a lesson in reality. (". . . and this is the sex.") This landscape of the body seems as fevered as any acreage on the Mississippi delta plain, with its mysterious shadows and weird foliage—the digestive tract, the reproductive tract, the respiratory tract, the alimentary canal. Stanley, whose colored lights leave something to be desired in the way of characterization, is never so convincing as when he is banging on the bathroom door and screaming about his kidneys. Shannon, the unfrocked priest of *Night of the Iguana*, keeps an all-night vigil with a woman who obviously—as she herself might say—feels more than friendship for him, and whiles away the long hours before dawn regaling her with stories, among which is the episode, observed in his travels, of a destitute beggar eating human offal. And earlier, he has described with similar precision how his moral turpitude stems from the moment his mother discovered him practicing the "little boy's vice."

The effectiveness of the beggar episode in the play—which is intended, it seems, to provide the final documentation of Shannon's and Williams' vision of life as hell—is considerably weakened by the fact that Shannon seems to have told his once devastating story numerous times before, in fact whenever he's had one too many, and its power as a Dantesque hallucination has run out. Earlier, Shannon—are we to take him as a ruined saint?—in a gesture of defiance against the bus-load of ladies who have been tormenting him with sexual or other claims, pees on everyone's luggage to the unbounded glee of the audience and of the two Mexican houseboys onstage who are retained by the management to crouch in feline postures and speak occasional sentences in Spanish. Only after he has accomplished these various demonic acts and been, in addition, lashed to his hammock in the most objectionable exploitation of Christian symbolism since Chance Wayne got castrated on Easter Sunday, does he go off to splash in the waves with Shelley Winters.

What, then, are we to make of the "serious" import of the play— with all this bathroom behavior mixed up with an apparent concern with the themes of the loss of faith and regaining of faith? To be sure, Shannon is provided with one of those incredible biographies that Williams gives his heroes-at-the-end-of-their-rope to explain how they got there. He was once a man of God who sinned in the attempt to find "purity." But when he hurls a challenge at God—"you senile delinquent"—and a perceptible stir goes through the audience, and when he later flings a crucifix to the ground, we are in the presence of nothing more than that most unpleasant of travesties—blasphemy without travail, without the prior justification of the loss of a deeply held faith: in short, a black mass with costumes by *Motley* for the titillation of a sensation-hungry audience. It is hard to judge whether the fraud or the foolishness cries out louder in this play, hailed by critics as Williams' "gentlest" thus far. There is always this distinct unease engendered by Williams' ultimate visions—Sebastian devoured by the street urchins, the castration of Chance Wayne, Val torn to pieces by the rabid mob, the madness of Blanche. It is not only because of their intrinsic unpleasantness. Mutilation and violent death are hardly news in an age whose experience of Gehenna makes even Williams' hallucinations seem pastel-colored. What turns the violent and shocking aspects of Williams' plays into something repellent is the sense one has of a disproportion. His view of life seems in excess of its own ostensible causes—rather as though a man were to do in a series of women because his girl friend had failed to keep an appointment. The plays simply do not seem sufficiently sombre or profound to warrant their catastrophes; they do not bear witness that the author has wrestled sufficiently with his own demons to give his vision authority. If he had, Williams might have succeeded in creating something like the tragic hero. Wistful, charming, poignant though his characters are, they lack a certain dignity, a grandeur appropriate to their own tragic ends. Instead of resisting them, shaping them, finally transcending them, Williams seems to welcome all too eagerly the most hectic images that flock to his imagination or come across his path in his various sojourns around the globe—as a very chic decorator welcomes something really new in the way of tropical decorations for the patio. And there is ultimately that particular unease produced by evasion—the feeling one always has that his most gothic revelations are themselves masks for a meaning still further hidden.

PERHAPS THE BEST illustration of this last point is provided by *Cat on a Hot Tin Roof*—Williams' best play since *The Glass Menagerie*. Here is Williams' finest writing—blessedly free of that false incantatory note and straining after effect which mark his other plays. It is lyric and authentic in its evocation of the American mythology of brilliant halfbacks, beauty queens, and sports announcers. There is an absence of the conspicuously "Southern" or of the Berlitz Italian or Spanish, that Williams usually depends upon for "earthy" atmosphere. Moreover, it is the last of Williams' important plays to be anchored in reality—that bedrock which the theater deserts at its peril—the reality of houses, families, marriage, children, money. Maggie the Cat is the best in Williams' gallery of jumpy Southern women, a more detailed and psychologically accurate portrait than Blanche, whom she somewhat resembles. In general, Williams seems to have written this play with a control that he has not had before or since. Yet the play is astonishingly flawed at its center. It appears to be an Ibsenian play of unmasking, of revelation, of the stripping away of lies to reveal truth. Yet at the crucial moment, the unmasking is evaded. Williams seems to have toyed with the keys of a locked door, dangling them one by one, only to decide at the end that what is behind the door had best remain hidden.

Cat on a Hot Tin Roof is about a marriage that is falling apart. The husband, Brick, who was once a star athlete and later a sports announcer is now an alcoholic who refuses to sleep with his wife, Margaret. His wife loves him and wants to have a child by him because (among other reasons) the inheritance of the family estate depends on it. But Brick refuses to yield, is interested in nothing but alcohol which gives him peace, that "click" in the head which signifies the end of struggle. Each member of the family has his own version of why Brick drinks and why he will have nothing to do with his wife, but all agree that his behavior is related to the recent death of Skipper, Brick's best friend. The hostile members of the family, Brick's brother and his wife, have hinted darkly that Brick's and Skipper's friendship was "not normal." Margaret knows further details. She believes that though Skipper loved her husband "that" way, her husband did not respond in kind. She feels herself responsible for having alienated her husband, because it was her attempted seduction of Skipper which triggered his collapse and death. Only Brick knows the truth, and he refuses to talk.

SINCE THE PLAY announces its theme to be that of "mendacity," and since the crucial scene is the confrontation between Brick and Big Daddy in which they both agree that final disclosures must now be faced, one expects that this scene will reveal the answer to the question that everyone is asking: is Brick homosexual or isn't he? Astonishingly enough, though the characters circle this question for almost the length of an act in a carefully choreographed minuet of confrontation and confession, the question remains unanswered. Big Daddy succeeds in extracting from Brick only the admission that a final conversation he had with Skipper was the immediate cause of his death. And this admission is made to seem sufficient. Brick in turn tells Big Daddy what everyone has kept from him—that he is dying—and there is a sense of the restoration of balance, a lie exchanged for a lie, a truth for a truth.

But the failure to answer the question of Brick's homosexuality makes the play totally incoherent. Is it a play about a man unjustly accused by a society which is right (yes, homosexuality is evil, but this wasn't it) or a play about a man justly accused by a society which is wrong (no, homosexuality is not evil, it is only wicked tongues that make it out to be so)? In place of what would seem to be Brick's obligatory speech—the one in which he faces the real nature of his feelings for Skipper one way or another—there is an eloquent and finely ironic explanation of how "pure" love is no less "abnormal" than homosexual love, being so rare. In view of the fact, however, that we do not know whether this speech proceeds from the lips of a man who is telling the truth or from the lips of a man who is alternatively either lying or self-deluded, we cannot credit it. If Brick were, in fact, homosexual, or were unable to face the fact that he is homosexual, the assertion would be patently false—there would then, indeed, be no such thing as "pure" love between men. If he were, on the other hand, neither lying nor self-deluded, then there might be. But the assertion cannot possibly hold for all three cases. It seems moreover crucial to the meaning of the play to know whether Brick is weak and self-deluded or whether he is the last example of the pure in heart. Are we to conclude from the author's ambiguities that he finds the two identical?

Most of the daily newspaper critics were so delighted to spot the old-fashioned well-made revelation scene that they missed the point that nothing was, in fact, revealed, and talked rhapsodically about how Williams had once again probed with his scalpel the most hidden places of the human heart, etc., etc. Only Walter Kerr of the New York *Herald Tribune* seemed to have noticed that the play evaded its own questions—that the love that dare not speak its name, so to speak, was still wearing a pseudonym. Williams answered by saying that ". . . some mystery should be left in the revelation of character in a play just as a great deal of mystery is always left in the revelation of character in life . . ." which is tantamount to saying that *Oedipus Rex* might on the whole have been a more profound tragedy if the rumor that Oedipus was sleeping with his mother had remained unconfirmed.

Why did Williams avoid answering this question in the play? Partly for the sake of expediency, the same expediency that permitted him to allow Kazan to tinker with the third act of the play so that it was sweetened, assuaged, and its real meaning—the bitterness and terror of marriage—somewhat masked. An audience that will accept the unproved allegation of homosexuality, that is even prepared to accept an absent or dead homosexual figuring in someone else's psychic drama, is still not quite prepared to accept a real live red-blooded American husband as homosexual, and one who moreover gets into bed with the heroine at the final curtain. By evading the real nature of Brick's feelings for Maggie—by leaving open the possibility that Brick's aversion for her is on ethical rather than psychological grounds—Williams avoided writing the important American play, the one about the American family and its woe-begone sons, the story of American adolescence which so frequently persists into middle age. But he managed instead neatly to insure the nice lady's comment to her husband when the curtain fell: ". . . how sweet, they've gotten together again. . . ."

Williams does not surrender to his audience; rather he establishes the communion between his myths and theirs. He avoided being specific about Brick's homosexuality not only because it is not "nice" to confront an audience with such home truths, but because he shares that curious American aversion to facts: the view that somehow or other people are different from what they do or say, from what experience has turned them into—that a man is defined by something other than his actions. America is after all the home of the new start, the second chance, and there is a kind of gloomy, adolescent optimism, reflected in the culture, which clings to the possibility that people may change—that with enough love (which means forgiveness) they may one day become beautiful, good, and happy. Williams' failure to pinpoint the character of Brick is a gesture of misguided benignity in his behalf. Like America, Williams lacks ultimately the conviction of his own neurosis.

This same hedging before specifics has always been evident in the critical reception of Williams. There are real and apparent themes in Williams, and the critics have invariably seized upon the apparent ones. They are easier to take, and by now sufficiently orthodox, even sacrosanct, to avoid danger: the failure of communication, the destruction of the dreamers by the practical men, how hellish life can be for the lonelies and the losers. Oddly enough, adumbrating these themes, reviewers frequently congratulate Williams on having once again "affirmed the dignity of the human spirit," the one thing that he has not succeeded in doing. For Williams has never created a character who recovered from the wounds and desolation of childhood.

A PLAY LIKE *Period of Adjustment*—Williams' rather touching attempt to adjust his world view to the comic and the domestic by sheer will power—is particularly revealing in the clarity with which it shows, or shows up, the true nature of his obsessions. It is a banal, ordinary, and even vulgar play about, of all things, how scary the wedding night can be. The play is in effect a mild dirty joke sustained for two acts; but the embarrassment that it occasions is the embarrassment of hearing a dirty joke told by someone fairly prudish. What emerges into the open is that shrinking and fastidious side of Williams which has made him so adept at capturing the ironic self-observations of women who are too smart to believe in their own delusions, but too weak to do anything about them, and who are sustained by a certain delicacy of hope. Though it has the requisite Williams touches, the play offers an entirely conformist, trivial view of love as a kind of soothing ointment. Its burden is that somehow or other human beings—weak, frail, tormented, and uncertain as they are—can offer each other at least the comfort of bodily warmth. The bride in the play is a nurse and the controlling image is that the world is a hospital.

THE PLAY is about false and true ideas of manhood, and here we observe a curious thing. Williams has always carried with him, in suspension as it were, the corrective to his own distortions of the masculine. He knows, as do most of us, the truth about the excessive blustering of American malehood—the notorious fear of seeming soft or sissyish, the mistrust of hair worn too long, of demonstrations of affection or tenderness among men, the longing to go off with the boys and all the other apparatus of stag party cameraderie—that all of this is not an expression of authentic masculinity, but of its opposite. Yet this knowledge has never inhibited Williams' more lurid perpetrations of the masculine ideal—the crudities of Stanley Kowalski, the grotesque cavortings of "normalcy" in *Cat* and *Streetcar,* the gratuitous obscenity of Big Daddy when he talks about women. It is as though Williams were aware of the reality, but helpless before the fantasy. Even in *Period of Adjustment,* which amounts to a course of instruction in that very truth, Williams stacks the cards to thwart his own purpose. He offers us two "typical" American couples engaged in working out the ambiguities and problematics of the married state. The first man is married to a woman presented as so incredibly homely that her appearance onstage in a nightgown instantly provokes gales of laughter from the audience; a laughter which is sustained by the author's relish for the details of synthetic correction that she has undergone to make herself bearable. The second man is in such an advanced state of anxiety that he literally has the shakes.

The play ends with an extraordinary scene. The stage is divided in two: on either side of the partition, two beds are invitingly made up, and the two protagonists, with many a backward glance, hop into the sack with their all-too-willing wives. After the first recoil the viewer comes to the astonishing realization that only in America could an entire play be constructed on the question of whether four consenting adults will or will not succeed in making love to one another on a given night. Where one would expect a domestic comedy by a sophisticated modern author in 1960 to begin, Williams' play ends.

And Williams has, one must recall, the reputation for being our sexiest American playwright. What could, in fact, be more innocent? Coprophilia, cannibalism, homosexuality, exhibitionism, fetishism, violation of the Mann Act, turn out in Williams to be masks for some other horror, darker than any of these: the catastrophe of normal adult sexuality. In the end, Williams' vision is revealed as a shocked outcry, a child's refusal to accept the fact of sex that, yes, grownups really do it. Perhaps this ultimately is what the ladies in flowered hats understand about Williams—that beneath the mantle of the swashbuckling libertine, the initiate, the participant in the dark mysteries, there beats a heart as virginal as their own, as their husbands', as America's—that country where the women's magazines on every newsstand carry side by side starry-eyed evocations of the "act of love" and "Eric's strong arms . . ." and the most lurid clinical how-to-do-it manuals of the practice and fulfillment of heterosexual love.

walter kerr

CHRISTOPHER FRY

IT IS POSSIBLE to respect the "natural" poetic imagery of a man like Tennessee Williams and still yearn for the day when this shall grow, stage by stage through action and character, into language that is admittedly, and powerfully, verse. Christopher Fry has, in a sense, overleaped our time. He has come out for verse now; it has got him into trouble, but it has also made our eyes pop and our ears perk up.

The most striking thing Mr. Fry has accomplished is to have discovered a twentieth-century verse form for comedy—of all things. Matters had got to the point where it was almost impossible to convince anyone that comedy *could* be written in verse, so strong is the stranglehold of prose upon our age. Lip service was still paid to the notion of verse tragedy, because both verse and tragedy seemed equally remote to us; but prose comedy had been galloping along at a successful rate and there seemed no reason to wish for anything better. Mr. Fry has given us something better—has found both an imagery and a rhythm for comedy which increases the intellectual and emotional range of things to be laughed at—and his work comes as a genuine surprise.

Broadway had to wait for Mr. Fry's second American showing to take his work to heart. The first Fry venture to appear here, *A Phoenix Too Frequent,* was apparently so ruinously directed and acted as to conceal completely the quality of the play. On the printed page *A Phoenix Too Frequent* seems to me the most perfect thing of its kind since *The Importance of Being Earnest* and, within its limited intention and shorter length, superior to *The Lady's Not for Burning.* It has a sharply defined narrative that is developed with alacrity and precision. By comparison, *The Lady's Not for Burning* seems talky and meandering. But the play has its own virtues and they represent an experimental advance for Fry. He has tried for more complexity and got a richer texture out of it. He has tried for a slightly more rounded characterization and picked up a bit of human warmth.

From *Pieces At Eight,* Simon and Schuster, New York. Reprinted by permission of The New York Herald Tribune, Inc.

Where the earlier play was a perfect joke, intellectual to the core, the new one is an imperfect but possibly more appealing attempt to capture nature on its own vexing, complicated, and fulsome terms. It keeps shifting gears, and pulling back into first rather too often, but when it gets where it is going you feel you have been with the people all the way. *A Phoenix Too Frequent* is an exercise in detachment; *The Lady's Not for Burning* is an experiment in participation. Fry asks you to accompany the characters rather than observe them.

There is a perpetual danger of Fry's becoming too fulsome. In one of his plays he has a character settle back and sigh happily, "It's nice that anyone can say anything at all."

And it is nice, now that verse has made it possible. But drama is still limited by the singleness of its action and the things said must have some relation to this singleness. Occasionally Mr. Fry forgets this and indulges himself in the pure delight of all that can be said. I am so grateful for the method of saying it that I am willing to indulge him his indulgence, but the audience isn't likely to, and he will do well to brake his verbal exuberance every now and then.

The effect of talkiness was accented by John Gielgud's performance in the production of *The Lady's Not for Burning* that was imported from England. Where the rest of the company, under Mr. Gielgud's own direction, read contemporary verse as though it were contemporary verse, Gielgud himself was frequently guilty of chanting. The immediate result was that Fry's verse was compared to Shakespeare's in some quarters, whereas the author's chief distinction is that he has found a new form instead of echoing an old one. If Fry is like anything, he is like Shaw in verse.

In a later and less successful play *Venus Observed*, the stuffy Dominic is informing his sister Perpetua that their charming father is a crook and likely to go to jail. Dominic expects his sister to be shocked, but she is a pleasant realist:

> PERPETUA: . . . *I was able to believe you at once.*
> *Poppadillo has the most beguiling*
> *Jackdaw look about him. But you think*
> *He wouldn't be happy in prison?*
> DOMINIC: *He wouldn't, but what*
> *Difference does that make? Would you be able*
> *To look anyone in the face, with a father jailed?*
> PERPETUA: *Oh, yes, if he were comfortable.*

That is like a dozen passages in Shaw, and Fry has much of the impudent love of paradox, the passion for plain sense, and the hopeful irony of his prose forbear. He has neither the romanticism of Shakespearean high comedy nor the lowness of Shakespearean bumpkin comedy. Even when, in *The Lady's Not for Burning,* he introduces two brothers who seem on the bumpkin side, they turn out to have the intellectual facility and emotional disillusionment of a couple of Shavian Caesars.

That third play, *Venus Observed,* did shake a number of Fry fans in various ways. By the time it appeared in America, in a rather sluggish production staged by Sir Laurence Olivier, two schools of thought about Fry had formed: one which held that the fanciful young comic poet had brought about a joyous rediscovery of the English language, and another which stubbornly held that his verbal dexterity was mere vaudeville, and difficult vaudeville at that.

I remain a Fry man myself, but I must confess that *Venus Observed* gave aid and comfort to the enemy. In the process of dazzling his contemporaries with the rare and rich antics through which obedient words can be put, Mr. Fry had apparently bedazzled, and perhaps even blinded, himself. The language was once more sent sailing through hoops; but it finally tumbled in a little clutter about the feet of some paper-thin people whose behavior was sometimes amusing, sometimes ingratiating, but almost always uncomfortably contrived.

No one should ask that a verse comedy, least of all the kind of fanciful conceit that Mr. Fry so pleasantly invents, be entirely level-headed about its people. And we should have been willing, momentarily at least, to accept as heroine a young lady who had spent a few years in America destroying such public objects as offended her aesthetic sense. We were, in fact, mildly entertained by the notion that she had spent some time in jail, making restitution. We may have been a little bewildered that she should suddenly draw a gun in a living room and shoot an apple out of a young man's hand, but we expected that Fry would sooner or later have some delectable point to make of the episode. And it was pleasant enough to watch the Duke of Altair, an aging rake who believed himself to have renounced all further conquests, fall in love with her.

But, having accepted all of the author's introductory whimsy, and having finally arrived at the moment of intimacy between Duke and girl, we were dismayed to discover that Mr. Fry had conceived no real relationship for them. No emotion fluttered upward to disturb the glossy verbal surface. Instead, the girl stood prettily in the center of the room and delivered a sparkling apostrophe to the glories of syntax. The speech ran on for forty-one lines, and while it was delivered (by Lilli Palmer) with some gaiety and some invention, it gave the whole show away. Mr. Fry had assembled his unlikely figures only to parse them.

At about the time that *Venus Observed* was being poorly received in this country, Mr. Fry was jotting down some thoughts of his own— for a small book called *An, Experience of Critics*—on the creative processes, the behavior and misbehavior of words, and, of course, the critics who had been commenting on his work.

Most playwrights who turn on their tormentors do so in the heat of passion. Smarting under the immediate sting of a set of bad notices, they tend to cast both caution and coherence to the winds, erupting into a breathless invective that is quite as unpersuasive as the play which has preceded it.

Mr. Fry was cannier. He permitted his critics to go on to new targets, fully frocked; he caused his own rancor, if he ever had any, to relax into the graceful coil of the sleeping serpent; he seemed to have taken his hemlock in small daily doses so as to build up a splendid tolerance for the stuff. Then, in his quiet and almost jolly way, he let us have it.

An Experience of Critics may have been only a temporary victory for Mr. Fry, but it was a juicy one. For one thing, Mr. Fry writes better than the people who write about his writing. And for another, he had thought long enough, calmly enough and trenchantly enough to have found some true and telling things to say.

On the critical treatment of still budding talent: "The newly sprouting acorn is dug up several times a week and solemnly told that whatever it may think to the contrary, it is not an oak tree."

On one of the occupational hazards of criticism, noted when Mr. Fry himself attempted to review a play: "I could scarcely hear a word of the play for the noise of my own mind wondering how I should write about it."

On the inadvisability of having infallible criticism: "No man in his senses expects a critic always to be right—indeed, it would be very disconcerting if he were: we should have to believe him."

On the howls that go up when critical thumbs go down: "An artist's sensitiveness to criticism is, at least in part, an effort to keep unimpaired the zest, or confidence, or arrogance, which he needs to make creation possible."

On the vision of versifier Fry at work, as conjured up by the newspaper notices: "I see a man reeling intoxicated with words; they flow in a golden—or perhaps pinchbeck—stream from his mouth; they start out at his ears; they burst like rockets and jumping crackers and Catherine-wheels round his head . . . his typewriter continues to chatter long after it has been put back in the case. Words will grow out of him, like finger-nails, for some time after his death."

The poet's morose account of how he turns from this sort of journalistic analysis of his work to the work itself, sitting like an ancient Indian for silent hour after silent hour until at last he is able to type out an inspired "How," is not only deliciously funny reading; it is also a sharp comment on the easy nonsense which critics often substitute for an accurate reading of a complex creative problem.

Meanwhile, our author was at work on the problem. Shortly thereafter he came up with a fourth major play, the "winter comedy" called *The Dark Is Light Enough,* in which one character turned to another at a fairly heated point in the verbal clamor and cried, "But that's only a word!"

"Still," replied someone who was obviously a friend of the playwright's, "a word stays in the mind—and has its children, too."

And at long last—and in spite of certain very real difficulties in the play—it did seem as though Mr. Fry's words were ready to give up philandering, settle down, and perhaps produce grandchildren. Until now, except for the hint of amiably rooted character in *The Lady's Not for Burning,* the unexpected poet had been having fun with the language—testing it, tormenting it, making it laugh in a manner to which it had been unaccustomed, and sometimes skyrocketing it right over the garden wall. If it had often been exhilarating, it had sometimes been irrepressible to the point of irresponsibility.

In *The Dark Is Light Enough*—my enthusiasm for this play is based on the British rather than the softer and sleepier American production—language was ready to come home and stay with people, even belong to them. As an Austrian countess of the 1860s chose to risk her life and endanger her loved ones in order to perform an entirely quixotic act of mercy, she spoke now with a quiet self-confidence ("I am always perfectly guilty of what I do"), now with tartness ("People are always ready to die for what death will take away from them"), now with humor ("Are you military by nature or misfortune?"). And each of the lines belonged not to a free flight of Mr. Fry's more errant invention but to the woman who was thinking it.

Elsewhere in this melodramatic poem in praise of human generosity there were further evidences of the author's beginning tryst with reality, his beginning fondness for dimension in addition to dexterity. Much of the second act was concerned with an elusive, tantalizing yet thoroughly alive relationship between a good-for-nothing deserter and a woman—the Countess' daughter—who had loved him, lost him, and was now risking the destruction of her second marriage by giving him the time of day and the kindness of her heart.

As these two moved clumsily, then impulsively, toward each other, we were never quite certain what this lingering affection meant, or where it was going to lead. But it existed. For the moment something very concrete, thoroughly clothed in flesh, was seen to be working out its peculiar destiny before us—and the moment meant that Mr. Fry had begun to see his characters in terms of their secrets rather than their syntax.

Thus, toward the end of the evening, when one of the puzzled people whose lives had been turned topsy-turvy by a meaningless war paused to remark that he knew a certain truth "in the still of my mind," it was possible to believe that these figures did have still reservoirs, places of rest, behind their bright and eager phrasemaking.

Mr. Fry was slowly and patiently putting flesh on those dancing bones.

❅   ❅   ❅

section iv
THE TERRITORY OF EXPERIMENT

frederick j. hoffmann

MR. ZERO AND OTHER CIPHERS: EXPERIMENTS ON THE STAGE

"I HAD THE curious experience with *The Great God Brown*," said Stark Young of the performance on January 23, 1926, "of being moved with something that I felt behind the play, but almost always untouched by the play itself." It was an "interesting" play, and there were moments when the restless experimenting with new theatrical devices succeeded. But these tricks were not in themselves wholly admirable: "When once a device is adopted in a drama and the expressive meaning of it has become clear, the continued significance or suggestiveness of its use will depend on the artist's imagination."

The American theater in the 1920s was overwhelmed by experiment of one kind and another: it tried to represent life more concretely through abstractions, tried to moralize, satirize, lyricize in terms of new manipulations of space and movement, new concepts and sequences of dialogue, new versions of characterization. It performed brilliantly in the matter of stage design; the settings in many cases proved more revealing of theme and motivation than the characters themselves. The newness was not exclusively a matter of techniques, but part of the general stir of experimental activity in the arts. The imagination had boundless opportunity to dramatize its imaginings.

When a group of strictly amateur playwrights gathered in a deserted old fish house in Provincetown, Massachusetts, in the summer of 1915, the "new theater" was launched. It was an act of defiance, to free the stage from the "commercial manager's interpretation of public taste." [1] With a firm conviction that creative imagination must be kept alive, the leader of the group, George Cram Cook, sponsored whatever new plays he could find, whatever old ones he thought were valuable. "Without [the creative imagination]," he affirmed,

From *The Twenties* by F. J. Hoffmann. Copyright 1948 © 1955 by Frederick J. Hoffmann. Reprinted by permission of The Viking Press, Inc.
[1] See Helen Deutsch and Stella Hanau, *The Provincetown: A Story of the Theatre* (1931).

"the wreck of the world cannot be cleared away and the new world shaped."

From Europe came the movement called most often *expressionism*. It affected all the arts, was especially striking in its demonstrations in German films and architecture. In the drama, as in the cinema and painting and sculpture, expressionism demonstrated the artist's dissatisfaction with naturalism or realism, with the limitations set upon the work of the artist by these schools. The aim of the expressionist was to project in outer symbols a state of mind, an inner crisis, a psychological condition. This also involved expressions of the dream state. One of the earliest expressionist dramas, Strindberg's *Dream Play* (written 1901–1902), attempted, as Strindberg explained in the prologue, to "imitate the disconnected but seemingly logical form of the dream. . . . Time and space do not exist. . . . The characters split, double, multiply, vanish, solidify, blur, clarify. But one consciousness reigns above them all—that of the dreamer; and before it there are no secrets, no incongruities, no scruples, no laws. There is neither judgment nor exoneration, but merely narration."

George H. Scheffauer, in *The New Vision in the German Arts* (1924), showed great excitement over what he thought was primarily a German art movement. He defined expressionism as "*direct action in art*—the forthright naked impulse, delivered without intermediaries from the imagination to the outer world—like a child from the womb." Scheffauer analyzed the products of German expressionism—the film *Dr. Caligari*, the plays of Max Reinhardt, Ernst Toller, and Georg Kaiser, especially the latter's *Gas*—and he concluded by saying that the movement, as headed by Kaiser, was "the American spirit idealized by a European artist, purged of its slag, of the trivial, the cynical and the ephemeral, and given power, voice, direction as an element in art."

Whatever the actual contribution of expressionism to "the American spirit," there is no doubt that it encouraged a remarkable variety of experiments, large and small, on the American stage. Some of its most successful effects were found in comedy, where its exaggerations and arrangements of abstractions in motion were especially useful. Elmer Rice's *The Adding Machine* (1923) was the most remarkable illustration of expressionist comedy. Stereotypes of character and setting illustrated the native stereotypes which the comedy satirized.

The main character of *The Adding Machine* is Mr. Zero. In his home he is surrounded by the clichés of modern life: installment-plan furniture, walls papered "with sheets of foolscap covered with columns of figures," and so on. His wife, his friends, his opinions, his desires, are similarly cliché extensions of the reality. His office is abstracted from the obvious setting of a small-time bookkeeper's life; his uncharming assistant is given the most glamorous of Hollywood names, Daisy Diana Dorothea Devore. Zero must endlessly mark down figures as she calls them out, and add them, a function he has mechanically performed for many years.

In the play's first crisis, "the Boss," another stereotype ("middle-aged, stoutish, bald, well dressed") announces the installment of adding machines, regrets that "for business reasons" Zero will have to be fired; after which the stage itself acts out Zero's murder of the Boss, as the stage directions indicate:

> His voice is drowned by the music. The platform is revolving rapidly now. Zero and the Boss face each other. They are entirely motionless save for the Boss's jaws, which open and close incessantly. But the words are inaudible. The music swells and swells. To it is added every offstage effect of the theater: the wind, the waves, the galloping horses, the locomotive whistle, the sleigh bells, the automobile siren, the glass-crash, New Year's Eve, Election Night, Armistice Day, and Mardi Gras. The noise is deafening, maddening, unendurable. Suddenly it culminates in a terrific peal of thunder. For an instant there is a flash of red and then everything is plunged into blackness.

This is violently comical, noisily "representative." *The Adding Machine*, in its expressionistic phases at least, abstracts from an abstraction. Mr. Zero, from birth a cipher, can give expression only to the limited variety of his cipherhood. Murdering the Boss is his rebellion; but after the interval of stereotyped bliss that follows the murder, Zero is put back on the track of his routine—again in an exaggerated form. In his next incarnation Zero operates a "super-hyper-adding machine" with "the great toe" of his right foot. In sum, the devices of repetition and abstraction all lead to the comic thesis of the play: that the soul of Zero is the soul of the small-time worker,[2] whose acts are duplicated a million times, in all phases of history, who doesn't grow at all but merely changes his work as mechanical progress dictates.

Expressionist comedy found an especially useful subject in the twin scapegoats of much criticism of the 1920s—the standardization of life in modern business and the standardization of morality in middle-class convention. *Beggar on Horseback* (1924), by George S. Kaufman and Marc Connelly, exploited both themes. The plot is as conventional as slick comedy can provide; it is the stage that makes

---

[2] "You're a failure, Zero, a failure. A waste product . . . the raw material of slums and wars—the ready prey of the first jingo or demagogue or political adventurer who takes the trouble to play upon your ignorance and credulity and provincialism."

the play. Undecided whether to marry a vulgar rich girl or a sensitive poor one, the hero takes time out to dream. The expressionist dream outlines his future life, should he choose the grossly wealthy Miss Cady; in his dream-exasperation he murders the entire family, is given a comic-opera trial, and is sentenced to hard labor in the Cady Consolidated Art factory, where he is forced to produce jingles in great numbers. The dream convinces him, and he is presumably doomed at the play's conclusion to live happily ever after with the poor but sensitive Cynthia.

This is vaudeville given an expressionist streamlining. Similar effects are gained in John Howard Lawson's *Roger Bloomer* (1923).[3] The Bloomer family at dinner—in Excelsior, Iowa—reiterate banal lines and gestures as they consume their food. In New York, to which Bloomer flees to escape the banality, he discovers that it persists; and his discovery is suitably externalized in a monotonously precise repetition of stage props. Lawson is in more deadly earnest than Rice or Kaufman and Connelly; Bloomer doesn't solve his problem easily. Aware that he is not for Wall Street, he tries suicide but fails; his sensitive companion tries and succeeds; and in the concluding dream scene she returns to him, encouraging him to continue "fighting through."

Parody and criticism of the economic order lent themselves remarkably well to the use of expressionist effects. Rice combined these again and again. In *The Subway* (1929), Mr. Zero has become George, who takes a correspondence course in SUCCESS ("Capacity plus perseverance spells success"); in the subway, Sophie, the heroine, is surrounded by men who wear identifying masks (a dog, a pig, a monkey, a wolf, a rat). Eugene, the sensitive one, plans a masterpiece, a "mad mechanistic dance" leading finally to the destruction of Western man; years later scientists, digging in the ruins, will find a few odds and ends (false teeth, a pair of jade earrings from the 5-and-10), "all that remains of Western civilization." In the final scene Sophie, dressed in nightgown and light coat, rushes to the subway station, is fascinated by the approaching train ("like the waves on the beach"), and jumps into its path.

The tendency, evident in the work of Rice and Lawson, to move from comedy to social tragedy was not uncommon in the history of expressionist drama. The Machine, implying "efficient" standardization of commercial life, was associated with class conflict in the plays of

[3] See also Lawson's *Processional* (1925) and *The International* (1928): the first, an anticipation of the proletarian play of the 1930s, treats the strike theme with a mixture of expressionist devices and vaudeville satire; the second is an expressionist fantasy of proletarian situations and dogma.

Kaiser, Reinhardt, and Toller. Toller's *Masse Mensch*,[4] Reinhardt's *The Machine-Stormers*, and Kaiser's *Gas* take advantage of the abstractions to be found in the life they criticize. The limitations of this type of drama lie in the very restricted use to which the abstractions can be put. Abstractions require an immense effort of the imagination to give them individuality and a meaning beyond the most generalized kind of cardboard editorial. Rice's characters are almost invariably fleeing from expressionistically defined circumstances; frequently they are victimized more by the stage setting than by life itself. The experiment has its own risks: in comedy it leads to a modernized kind of vaudeville sequence; in tragedy, the devices of the "new stage" get in the way of a proper consideration of the characters, even though they are there supposed to clarify and explain them.[5]

The most remarkable American experiment in the expressionist drama was E. E. Cummings' *Him* (1927). The two main characters, Him and Me, are types. Him is an artist-creator; Me is his mistress, an expressionist idealization of the Cummings *"Weiblichkeit."* They are surrounded, victimized, annoyed, by representatives of modern evils. Him's great distinction is that he is not successful, "hasn't been favored by fate." He is the circus man, the acrobat, the clown: "an artist, a man, and a failure." The Man in the Mirror is an ideal representation of Him's bohemian nature; this man, this part of Him, puts on a play of nine scenes, drawn inconsequentially from aspects of the contemporary scene: Prohibition, soap-box oratory, nostrums and patent medicines, the business "unlife," the censorship ("Mr. John Rutter, President pro. tem. of the Society for the Contraception of Vice"), and fascism.

The individual scenes push hard (though often with extreme cleverness) the thesis of man's need to realize himself in spite of circumstance and his own fear of self-knowledge. The final act represents the positive values identified with Him and Me: their love for each other, her great gift of feeling, the way toward "honest" beauty and passion, the miracle of birth, the beauty of little children. Scene vi presents a great sideshow; Me, holding a newborn baby, shocks the crowd with this vision of life, and it turns away in disgust and

---

[4] See Scheffauer, *The New Vision in the German Arts* (1924): "The characters are nameless—Workmen, Workwomen, the Nameless One, Officer, Priest, Man, Bankers, Prisoners, Guards, Shadows. Only the heroine, Sonia Irene L., a woman of the caste of officials who makes common cause with the workers, is given a name—significantly Russian."

[5] Cf. Stark Young (*Immortal Shadows*, 1948): "You could take a knife and fork to represent a man and wife. But to achieve anything important there must then be imagination exercised in the use of these symbols, otherwise you have only the regular story, plus the knife and fork instead of man and wife, and have achieved nothing beyond the first device, the initial metaphor."

terror. She is a freak in the sideshow, but the conclusion of the play is that the freaks are important; they are the elements of life put aside by the crowd. The dominating symbol of the circus acrobat and clown enforces this conclusion: the acrobat describes in his action the grace of movement which is expression in art; the clown is the humorist who gets his laughs because he is absurd and utterly unlike the conventional audience who laughs at him. It is a simple thesis, but it is particularized in brilliant dramatic fragments, which are interrelated in terms of what each adds to the sum of meaning. Perhaps this is the best that can be done with expressionism; at any rate, *Him* succeeds because of, rather than in spite of, its wealth of dramatic variations.

One may almost say that the American drama of the 1920s was O'Neill's drama: he was so valuable an asset to the Provincetown Players and subsequent groups; he seemed capable of so many new ideas for the theater; his plays were so much the expression of dramatic experiment and innovation. He had decided on the theater as a career after having read the plays of Strindberg, Wedekind, Kaiser, and other Europeans during a five-month convalescence in 1912–1913. He spent a semester at Harvard, working in George Pierce Baker's "Workshop 47" (fall of 1914). He was ready for the Provincetown Players when he joined them in the summer of 1916—with plays, most of them one-acters based on life at sea.

Expressionist effects were first made noticeably a part of his drama in *The Emperor Jones* (1920), a remarkably skillful projection of its hero's inner consciousness. From that point O'Neill moved to bolder and more varied experiments. In *The Hairy Ape* (1922), expressionist devices and settings combined with strictly naturalistic details, so that the "real" achieved a symbolic quality through formal repetition and exaggeration. In *The Great God Brown* (1926) he tried the addition of masks as an experiment in dramatic effects. They were the best way, he explained (*American Spectator*, November 1932), for the dramatist to express "those profound hidden conflicts of the mind which the probings of psychology continue to disclose to us." *Lazarus Laughed* (1928) carried the use of masks to an extreme of complication: seven masked choruses representing seven periods of life, each of which contained seven types of character. He also experimented with that unwritten agreement between audience and playwright concerning the play's tolerable length. The performance of *Strange Interlude* (1928) lasted from 5:30 until after 11:00, with an eighty-minute intermission; the trilogy, *Mourning Becomes Electra* (1931), was supposed to be performed in a single evening; and, in 1936,

O'Neill wrote Barrett Clark that he was working on a series of nine plays to be produced on nine successive nights.

O'Neill was, in short, extremely versatile. The range of his plays, from a one-acter like *Before Breakfast* (1916), in which there is only one character on stage, to the complications of *Lazarus Laughed,* testifies to his great talent for surprise and innovation. There is scarcely a dramatic idea, device, trick that he did not try. While he borrowed from expressionism, he invented his own original variants.

A driving intellectual ambition to "get at the root" of human desires and frustrations was ever present in O'Neill. He tried to explore the complexes of the human spirit, the psychology of human motive and obsession (*Diff'rent,* 1920; *Desire under the Elms,* 1924; *Mourning Becomes Electra*); the tensions of race differences (*All God's Chillun' Got Wings,* 1924); the comedy of modern commercial life (*Marco Millions,* 1928). In 1929 he announced a new trilogy of "the human spirit," a "trilogy that will dig at the roots of the sickness of today as I feel it—the death of an old God and the failure of science and materialism to give any satisfactory new one for the surviving religious instinct to find a meaning for life in, and to comfort its fear of death with." Two plays were completed, *Dynamo* (1929) and *Days Without End* (1934).

Not only is O'Neill burdened with this sense of "profound mission," but his characters are almost invariably disturbed by it; not infrequently the disturbance and the stagecraft are all the play has to offer. Jim Harris of *All God's Chillun',* for example, is troubled by the problem of his personal relationship with God. "Maybe He can forgive what you've done to me," he says to Ella, his wife, "and maybe He can forgive what I've done to you; but I don't see how He's going to forgive—Himself." There are numerous speeches of this kind in the most ambitious of O'Neill's plays. The characters share his perplexity about the human state—as the devices of the stage represent it—and are so often urged to comment upon it that the plays become entangled in the confusion and torture of explaining themselves. The experiments often get in the way of the drama; they give an impression of a depth and complexity they only infrequently possess. Occasionally, as in *The Emperor Jones,* the experiment and the theme are almost perfectly integrated. The hero does not become an amateur philosopher but remains a man victimized by his fears and struggling vainly to escape his danger; he grows in terms of, and as a result of, the skillful and controlled use of dramatic experiment. That balance O'Neill rarely achieved.

O'Neill's reputation was based upon his love of experiment; he kept his public in a state of excitement over his restless and clever experimenting. His failure as a dramatist may also be identified with the general failure of expressionism itself. In its effort to objectify inner states of mind and emotion, it forced the dramatist to devote too much of his attention, energy, and imagination to problems of new stage conventions, to the neglect of the essential concerns of any literature.

robert w. corrigan

THORNTON WILDER AND THE TRAGIC SENSE OF LIFE

OF ALL modern American dramatists, none is more difficult to pin down than Thornton Wilder. He is thought of, together with O'Neill, Miller, and Williams, as one of our "Big Four," and yet his reputation is based on only three full-length plays and was made on one. And whereas reams of criticism have been written on the other three playwrights, only an occasional article on Wilder is published. This is all the more surprising since no one seems to agree about his work. For some he is the great American satirist; for others he is a soft-hearted sentimentalist; and for still others he is our only "religious" dramatist. Furthermore, no American playwright is more respected by contemporary European dramatists than is Wilder; Brecht, Ionesco, and Duerrenmatt have all acknowledged their debt to this "great and fanatical experimentor." Therefore, it is about time that we reëvaluate his work.

From his earliest volumes of one-acts, *The Angel That Troubled the Waters* and *The Long Christmas Dinner*, to his last play, *The Matchmaker*, Wilder has dealt boldly and affirmatively with the themes of Life, Love, and Earth. Each of his plays is a hymn in dramatic form affirming life. But the important question is: What is the nature of this affirmation? It is not, as some would have it, Christian. To begin with, Wilder has no belief—at least in his plays—in a religion that is revealed or historical. These are basic premises of Christianity. To be sure Wilder is deistic, but as almost all of his critics have pointed out, he is essentially a religious Platonist; and this position must ultimately reject the historic dimension as meaningful. Francis Fergusson ties these two ideas together when he writes:

> The plays are perfectly in accord with the Platonic kind of philosophy which they are designed to teach. The great Ideas are timeless, above the history of the race and the history of actual individuals.

From *Educational Theatre Journal*, Vol. XIII. Reprinted by permission.

Any bit of individual or racial history will do, therefore, to "illustrate" them; but history and individual lives lack all real being; they are only shadows on the cave wall.

Mary McCarthy approaches this another way when she writes of *The Skin of our Teeth:*

> In other words, if George misses the five-fifteen, Chaos is come again. This is the moral of the piece. Man, says Mr. Wilder, from time to time gets puffed up with pride and prosperity, he grows envious, covetous, lecherous, forgets his conjugal duties, goes whoring after women; portents of disaster appear, but he is too blind to see them; in the end, with the help of the little woman, who has never taken any stock in either pleasure or wisdom, he escapes by the skin of his teeth. *Sicut erat in principio. . . .*
>
> It is a curious view of life. It displays elements of Christian morality. Christ, however, was never so simple, but on the contrary allowed always for paradox (the woman taken in adultery, the story of Martha and Mary, "Consider the lilies of the field") . . . No, it is not the Christian view, but a kind of bowdlerized version of it, such as might have been imparted to a class of taxpayer's children by a New England Sunday School teacher forty years ago.

Now, I happen to believe that both Fergusson and Miss McCarthy (even in their admiration for Wilder) overstate their arguments, because Wilder, except in his preface to *The Angel That Troubled the Waters,* has never thought of himself as a Christian or a religious playwright. He best states his position when he writes: "*Our Town* is not offered as a picture of life in a New Hampshire village; or speculation about the conditions of life after death. . . . It is an attempt to find a value above all price for the smallest events of daily life." Wilder is talking about *Our Town,* but what he says applies to all of his work. In short, Wilder is a humanist, an affirming humanist—a "yea-sayer to life" as Barnard Hewitt calls him—but nonetheless a humanist.

When we examine the nature of Wilder's humanistic affirmation, what do we discover? His plays celebrate human love, the worth and dignity of man, the values of the ordinary, and the eternity of human values. From the little boy in Wilder's first play who says: "I am not afraid of life. I will astonish it!" to Dolly Levi and her cohorts in adventure in *The Matchmaker,* Wilder has always been on the side of life and life is seen to be most directly affirmed through love. Love, then, is his most persistent theme and it has been for him an inexhaustible subject. Of its worth he is convinced, but it is interesting to note that Wilder has never been able to make any commitments as to the reasons for its worth. Wilder can deal with life and love directly and concretely; but when he moves to the edges of life, the focus becomes less sharp. Certainly, Wilder deals with death—he is not afraid of it, but death in his plays is terminal. When Mrs. Soames says in Act Three of *Our Town:* "My, wasn't life awful—and wonderful," Wilder is reminding us that beauty is recognizable because of change and life is meaningful because of death. But as both John Mason Brown and Winfield Townley Scott have pointed out, Wilder never deals adequately with Death's own meaning. And as for what's beyond death? The Stage Manager in *Our Town* tells us:

> You know as well as I do that the dead don't stay interested in us living people for very long. Gradually, gradually, they let go of the earth. . . . They get weaned away from the earth—that's the way I put it,— weaned away. Yes, they stay here while the earth-part of 'em burns away, burns out, and all that time they slowly get indifferent to what's going on in Grover's Corners. They're waitin'! They're waitin' for something that they feel is comin'. Something important and great. Aren't they waitin' for the eternal part in them to come out clear?

But what is this eternal part, this Platonic essence, which in our imperfect awareness of living is only a shadow on the wall of the cave? What is death's meaning? The Stage Manager has just told us:

> everybody knows that *something* is eternal. And it ain't houses and it ain't names, and it ain't earth, and it ain't even the stars . . . everybody knows in their bones that *something* is eternal, and that something has to do with human beings. All the greatest people ever lived have been telling us that for five thousand years and yet you'd be surprised how people are always losing hold of it. There's something way down deep that's eternal about every human being.

So, we are right back where we started: Life is reality and eternity is the perfected essence of that reality to which we are too often blind and of which we can't stand too much.

It is this tendency—a tendency consistent with his Platonism— to reduce the dimension of eternity so that it can be encompassed by life itself, that has lead me to believe—although he has written no tragedies—that Wilder has essentially a tragic rather than a Christian or even religious view of life. Why his plays are not tragedies I shall come to, but first I should like to describe briefly what I mean by the tragic view of life. Scott Fitzgerald described it in a letter to his daughter as "the sense that life is essentially a cheat and its conditions are those of defeat." It seems to me that the awareness of the tragic nature of things informs every serious outlook. You can escape it in play or other forms of illusion; you can transcend it in religion; or you can celebrate it in exaltation; but it is always there! It is the backdrop of fate which insists that part, if not all, of life's glory is in its doom.

The tragic view of life is derived from that form of Greek mysticism known as gnosticism. The simplest statement of the gnostic attitude that I know of—and Wilder is very pertinent here—is Hegel's "the truth is in the whole!" What this means is that any adequate philosophy of life must not only include everything, but affirm everything. It must not suppress any aspect of reality because some moral code finds it offensive or ignoble; or because some human emotion or action is unpleasant or shocking; nor can it prefer some aspect of life because it is beautiful, noble, or good. In short, if the truth is in the whole, then reality is neutral, not partisan—it is beyond good and evil. But life as it is lived is fragmentary and denies the possibility of neutrality: flesh-and-blood men are always partisan. Living is taking sides; and neutrality in life is always the taking of sides by default. Thus, if "the truth is in the whole," it is mocked by life as it destroys it. Life depends on the interplay of polar opposites, and this fact is the lowest common denominator of the tragic view of life. The differences in tragedy are the differences in the way the clash is conceived. But finally, the very existence of separate, discrete individuals is itself sufficient to set up a tragic conflict. Tragedy is the inevitable result of our ontological solitude. As long as, to use Rilke's phrase, "I am I and you are you and we are separated by a void," the possibility of tragedy exists. For Thomas Wolfe was right when he saw: "Naked and alone we came into exile. In her dark womb we did not know our mother's face; from the prison of her flesh have we come into the unspeakable and uncommunicable prison of this earth. Which of us has known his brother? Which of us has looked into his father's heart? Which of us is not forever a stranger and alone?"

For this reason the stage of tragic drama consists of two ever-shifting backdrops or perspectives: the ultimate perspective which is neutral and beyond good and evil, and in which all experience is equally valid and real; and the finite perspective of men in action; the perspective of life's strife, tensions, and contradictions. And man, being finite, will of necessity always challenge the ultimate perspective, and tragedy is the dramatization of that conflict. It is for this reason that man's pride, whether it be in the form of an inordinate pursuit of a finite goal or the suicidal aspiration toward the infinite, should not be viewed as a character defect of egotism, or as a tragic flaw. Rather it is a part of human nature, the necessary counterpart of man's creative capacity as a rational being.

Tragedy, then, sees man as the questioner—naked and alone—facing the mysterious forces of life, and particularly those irreducible forces of suffering and death. We must understand that tragedy does not attempt to abolish the suffering of pain, fear, and sadness, rather it embraces that suffering as the fulfillment of maturity and self-understanding. The tragic vision impels man to fight against his destiny. It impels the hero, the playwright, and finally the audience into "boundary situations." Those situations where man is at the limits of his sovereignty: Job on the ash-heap; Prometheus on the crag; Oedipus discovered; Lear on the heath; Ahab on the quarter-deck. Here, with all the protective coverings stripped off, the hero faces—as if no man had ever faced it before—the existential question: Job's "What is man?"; Lear's "Is man no more than this?" The tragic writer always presses these boundary situations to their fullest yield, and this is the discovery of tragedy. The hero discovers through this suffering not God, or Nature, but himself. In tragedy, action is carried to the uttermost limits, in order that the farthest reaches of human possibility may be explored. And in so doing the hero's defeat is vindicated by his capacity to impose meaning on the void, even while in the act of falling.

Now, Wilder has not created any Ahabs or Lears, but this is not because he hasn't a tragic view of life. He happens to believe—as did Maeterlinck—that the tragedy of life can best be seen in the drama of the everyday—in life's smallest events. For this reason he does not dramatize great conflicts in order to capture the quintessence of tragedy, for there are times in each of our lives when we are conscious of moving into boundary situations. I think it is important to see the validity of this, although we must point out that this is tragic but not always dramatic. And this, I think, accounts for the fact that Wilder's plays are usually called "hymns," "odes," "songs," and so on, and most critics feel that there isn't much conflict in their plots. It might be helpful to take a specific example to illustrate Wilder's position on this matter.

Over and over again in Wilder's work, the belief is stated directly and indirectly that "life is what you make of it." The fullest discussion of the idea is in *The Ides of March*, where Caesar says: "Life has no meaning save that which we confer upon it." Later he says:

> Am I sure that there is no mind behind our existence and no mystery anywhere in the universe? I think I am. . . . How terrifying and glorious the role of man if, indeed, without guidance and without consolation he must create from his own vitals the meaning for his existence and the rules whereby he lives.

Many of us believe this idea when stated in its simpler form: "Life is what we make of it." But we are unaware that this is really an existential position and that Wilder is very close to Sartre's "Man is condemned to be free."

In fact, upon reflection, we discover that in starting from "Life is what we make of it," Wilder is really in the mainstream of the modern drama beginning with Ibsen and Strindberg. And this is a dangerous position and usually in the drama has led to despair. The image of man in this drama is an image of collapse. Certainly, Kierkegaard saw this when he wrote in *Fear and Trembling*:

> If there were no eternal consciousness in a man, if at the foundation of all there lay only a wildly seething power which writhing with obscure passions produced everything that is great and everything that is insignificant, if a bottomless void never satiated lay hidden beneath all— what then would life be but despair.

Most modern dramatists have answered with "that's all!" But Wilder hasn't, even though he holds a position that should lead this way. I think he averts despair—and also tragedy, even though his view of life is essentially tragic—with a kind of Santayana-like belief in life. In fact, Wilder's Platonism can make sense only if it is seen as coming through Santayana. Wilder is—as probably most of us are—saved from despair and its paralyzing effects by what Santayana calls "animal faith." We admit that life may be only an irrational nightmare and there is no reality except that which we imagine, but the animal faith which bids us believe in the external world is much stronger than all the logical arguments which would make life absurd. As Joseph Wood Krutch put it: "Everybody acts as though he believed that the external world exists; nearly everybody acts as though he believed that his version of it is a dependable one; and the majority act as though they could also make valid value judgments about it." It is this belief, this animal faith, that permits Wilder to say "Life is what you make of it," and still come up in affirmation on this side of despair. All his plays might be described by that verse of Theodore Spencer's (and I think Wilder and Spencer have great affinities):

> Oh how to praise that No,
> When all longing would press
> After the lost Yes!
> Oh how redress
> That disaster of No?

But although Wilder can assert meaning to life, the meaning is almost in the assertion itself and this is not a very comfortable position to be in. One gets the feeling that Wilder has to keep saying it to make sure that it is true. The danger of this position is that it lacks the necessary polarity and tension for full meaning; the tension between an ultimate perspective and a finite one. This in itself keeps Wilder from being a religious dramatist. In all great religious drama: the works of Sophocles, Calderón, *Everyman,* and in more recent times the later plays of Hofmannsthal, Eliot and even Fry, there is the back-drop of religious belief which gives meaning to and informs the hero's "life is what you make of it." There is the greater stage. The medieval theatre and the Spanish theatre of Calderón exhibit this, and this is what Hofmannsthal tried to achieve at the Salzburg festivals with his productions of *Everyman, The Great World Theatre,* and *The Tower.* In all of these plays the actors—man—are faced with a moral choice under the very eyes of God and his angels upstage. The scaffold of these multiple stage structures not only serves as a magic mirror for the visible world and its invisible order, but the invisible order is made visible. For in these plays the idea of man as a player on the world's stage becomes the very principle of the *mise-en-scène.* For God, the master, speaking from the top of the scaffold, actually orders the world to produce a play under his eyes, featuring man who is to act out his part on earth.

More important than the absence of a religious dimension to Wilder's work, however, are the many experiments he has made in theatrical technique to compensate for this lack of an ultimate per-spective. It is a commonplace in talking about modern literature to comment on the loss of a community of values and the disappearance of public truths in our time. It is equally well known that writers tend to compensate for the lack of a community of belief with new tech-niques of expression. The problem for the dramatist is how to make a highly individual standard of values appear to the audience to be a natural objective standard. Most of the modern dramatists have at-tempted to meet this problem by focussing on the psychology of their characters. In so doing they leave begged the question of value by confining the world of the play to the limits of an individual character's mind and then assessing value solely in terms of the consciousness of that mind. Thus, an incident in *Hedda Gabler* may not be important by any communicable standard of human significance, but if the universe is confined to her mind and Ibsen makes us look deeply enough into it, we can at least see it as important in that tiny context. In this way psychology makes possible such a drastic limitation of context that a private world can be the subject of a tragedy. Further-more, by new techniques of presentation that private world and its values can be made, at least for the duration of the performance, convincing.

Wilder has not been interested in psychology and has never

used psychological techniques to solve the "modernists'" problems in the theatre. This accounts, I think, for his great influence on the continental avant-garde dramatists who are rebelling against our psychologically oriented theatre. Wilder sought to achieve the sense of an ultimate perspective by immaterializing the sense of dramatic place on stage. The bare stage of *Our Town* with its chairs, tables, and ladders, together with the Stage Manager's bald exposition, are all that he uses to create the town. The same is true of *The Skin of Our Teeth;* you never really know where the Antrobuses live—nor when. This is his second dominant technique; by destroying the illusion of time, Wilder achieves the effect of any time, all time, each time. But this is risky business, for without the backdrop of an ultimate perspective to inform a play's action, it can very easily become sentimental or satirical, or even pretentious. Wilder at his best keeps this from happening, but his only weapons are wit and irony. And a production which does not succeed in capturing these qualities (as alas most college and school productions do not) is bound to turn out bathetic and sentimental; when technique is used as a compensation for the ultimate perspective, the resultant work of art always lies precariously under a Damoclean sword.

It is important that we see the dangers in Wilder's methods, but that a tragic sense of life informs his plays is best illustrated by his sense of destiny. In Wilder's novel, *The Woman of Andros,* Chrysis tells her guests a fable of the dead hero who receives Zeus' permission to return to earth to relive the least eventful day of his life, on the condition that he see it both as onlooker and participant.

> Suddenly the hero saw that the living too are dead and that we can only be said to be alive in those moments when our hearts are conscious of our treasure; for our hearts are not strong enough to love every moment.

He quickly asks to be released from this experience, and it is the opinion of Chrysis that

> All human beings—save a few mysterious exceptions who seemed to be in possession of some secret from the gods—merely endured the slow misery of existence, hiding as best they could their consternation that life had no wonderful surprises after all and that its most difficult burden was the incommunicability of love.

Eight years later Wilder incorporated this into the last scene of *Our Town.* When Emily comes back on her twelfth birthday, she discovers that "we don't have time to look at one another. I didn't realize. So all that was going on and we never noticed . . . Oh, earth you're too wonderful for anybody to realize you. Do any human beings ever realize life while they live it? —every, every minute?" The answer, of course, is "no," and Emily must conclude with "That's all human beings are!—Just blind people."

What Wilder is saying here is that human beings cannot stand to have a sense of destiny—the awareness that there is a continuity in all our acts, the awareness that every present moment comes from a past and is directed to a future. Only at moments—usually of emotional crisis—do we have this sense of destiny, this sense of awareness of the future. It is this sense of destiny that is the great human reality and the tragedy of life lies in our fragmentary and imperfect awareness of it. Wilder is aware, like Eliot, that "human kind cannot bear very much reality," but his plays fall short of tragedy because he takes the Platonic escape, he moves into a world that denies the reality and the nemesis of destiny. Nor does he have the solution of an Eliot. For in denying, finally, the reality of destiny he shuts out the possibility of ever providing the means to perfect our fragmentary and imperfect vision. He fails, to use Karl Jaspers' phrase, to go "Beyond Tragedy." That Wilder lacks this dimension, is not to discredit him, however, for no other American dramatist more fully affirms that miracle of life which so much modern drama would deny.

martin esslin

THE THEATRE OF THE ABSURD

THE PLAYS of Samuel Beckett, Arthur Adamov, and Eugène Ionesco
have been performed with astonishing success in France, Germany,
Scandinavia, and the English-speaking countries. This reception is all
the more puzzling when one considers that the audiences concerned
were amused by and applauded these plays fully aware that they
could not understand what they meant or what their authors were
driving at.

At first sight these plays do, indeed, confront their public with
a bewildering experience, a veritable barrage of wildly irrational,
often nonsensical goings-on that seem to go counter to all accepted
standards of stage convention. In these plays, some of which are
labeled "anti-plays," neither the time nor the place of the action are
ever clearly stated. (At the beginning of Ionesco's *The Bald Soprano*
the clock strikes seventeen.) The characters hardly have any individuality and often even lack a name; moreover, halfway through the
action they tend to change their nature completely. Pozzo and Lucky
in Beckett's *Waiting for Godot*, for example, appear as master and
slave at one moment only to return after a while with their respective
positions mysteriously reversed. The laws of probability as well as
those of physics are suspended when we meet young ladies with two
or even three noses (Ionesco's *Jack or the Submission*), or a corpse
that has been hidden in the next room that suddenly begins to grow
to monstrous size until a giant foot crashes through the door onto
the stage (Ionesco's *Amédée*). At a result, it is often unclear whether
the action is meant to represent a dream world of nightmares or real
happenings. Within the same scene the action may switch from the
nightmarish poetry of high emotions to pure knock-about farce or
cabaret, and above all, the dialogue tends to get out of hand so that
at times the words seem to go counter to the actions of the characters
on the stage, to degenerate into lists of words and phrases from a

From the *Tulane Drama Review*, May, 1960. Reprinted with the permission of the
Tulane Drama Review.

dictionary or traveler's conversation book, or to get bogged down in endless repetitions like a phonograph record stuck in one groove. Only in this kind of demented world can strangers meet and discover, after a long and polite conversation and close cross-questioning, that, to their immense surprise, they must be man and wife as they are living on the same street, in the same house, apartment, room, and bed (Ionesco's *The Bald Soprano*). Only here can the whole life of a group of characters revolve around the passionate discussion of the aesthetics and economics of pinball machines (Adamov's *Ping-Pong*). Above all, everything that happens seems to be beyond rational motivation, happening at random or through the demented caprice of an unaccountable idiot fate. Yet, these wildly extravagant tragic farces and farcical tragedies, although they have suffered their share of protests and scandals, do arouse interest and are received with laughter and thoughtful respect. What is the explanation for this curious phenomenon?

The most obvious, but perhaps too facile answer that suggests itself is that these plays are prime examples of "pure theatre." They are living proof that the magic of the stage can persist even outside, and divorced from, any framework of conceptual rationality. They prove that exits and entrances, light and shadow, contrasts in costume, voice, gait and behavior, pratfalls and embraces, all the manifold mechanical interactions of human puppets in groupings that suggest tension, conflict, or the relaxation of tensions, can arouse laughter or gloom and conjure up an atmosphere of poetry even if devoid of logical motivation and unrelated to recognizable human characters, emotions, and objectives.

But this is only a partial explanation. While the elements of "pure theatre" and abstract stagecraft is certainly at work in the plays concerned, they also have a much more substantial content and meaning. Not only *do* all these plays make sense, though perhaps not obvious or conventional sense, they also give expression to some of the basic issues and problems of our age, in a uniquely efficient and meaningful manner, so that they meet some of the deepest needs and unexpressed yearnings of their audience.

The three dramatists that have been grouped together here would probably most energetically deny that they form anything like a school or movement. Each of them, in fact, has his own roots and sources, his own very personal approach to both form and subject matter. Yet they also clearly have a good deal in common. This common denominator that characterizes their works might well be described as the element of *the absurd*. "Est absurde ce qui n'a pas de but . . ." ("Absurd is that which has no purpose, or goal, or objective"), the definition given by Ionesco in a note on Kafka,[1] certainly applies to the plays of Beckett and Ionesco as well as those of Arthur Adamov up to his latest play, *Paolo Paoli,* when he returned to a more traditional form of social drama.

Each of these writers, however, has his own special type of absurdity: in Beckett it is melancholic, colored by a feeling of futility born from the disillusionment of old age and chronic hopelessness; Adamov's is more active, aggressive, earthy, and tinged with social and political overtones; while Ionesco's absurdity has its own fantastic knock-about flavor of tragical clowning. But they all share the same deep sense of human isolation and of the irremediable character of the human condition.

As Arthur Adamov put it in describing how he came to write his first play, *La Parodie* (1947):

> I began to discover stage scenes in the most common-place everyday events. [One day I saw] a blind man begging; two girls went by without seeing him, singing: "I closed my eyes; it was marvelous!" This gave me the idea of showing on stage, as crudely and as visibly as possible, the loneliness of man, the absence of communication among human beings.[2]

Looking back at his earliest effort (which he now regards as unsuccessful) Adamov defines his basic idea in it, and a number of subsequent plays, as the idea "that the destinies of all human beings are of equal futility, that the refusal to live (of the character called N.) and the joyful acceptance of life (by the employee) both lead, by the same path, to inevitable failure, total destruction." [3] It is the same futility and pointlessness of human effort, the same impossibility of human communication which Ionesco expresses in ever new and ingenious variations. The two old people making conversation with the empty air and living in the expectation of an orator who is to pronounce profound truths about life, but turns out to be deaf and dumb (*The Chairs*), are as sardonically cruel a symbol of this fundamentally tragic view of human existence as Jack (*Jack or the Submission*), who stubbornly resists the concerted urgings of his entire family to subscribe to the most sacred principle of his clan—which, when his resistance finally yields to their entreaties, turns out to be the profound truth: "I love potatoes with bacon" ("J'adore les pommes de terre au lard").

The Theatre of the Absurd shows the world as an incomprehen-

---

[1] Ionesco, "Dans les Armes de la Ville," *Cahiers de la Compagnie Madeleine Renaud-Jean-Louis Barrault,* No. 20 (October, 1957).
[2] Adamov, "Note Préliminaire," *Théâtre II,* Paris, 1955.
[3] *Ibid.*

sible place. The spectators see the happenings on the stage entirely
from the outside, without ever understanding the full meaning of
these strange patterns of events, as newly arrived visitors might watch
life in a country of which they have not yet mastered the language.[4]
The confrontation of the audience with characters and happenings
which they are not quite able to comprehend makes it impossible for
them to share the aspirations and emotions depicted in the play.
Brecht's famous "Verfremdungseffekt" (alienation effect), the inhibi-
tion of any identification between spectator and actor, which Brecht
could never successfully achieve in his own highly rational theatre,
really comes into its own in the Theatre of the Absurd. It is impossible
to identify oneself with characters one does not understand or whose
motives remain a closed book, and so the distance between the public
and the happenings on the stage can be maintained. Emotional identification with the characters is replaced by a puzzled, critical attention. For while the happenings on the stage are absurd, they yet
remain recognizable as somehow related to real life with *its* absurdity,
so that eventually the spectators are brought face to face with the
irrational side of their existence. Thus, the absurd and fantastic
goings-on of the Theatre of the Absurd will, in the end, be found to
reveal the irrationality of the human condition and the illusion of
what we thought was its apparent logical structure.

If the dialogue in these plays consists of meaningless clichés and
the mechanical, circular repetition of stereotyped phrases—how many
meaningless clichés and stereotyped phrases do we use in our day-
to-day conversation? If the characters change their personality halfway
through the action, how consistent and truly integrated are the people
we meet in our real life? And if people in these plays appear as mere
marionettes, helpless puppets without any will of their own, passively
at the mercy of blind fate and meaningless circumstance, do we, in
fact, in our overorganized world, still possess any genuine initiative or
power to decide our own destiny? The spectators of the Theatre of the
Absurd are thus confronted with a grotesquely heightened picture of
their own world: a world without faith, meaning, and genuine freedom
of will. In this sense, the Theatre of the Absurd is the true theatre of
our time.

The theatre of most previous epochs reflected an accepted moral
order, a world whose aims and objectives were clearly present to the
minds of all its public, whether it was the audience of the medieval

[4] It may be significant that the three writers concerned, although they now all live in
France and write in French have all come to live there from outside and must have
experienced a period of adjustment to the country and its language. Samuel Beckett
(b. 1906) came from Ireland; Arthur Adamov (b. 1908) from Russia, and Eugène
Ionesco (b. 1912) from Rumania.

mystery plays with their solidly accepted faith in the Christian world order or the audience of the drama of Ibsen, Shaw, or Hauptmann with their unquestioned belief in evolution and progress. To such audiences, right and wrong were never in doubt, nor did they question the then accepted goals of human endeavor. Our own time, at least in the Western world, wholly lacks such a generally accepted and completely integrated world picture. The decline of religious faith, the destruction of the belief in automatic social and biological progress, the discovery of vast areas of irrational and unconscious forces within the human psyche, the loss of a sense of control over rational human development in an age of totalitarianism and weapons of mass destruction, have all contributed to the erosion of the basis for a dramatic convention in which the action proceeds within a fixed and self-evident framework of generally accepted values. Faced with the vacuum left by the destruction of a universally accepted and unified set of beliefs, most serious playwrights have felt the need to fit their work into the frame of values and objectives expressed in one of the contemporary ideologies: Marxism, psychoanalysis, aestheticism, or nature worship. But these, in the eyes of a writer like Adamov, are nothing but superficial rationalizations which try to hide the depth of man's predicament, his loneliness and his anxiety. Or, as Ionesco puts it:

> As far as I am concerned, I believe sincerely in the poverty of the poor, I deplore it; it is real; it can become a subject for the theatre; I also believe in the anxieties and serious troubles the rich may suffer from; but it is neither in the misery of the former nor in the melancholia of the latter, that I, for one, find my dramatic subject matter. Theatre is for me the outward projection onto the stage of an inner world; it is in my dreams, in my anxieties, in my obscure desires, in my internal contradictions that I, for one, reserve for myself the right of finding my dramatic subject matter. As I am not alone in the world, as each of us, in the depth of his being, is at the same time part and parcel of all others, my dreams, my desires, my anxieties, my obsessions do not belong to me alone. They form part of an ancestral heritage, a very ancient storehouse which is a portion of the common property of all mankind. It is this, which, transcending their outward diversity, reunites all human beings and constitutes our profound common patrimony, the universal language. . . .[5]

In other words, the commonly acceptable framework of beliefs and values of former epochs which has now been shattered is to be replaced by the community of dreams and desires of a collective unconscious. And, to quote Ionesco again:

[5] Ionesco, "L'Impromptu de l'Alma," *Théâtre II*, Paris, 1958.

. . . the new dramatist is one . . . who tries to link up with what is most ancient: new language and subject matter in a dramatic structure which aims at being clearer, more stripped of inessentials and more purely theatrical; the rejection of traditionalism to rediscover tradition; a synthesis of knowledge and invention, of the real and imaginary, of the particular and the universal, or as they say now, of the individual and the collective . . . By expressing my deepest obsessions, I express my deepest humanity. I become one with all others, spontaneously, over and above all the barriers of caste and different psychologies. I express my solitude and become one with all other solitudes. . . .[6]

What is the tradition with which the Theatre of the Absurd— at first sight the most revolutionary and radically new movement—is trying to link itself? It is in fact a very ancient and a very rich tradition, nourished from many and varied sources: the verbal exuberance and extravagant inventions of Rabelais, the age-old clowning of the Roman mimes and the Italian *Commedia dell'Arte,* the knock-about humor of circus clowns like Grock; the wild, archetypal symbolism of English nonsense verse, the baroque horror of Jacobean dramatists like Webster or Tourneur, the harsh, incisive and often brutal tones of the German drama of Grabbe, Büchner, Kleist, and Wedekind with its delirious language and grotesque inventiveness; and the Nordic paranoia of the dreams and persecution fantasies of Strindberg.

All these streams, however, first came together and crystallized in the more direct ancestors of the present Theatre of the Absurd. Of these, undoubtedly the first and foremost is Alfred Jarry (1873–1907), the creator of *Ubu Roi,* the first play which clearly belongs in the category of the Theatre of the Absurd. *Ubu Roi,* first performed in Paris on December 10, 1896, is a Rabelaisian nonsense drama about the fantastic adventures of a fat, cowardly, and brutal figure, *le père* Ubu, who makes himself King of Poland, fights a series of Falstaffian battles, and is finally routed. As if to challenge all accepted codes of propriety and thus to open a new era of irreverence, the play opens with the defiant expletive, "*Merdre!*" which immediately provoked a scandal. This, of course, was what Jarry had intended. *Ubu,* in its rollicking Rabelaisian parody of a Shakespearean history play, was meant to confront the Parisian bourgeois with a monstrous portrait of his own greed, selfishness, and philistinism: "As the curtain went up I wanted to confront the public with a theatre in which, as in the magic mirror . . . of the fairy tales . . . the vicious man sees his reflection with bulls' horns and the body of a dragon, the projections

[6] Ionesco, "The Avant-Garde Theatre," *World Theatre,* VIII, No. 3 (Autumn, 1959).

of his viciousness. . . ." [7] But Ubu is more than a mere monstrous exaggeration of the selfishness and crude sensuality of the French bourgeois. He is at the same time the personification of the grossness of human nature, an enormous belly walking on two legs. That is why Jarry put him on the stage as a monstrous potbellied figure in a highly stylized costume and mask—a mythical, archetypal externalization of human instincts of the lowest kind. Thus, Ubu, the false king of Poland, pretended doctor of the pseudoscience of Pataphysics, clearly anticipates one of the main characteristics of the Theatre of the Absurd, its tendency to externalize and project outwards what is happening in the deeper recesses of the mind. Examples of this tendency are: the disembodied voices of "monitors" shouting commands at the hero of Adamov's *La Grande et la Petite Manoeuvre* which concretizes his neurotic compulsions; the mutilated trunks of the parents in Beckett's *Endgame* emerging from ashcans—the ashcans of the main character's subconscious to which he has banished his past and his conscience; or the proliferations of fungi that invade the married couple's apartment in Ionesco's *Amédée* and express the rottenness and decay of their relationship. All these psychological factors are not only projected outwards, they are also, as in Jarry's *Ubu Roi*, grotesquely magnified and exaggerated. This scornful rejection of all subtleties is a reaction against the supposed *finesse* of the psychology of the naturalistic theatre in which everything was to be inferred between the lines. The Theatre of the Absurd, from Jarry onwards, stands for explicitness as against implicit psychology, and in this resembles the highly explicit theatre of the Expressionists or the political theatre of Piscator or Brecht.

To be larger and more real than life was also the aim of Guillaume Apollinaire (1880–1918), the great poet who was one of the seminal forces in the rise of Cubism and who had close personal and artistic links with Jarry. If Apollinaire labeled his play *Les Mamelles de Tiresias* a *"drame surrealiste,"* he did not intend that term, of which he was one of the earliest users, in the sense in which it later became famous. He wanted it to describe a play in which everything was *larger than life,* for he believed in an art which was to be "modern, simple, rapid, with the shortcuts and enlargements that are needed to shock the spectator." [8] In the prologue to *Les Mamelles de Tiresias,* a grotesque pamphlet purportedly advocating an immense rise in the French birthrate, Apollinaire makes the Director of the Company of Actors who perform the play, define his ideas:

[7] Jarry, "Questions de Théâtre," in *Ubu Roi, Ubu Enchaîné,* and other Ubuesque writings. Ed. Rene Massat, Lausanne, 1948.
[8] Apollinaire, *Les Mamelles de Tiresias,* Preface.

For the theatre should not be an imitation of reality
It is right that the dramatist should use
All the illusions at his disposal . . .
It is right that he should let crowds speak, or inanimate objects
If he so pleases
And that he no longer has to reckon
With time and space
His universe is the play
Within which he is God the Creator
Who disposes at will
Of sounds gestures movements masses colors
Not merely in order
To photograph what is called a slice of life
But to bring forth life itself and all its truth . . .

Accordingly, in *Les Mamelles de Tiresias* the whole population of Zanzibar, where the scene is laid, is represented by a single actor; and the heroine, Thérèse, changes herself into a man by letting her breasts float upwards like a pair of toy balloons. Although *Les Mamelles de Tiresias* was not a surrealist work in the strictest sense of the term, it clearly foreshadowed the ideas of the movement led by André Breton. Surrealism in that narrower, technical sense found little expression in the theatre. But Antonin Artaud (1896–1948), another major influence in the development of the Theatre of the Absurd, did at one time belong to the Surrealist group, although his main activity in the theatre took place after he had broken with Breton. Artaud was one of the most unhappy men of genius of his age, an artist consumed by the most intense passions; poet, actor, director, designer, immensely fertile and original in his inventions and ideas, yet always living on the borders of sanity and never able to realize his ambitions, plans, and projects.

Artaud, who had been an actor in Charles Dullin's company at the Atelier, began his venture into the realm of experimental theatre in a series of productions characteristically sailing under the label *Théâtre Alfred Jarry* (1927–29). But his theories of a new and revolutionary theatre only crystallized after he had been deeply stirred by a performance of Balinese dancers at the Colonial Exhibition of 1931. He formulated his ideas in a series of impassioned manifestoes later collected in the volume *The Theatre and Its Double* (1938), which continues to exercise an important influence on the contemporary French theatre. Artaud named the theatre of his dreams *Théâtre de la Cruauté*, a theatre of cruelty, which he said, "means a theatre difficult and cruel above all for myself." "Everything that is really active is cruelty. It is around this idea of action carried to the extreme that the theatre must renew itself." Here too the idea of action larger and more real than life is the dominant theme. "Every performance will contain a physical and objective element that will be felt by all. Cries, Wails, Apparitions, Surprises, *Coups de Théâtre* of all kinds, the magical beauty of costumes inspired by the model of certain rituals. . . ." The language of the drama must also undergo a change: "It is not a matter of suppressing articulate speech but of giving to the words something like the importance they have in dreams." In Artaud's new theatre "not only the obverse side of man will appear but also the reverse side of the coin: the reality of imagination and of dreams will here be seen on an equal footing with everyday life."

Artaud's only attempt at putting these theories to the test on the stage took place on May 6, 1935 at the Folies-Wagram. Artaud had made his own adaptation ("after Shelley and Stendhal") of the story of the Cenci, that sombre Renaissance story of incest and patricide. It was in many ways a beautiful and memorable performance, but full of imperfections and a financial disaster which marked the beginning of Artaud's eventual descent into despair, insanity, and abject poverty. Jean-Louis Barrault had some small part in this venture and Roger Blin, the actor and director who later played an important part in bringing Adamov, Beckett, and Ionesco to the stage, appeared in the small role of one of the hired assassins.

Jean-Louis Barrault, one of the most creative figures in the theatre of our time, was in turn, responsible for another venture which played an important part in the development of the Theatre of the Absurd. He staged André Gide's adaptation of Franz Kafka's novel, *The Trial,* in 1947 and played the part of the hero K. himself. Undoubtedly this performance which brought the dreamworld of Kafka to a triumphant unfolding on the stage and demonstrated the effectiveness of this particular brand of fantasy in practical theatrical terms exercised a profound influence on the practitioners of the new movement. For here, too, they saw the externalization of mental processes, the acting out of nightmarish dreams by schematized figures in a world of torment and absurdity.

The dream element in the Theatre of the Absurd can also be traced, in the case of Adamov, to Strindberg, acknowledged by him as his inspiration at the time when he began to think of writing for the theatre. This is the Strindberg of *The Ghost Sonata, The Dream Play* and of *To Damascus.* (Adamov is the author of an excellent brief monograph on Strindberg.)

But if Jarry, Artaud, Kafka, and Strindberg can be regarded as the decisive influences in the development of the Theatre of the Absurd, there is another giant of European literature that must not be omitted from the list—James Joyce, for whom Beckett at one time is supposed to have acted as helper and secretary. Not only is the Nightgown episode of *Ulysses* one of the earliest examples of the Theatre of the Absurd—with its exuberant mingling of the real and the nightmarish, its wild fantasies and externalizations of subconscious yearnings and fears, but Joyce's experimentation with language, his attempt to smash the limitations of conventional vocabulary and syntax has probably exercised an even more powerful impact on all the writers concerned.

It is in its attitude to language that the Theatre of the Absurd is most revolutionary. It deliberately attempts to renew the language of drama and to expose the barrenness of conventional stage dialogue. Ionesco once described how he came to write his first play. (Cf. his "The Tragedy of Language," *TDR*, Spring, 1960.) He had decided to take English lessons and began to study at the Berlitz school. When he read and repeated the sentences in his phrase book, those petrified corpses of once living speech, he was suddenly overcome by their tragic quality. From them he composed his first play, *The Bald Soprano*. The absurdity of its dialogue and its fantastic quality springs directly from its basic ordinariness. It exposes the emptiness of stereotyped language; "what is sometimes labeled the absurd," Ionesco says, "is only the denunciation of the ridiculous nature of a language which is empty of substance, made up of clichés and slogans. . . ." [9] Such a language has atrophied; it has ceased to be the expression of anything alive or vital and has been degraded into a mere conventional token of human intercourse, a mask for genuine meaning and emotion. That is why so often in the Theatre of the Absurd the dialogue becomes divorced from the real happenings in the play and is even put into direct contradiction with the action. The Professor and the Pupil in Ionesco's *The Lesson* "seem" to be going through a repetition of conventional school book phrases, but behind this smoke screen of language the *real* action of the play pursues an entirely different course with the Professor, vampire-like, draining the vitality from the young girl up to the final moment when he plunges his knife into her body. In Beckett's *Waiting for Godot* Lucky's much vaunted philosophical wisdom is revealed to be a flood of completely meaningless gibberish that vaguely resembles the language of philosophical argument. And in Adamov's remarkable play, *Ping-Pong*, a good deal of the dramatic power lies in the contrapuntal contrast between the triviality of the theme—the improvement of pinball machines—and the almost religious fervor with which it is discussed. Here, in order to bring out the full meaning of the play, the actors have to act

[9] Ionesco, "The Avant-Garde Theatre."

against the dialogue rather than with it, the fervor of the delivery must stand in a dialectical contrast to the pointlessness of the meaning of the lines. In the same way, the author implies that most of the fervent and passionate discussion of real life (of political controversy, to give but one example) also turns around empty and meaningless clichés. Or, as Ionesco says in an essay on Antonin Artaud:

> As our knowledge becomes increasingly divorced from real life, our culture no longer contains ourselves (or only contains an insignificant part of ourselves) and forms a "social" context in which we are not integrated. The problem thus becomes that of again reconciling our culture with our life by making our culture a living culture once more. But to achieve this end we shall first have to kill the "respect for that which is written" . . . it becomes necessary to break up our language so that it may become possible to put it together again and to reëstablish contact with the absolute, or as I should prefer to call it, with multiple reality.[10]

This quest for the multiple reality of the world which is real *because* it exists on many planes simultaneously and is more than a mere unidirectional abstraction is not only in itself a search for a reëstablished *poetical* reality (poetry in its essence expressing reality in its ambiguity and multidimensional depth); it is also in close accord with important movements of our age in what appear to be entirely different fields: psychology and philosophy. The dissolution, devaluation, and relativization of language is, after all, also the theme of much of present-day depth-psychology, which has shown what in former times was regarded as a rational expression of logically arrived at conclusions to be the mere rationalization of subconscious emotional impulses. Not everything we say means what we intend it to mean. And likewise, in present-day Logical Positivism a large proportion of all statements is regarded as devoid of conceptual meaning and merely emotive. A philosopher like Ludwig Wittgenstein, in his later phases, even tried to break through what he regarded as the opacity, the misleading nature of language and grammar; for if all our thinking is in terms of language, and language obeys what after all are the arbitrary conventions of grammar, we must strive to penetrate to the real content of thought that is masked by grammatical rules and conventions. Here, too, then is a matter of getting behind the surface of linguistic clichés and of finding reality through the break-up of language.

In the Theatre of the Absurd, therefore, the real content of the play lies in the action. Language may be discarded altogether, as in

[10] Ionesco, "Ni un Dieu, ni un Demon," *Cahiers de la Compagnie Madeleine Renaud-Jean-Louis Barrault,* No. 22–23 (May, 1958).

Beckett's *Act Without Words* or in Ionesco's *The New Tenant,* in which the whole sense of the play is contained in the incessant arrival of more and more furniture so that the occupant of the room is, in the end, literally drowned in it. Here the movement of objects alone carries the dramatic action, the language has become purely incidental, less important than the contribution of the property department. In this, the Theatre of the Absurd also reveals its anti-literary character, its endeavor to link up with the pre-literary strata of stage history: the circus, the performances of itinerant jugglers and mountebanks, the music hall, fairground barkers, acrobats, and also the robust world of the silent film. Ionesco, in particular, clearly owes a great deal to Chaplin, Buster Keaton, the Keystone Cops, Laurel and Hardy, and the Marx Brothers. And it is surely significant that so much of successful popular entertainment in our age shows affinities with the subject matter and preoccupation of the avant-garde Theatre of the Absurd. A sophisticated, but nevertheless highly popular, film comedian like Jacques Tati uses dialogue merely as a barely comprehensible babble of noises, and also dwells on the loneliness of man in our age, the horror of overmechanization and overorganization gone mad. Danny Kaye excels in streams of gibberish closely akin to Lucky's oration in *Waiting for Godot.* The brilliant and greatly liked team of British radio (and occasionally television) comedians, the Goons, have a sense of the absurd that resembles Kafka's or Ionesco's and a team of grotesque singers like "Les Frères Jacques" seems more closely in line with the Theatre of the Absurd than with the conventional cabaret.

Yet the defiant rejection of language as the main vehicle of the dramatic action, the onslaught on conventional logic and unilinear conceptual thinking in the Theatre of the Absurd is by no means equivalent to a total rejection of all meaning. On the contrary, it constitutes an earnest endeavor to penetrate to deeper layers of meaning and to give a truer, because more complex, picture of reality in avoiding the simplification which results from leaving out all the undertones, overtones, and inherent absurdities and contradictions of any human situation. In the conventional drama every word means what it says, the situations are clearcut, and at the end all conflicts are tidily resolved. But reality, as Ionesco points out in the passage we have quoted, is never like that; it is multiple, complex, many-dimensional and exists on a number of different levels at one and the same time. Language is far too straightforward an instrument to express all this by itself. Reality can only be conveyed by being *acted out* in all its complexity. Hence, it is the theatre, which is multidimensional and more than merely language or literature, which is the only instrument to express the bewildering complexity of the human condition. The human condition being what it is, with man small, helpless, insecure, and unable ever to fathom the world in all its hopelessness, death, and absurdity, the theatre has to confront him with the bitter truth that most human endeavor is irrational and senseless, that communication between human beings is well-nigh impossible, and that the world will forever remain an impenetrable mystery. At the same time, the recognition of all these bitter truths will have a liberating effect: if we realize the basic absurdity of most of our objectives we are freed from being obsessed with them and this release expresses itself in laughter.

Moreover, while the world is being shown as complex, harsh, and absurd and as difficult to interpret as reality itself, the audience is yet spurred on to attempt their own interpretation, to wonder what it is all about. In that sense they are being invited to school their critical faculties, to train themselves in adjusting to reality. As the world is being represented as highly complex and devoid of a clear-cut purpose or design, there will always be an infinite number of possible interpretations. As Apollinaire points out in his Preface to *Les Mamelles de Tiresias:* "None of the symbols in my play is very clear, but one is at liberty to see in it all the symbols one desires and to find in it a thousand senses—as in the Sybilline oracles." Thus, it may be that the pinball machines in Adamov's *Ping-Pong* and the ideology which is developed around them stand for the futility of political or religious ideologies that are pursued with equal fervor and equal futility in the final result. Others have interpreted the play as a parable on the greed and sordidness of the profit motive. Others again may give it quite different meanings. The mysterious transformation of human beings into rhinos in Ionesco's latest play, *The Rhinoceros,* was felt by the audience of its world premier at Duesseldorf (November 6, 1959) to depict the transformation of human beings into Nazis. It is known that Ionesco himself intended the play to express his feelings at the time when more and more of his friends in Rumania joined the Fascist Iron Guard and, in effect, left the ranks of thin-skinned humans to turn themselves into moral pachyderms. But to spectators less intimately aware of the moral climate of such a situation than the German audience, other interpretations might impose themselves: if the hero, Bérenger, is at the end left alone as the only human being in his native town, now entirely inhabited by rhinos, they might regard this as a poetic symbol of the gradual isolation of man growing old and imprisoned in the strait jacket of his own habits and memories. Does Godot, so fervently and vainly awaited by Vladimir and Estragon, stand for God? Or does he merely represent the ever elusive tomorrow, man's hope that one day something will happen that will render his existence meaningful? The force and poetic power of the play lie precisely in the impossibility of ever reaching a conclusive answer this question.

Here we touch the essential point of difference between the conventional theatre and the Theatre of the Absurd. The former, based as it is on a known framework of accepted values and a rational view of life, always starts out by indicating a fixed objective towards which the action will be moving or by posing a definite problem to which it will supply an answer. Will Hamlet revenge the murder of his father? Will Iago succeed in destroying Othello? Will Nora leave her husband? In the conventional theatre the action always proceeds towards a definable end. The spectators do not know whether that end will be reached and how it will be reached. Hence, they are in suspense, eager to find out *what* will happen. In the Theatre of the Absurd, on the other hand, the action does not proceed in the manner of a logical syllogism. It does not go from A to B but travels from an unknown premise X towards an unknowable conclusion Y. The spectators, not knowing what their author is driving at, cannot be in suspense as to how or whether an expected objective is going to be reached. They are not, therefore, so much in suspense as to *what* is going to happen *next* (although the most unexpected and unpredictable things do happen) as they are in suspense about what the next event to take place will add to their understanding of *what is happening*. The action supplies an increasing number of contradictory and bewildering clues on a number of different levels, but the final question is never wholly answered. Thus, instead of being in suspense as to what will happen next, the spectators are, in the Theatre of the Absurd, put into suspense as to *what* the play *may mean*. This suspense continues even after the curtain has come down. Here again the Theatre of the Absurd fulfills Brecht's postulate of a critical, detached audience, who will have to sharpen their wits on the play and be stimulated by it to think for themselves, far more effectively than Brecht's own theatre. Not only are the members of the audience unable to identify with the characters, they are compelled to puzzle out the meaning of what they have seen. Each of them will probably find his own, personal meaning, which will differ from the solution found by most others. But he will have been forced to make a mental effort and to evaluate an experience he has undergone. In this sense, the Theatre of the Absurd is the most demanding, the most intellectual theatre. It may be riotously funny, wildly exaggerated and oversimplified, vulgar and garish, but it will always confront the spectator with a genuine intellectual problem, a philosophical paradox, which he will have to try to solve even if he knows that it is most probably insoluble.

In this respect, the Theatre of the Absurd links up with an older tradition which has almost completely disappeared from Western culture: the tradition of allegory and the symbolical representation of abstract concepts personified by characters whose costumes and accoutrements subtly suggested whether they represented Time, Chastity, Winter, Fortune, the World, etc. This is the tradition which stretches from the Italian *Trionfo* of the Renaissance to the English Masque, the elaborate allegorical constructions of the Spanish *Auto sacramental* down to Goethe's allegorical processions and masques written for the court of Weimar at the turn of the eighteenth century. Although the living riddles the characters represented in these entertainments were by no means difficult to solve, as everyone knew that a character with a scythe and an hourglass represented Time, and although the characters soon revealed their identity and explained their attributes, there was an element of intellectual challenge which stimulated the audience in the moments between the appearance of the riddle and its solution and which provided them with the pleasure of having solved a puzzle. And what is more, in the elaborate allegorical dramas like Calderón's *El Gran Teatro del Mundo* the subtle interplay of allegorical characters itself presented the audience with a great deal to think out for themselves. They had, as it were, to translate the abstractly presented action into terms of their everyday experience; they could ponder on the deeper meaning of such facts as death having taken the characters representing Riches or Poverty in a Dance of Death equally quickly and equally harshly, or that Mammon had deserted his master Everyman in the hour of death. The dramatic riddles of our time present no such clear-cut solutions. All they can show is that while the solutions have evaporated the riddle of our existence remains—complex, unfathomable, and paradoxical.

ward hooker

IRONY AND ABSURDITY IN
THE AVANT-GARDE THEATRE

IN TRAGIC plays, dramatic irony manifests itself in plausible speeches
—innocent questions about lost handkerchieves, informative hints
about pierced ankles. In comedy, on the other hand, dramatic irony
often manifests itself in the absurd. France has always been considered
the very home of *double entendre,* and in recent years absurdity has
become a marked feature of the French stage. It is conceivable, then,
that the study of the few typical samples of absurdity from modern
French comedy in ironic vein might throw light on that perennial
puzzle, Samuel Beckett's "tragi-comedy" *Waiting for Godot.*

Dramatic irony is usually defined as speech or action which is
more fully understood, or differently understood by the audience
than by the speaker. Sometimes the audience apprehends the irony
directly, as for instance when Shakespeare presents Malvolio reading
his "love letter" in *Twelfth Night;* sometimes there is a contrasting
character, supposedly more discerning, to "draw out" the ironic
speeches, as Prince Hal does with Falstaff or Touchstone with Audrey
and William. The difference in understanding may be slight or subtle,
as in a play like *The Cocktail Party;* it may be great, as in *The School
for Wives;* if it is great enough, the resulting phenomenon may be
called "absurdity." This term, for the ordinary playgoer, may be taken
to mean the extremely incongruous, inadequate, or irrelevant. And our
concern is with the playgoer, particularly with his emotional and
intellectual participation in the irony of the passages to be examined.

MAITRE BLAISE: Well, my girl, how do I stand with Angélique?

LISETTE: Just where you stood before.

MAITRE BLAISE, *laughing:* Why, then, so much the worse?

LISETTE: Aren't you going to tell me what you mean by laughing
when you say "so much the worse"?

MAITRE BLAISE: Oh, I laugh at everything, ducky.

LISETTE: Anyway, . . . as things stand, if you keep on courting
her, apparently you will win her.

From *The Kenyon Review,* Vol. XXII. Reprinted by permission.

MAÎTRE BLAISE, *sadly:* Do you think so? Well, so much the better.

LISETTE: Oh, you provoke me with your sad "so much the betters" and your cheerful "so much the worses." . . .

Marivaux, *L'Epreuve*

However puzzled Lisette may have been at the absurdities of Maître Blaise's behavior, Marivaux's audience understood them very well, having witnessed a scene in which Lucidor, the proper *amant*, promised Maître Blaise twelve thousand pounds if Blaise sued for the hand of Angélique and was rejected. It was an audience well accustomed to the intricacies of Marivaux's plots. No doubt Maître Blaise's "tant pire" was accompanied by just such an oafish giggle as may be heard when Jean-Louis Le Goff takes the part nowadays at the *Comédie française.* One might suppose that a giggle would be enough to call attention to the absurdity, but notice that Marivaux provided Lisette with *two* indignant protests. Did he do this just in case some complete clod had strayed into his audience (a most unlikely *contretemps*)? More probably Marivaux was following the practice of Molière, which seems to be based on a theory that the enjoyment of irony increases with the *continued* mystification of its victim on the stage. At any rate, Marivaux's audience could hardly have been burdened or dismayed by the intellectual demands made upon it in that scene.

> *Enter the Life-Saver of the Alma bridge carrying a body.*
>
> THE PROSPECTOR: It's Pierre! What has happened? . . . You, there, what are you carrying?
>
> THE LIFE-SAVER: A drowned man. My first drowned man. I'm the new life-saver of the Alma bridge.
>
> MARTIAL: He looks more as though he'd been slugged. His clothes are dry.
>
> THE LIFE-SAVER: Slugged is also correct. . . . I slugged him so that he wouldn't struggle. Our instructions are very specific: Stun the drowned man so that he cannot drag you under water.
>
> MARTIAL: But since he was on dry land. . . .
>
> THE PROSPECTOR: The young idiot is going to expose us! . . . (*The Life-saver breathes into the young man's mouth, and applies artificial respiration. The Prospector approaches*) What are you doing to him?
>
> THE LIFE-SAVER: I am exercising his thorax. I am forcing my breath into his pharynx. First-aid to the drowned. . . .
>
> THE PROSPECTOR: But he isn't drowned.
>
> THE LIFE-SAVER: He thinks he's drowned.
>
> THE PROSPECTOR: He thinks he's drowned. But he is drowned on land. Your first-aid for those drowned in water won't do anything for him.

THE BARON: Bravo, Prospector! I understand. . . .

THE LIFE-SAVER: But how can I make my first-aid work, then?

THE PROSPECTOR: Throw him back in the Seine. Wait until he is really drowned. Then it will work.

THE LIFE-SAVER: Why, yes. That's logical.

Giraudoux, *The Madwoman of Chaillot*

Logical indeed, but by a strictly Giralducian logic which allows the dialogue to ramble on to the topics of intra-uterine activity and bee-keeping, before settling down to its main business.

Marivaux's irony depended on memory of plot and also furthered his plot. If it yielded any such by-products as character sketches, they required little more than recognition of established comic types, the mercenary farmer (Blaise) and the husband-huntress (Lisette). Giraudoux's irony is a great deal richer in by-products and less contributory to plot. True, we can understand that the dramatist is ironically prolonging the anxiety of the Prospector and his cohorts to get rid of the would-be suicide, whom they had hired to commit a crime. We shall also be able to see in retrospect that the scene had a definite function, in giving Countess Aurélie, *la folle de Chaillot*, occasion to convince the *"noyé de terre"* (and the audience) that life is worth living. But in the meantime, what are we to make of these absurd people onstage? They are not characters, not types, not even *caractères;* they are Giralducian "absolutes," impressionistic sketches in which a human quality or condition is reduced to its quintessence. This Prospector is the human engineer who has achieved the ultimate efficiency rating, a *"mec"* or pimp at the summit level. Is the French public service hampered by well-meaning theorists who substitute logic for common sense? Giraudoux will tell us so by bringing into his play this astonishing Life-saver who has given the closest attention to his "formal instructions" but, as we shall find, has neglected to learn to swim. He will shortly be joined by a Health Officer, a man of extraordinarily useless learning, who will choose this critical moment to begin a discussion of the intra-uterine life.

In these impressionistic sketches dramatic irony reaches a very high degree of complexity and richness. There are crowded scenes in which every character is viewed ironically, every speech evaluated in several different ways. "Bravo, Prospecteur!" cries the Baron when the Prospector begins his nonsensical reasoning, "I understand." He does see a point, in his little way; but the irony does not consist merely in contrasting his "understanding" with the Life-saver's naiveté, for the audience reaction comprises many simultaneous evaluations. The audience knows that what the Baron "understands" is actually incomprehensible, absurd: perhaps the Life-saver's unwisdom has more real clarity. The audience "understands" the Prospector differently; it also doubts the possibility of any such super-exploiter, but suspects that if things go on the way they are going, one of these days he may appear. In this three-ring circus so many preposterous characters have such an authentic air of belonging exactly where they are, that we are momentarily convinced of the reality of Giraudoux's world, or at least of this corner of Paris. Essences have, in a way, more reality than photographs.

> THE CURE: . . . We must arm ourselves with patience and courage.
>
> THE GENERAL: I've never had any patience. I shall not change my nature. As for courage, I try. (*He suddenly picks up a piece of red blotting-paper from the desk and chews it, offering an end of it to the Curé*) Do you want a bit?
>
> THE CURE, *bewildered:* A bit of what? Is that something to be eaten?
>
> THE GENERAL *bursts out laughing at the sight of the Curé, who is looking mistrustfully at his piece of blotting-paper:* Yes, M. le Curé. But it's just the same as with the Almighty, you have to have faith! (*He cries out, facetiously but in some confusion*) Oh, what a rotten taste this one has! But that doesn't hinder its effect on the spirit, does it!
>
> *Suddenly he embraces the Curé. Aunt Bise enters in a great hurry, but stops at the door crying, 'Ludovic!'*
>
> THE GENERAL, *startled in spite of himself:* What do you mean, 'Ludovic!' It's Monsieur le Curé! (*turning to him*) I must tell you, the last time, my sister surprised me in the act of embracing the maid. (*He corrects himself*) With only the most honorable intentions. Otherwise, I wouldn't have told you, Monsieur le Curé! The girl had just told me that she was expecting a child. (*He stops and tries again*) A child of the mailman, of course. What's more, the proof has come out, thank God! the child resembles him. He has already developed a red nose. . . .
>
> Anouilh, L'Hurluberlu

Anouilh's use of absurdity in characterization seems at first glance much like Giraudoux's. We may recognize in this central character, the scatter-brained general, another haunting survivor of the old regime, at odds with the modern world, another *folle de Chaillot*. His mysterious blotting-paper which gives courage to anyone who eats it reminds one somewhat of the Countess's basket of bones; and the monologue begun in this excerpt rambles on in Giralducian style to such assorted topics as first names, the religious fervor of the P.T.T., and the superiority of old bicycles to new ones.[1]

But closer study of the two dramatists will reveal great differences in both method and purpose. Consider for a moment, as an illustration of Anouilh's technique, the General's blotting-paper. An absurd whim, no doubt, but it is also an excellent symbol for the obscure well-spring of courage, to tell us that courage has to be made out of nothing, or of some trivial commodity one might find around the house. In the long run, perhaps, a more valid symbol than Cyrano's white plume, and it is especially good because the General has given it a name, *mininistafia*, which is Anouilh's way of signifying that every man has to find his own private source of courage. We should, therefore, recognize irony in the exposure of the General's mistakenness when he offers his *mininistafia* to the Curé; but perhaps we only recognize the General's quixotic nature. Continuing the monologue, the General equates his blotting-paper with the Curé's religious faith, laughs at his mystification, but then finds it so touching that he *must* embrace the Curé, with embarrassing results which he does not, however, allow to embarrass him. By the time Anouilh has completed the development of this absurd symbol, the more alert members of the audience will have learned a great deal about a complex human being.

The purpose served by Anouilh's irony is character revelation, the same goal which Ibsen pursued (though without absurdity or comic effect) in *Hedda Gabler;* and this is quite different from the purpose of *The Madwoman of Chaillot.* Giraudoux was a Platonist, with an uncanny ability to persuade us of the superior reality of his ideals and essences. Anouilh is an Aristotelian, intent on studying the world as it is, and his sketch of the General has the completeness and penetration which are necessary in psychological analysis. Like other realists he comes to a bitter conclusion about the world as it is, even though he had started his sketch in a gayer mood. For *L'Hurluberlu* follows the tradition of the earlier Anouilh plays by turning sour, not with the acrid sourness of *The Rehearsal,* but with the sad-autumnal sourness of *The Waltz of the Toreadors.* The resemblance between the General and Giraudoux's Countess Aurélie as disoriented "survivors of the old régime" disappears, for whereas the mad Countess triumphed over the modern world, the General only became more and more ill at ease.

[1] My example of Anouilh's work is chronologically out of order with the two examples which follow it. *Time Remembered* or *Thieves' Carnival* would have furnished excellent examples, but I thought a comment on Anouilh's current play might be of interest, and his style and dramatic construction have not changed greatly.

MR. SMITH: . . . Poor Bobby, he had been dead for four years and he was still warm. A veritable living corpse. And how gay he was!

MRS. SMITH: Poor Mrs. Bobby.

MR. SMITH: You mean poor Bobby.

MRS. SMITH: No, it is his wife I am thinking of. She too was named Bobby, Bobby Watson. Since they both had the same name, they could never be distinguished from each other when they were seen together. It was only after his death that one could really tell which was which. Even so, there are still people today who have her mixed up with the deceased and offer condolences to him. Do you know her?

MR. SMITH: I have met her only once, by chance, at Bobby's funeral.

MRS. SMITH: I have never seen her. Is she pretty?

MR. SMITH: She has regular features, but yet it can't be said that she is pretty. She is too tall and heavy. Her features are not regular, but yet one may say that she is very pretty. She is a bit too short and too thin. . . .

Ionesco, *The Bald Soprano*

With Ionesco we enter a grey realm of intellectual abstraction in which neither plot nor characterization will provide a key to the ironic dialogue. What is said here does not gain point from what has been said before; likewise there is no need to remember from this passage what the Watsons were like, since neither they nor their numerous relatives (all named Bobby Watson) will appear before us. Nor, for that matter, will any bald sopranos. An indication of what to expect of the plot is given by the subtitle *"anti-drame"*: the play mirrors life which is not dramatic but repetitious and inconsequential. We are given the impression that the play could start at either end, the scenes could be arranged in any order; time is marked by an extremely erratic clock which on one occasion strikes 29 times, and there are often silences when it seems to stand still.

As to characterization, we can hardly miss the point of the dialogue quoted above, that in the Watson household characters were indistinguishable. If M. Watson proved to be the same dead as alive, it will be useless to entertain better hopes for Madame, with her medium build and *mas o menos* features. Before long another couple, the Martins, will appear to give us a similar demonstration of what life in a bourgeois ménage is like, with an additional suggestion that married couples are the same asleep as awake. Our present speakers, M. and Mme. Smith, are indistinguishable in this passage; and elsewhere in the play they deviate only far enough to show that it takes two to make a quarrel, not far enough to establish a difference between masculinity and femininity. There is one character of greater warmth and truer sociability, the symbolic Fireman, who seems to have been brought into this domestic treadmill to provide, by his cheerful clowning, a contrast with the pompous ineptitudes of the rest.

However bloodless, however anti-dramatic *The Bald Soprano* may be, it is still quite possible to understand the irony of its absurd dialogue. The point of reference is the *theme* of the play, which may be stated thus: bourgeois people are characterless, indistinguishable; therefore they cannot communicate with each other except in meaningless *clichés*, and their lives are tedious and unprofitable. Stemming as it does only from this intellectual idea, the ironic tone keeps the play uniformly on the level of comedy, and neither Ionesco nor his audience is disturbed by emotional reactions to the characters or to what they say.

Much has been made of Ionesco's "bitterness." Professor David Grossvogel in his recent study[2] tells us that Ionesco's "world is informed by anger. His is a noisy . . . meaninglessly frenzied . . . cruel theatre, one of physical torture." As for its tone, and theme:

> Indeed, the drama of Ionesco is monochromatic. Not only does it reflect too consistently a single one of the author's moods (and drama is poor in proportion to its refusal to exploit its many modulations), but it is poor as well in its subject matter. Choubert[3] tells the spectator that this drama will reject subject matter and plot for they have made detective stories of classical and conventional drama alike. But a completely gratuitous theatre is so difficult a notion to conceive that even enlightened readers of Ionesco . . . are tempted to see the development of a specific idea in these 'anti-plays.' Renée Saurel detects in *La Cantatrice chauve* the embryonic tragedy of the married couple, and indeed, the play expresses this idea if it has any claim at all to validity.

In his opinion the play fails to substantiate this claim, because "the probing is circumscribed, virtually nonexistent"; but why should we suppose that Ionesco made any claim to "validity" in this pure comedy? "Enlightened readers" may build such theories and make vain demands for tragic effect, but I am sure the audience at the *Huchette* will only go on laughing at the play, as it has for the past three years. It should be noted that the two most successful plays of Ionesco are also the funniest (though I must admit having noticed in several audiences a certain nervousness in the hilarity provoked by *The Lesson*), and that Ionesco's "gratuitous" theatricality may be enjoyed for its own sake. We are not called upon to believe in the characters, any more than we are in those of Gilbert and Sullivan; we are not

[2] *The Self-Conscious Stage in Modern French Drama*, N.Y., 1959.
[3] A character in Ionesco's *Victimes du devoir*.

asked to react emotionally to them, so why take them seriously? Where there is no subtlety, no intensity nor richness of suggestion in the ironic dialogue, there can be no bitterness, and even tedium can become amusing.

> POZZO: . . . (*he fumbles in his pockets*) let me wish you . . . (*fumbles*) . . . wish you . . . (*fumbles*) . . . what have I done with my watch? (*Fumbles*) A genuine half-hunter, gentlemen, with dead-beat escapement! (*Sobbing*) 'Twas my granpa gave it to me! (*He searches on the ground, Vladimir and Estragon likewise. Pozzo turns over with his foot the remains of Lucky's hat.*) Well, now isn't that just—
>
> VLADIMIR: Perhaps it's in your fob.
>
> POZZO: Wait! (*He doubles up in an attempt to apply his ear to his stomach, listens. Silence.*) I hear nothing. (*He beckons them to approach. Vladimir and Estragon go over to him, bend over his stomach.*) Surely one should hear the tick-tick.
>
> VLADIMIR: Silence! (*All listen, bent double.*)
>
> ESTRAGON: I hear something.
>
> POZZO: Where?
>
> VLADIMIR: It's the heart.
>
> POZZO: (*disappointed*) Damnation!
>
> VLADIMIR: Silence!
>
> ESTRAGON: Perhaps it has stopped. (*They straighten up.*)
>
> POZZO: Which of you smells so bad?
>
> ESTRAGON: He has stinking breath and I have stinking feet.
>
> POZZO: I must go.

Beckett, Waiting for Godot,[4] I

Coming at last to Beckett, we may find in this brief passage some of the characteristic brilliance and ambiguity of his comedy. Neither Charlot nor the music-hall ever created anything more neatly absurd than these three men bent anxiously over Pozzo's ample midriff, or Pozzo's disappointment. And the little scene echoes with ironic overtones: there is, for instance, the surprise that Pozzo *has* a heart. He has been pre-eminently the Man of Property, self-assured, condescending, cruel, unduly concerned with his valuables. We are here witnessing his gradual disintegration; he has already mislaid his pipe and vaporiser; later he will suffer the losses of his vision, his equilibrium, his sense of time (the theme is extended on into *Endgame,* where the central character exists, apparently, only to disintegrate). One is tempted to find an ironic contrast between the vulnerable man of property and the completely destitute Vladimir and Estragon. For them, the scene is a particularly endearing one; though humble and

---

[4] This and the following English translations are by Beckett himself, published in 1954 by Grove Press.

amiable as usual, they are here experiencing an almost unique moment of certainty, a rare flash of discernment—on the subject of how they smell bad. But however aware we may be of these overtones, the irony of the passage will not lead us anywhere. At the end of the play Pozzo will not be any more miserable than the two bums who are left frozen in immobility at the last curtain, so that we shall not reach any conclusion about burdensome property. Nor will the irony give us a clue to the character of Pozzo, who will continue to be inconsistent, nor real knowledge of Vladimir and Estragon, whom we shall like more and more without knowing why. Perhaps another passage may prove more illuminating.

> VLADIMIR: (*triumphantly, pointing to the boots*). There they are! (*Estragon looks at the boots.*) At the very spot where you left them yesterday! (*Estragon goes towards the boots, inspects them closely.*)
>
> ESTRAGON: They're not mine.
>
> VLADIMIR: (*Stupefied*) Not yours!
>
> ESTRAGON: Mine were black. These are brown.
>
> VLADIMIR: You're sure yours were black?
>
> ESTRAGON: Well, they were a kind of gray.
>
> VLADIMIR: And these are brown. Show.
>
> ESTRAGON: (*picking up a boot*)—Well, they're a kind of green.
>
> VLADIMIR: Show. (*Estragon hands him the boot. Vladimir inspects it, throws it down angrily.*) Well, of all the—
>
> ESTRAGON: You see, all that's a lot of bloody—
>
> VLADIMIR: Ah! I see what it is. Yes, I see what's happened.
>
> ESTRAGON: All that's a lot of bloody—
>
> VLADIMIR: It's elementary. Someone came and took yours and left you his.
>
> ESTRAGON: Why?
>
> VLADIMIR: His were too tight for him, so he took yours.
>
> ESTRAGON: But mine were too tight.
>
> VLADIMIR: For you. Not for him.
>
> ESTRAGON: (*having tried in vain to work it out*). I'm tired! (*Pause*) Let's go.
>
> VLADIMIR: We can't.
>
> ESTRAGON: Why not?
>
> VLADIMIR: We're waiting for Godot.
>
> ESTRAGON: Ah! . . .
>
> Beckett, *Waiting for Godot*, II

After taking part in the long, futile quest of Vladimir and Estragon for the right shoes, we may detect that they are not only funny but very human. These Chaplinesque characters are totally different from Ionesco's wooden figures, totally lacking in the fatuousness which made the Smiths and Martins natural victims of irony. Here the irony appeals primarily to the emotions; our intellectual grasp of its meaning is liable to become as tenuous as Estragon's memory. What is absurd? That there has been so much bother about shoes, hats, carrots and radishes. That Vladimir and Estragon have such a hard time keeping track of their valuables, and so little certainty that they are valuable. It ought to be easier to distinguish the color of shoes, and the effort of following Vladimir's logic really should not have left Estragon utterly exhausted. It should be noted also that the conversation about shoes is ironic as well as absurd. The audience knows that these are Estragon's shoes: they have been there for some time, peeping out beneath the curtain during the *entr' acte;* it may remember also Vladimir's philosophic remark very early in the play: "There's man all over for you, blaming on his boots the faults of his feet." Yet *he* is showing the anger here.

The last five lines of this passage should also stir our memory, since this is the fifth time that the question-and-answer formula about waiting for Godot has been heard in the play (it will be heard, with slight variations, some twelve times before the end). But is this repetition ironic in the same sense? Who knows any more than Vladimir and Estragon about the identity, existence, attitude, or future plans of M. Godot? At this point the laughter of the audience may well change to sickening doubt—perhaps not abruptly, since Godot might just be a man, but is much more probably God. The uncertainty about shoes was one thing; this uncertainty, which spreads from the addled minds of Vladimir and Estragon to engulf the audience too, is quite another.

Both of these passages from *Waiting for Godot* lead us, then, to the same puzzling question about Beckett's use of irony: what is its function in his play? Since it was postulated that the audience must "understand" irony, the question is fundamental enough to justify more study of Beckett's use of irony in plot, characterization, and theme. As to plot, the play is like *The Bald Soprano* in that its pattern of action is based on repetition. But whereas Ionesco's play went around in a circle, Beckett's goes around in two circles. Each of the two acts begins with a struggle over Estragon's shoes, which serve as a kind of symbol of misery. The subsequent action or inaction consists of fruitless projects to pass the time while waiting—projects for satisfying hunger or curiosity—or to end the waiting altogether by suicide. In the middle of each act comes the strange visit of Pozzo and Lucky, not so strange or exciting the second time. This is always followed by a climactic visit from the Boy with the message from Godot, and then we return to the same inaction and waiting with which the play began. The audience will undoubtedly realize that Act II has the same pattern as Act I, but may we say that this ironic recognition gives the plot significance? Not exactly. It is ironic to observe, *"Plus ça change, plus c'est la même chose,"* but only tautological to say *"Plus ça ne change pas, plus c'est la même chose."*

In character revelation Beckett's irony makes a clearer impression on the audience, though here too there is an element of mystery: a slight majority of the *dramatis personae* are incomprehensible either as human beings or as abstractions. Even the central characters present a kind of enigma, as was indicated by the remark that "we shall like Vladimir and Estragon more and more without knowing why." In the creation of these two characters Beckett worked from a familiar music-hall tradition. His Vladimir is fundamentally the old vaudeville comedian, his Estragon the old straight man, as many commentators have noted; and the play is full of mimetic tricks involving bowler hats, fallen pants, and sudden collapses. At times the irony seems to serve the sole purpose of exploiting the absurdity of Estragon, the simple and humble victim, for comic effect. But actually, both characters develop to a certain extent: Estragon toward sophistication, protest, even vindictiveness; Vladimir toward kindliness and responsible concern. In the course of the play they both come to realize that they are destitute of everything save each other, and though Vladimir had an analytical mind to begin with, he finds himself at the end not far behind his fellow-sufferer on the road to Uncertainty, Amnesia and Oblivion. Both figures are so thoroughly natural that they have been taken to represent a composite portrait of Man in Our Time, Vladimir standing for the soul, the mind, Estragon for the heart or emotion (though they are capable of exchanging these delineations).

Accepting this interpretation, we may hope that we discern a point in the ironic presentation of their disappointments. Vladimir and Estragon, waiting with increasing anxiety for a Godot who never comes, represent Man in search of lost faith and sense of purpose, groping for security in the moribund, hostile, modern world. There is much evidence to support this view, such as Vladimir's anxiety about the discrepant accounts of the Savior's mercy toward the thief at Calvary, Estragon's acknowledgement that he has always compared himself to Jesus, the mournful dialogue on *la nature morte,* and the endless debates to ascertain their position in time and space. The "point" must be that God will forever elude people who seek after Him, in this life at least.

If Vladimir and Estragon are to carry this vast weight of symbolism, it matters whether they adequately represent "people." Why are they bums? A skeptical playgoer might refuse to recognize modern man in these eaters of raw carrots and turnips, afflicted with ill-fitting shoes. Why was the harmless Estragon destined to be beaten in a

ditch every night by unknown ruffians? Is the mugger of tramps a
major highway hazard in our time? The answer to these questions is
simply that Beckett was not writing a problem or thesis play for the
naturalistic theatre, and his symbolic characters must be allowed some
leeway. If his two tramps are homeless, uncomfortable, hungry and
neurotic, it is probably because modern man has lost his attachment
to home, his satisfaction with mechanized comforts and tasteless food-
stuffs, his sense of purpose. If Estragon is beaten unjustly and has
swollen, ill-smelling feet, it may be because violence and bestiality
still often overwhelm us however "harmless" we may wish to be. No,
these tramps are not bums at all. Their way of life is an absurdity
which Beckett used to ensure that they would not resemble too closely
Christian and Faithful. Estragon sometimes inclines toward begging,
but is always sharply checked by Vladimir. Their conversation sometimes veers toward the trivial, once toward the bawdy, but comes back
quickly to the persistent preoccupations of their minds, the highest
aspirations and gravest concerns of man. These are not easily recognized as "high" or "grave" because usually the lines are very short,
the subject matter being divided between the two in the style of music-
hall patter. Thus is established an ironic contrast: the manner or
effect is often absurd, the content or import serious. Here is an example
of what I mean:

> VLADIMIR: . . . Yes, in this immense confusion one thing alone is
> clear. We are waiting for Godot to come—
> ESTRAGON: Ah!
> POZZO: Help!
> VLADIMIR: Or for night to fall. (*Pause*) We have kept our appoint-
> ment and that's an end to that. We are not saints, but we have kept
> our appointment. How many people can boast as much?
> ESTRAGON: Billions.
> VLADIMIR: You think so?
> ESTRAGON: I don't know.
> VLADIMIR: You may be right.

Beckett, *Waiting for Godot*, II

The idealism of Vladimir's claim is absolutely inherent and essential
to the play—but so is the humor in Estragon's deflating answer and
in Vladimir's rueful admission.

The irony in Beckett's presentation of these two central characters is not, then, beyond the grasp of the audience; their human
traits are recognizable and can evoke a sympathetic reaction. But the
other creatures of Beckett's imagination—Pozzo, Lucky, and the Boy
—are so utterly baffling that it would be profitless to analyze them
by psychological methods. They are not "characters," but rather instruments in the development of the *theme* of "waiting" for "Godot,"

and their inscrutability must result from obscurity in the theme itself.

Even if the title did not announce this theme of "waiting," it would not take the audience long to realize that Vladimir and Estragon are, like most of us, by nature waiters, not men of initiative. And one begins to suspect early in the play that their waiting is not going to be rewarded, so that the proceedings are bound to be viewed ironically. But what about "M. Godot"? Both the "Monsieur" and the "-ot" ending blur the identification of their vigil with a quest for religious salvation, although both have been accounted for by many interpreters as meaning "the poor man's God," "the little man's diminutive deity," etc. Much more important for the audience is the fact that Vladimir and Estragon establish the theme of a religious quest by their preoccupations at the beginning of the play. Vladimir wants to satisfy himself as to whether Christian mercy was extended to the thief crucified *"en même temps que le Sauveur"*—"at the same time as our Saviour" in Beckett's English version.—"Our what?" asks Estragon, thus pointing up ironically the improbability of their having been or ever being saved. We then have the first of the many statements of the *leitmotif* quoted above, "Let's go . . . We can't . . . We're waiting for Godot." This is followed by some conversation about the mysterious tree (the scene indications are sparse: A county road. A tree), whose species defies identification but which looks to the audience rather like a Cross, and to them rather like a good place for suicide by hanging. After a brief quarrel, the two come back to an exhaustive pursuit of the question of Godot and this time it is Estragon who is preoccupied with the metaphysical problem, *"est-on lié"* ("if we're tied"); what are Godot's requirements and man's responsibilities toward them? Though this is interrupted by some talk of Estragon's favorite food, carrots, the main theme should be established by now. The play is a religious allegory, and anyone who happens onstage from this time forth is sure to be frisked for doves, crowns of thorn, and assorted thunderbolts both by the two waiters and by the audience.

But of the people who happen onstage after this portentous introduction, all that may safely be said is that they are not only witless in themselves, but the cause that witlessness is in other men. The first visitor, Pozzo, introduces himself with Olympian self-assurance and is of course immediately mistaken for Godot. He maintains, for a short time, a kind of intellectual superiority over Vladimir and Estragon, and a very marked (though meaningless) economic and social superiority over his bestial servant Lucky—but the assurance and superiority are built up only so that they can vanish later, for no visible reason. Pozzo invites new interpretations with every speech he makes; he is now Lord Keynes, now the Grand Inquisitor, now King Midas; he tries to encompass the fascination of Iago, the stigma of Cain, the pathos of Oedipus. All that is certain, however, is that he exists to provide uncertainty and deception for the anxious waiters. Similarly, Lucky is developed as a pitiable, suffering victim, with some suggestion of the divine burden-bearer about him, only to reward the pity which the tramps extend to him by giving Estragon a very animal kick in the leg. The third visitor, the Boy with the Message from Godot, also comes on trailing clouds of glory which promptly dissolve. He appears as an intermediary between God and man, bringing momentary hope to the waiters, but only to disappoint them more cruelly when he vanishes, along with the sun, "like an arrow."

The effect of these visits, then, is to darken what light had been thrown on Vladimir and Estragon in the earlier part of each act. The dramatic irony of their absurd dialogue had clarified them as human beings; the absurdity of Pozzo, Lucky and the Boy now renders meaningless the experience of these human beings in the world. It may be claimed that the scenes are arranged so as to produce a climax; the comic and incongruous frustrations of Act I lead on, by repetition in Act II, to emotions of more profound despair. And the despair is authentic, heart-felt: it results from the tremendous human appeal of Gogo and Didi. Perhaps Beckett meant the audience to reassure itself at the end that the tramps have really found their Godot, that the significance of their quest was in the seeking. But no such confidence can be based on the action of the play; the arena for the performance of their "good works," peopled as it is by Pozzo and the rest, can be no more than a pseudo-world. If we consider the irony of this resolution of the "waiting" theme, it must be acknowledged that we never have the key to it; we are called upon to observe the confusion of our much-loved Gogo and Didi about people and actions which confuse us just as much. Modern Man is baffled by something baffling. It is as though Beckett extended to his audience an austere summons: "We need your muddled head in our muddled business."

M. Jean Tardieu has written a satirical playlet presenting two characters who discuss an intrigue about which the audience is never informed, and which is brought to an incomprehensible dénouement. The object of satire in this hilarious *pièce de chambre*, entitled *Eux seuls le savent* (They are the Only Ones who Know), is the theatre of innuendo: the audience is being challenged to solve an insoluble puzzle before going to sleep. It may be that M. Tardieu was parodying Beckett, but if that was his intention, the parody lacks the necessary exaggeration. For in M. Tardieu's play *someone knew;* in Beckett's, no one knows. We come at last to a curious phenomenon of the drama: irony in a vacuum.

robert brustein

GENET'S CALL TO THE COLORS

CONSIDERING THE fact that *The Blacks* is a ritual of murder, violence, and crime, enacted by Negro supremacists, and culminating in the ceremonious slaughter of the entire White race, its thunderous success here is really rather astonishing. One would hardly be surprised if Genet's celebration of race hatred found favor with an audience of Black Muslims; but the play is now being praised by the same liberal community which so heartily applauded *Raisin in the Sun* for its moderation, charity, and racial togetherness. It could be, of course, that *The Blacks* has simply been misunderstood—after all, the *Times* reviewer seemed to interpret the work as a plea for inter-racial harmony. Then, again, perhaps the insularity of our stage is so complete that nobody cares what a play says as long as it fulfills the aesthetic requirements of "good theater." I am inclined to opt, hopefully, for a third possibility; namely, that audiences have become so surfeited with the liberalistic pieties, platitudes, and exhortations always mouthed in American plays about Negroes that they are finally open to a more radical treatment of race, one closer to the uncensored stuff of dreams than to the official doctrines of the NAACP. Whatever the explanation, *The Blacks* is a depth charge of evil which sinks the spectator well below the placid surface of social benevolence to the dark sea floor of the unconscious, leaving him totally submerged beneath a torrent of primitive impulses, sado-masochistic hallucinations, and myths of danger. As such, the play may do a great deal of harm to the cause of inter-race relations, but it is cut to order for that alchemical theater of cruelty envisioned by Antonin Artaud where the spectator's "taste for crime, his erotic obsessions, his savagery, his chimeras . . . even his cannibalism" would be vicariously indulged, and, thereby, momentarily purged.

Genet's genius for cruel myth-making is evident from the opening moments of the play when eight Negroes and Negresses, dressed in the height of flouncy elegance, begin dancing a stately minuet around a

From *The New Republic*, May 29, 1961. Reprinted by permission.

catafalque supposedly containing the corpse of a white woman, freshly killed for the performance. These are the props and actors in a ritual rehearsal of an earlier murder, to be re-enacted by the murderer, Deodatus Village, and judged by a White Court consisting of the Great Figures of European colonialism: Queen, Queen's valet, Judge, Missionary, and Governor. The entire affair, however (including the corpse which later turns to be non-existent) is a fake—a masquerade performed by ritual celebrants who keep their true identity carefully concealed. For the actors (all of them Europeanized Negroes in middle class professions) are determined to expose not their individual lives but their collective racial identity: the Blacks by "negrifying" themselves "to the point of madness in what they're condemned to be," and the Whites (Negroes in masks) by satirically celebrating, through hyper-cultured postures and inflections, the various triumphs of European civilization. Consistent with these roles, the Blacks labor to caricature or suppress all "white" ideas like love and tenderness, intensifying their atavistic poetry, savagery, and cannibalism, and finding their meaning solely through acts of hatred and revenge, while the Whites preside over the events from a raised platform, contemplating their failing racial authority ("have courage, Madame, God is White"), exploiting Africa's resources and manpower, and covertly admiring Negro sexuality, spontaneity, and beauty.

Behind this stage ceremony, however, a series of real events—periodically and cryptically reported by a Messenger, appropriately named Newport News—is taking place offstage: first the trial and execution of a Negro traitor, and then the emergence of a new Black Hero to carry on the battle against White supremacy. The theatrical ritual, in short, exists only to mask secret preparations for a Negro uprising, but at the same time that it draws attention from these preparations, it predicts their outcome. For Village's murder of a Woman (played by a scapegoat Negro curate in blonde curls and a pasty mask) symbolizes the massacre of Europe by African hordes, the Woman being nothing less than the Mother of the White Race (before she is disembowelled, she gives birth to dolls representing all the Great Figures). Proceeding into the jungle to avenge this archetypal crime, the Great Figures are themselves exterminated, as a crowing cock signals the beginning of a new era. But Genet's theory of history is cyclical, and, as inevitably as night gives way to day, the Whites will return again in ten thousand years to renew the conflict. The play ends with a repetition of the minuet around the catafalque—this time without the Whites, the Black prophecy having been fulfilled and the ritualistic vision a mythic rite of a past historic event.

The Blacks no doubt sounds impossibly complicated, and perhaps the play is ultimately too dense and opaque to be called a totally successful work of art. Genet has a Pirandellian obsession with the idea that human identity is defined by play-acting; and *The Blacks*, like *The Balcony* (which it resembles in so many other ways), examines the artificiality of human behavior in a world of rigid definitions. But whereas this philosophical probing enriched the vision of sham in *The Balcony*, it merely muddies the ritualistic line of *The Blacks*, and sometimes even produces puzzling contradictions (for example, at times the Negroes are enacting their own definition of Black, at other times, that of the White audience). Because of Genet's failure to integrate his conscious preoccupations with his unconscious fantasies, *The Blacks* remains an elusive enigma. But while it fails as a philosophical drama, it stands triumphant as a cruel purgative myth, enlivened by a fierce imagination, a rich theatrical sense, and some of the most superb imagery in all modern drama.

It is the fantastic, ritualistic element of the work that is best realized in Gene Frankel's production. Working with a scimitar-shaped ramp which leads from an open stage to a raised platform, Frankel has staged the play with an uncanny eye for handsome effects, and paced the scenes with a kind of voodoo frenzy to the accompaniment of jungle sounds, African chants, and native dances. Obviously, Mr. Frankel's stage technique is now impeccable, but his theatricalist emphasis does not help to clarify Genet's thematic line, and his actors—except for Roscoe Lee Browne and James Earl Jones—are not always very strong, or penetrating, or even well cast. On the other hand, this is surely the best production of a Genet work yet seen in New York—superior to Quintero's interpretation of *The Balcony* in that it is highly imaginative *without* sacrificing the text. As for this text, whatever its failings, it clearly displays the mind of a genius; and whatever the evil implications of the play, it is a welcome tonic for a theater where the Negro lacks any substantiality at all, being either transparent—which is to say, discernible only as an object of White guilt, prejudice, and benevolence—or totally invisible—which is to say, exactly the same as everyone else. In restoring to the Negro his high visibility, Genet inadvertently halts, if only for a moment, that inexorable process of mass assimilation which is draining the color from us all.

john russell brown

MR. PINTER'S SHAKESPEARE

WE USED to be taught that every play could be analysed as 'Exposition', 'Development' and 'Conclusion'. Sometimes a conclusion would be weak, but the first two parts remained essential. But now, within the last ten years, a kind of drama has appeared which challenges these judgments. If Development is story or argument, the plays of Mr. Pinter, for example, have very little: it is more accurate to say that Exposition has become Development, and Conclusion as well.

His *Caretaker, Slight Ache, Dumb Waiter* and *Collection* have minimal plots and the slightest argument; but they progressively reveal the inner nature of their characters. The audience's attention is held by small, disconnected incidents while the play-long interests are being manifested at a different level of consciousness. So Pinter times the comings-and-goings with the nervous alertness of American gangster films, yet the plays do not end with a 'catch'. He directs that water should drip into a suspended bucket at crucial moments, yet the bucket is never filled and never emptied; the drips add up to nothing. Sometimes he gives two flatly contradictory pieces of information, or ensures that doubt is thrown on the simplest piece of factual exposition, as the name of a character, or his home town, or his trade, or whether or not he is married. These devices ensure that the audience is kept alert and curious, even perplexed, throughout the play and, being unable to 'follow the story' or 'get the message', may discern a progressive disclosure of antagonisms, desires or appetites which were hidden at the beginning. Devices which have caused these plays to be labelled 'Comedy of Menace', 'Theatre of the Absurd' or 'Theatre of Non-Communication' are matters of a moment: the whole play is 'Exposition'.

In a lecture printed in *The Sunday Times* on 4th March, 1962, Harold Pinter quarrelled with the label 'Failure of Communication':

> I'm not suggesting that no character in a play can ever say what he in fact means. Not at all. I have found that there invariably does come a moment when this happens, where he says something, perhaps which he has never said before. And where this happens, what he says is irrevocable, and can never be taken back.

Reprinted from *The Critical Quarterly*, Autumn, 1963, by permission.

The business of a play, for Pinter, is to reach this statement.

A Slight Ache (1959) is the simplest of his plays. An intruding wasp and a stationary, mysterious matchseller set off the interplay between husband and wife, Edward and Flora. This is ordinary bickering, Flora taking the punishment. But when the matchseller is brought into the house and remains silent, each character becomes more uneasy. Their rivalry is deep enough to force them to overcome fears, and each contrives to speak with the matchseller alone. Then, irritated and challenged by his continual silence, they express their thoughts compulsively and powerfully; their habitual reserve is broken and they utter their hidden, irrational fears and demands, as if by possession. Flora treats the stranger as a lover and as a husband to be cossetted, while Edward tries to justify himself in the stranger's eyes by bragging of his own physical achievements, and in this earlier phrases are repeated, now 'respoken' or revealing their true motivation. The play ends when Flora re-enters, talking with ease to the silent man, and takes him off to lunch; she pauses only to give Edward the tray of matches to hold. Here the expression of hidden resources of character at the end gives the play a brief development in the usual sense of that word.

The conclusion of *The Dumb Waiter* (1958) is brought about by a melodramatic intervention outside the room in which we have seen the two gunmen, Ben and Gus. It is over in a moment as Gus stumbles in, stripped of his coat, tie, holster and revolver; there follows only a long silence in which the two men stare at each other. They have no further move to make, for the interplay between them, as the strange behaviour of the dumb waiter has heightened the momentary excitements, has already revealed all. Immediately before the catastrophe, each in turn has held the stage alone for a longer time and with clearer reactions than elsewhere in the play. As his sense of danger has increased with new orders delivered by the dumb waiter, Ben tried to placate the unknown by subservience and correctitude: 'Yes. Yes . . . Yes certainly. Certainly. Right away'; and he was pleased to think he had been proved right about a trivial detail. Against first impressions he is the weaker of the two. Gus, with the same provocation, tried to puzzle out the situation: 'Why did you send him up all that stuff? (*Thoughtfully.*) Why did I send it up? (*Pause.*) Who knows what he's got upstairs? . . .' On the next descent of the dumb waiter with an order, he could rebel reasonably: 'WE'VE GOT NOTHING LEFT! NOTHING! DO YOU UNDERSTAND?' As in *A Slight Ache*, trivial phrases or words are repeated from earlier in the play in these last demonstrations of character, so that the more casual reactions are summed up and given new and deeper interpretations. The bickering of husband and wife and the talk to pass the time as the gunmen await instructions are revalued, the apparently inconsequential duologue becoming one with the expression of inner antagonisms, strengths and weaknesses.

While the true development of *The Dumb Waiter* must be described in terms of Exposition, it firmly controls the play as a whole. Pinter's wish to express hidden natures has determined structure, tempo and proportion. In one way this drama is like the first movement of Sibelius' *Second Symphony:* the 'subject' is introduced fragmentarily and not stated fully until the conclusion. But we must add that the early intimations are not distinguished as 'subject'. The audience is perplexed and its attention drawn away to momentary interests that seem more compelling, so that when the 'statement' comes it carries more assurance by the recognition it brings of the play's entire form.

The Caretaker (1960) has three acts and three characters, but its more complex structure is organized on the same lines. At the end of Act I Davies, who has been given hospitality by Aston, reveals a critical truthfulness not seen before, and the curtain falls as he is suddenly confronted with his host's brother, Mick, and the question, 'What's the game?' At the end of Act II, Aston, in a long monologue, reveals his sense of a cruel world around him while Mick is still known only in a perplexing way. Before the end of Act III there have been various changes of fortune as Davies has become aggressive, lost Aston's support, and tried to insinuate himself with the other brother; but the conclusion comes with a revelation of Mick's intense concern with himself:

> THAT'S WHAT I WANT!
>> *He hurls the Buddha* [*Aston's*] *against the gas stove. It breaks.* (*To himself, slowly, broodingly.*) Anyone would think this house was all I got to worry about. I got plenty of other things I can worry about. I've got other things. I've got plenty of other interests. I've got my own business . . .

This statement has been sparked off by Davies' insinuation that Aston is 'nutty'; the belittlement of his brother has been an unwitting and almost unrecognized challenge to Mick. Aston enters immediately and the brothers say nothing; they look at each other: '*Both are smiling, faintly.* MICK *begins to speak, stops, goes to the door and exits.*' They must move apart, even when they understand each other. Davies and Aston remain for two more revelations. The visitor now placates, insinuates, whines, shows his helpless dependence; if he got his papers— if they exist—from Sidcup he still would need Aston. On this thought, he becomes incoherent, and then silent. And the host, having probed the plug again, speaks of the shed he wishes to build, and then replies with curt 'No's' to Davies' entreaties and stands looking away from him, out of the window towards the overgrown garden behind the house. After a long silence, the curtain falls: Aston will live by his aspiration, expressed casually at first, in Act I: 'I might build a shed out the back'.

The inner needs of the characters have been revealed. This is more than a disclosure of hidden motives, as a comparison with Stanislavsky's use of the word 'sub-text' illustrates. In *The Caretaker* there is often a sub-conscious sub-text, a conscious one, and the text itself. In many plays of Stanislavsky's time the sub-text is finally acknowledged in the text: here the sub-conscious sub-text becomes manifest indirectly, by added forcefulness rather than by textual explicitness. Pinter's characters have been 'taking care' of desires and needs, without recognizing them as such: and even when their 'infra-textual' tensions are revealed to the audience, they do not seem to realise what has happened. They know that some destination has been reached, but they are not heroes who can describe this termination.

The Caretaker is a more complex play than the others, for it reveals unacknowledged relationships as well as individual natures. We do not know whether Davies stays or departs, or whether Mick will return: the small narrative interest remains unconcluded. But the curtain is final because the audience has seen the characters and their mutual situations so intensely that no new incident could alter or increase that understanding. The audience has been perplexed throughout the play on several levels of understanding in order to ensure an intent view of the stage. It is perplexed no longer on the level of its true development or Exposition.

A progressive expression of unacknowledged situation and character, with a climactic revelation at the conclusion, is the form of many of the 'new' plays. Even when Pinter gives greater importance to narrative in *The Birthday Party* (1958), his first and third Acts conclude with character-revelations, rather than turns in the story. At the end of the first, Stanley surprizingly beats a drum in savage 'possession', and the play ends, not with his departure under arrest, but with a manifestation of Meg's selfish optimism and self-delusion— until this moment she had seemed capable of affection for Stanley. The third Act of this play has been criticised for failing to sustain the narrative interest. But Pinter probably hoped that the disclosure of inner natures would hold the audience's attention: McCann, Goldberg, Lulu, Petey and, lastly, Meg are all so revealed. Perhaps the inability of his audience to transfer its interest away from narrative towards inner-development led Pinter to write later plays with only momentary and perplexing plot-interest.

Other playwrights have made similar decisions. No one could follow with assurance or delight all the negotiations presented in Adamov's *Paolo Paoli*; here it is behind an impenetrable maze of plot and counter-plot that a situation is progressively revealed—a social subject this time, rather than one based on individual characters. Ionesco, in *The Chairs* (1952), anticipated Pinter's silent matchseller as a device to draw out a true expression of character. His technique is even more surprising, for the man and wife of his play are surrounded with persons, including an Emperor, who have no physical presence at all. His two *dramatis personae* live their last hours in a reality that corresponds to their dreams, seen and heard by themselves alone. In this freedom, the woman of ninety-four years of age reveals a new range of behaviour:

> *throwing her head back, hands on hips, uttering erotic cries, thrusting her pelvis forward, standing with legs apart, she laughs like an old whore.*

The old people, separated from each other by a roomful of imaginary guests, tell wildly contradictory versions of their past, to satisfy their different selves. The husband, who is customarily proud of his intellect and is about to give an important message to the world, confesses to constant humiliation. These revelations are more explicit than Pinter's: in the fantastic situation it is appropriate that these players should realize that they are trying to 'tell all'. And the conclusion comes some time after man and wife have committed suicide by jumping out of opposite windows: then an 'Orator' completes the petty narrative by stuttering and writing a message, mixed with incoherent nonsense: 'ANGELBREAD' (or, possibly, 'ANGELFOOD'; the French is 'ANGE-PAIN') and 'ADIEU'. In this play Ionesco tells a fable, as well as expressing character, so that there is some ordinary development. He is indeed more concerned to make intellectual points than Pinter; at the end of *The Killer* he has directed that the text of Berenger's speech to the Killer:

> Should be interpreted in such a way as to bring out the gradual breaking-down of Berenger, his falling apart and the vacuity of his own rather commonplace morality, which collapses like a leaking balloon. In fact Berenger finds within himself, in spite of himself and against his own will, arguments in favour of the killer.

Samuel Beckett uses a play-length Exposition boldly and subtlely. In *Krapp's Last Tape* (1958), the single character listens to a fragment of his autobiography that he recorded thirty years before and then dictates a further passage. At first he laughs at the recorded pretensions and philosophizings of his younger self, but then he increasingly fixes his attention on the account of sensual experiences. He re-plays the old tape, cursing until he finds the incident of the girl in a punt. The play ends with Krapp brooding and the tape-recorder running on in silence; it has finished the spool which contained the desired story as well as the now-unheeded comment showing an intellectual confidence in what had then been the future. The short play is called *Krapp's LAST Tape*, so the deadlock between past and present may give a slight development with Krapp's death as well as completing its Exposition of the true motivation of Krapp's philosophizing.

In the earlier *Waiting for Godot* Beckett's technique is less obvious. Its two Acts tell a minimal story: Godot is awaited and in each Act a messenger comes from him; twice the sun sets and a moon rises. In the first set a tree is bare and in the second it has leaves; the first finishes with the two tramps, Estragon and Vladimir, sitting silent together, the second with them standing silent together. The most startling change is off-stage between Acts: Pozzo has been going to the fair to sell Lucky, but they return together and Pozzo is blind, Lucky dumb. In brief, the 'plot' shows repetitions and some alterations, rather than developments or resolutions. The audience is constantly reminded that the action could be repeated with minor differences any day. When Vladimir tries to trace a process he is reproved by Pozzo:

> When! When! One day, is that not enough for you, one day like any other day, one day he went dumb, one day I went blind, one day we'll go deaf, one day we were born, one day we'll die, the same day, the same second, is that not enough for you?

Left alone Vladimir acknowledges that there is little 'truth' in describing the happenings of any one day:

> . . . We have time to grow old. The air is full of our cries. (*He listens.*) But habit is a great deadener. (*He looks again at* ESTRAGON [*who is sleeping*].) At me too someone is looking, of me too someone is saying, 'He is sleeping, he knows nothing, let him sleep on.' (*Pause.*) I can't go on! (*Pause.*) What have I said?
>   *He goes feverishly to and fro, halts finally at extreme left, broods.*

These attitudes are reflected in the organization of the play: almost every event has been 'deadened' by habit:

—Certainly they beat me.
—The same lot as usual?
—The same? I don't know.

—That passed the time.
—It would have passed in any case.
—Yes, but not so rapidly.

—I've seen you before, haven't I? . . .

—You again!

—It would be better if we parted.
—You always say that, and you always come crawling back.

Interest is not sustained by narrative, for the various incidents are presented in ways that prevent the audience from believing that they are witnessing any unique crisis. The continuous and developing interest comes from the revelation of the unacknowledged natures of the characters and their inter-relations, and also—here Beckett has a wider subject than Pinter—also the revelation of their true mode of existence.

The most straightforward revelation is of Pozzo as he tries to gain the attention of Vladimir and Estragon while giving next to nothing in exchange; he is led on, like characters in *The Chairs* and *A Slight Ache,* to talk about his secret defeat. But generally the disclosures are made less consciously and without long, climactic speeches. Most of the dialogue is short-phrased, and would be trivial if it were heard outside the dramatic context built up throughout the play. By repetitions and a slow accumulation of significances, the bare bones live, showing progressively the true life and dependencies of the characters. At the final curtain Beckett does not introduce eloquence or elaboration, keeping the interchanges of the duologue as apparently simple as they have ever been. But the audience will recognize the end of the play. For this day the two tramps have tried most of the responses in their repertoire, the last being to stand side-by-side silent, without argument: this is their resource when they have no more words or actions. As the moon rises, Estragon's childishness and Vladimir's attempted dignity have yielded, like Krapp's philosophizing, to a revelation of their deeper and more permanent attributes, their acceptance of each other's presence and a kind of stoicism as necessary comforts.

Of these dramatists Ionesco is the most articulate about his purposes, so he may speak as their representative. He says that his plays 'magnify' those aspects of human behaviour which are normally observed through 'nuances' alone, that they are a projection on to the stage of internal and obscure desires, anxieties, contradictions. They are realized psychic conflicts or 'realized dreams'. Their source is:

> a mood and not an ideology, an impulse not a programme; the cohesive unity that grants formal structure to emotions in their primitive state satisfies an inner need and does not answer the logic of some structural order imposed from without; not submission to some pre-

determined action, but the exteriorization of a psychic dynamism, a projection onto the stage of internal conflict, of the universe that lies within: . . . it is in the deepest part of myself, of my anguish and my dreams, it is in my solitude that I have the best chance of rediscovering the universal, the common ground.[1]

In an introduction to *The Chairs,* he says that the play:

progresses not through a predetermined subject and plot, but through an increasingly intense and revealing series of emotional states.[2]

The other 'new' dramatists do not rely so completely on introspection for the source of their drama, nor do they charge emotions so highly, but they would be at one with Ionesco in claiming freedom from plot or clear thematic development. And they do so for the same reason: to show a more inward, a deeper, a wider or a more precarious reality than can easily be viewed in life or in the exhibition of some clear narrative upon the stage. Pinter says that there 'comes a moment' when something 'irrevocable' is said.

The new dramatists have had to create a new audience by which they can be appreciated. And in ten years much has been accomplished. This audience now knows that it is responding helpfully when it cannot recognize a simple theme or continuous story, or when it notices repetitions, long hesitations or the forceful speaking of trivial phrases and thus begins to sense the infra-textual subject. This is a major change, for these reactions to other plays would all be signs that something was going wrong. The audience is reassured and discovers that its perception is deepened and refined. It has become quicker to respond to the early passages, where the inner-development is necessarily slight. It has learnt to appreciate the almost musical form, whereby proportion and tempo accentuate the inner-drama and sometimes become an essential part of its expression. It is able to recognize the climactic revelations of character and situation and to give its attention more wholly to them. The result is that the new plays have seemed to grow in stature; *The Birthday Party,* for example, drew and held an audience of millions in a television production only a few years after its total failure in London. An audience with new powers of perception has been conjured into existence.

And this audience is part of the larger one that sees Shakespeare's plays. Will there be a new response? New perceptions? We know, now, that Exposition may not be complete until the very last moment of the play, and that the audience's deeper realisation of character and situation can form a sufficient Conclusion. This is a discovery

1 Forward, *Plays*, i, tr. D. Watson (1958), pp. viii–ix.
2 'The World of Eugene Ionesco', *International Theatre Annual*, ii (1957).

about the basic resources of the theatre and it is possible that Shakespeare had already sensed this and relied upon its power in shaping his plays.

There are obvious differences between this 'Ancient' and the 'Moderns', of course. Shakespeare never dispensed with a strong narrative Development: journeys end in lovers' meetings; the king is killed and the king is crowned. But a new audience may discover something more. Being aware of the holding power of drama without a clear plot or theme it will be able to recognize Shakespeare's progressive demonstration of character and situation within his fables. Taught to respond to the climatic nature of speeches which are not direct expressions of intention or feeling, this audience may observe an inward drama in Shakespeare's plays, the 'enlarged nuances' which, in the theatre, can project subconscious antagonisms.

That is to say the new audience will rediscover Shakespeare's presentation of human nature, his intuitive skill in using the stage as a means of viewing deeply and widely. It will respond, for example, to his characters' 'motiveless insistences'. Macbeth's elaborate persuasion of the murderers to kill Banquo when they are obviously ready for the deed, his enumeration of the catalogue of dogs and men, his counsel that they should 'resolve' themselves apart when they are resolved already, are uneconomical as narrative or direct expression of the apparent situation. They are, however, a means of showing the strength of Macbeth's inner conflict. He speaks at this length, and with this insistence and complexity, because while he thinks he is practically discussing terms with paid assassins he is, in fact, expressing his own sub-conscious fears and half-conscious scruples.

Or observe Hamlet on the approach of the players. This is not a moment which is often considered as some 'necessary question of the play': Professor Lawlor's sensitive analysis of Hamlet's attitude to the call for revenge does not mention it; nor does Professor Bowers' examination of Hamlet's religious consciousness; nor yet the statement of a 'Psycho-Analytical Solution' by Dr. Ernest Jones.[3] Yet to the 'new audience' it is an important revelation. It is true that the dialogue at this point seems casual, but so does Pozzo's discourse on the twilight or his insistence on pipe-smoking. It is true that its concerns seem far removed from the practical demands of the situation, but so do Davies' explanations of his pseudonym or Mick's disquisition on London bus routes. We now understand how these characteristics can enhance the force and meaning of a speech. Moreover, we can see how strongly Hamlet's disquisition on the players is placed; he

[3] J. Lawlor, *The Tragic Sense in Shakespeare* (1960); F. Bowers, 'Hamlet as Minister and Scourge', *PMLA*, lxx (1955), 740–9; and E. Jones, *Hamlet and Oedipus* (1949 and 1955).

has been taunted by Polonius' interference and his friends' double-talk, and he has spoken of dreams and the insubstantial nature of human good; he is alert, excited, uncommonly aware of his situation:

> HAMLET: Why did you laugh then, when I said 'man delights not me'?
> ROSENCRANTZ: To think, my lord, if you delight not in man, what lenten entertainment the players shall receive from you: . . . hither are they coming, to offer you service.

With the freedom of feigned madness perhaps, yet with logical elaboration, his mind transfers easily from one subject to another; and so the idea of the players—they are still off-stage—immediately suggests an ideal world containing loyalties, affections and satisfactions:

> ROSENCRANTZ: . . . hither are they coming, to offer you service.
> HAMLET: He that plays the king shall be welcome; his majesty shall have tribute of me; the adventurous knight shall use his foil and target; the lover shall not sigh gratis; the humorous man shall end his part in peace; the clown shall make those laugh whose lungs are tickle o' the sere; and the lady shall say her mind freely . . .

There follows a declension to ordinary bantering, and the new audience may believe that some deep concern is being 'covered' by cheap humour:

> . . . the lady shall say her mind freely, or the blank verse shall halt for't. What players are they? (II.ii.332–40)

This speech is by no means as famous as the one immediately preceding, 'What a piece of work is man! how noble in reason! . . .' which seems to bear directly on Hamlet's predicament; yet 'He that plays the king . . .' *follows* this apparent climax and is an instantaneous response to a new turn in the action. Its elaboration is made to appear the more remarkable because it springs fully grown at the instant of suggestion, in response to a notion which does not originate with Hamlet's conscious thoughts as did the subject of the earlier speech. And we may notice that, in contrast with those of the philosophic monologue, its terms are exact, not evasively general. All these elements of the theatrical moment give forcefulness, size and added meaning; in performance 'He that plays the king . . .' is an 'irrevocable statement'.

The new audience will attend closely, and it will find all Hamlet's personal and social interests implicit in its words: the king, the hero, the lover, the philosophizer, the 'jack o' dreams', the lady-mother. Accepting the implicit references, it will also notice that all these precise concerns are linked with ideal longings and expressed with surprizing clarity, promptness and completeness. We may remember that Hamlet has been taken off-guard and probably forgets to deceive his hearers or himself. We may judge that this speech does not bring a change of subject, as at first appeared, but a release from the censorship of the conscious mind, a fuller revelation of the complex antagonisms of his inward nature. The apparent topic of the actors has allowed him to speak largely. The words should be delivered as if the speaker were indulging, probably unknown to himself, his deepest and fullest desires. It is a still, surprizing, expressive climax, like the revelations of the new drama. The dialogue continues to refer to the actors less remarkably, but with traces of residual energy, and, finally, Hamlet acknowledges the inadequacy of conscious thought: ' 'Sblood, there is something in this more than natural, if philosophy could find it out.' When the actors enter the stage, Hamlet gives them his entire attention.

The moment of revelation is not lost. Hamlet recurs to actors and acting throughout the play, as Vladimir repeatedly fiddles with his hat or Aston speaks of the shed he wants to build. Thus the new audience can respond to a progressive expression of the hero's need for a perfect action that 'passeth show' and ends 'in peace', that speaks eloquently to those who are but 'mutes and audience'. Among his other achievements, Shakespeare has contrived a developing exposition of a part of Hamlet's being that remains a nuance in his direct and conscious elaborations of thought; in this he is like the new dramatists and uses similar devices.

Some parts of Shakespeare's comedies have been called 'scenes of idle clowning', or 'sallets for the groundlings', or 'actors' interpolations of hackneyed material'. When such incidents contain obsolete word-play they are often cut in performance today and the audience is not aware of the loss. None has much narrative interest or obvious thematic importance, and critics pay them little attention. But the new audience will be interested, for here Shakespeare's techniques are closer to those of Beckett and Pinter and their generation.

Consider, for example, the role of Launcelot in *The Merchant of Venice*. In one of the very few discerning studies of the early comedies, Dr. Muriel Bradbrook notices how Launcelot's debate with the fiend about leaving his master, Shylock ('who, God bless the mark, is a kind of devil'), is a parody of Jessica's quick decision to leave her home.[4] Similarly, when Launcelot 'tries confusions' with his father, the comic dialogue could be justified as an analogy of that choice 'by outward show' which is the business of the casket scenes; long ago a scholar suggested that it awakens a memory of Isaac's recognition of Jacob and so reflects on the play's whole action which is about possession and a Jew. Old Gobbo's gift of a 'dish of doves' when

[4] See M. C. Bradbrook, *Shakespeare and Elizabethan Poetry* (1951), p. 188.

his son wishes to become Bassanio's servant might be said to contrast with the 'giving and hazarding of all' which is the condition for winning Portia. These incidents in Launcelot's role serve the main narrative development very slightly, but they clarify its themes in the medieval analogical manner which Shakespeare had made his own. Yet the clown has more 'set down' for him to say and do, long after he has performed these functions. Critics seeking the 'meaning' of the comedies have not explained how his talk with Jessica about being damned for her father's or mother's sins (III.v) contributes notably to the thematic development. The same is true of his condemnation of Lorenzo for making more Christians and so raising the price of hogs. Playing on words has perhaps some analogical significance before the trial scene, for Launcelot 'defies the matter' for a 'tricksy word' (III.v.74–5) and so does Shylock in claiming 'justice' according to the word of his bond when truly he is trying to 'have the life' of his adversary; and Portia, defending Antonio, turns the words of the bond yet another way. But there's little in the situation or Launcelot's ostensible subject which could enforce this very general analogy. The clown's last entry bringing news of Bassanio's return to Belmont is necessary for the narrative, but the utmost ingenuity would be required to show how his crying out as if hunting or his failing to see Lorenzo when he speaks to him reflect on the themes of the final Act. Launcelot's two appearances at Belmont will seem uneconomical in the play as a whole if they have to be justified by narrative or thematic relevance. Indeed, when the play is seen in performance even the neatest and most obvious of the analogical significances may seem over subtle, bearing only a little relation to the actual response of an audience. In the theatre, an observer trained by the critics may notice the analogies, and yet recognize that they are only a part of a larger phenomenon. It is just here that the new audience, accustomed to Exposition rather than Development of theme or narrative, can appreciate more fully (and explain, if they wish). In these last appearances Launcelot is revealed independently of others, and more certainly and more deeply: he is restless, always on the move, and his energy is ridiculously uncontrolled, except by a simple, irrational sense of loyalty. His earlier words and actions, especially his leave-takings, are revalued and his character clarified as he rushes off-stage in Act V, regardless of Lorenzo's presence.

We may now see that Shakespeare was also aiming at a progressive exposition of the inner natures of these comic characters. In some plays this can be accepted easily, for the climactic scene of character-presentation is the point at which the clown's thematic contribution is most obvious. In *The Two Gentlemen of Verona*, the audience has to wait for Launce's last entry, in IV.iv, before it fully understands his dependence on his dog, Crab; and it is also here that he prefigures Valentine's forgiveness and embarrassed generosity in the last scene by his talk of being whipped for his dog ('How many masters would do this for his servant?') and of offering him to Silvia. In *A Midsummer-Night's Dream*, Bottom is the last to be freed from the wood's enchantments in IV.i, and he then speaks of his companions and his 'vision'. Thematically, the critics agree, this speech is of utmost importance. Professor Kermode notes:

> the final awakening of this superbly arranged climax . . . is Bottom's. And here the 'moral' defies comfortable analysis; we suddenly leave behind the neat love-is-a-kind-of-madness pattern and discover that there is more to ideas-in-poetry than ideas and verse.[5]

Bottom's words serve both narrative and theme:

> I have had a most rare vision. I have had a dream, past the wit of man to say what dream it was . . . The eye of man hath not heard, the ear of man hath not seen, man's hand is not able to taste, his tongue to conceive, nor his heart to report what my dream was.

Impressive echoes of I Corinthians (ii.9ff) can be heard:

> Eye hath not seen, or ear heard, neither have entered into the heart of man the things which God hath prepared for them that love him.

Professor Merchant has noted a further hint of the vision of St. John's first Epistle:[6]

> That which we have seen with our eyes, which we have looked upon, and our hands have handled, of the Word of Life.

The thematic importance of part of Bottom's soliloquy is so obvious, and so often drawn to our attention, that we may have to remind ourselves of the whole:

> When my cues come, call me, and I will answer: my next is, 'Most fair Pyramus'. Heigh-ho! Peter Quince! Flute, the bellows-mender! Snout, the tinker! Starveling! God's my life, stolen hence, and left me asleep! I have had a most rare vision. I have had a dream, past the wit of man to say what dream it was: man is but an ass, if he go about to expound this dream. Methought I was—there is no man can tell what. Methought I was,—and methought I had,—but man is but a patched fool, if he will offer to say what methought I had. The eye of man hath not heard, the ear of man hath not seen, man's hand is not able to taste, his tongue to conceive, nor his heart to report, what my dream was. I will get Peter Quince to write a ballad of this dream: it shall

---

[5] F. Kermode, 'The Mature Comedies', *Stratford-upon-Avon Studies, III: Early Shakespeare* (1961), p. 218.
[6] See W. M. Merchant, '*A Midsummer-Night's Dream:* a Visual Re-creation', *Stratford-upon-Avon Studies, III: Early Shakespeare* (1961), pp. 184–5.

be called Bottom's Dream, because it hath no bottom; and I will sing it in the latter end of a play, before the duke: peradventure, to make it the more gracious, I shall sing it at her death.

The soliloquy is also a climactic and uniquely full expression of Bottom's nature: practical, courageous and egotistically romantic. It reveals his unexpressed need to be glorious in good company. To affect this, Shakespeare has interweaved echoes of Bottom's earlier talk at rehearsals. Casual business and jokes are here remembered and revalued: they were necessary to Bottom, because they were partly suggested by his *inner* dream—the one he will have with him always—by his unexpressed fears and desires. The soliloquy begins and ends with amateur theatricals, and at its climax the mention of a 'patched fool' (Bottom's true role from another point of view) is a reminder of his less direct expressions of the precarious nature of his attempt to act seriously according to the truth of his imagination.

In the economy of the play as a whole, the character-revelation of this soliloquy is as important as its thematic clarification, for it modifies the audience's response to Bottom. When he gives his performance as Pyramus in the last Act, the audience will watch him fulfil his deepest desires as well as his role in the play-within-the-play. So, in the words of Theseus, it will 'imagine no worse' of the amateur actor than he of himself, and he will 'pass as an excellent man'. We might argue that Bottom's part in the comedy reaches a fuller conclusion than that of the lovers; they go, 'sweet friends', to bed, with nothing more to say, and so they serve both plot and theme at the close, but, because of the effect of his soliloquy, Bottom's last triumphant dance with his fellows completes the less obvious Exposition of character, as well as concluding the developed narrative and theme.

In *Much Ado About Nothing*, Dogberry has a climactic speech which is placed, like Launce's and Bottom's, at the end of Act IV. But here the critics cannot point to any obvious thematic relevance:

Dost thou not suspect my place? dost thou not suspect my years? O that he were here to write me down an ass! But, masters, remember that I am an ass; though it be not written down, yet forget not that I am an ass. No, thou villain, thou art full of piety, as shall be proved upon thee by good witness. I am a wise fellow, and, which is more, an officer, and, which is more, a householder, and, which is more, as pretty a piece of flesh as any is in Messina, and one that knows the law, go to; and a rich fellow enough, go to; and a fellow that hath had losses, and one that hath two gowns and every thing handsome about him. Bring him away. O that I had been writ down an ass!

This starts a minor narrative trail to keep the plotting full to the end of the play, but Dogberry's demand to be writ down an ass is not the centre or climax of the speech. Because the watchmen and the two prisoners are silent as he addresses them in turn, they all— like the silent matchseller in *A Slight Ache* or the silent Killer in Ionesco's play—draw out the depths of Dogberry's consciousness: in a rarely contrived mixture of elation and frustration, he rises to an expression of his last resources. Echoes of the scene with the watchmen are heard in the speech, as catch-phrases from the rehearsal scenes were repeated in Bottom's awakening, and they help to sustain two climaxes. The first is: 'as pretty a piece of flesh as any is in Messina'; and then, after a reversion to the affairs of a Constable, there is the second: 'a rich fellow enough, go to: and a fellow that hath two gowns and every thing handsome about him'. Dogberry *needs* to be well esteemed. In a play about the ados and nothings of love, the comic constable is revealed as proud of his 'flesh', considering it as 'pretty' as any he has seen. He also recognizes that wealth and loss are closely associated; this is a strange juxtaposition of ideas unless he senses the exposure to risk, and the fear, which pride involves. Dogberry is soon to leave the play, effusing generous sentiments on the receipt of a tip but, in a comedy so full of disguises, this delayed and 'irrevocable' statement of a clown's inner needs will contribute to the reception of the conclusion. Dogberry plays a part in establishing the deep psychological perspective against which all the characters are seen, the hidden ground of pride and fear.

The new dramatists can teach us about the structure of Shakespeare's plays. His Exposition is not always complete when the initial situation of the narrative has been established and dominant themes suggested. The expression of character in subconscious existence and in the deeper recesses of consciousness is necessarily a subtle and slow process. Even though Shakespeare was a master of plot-development he sometimes introduced scenes with only the slightest narrative interest in order to sustain an inner-development of this sort. He used repetitions, silences, sudden intensities and insistences that are apparently without motive, devices that we may now recognize as means of sustaining a play-long Exposition.

Mr. Pinter's Shakespeare is a discovery that can alter our presuppositions. We should not talk slightingly of 'mere comic relief'. We should not be certain that we have grasped Shakespeare's achievement when we recognize the themes of a play, the 'pattern in the carpet'. We must know *how* characters are presented and how they are perceived by the audience; we must appreciate 'enlarged nuances' and recognize 'an increasingly intense or revealing series of emotional states'.

lionel abel

TRAGEDY—OR METATHEATRE?

THE GREATEST playwright in the nineteenth century was, no doubt, influenced by Goethe's *Faust* in writing his own piece of metatheatre, *Peer Gynt*. Here again we have a drama of philosophical depth expressed in fantasy, mixing comedy and satire. And again we have a self-referring character, Peer Gynt, a kind of milder, more mediocre, and more bourgeois Faust. Shaw thought Ibsen's play the greatest comedy ever written; Shaw, however, was wrong in calling it a comedy; Ibsen's gift for comedy was not marked. But in *Peer Gynt* the seriousness of the great Norwegian, shining through all of his plays, becomes exceptionally subtle, evocative, and delicate.

Ibsen did not later continue to work with the form he handled so masterfully in *Peer Gynt*. He was attracted on the one hand by the new realistic vision of life already expressed in the European novel, and on the other by the necessitarian structure of fated events which he found in Greek tragedy. And he devoted his genius, for much of his life, to unifying his critical and highly realistic observations of middle-class life in Norway with a dramatic form derived from Sophocles.

There was a great perception in this effort of Ibsen's. He must have realized that no form of drama gives such a compelling effect of the real as does the form of tragedy. Why not utilize that form along with direct observation of people and places? Why not combine the realist's critical attitude of mind with the tragic poet's feeling for the ultimately real in action, and thus produce the most overpowering illusion of reality ever achieved by any dramatist? Such must have been Ibsen's hope in writing *Ghosts, Hedda Gabler, The Wild Duck, Rosmersholm*, and *The Master Builder*.

So stated, Ibsen's objective seems a valid one. It always seems a valid hope to combine widely separate modes of thinking into a new pattern. Yet the strength of the human mind is not expressed in marriages of convenience, but I think, as Ibsen might have learned from Kierkegaard, in the resolute confrontation of a real "either, or." I believe that it is in the light provided by the burning of its own bridges that the mind can best see. When Pizarro burned his own ships, he had all Peru at his mercy.

What did Ibsen achieve in the realistic "tragedies" of his most

From *Metatheatre: A New View of Dramatic Form* by Lionel Abel. Copyright © 1963 by Lionel Abel. Reprinted by permission of Hill and Wang, Inc.

productive period? He never convinces us of the necessity for the fate of Oswald in *Ghosts*, of Hedda Gabler in his play about her, of Hedvig in *The Wild Duck*, of Solness in *The Master Builder*, of Rosmer and Rebecca West in *Rosmersholm*. His critically observed characters are alive, and today his plays still live. But the "fatality" suggested in his dramas remains suggested, and does not convince us finally. Take *Ghosts*. The play would be just as moving and much truer to its real subject, the rigidity of Norwegian middle-class society, if Oswald did not have hereditary syphilis and were simply "disturbed" —he is that anyway—as a result of his separation from parents whose marriage was unsatisfactory.

There is an artificial imposition of fate on his characters, which today makes us feel some of Ibsen's greatest works are clumsy and contrived—often unreal. In a certain sense, the truth of Ibsen is in Chekhov, who, powerfully influenced by Tolstoy's insistence on utter truthfulness, deliberately softened the oppositions in his plays, toned down their climaxes, broke up the structure of the "well-made play," of which Ibsen was so proud, and eliminated altogether any suggestion that what happened to his characters happened because of fate. Interestingly enough, Chekhov was able to do all this and yet produce plays which have some dynamism because of an accidental fact of history: the characters he presents are derived from the Russian intelligentsia, which European history, long before Chekhov became a dramatist, had already placed on the stage.

Thus Chekhov could produce a kind of metatheatre while remaining genuinely realistic. The characters he described were already theatrical. Social forces had doomed the Russian intelligentsia to extinction; their consciousness of this, though, was what interested Chekhov, not the fatefulness of their situation. And insofar as Chekhov ever yields to the sense of fatality—as he does in *The Cherry Orchard* —instead of magnifying it or making it more drastic, his whole effort is to render it delicately. He understood, no doubt, that there was no such thing as fate even in the historical sense of that term, without the willing collaboration of men.

There is another point I want to make about Ibsen's peculiar effort and the results of that effort on subsequent dramatists. There is something else about tragedy which is interesting besides the fact that it thrusts one against the ultimate real: in a true tragedy one is beyond thought. Thus the writer of a tragedy does not have to express ideas. He only has to have, as the phrase goes—I do not think it a good one—"a tragic view of life." Actually, Ibsen, supposedly an intellectual playwright, was strikingly lacking in ideas. When in *Rosmersholm* Rosmer speaks of carrying out "the new ideas" one never knows what he has in mind. *The Wild Duck* becomes absurd insofar as Gregers Werle has no genuinely intellectual motive for making the revelation he makes to Hjalmar Ekdal, which results in the painful suicide of Hedvig. In *Ghosts*, Ibsen makes Mrs. Alving too easily superior to Pastor Manders for any real criticism of the Protestant clergy to emerge in that play. When Kierkegaard attacked the Protestant church, he attacked the greatest Protestant pastors of Denmark; Ibsen's Pastor Manders is a plain fool. How could the Protestant church be made ridiculous by the exhibition of Manders' mainly personal folly?

If the truth of Ibsen is in Chekhov, Ibsen's false tragedy is to be found particularly in the American theatre, whose outstanding playwrights so far, Eugene O'Neill, Tennessee Williams, and Arthur Miller, are all continuers and imitators of Ibsen. Here (for once) I agree with Mary McCarthy, who has pointed up the dependence of the realistic school of American playwrights on the work of the great Norwegian. Miss McCarthy is quite wrong, however, in saying that all realistic plays are badly written. O'Neill and Tennessee Williams, at least, are excellent writers; Ibsen was a great writer and, as Eliot said, actually made prose do what before him only the verse form could.

What *is* true of O'Neill, Tennessee Williams, and Arthur Miller, though, is that all of them were attracted to Ibsen's form because it suggests the possibility of a serious play without the dramatist's having any need to think—except dramatically. Like Ibsen, and thanks to him, these playwrights have accomplished what they have without the need for ideas.

If Shaw, who admired Ibsen so greatly, was never an imitator of Ibsen, this was because Shaw had a gift for comedy, which Ibsen lacked, and also because Shaw had an interest in expressing ideas. There is an intellectual structure in most of Shaw's important plays which we do not find in Ibsen at all. Moreover, in addition to his irrepressible and beneficent humor, the Irish playwright had a feeling for philosophical drama. Thus I account for his having written works of metatheatre without having thought seriously of going beyond the form of comedy. The *Don Juan in Hell* episode (a complete play in itself), *Pygmalion*, and *Saint Joan* are not comedies, but metaplays.

When Shaw saw a performance of Pirandello's *Six Characters in Search of an Author*, he is said to have remarked: "This playwright is greater than I am." If true, the story would indicate that Shaw was sensitive to a dramatic form irrelevant to his own social and moral purposes. For the effect of Pirandello's *Six Characters in Search of an Author* is not at all upon the critical reason, but almost entirely on the metaphysical imagination. In fact, the Italian dramatist is lacking in moral interest: his dramaturgy counts only when he is excited by the metaphysical side of a conflict.

One might say that Pirandello was the epistemologist of metatheatre, not its ontologist. Pirandello is always interesting when he explores dramatically our inability to distinguish between illusion and reality; he was not prepared to assert, though, that the unreal *is*. Illusion, for Pirandello, was that which defines the limits of human subjectivity. But for the contemporary playwright, Jean Genet, illusion is something objective, something splendid, too, not an error. Thus in *The Balcony,* the characters are most real when dressed up for their peculiar roles. In *The Blacks,* the Negroes are presented not as perhaps Negroes feel themselves to be, but as they see themselves reflected in the mirror of the white race.

The logician of metatheatre was Bertolt Brecht. He took care to order not only his plays but also their décor and the style of acting he needed for them. He introduced an antinaturalistic logic into acting and stage design as well as into his own dramatic construction. His characters are his puppets, to be sure, but he insists on the fact that they are puppets, does not try to pass them off as real people, and delights in exhibiting their mechanisms. The cynicism which modern dictators have shown toward real people was in Brecht; he showed it toward his own characters. Never could he have succeeded in doing so had he relied on a realistic or naturalistic form of drama. What led him to metatheatre? Certainly it was not reflection on past art, nor was it some deep intuition of the importance of consciousness. But he did come to metatheatre; and having come to it, he was more thorough about it than any other playwright of his time.

So there are two trends in contemporary drama, one going back to the Shaw of *Don Juan in Hell* and *Saint Joan,* to Ibsen's *Peer Gynt,* and still further back to Shakespeare and Calderón; the other springing from the realistic period of Ibsen's so-called tragedies. This second trend does not go, and cannot go, further back than Ibsen's works, for authentic tragedy, which can give a stronger feeling of reality than "realism," implies an acceptance of values which contemporary writers are unlikely to hold. I shall not say that tragedy is impossible, or, as George Steiner has suggested, dead. If Shakespeare, with his skepticism, could write even one tragedy, there is no reason at all to assert that the form is impossible to any modern dramatist, whatever his cast of mind. A dramatist may appear to whom the Furies are real—and I do not mean just symbolically real—and still uncompromising in their demands for blood vengeance, as they were before Aeschylus pacified them in the third part of his *Oresteia.*[1] Hegel thought that

---

[1] Are not the witches in *Macbeth* something like the Furies of the *Oresteia,* but more morally ambiguous, more symbolical, more literary, if you please, than the terrible figures in Aeschylus' work? Also, did not Shakespeare, to find them, have to plunge into a darker and more superstitious past, whereas Aeschylus was able to go with his Furies into

after *Hamlet*, all modern tragedies would be tragedies of the intellectual. I think he should have said tragedy would be replaced by metatheatre.

To summarize the values and disvalues of tragedy and metatheatre:

Tragedy gives by far the stronger sense of the reality of the world. Metatheatre gives by far the stronger sense that the world is a projection of human consciousness.

Tragedy glorifies the structure of the world, which it supposedly reflects in its own form. Metatheatre glorifies the unwillingness of the imagination to regard any image of the world as ultimate.

Tragedy makes human existence more vivid by showing its vulnerability to fate. Metatheatre makes human existence more dreamlike by showing that fate can be overcome.

Tragedy tries to mediate between the world and man. Tragedy wants to be on both sides. Metatheatre assumes there is no world except that created by human striving, human imagination.

Tragedy cannot operate without the assumption of an ultimate order. For metatheatre, order is something continually improvised by men.

There is no such thing as humanistic tragedy. There is no such thing as religious metatheatre. George Lukacs has said that the principal spectator of tragedy is God. I cannot imagine God present at a play of Shaw, Pirandello, or Genet. I cannot imagine Godot enjoying *Waiting for Godot*.

Tragedy, from the point of view of metatheatre, is our dream of the real. Metatheatre, from the point of view of tragedy, is as real as are our dreams.

Nicolai Hartmann distinguishes the "depth of succession" from the "breadth of simultaneity." The first is the province of tragedy. The second belongs to metatheatre.

Tragedy transcends optimism and pessimism, taking us beyond both these attitudes. Metatheatre makes us forget the opposition between optimism and pessimism by forcing us to wonder.

Shall we not stop lamenting the "death" of tragedy and value justly the dramatic form which Western civilization—and that civilization only—has been able to create and to refine?

---

the clear light of Athenean society? Certainly, the pacification of the Furies in the *Oresteia* made problematic the future of tragedy as an art form. Modern dramatists, trying to restore that form, have been forced to seek it among primitives: the Irish peasantry (Synge), the Spanish peasants (Lorca), half-mad sinners of the sixteenth century (Ghelderode), and, in America, culturally deprived characters like the protagonists of *Death of a Salesman* and *A View from the Bridge*.

NOTES ON CONTRIBUTORS

Lionel Abel is a playwright and drama critic. His criticism has appeared in *Partisan Review, Kenyon Review, Commentary,* and *The New Republic.* His plays have been produced off Broadway and have won praise from Albert Camus and Harold Clurman, among others. In 1958, he received a Guggenheim fellowship for drama.

Mr. Alvarez's criticism appears frequently in British and American journals. In 1958, he was D. H. Lawrence Fellow at the University of New Mexico.

William Archer (1856–1924), British dramatist and critic, translated and popularized Ibsen. He collaborated with Shaw on the first draft of *Widower's Houses* and was much respected by Wilde, Pinero, and Shaw.

Eric Bentley is Brander Matthews Professor of Dramatic Literature at Columbia University. He is the author of several books on the theater, including *The Playwright as Thinker* (1946), *In Search of Theater* (1953), and *The Dramatic Event* (1954). He has also directed plays.

John Russell Brown teaches at the University of Birmingham, England, and has been a visiting professor at several American universities. He has written *Shakespeare and His Comedies* (1962) and edited a number of Elizabethan plays. He is also active in theater production.

Robert Brustein, who teaches at Columbia University, is the theater critic for *The New Republic* and has contributed drama criticism to other magazines.

James H. Clancy is a professor in the Department of Speech and Drama at Stanford University, and is a former editor of *Educational Theatre Journal.*

Harold Clurman has served as drama critic for *The Nation* since 1953. A founder of the Group Theater, he has directed many famous American plays. His account of his work with the Group Theater appears in *The Fervent Years* (1945).

Robert Corrigan, a former editor of *The Tulane Drama Review,* has taught drama at several colleges and universities, and has been Andrew Mellon Professor and head of the Department of Drama at Carnegie Institute of

Technology. He is now Professor of Dramatic Literature at New York University.

Herbert H. Coston is Assistant Professor of Speech and Theatre at the C. W. Post College of Long Island University.

Martin Esslin is the author of *Brecht: the Man and His Work* (1960) and of *The Theatre of the Absurd* (1961). He lives in England.

Wallace Fowlie is Professor of French at the University of Colorado. Among his books are *A Guide to Contemporary French Literature* (1957) and *Mid-century French Poets* (1955).

Morris Freedman, editor of this volume, is Professor of English at the University of New Mexico. His articles on the drama have appeared in academic journals and quarterlies. His books include *Confessions of a Conformist* (1961) and *Chaos in Our Colleges* (1963).

John Gassner, Sterling Professor of Playwriting and Dramatic Literature at Yale University, has written and edited many books on drama and the theater. Among these are *Best American Plays* (various years), *Form and Idea in Modern Theatre* (1956), and *Theatre at the Crossroads* (1960).

F. J. Hoffmann is Professor of English at the University of California, Riverside. He has written several studies of modern literature, among them *Freudianism and the Literary Mind* (1945) and *Modern Novel in America* (1956).

A poet in his own right, Edwin Honig is one of the leading interpreters of Lorca. He has taught at various universities in the United States, including the University of New Mexico and Harvard.

Ward Hooker is Professor of English at Bucknell University. His criticism appears regularly in literary journals.

Walter F. Kerr has been drama critic for *Commonweal* and is now critic for *The New York Herald Tribune*. He has also written and directed plays.

Joseph Wood Krutch was for many years drama critic of *The Nation* and Brander Matthews Professor of Dramatic Literature at Columbia University. He now lives in Tucson, Arizona. His books on the theater include *The American Drama Since 1918* (1939) and *Comedy and Conscience after the Restoration* (1949).

Mary McCarthy was for many years the drama critic of *Partisan Review*. She is also well known for her fiction. Among her books are *The Groves of Academe* (1952) and *On the Contrary* (1961).

David Magarshack is an English critic and translator who specializes in Russian literature. In addition to a critical study of Chekhov's plays, he has also written a biography, *Chekhov: a Life* (1943).

Marion Magid, a young New York critic, has been an assistant editor of *Commentary*.

F. O. Matthiessen (1902–1950) was one of the leading students of American literature. He taught at Harvard for many years. His works included *American Renaissance* (1941) and *The Responsibilities of the Critic*.

H. L. Mencken (1880–1956) with George Jean Nathan, the founders and editors of the original *American Mercury*, achieved distinction as one of America's great critics of life and letters. Some of his essays appear in *A Mencken Chrestomathy* (1949).

Henry Popkin, who has taught at Brandeis University and at New York University, covers the New York theatrical scene for a number of publications.

George Bernard Shaw (1856–1950) was a great drama and music critic as well as playwright. His *The Quintessence of Ibsenism* remains one of the best critical studies of Ibsen, whom Shaw acknowledged as one of his masters.

Lionel Trilling, one of America's leading critics of literature and culture, is Professor of English at Columbia University. His books include *Matthew Arnold* (1939), *The Liberal Imagination* (1950), and *The Opposing Self* (1955).

Kenneth Tynan has been drama critic for *The Spectator* and *The Observer*, British publications, and was *The New Yorker's* drama critic from 1958 to 1960.

Domenico Vittorini, an Italian-American scholar, died in 1958. Among his books were *The Age of Dante* (1957) and *High Points in the History of Italian Literature* (1958).

Robert Warshow, who was born in 1917, had become before his death in 1955, one of the most original and perceptive critics of American popular culture, including the movies and the theater. His essays are collected in *The Immediate Experience* (1962).

Drama critic and historian Gerald Weales frequently writes on drama and the theater for *The Hudson Review* and other publications. He teaches at the University of Pennsylvania. He has written *Religion in Modern English Drama* (1961) and *American Drama Since World War II* (1962).

Stark Young was drama critic for *The New Republic* from 1925 to 1947. Before his death, in 1963, he had written widely on the theater, including one book, *Immortal Shadows* (1949). He has also published modern translations of Chekhov's plays.